PEERING OVER THE EDGE

THE PHILOSOPHY OF MOUNTAINEERING

MIKEL VAUSE, EDITOR

MOUNTAIN N' AIR BOOKS
LA CRESCENTA, CA 91224
USA

Peering Over the Edge
The Philosophy of Mountaineering
Edited by Mikel Vause, 1951—
First edition: 2005

Published in the United States of America by
Mountain N' Air Books
P.O. Box 12540
La Crescenta, CA 91224
USA

Phones: (818) 248-9345 or (800) 446-9696
Faxes: (818) 248-6516 or (800)303-5578
E-mail Address: publishers@mountain-n-air.com

Cover and book layout/design by Gilberto d' Urso
Cover photo: Sir Chris Bonington, CBE—Shivling—first ascent—SW Summit,
Gangotri Himilaya, 1983.
Back Cover: Doug Scott, CBE—Diamond Couloir, Mt. Kenya, 1976.
All reprints were granted permition by the authors and/or publishers.

This book is an original paperback, published electronically and printed on demand.

Library of Congress Control Number: 2005924443

Peering Over the Edge. Vause, Mikel, 2. Literature, mountaineering, adventures

Other titles by Mikel Vause
Rock and Roses ISBN: 1-879415-28-3
On Mountains and Mountaineers ISBN: 1-879415-06-2
I Knew it Would Come to This ISBN: 1-879415-30-5

ISBN[13]: 978-1-879415-42-3

ISBN 1-879415-42-9

TABLE OF CONTENTS

Nothing Ventured, Nothing Gained: Vocation and Advocation United

Peering Over the Edge: The Philosophy of Mountaineering

PREFACE

For the past thirty or so years it has been my lot in life to read and re-read many of the classics of mountaineering literature. It all began with my childhood interest in adventure and exploration. When I was in elementary school my parents ordered me a series of books called *We Were There*.... These books told the stories of the launching of the first nuclear submarine, the first manned space flight, and the discovery of the North Pole. They were wonderful, fascinating stories of human adventure, of exploration, of humans going to extremes, and I loved them. Such reading caused me, as I grew older, to search out books that would make me feel the same thrill as I did when I was young. When I was old enough to go to Saturday matinee movies I was thrilled to see such titles as "Journey to the Center of the Earth," and "Twenty Thousand Leagues Under the Sea" and "The White Tower" and "Third Man on the Mountain," and I was even more excited when I learned that those movies, and many others like them, were derived from books. I devoured the works of Jules Verne and James Ramsey Ullman and was in constant search of similar books that would stir my soul. The more I read and the more I wanted to emulate those characters in the books. For example, I wanted in the worst way to be as brave as Rudy Matt, the young hero of Ullman's *Banner in the Sky* and Disney's film "Third Man on the Mountain," who followed both his father and his heart into the mountains. As a boy I would look out my bedroom window at the Wasatch Mountains and imagine climbing routes up the shear faces. In the winter time I would take my sled and hike in the foothills above 9th Street Park in Ogden, Utah and pretend I was Robert Peary or Roald Amundsen pushing my way to one of the poles as the wind would blow the fine Utah powder snow in my face. There was something exciting about feeling my eye lashes freeze. So one can hardly wonder at the excitement I felt when the faculty of the graduate school of English at Bowling Green University approved my request to write a doctoral dissertation on mountaineering literature.

Some may find it ironic that a boy who grew up at the base of the Rocky Mountains, but was never encouraged to read about the mountains or mountaineering in school or college, would end up in Bowling Green, Ohio, possibly the flattest place in North America, writing a dissertation on mountaineering literature. I felt then and continue to feel today that I am extremely lucky to have, as Robert Frost advises in his poem "Two Tramps in Mud Time," been able to "unite advocation and vocation."

Over the many years of reading and analyzing literature having to do with exploration generally and mountaineering specifically, I have collected a number of essays and stories that I feel are unique and represent fine writing as well as excellent storytelling. It is from those that this collection is comprised. Some of the stories I have found in old, out of print books or journals, some have appeared in other anthologies of years ago such as Leslie Stephen's "Regrets of a Mountaineer" which I first came across in a turn of the century college reader entitled *The World's Greatest Literature*; G. W. Young's "The Influence of Mountains upon the Development of Human Intelligence" I found in the Special Collections Library of Augustana College in Rock Island Illinois; Steve Roper's "Dresden" was first published in an early seventies issue of the Sierra Club's mountaineering journal *Ascent*. Others I found in original texts, many of which are out of print. Some I collected from the authors, like Hamish Brown, Andrew Greig, Ian Mitchell, Maggie Body, and Paul Pritchard, after hearing them read at The International Mountaineering Literature Festival at Bretton Hall College in England. Along with reading and collecting mountain writing, it has been my good fortune to meet, climb and develop friendships with many of the contributors to this collections such as Chris Bonington, Doug Scott, Terry Gifford, Doug Robinson, and Greg Child, to name a few. Those included in this anthology, past and present, were and are not only fine writers, but many are great mountaineers as well. It is to them specifically, and to all mountaineers generally, that I dedicate this book.

—Mikel Vause
Weber State University
Ogden, Utah

Mikel Vause, editor

To Janis
Thanks for these 30
wonderful years

Note: To work as an editor can be, and many times, is quite rewarding. That being said, there are those times when editorial work is frustrating, even painful which is many times true when working with climbers. In most cases, mountaineers would prefer to be doing a climb rather than talking about climbing. And, trying to get them to write about climbing is even more difficult. No one knows these feelings better than Margaret Body. Maggie has had the opportunity to edit the writing of many of mountaineering's more recognizable names–everyone from Smyth and Shipton to Bonington and Scott just to name some of the more obvious. In 1996 Maggie presented her side of the experience in the essay "Recollections of an Editor." I first heard it at the International Mountaineering Literature Festival at Bretton Hall and a short time later as a keynote address at the annual Alpine Club meeting at St. Bart's Hospital in London. Both times she "brought down the house." I don't think anyone can better express what it is to do the work of an editor of mountaineering literature than can Maggie Body. It is for this reason that I am using her essay to introduce this collection.

—Mikel Vause

MARGARET BODY:
RECOLLECTIONS OF AN EDITOR

"Some Everesters I Have Known"

"Snow conditions bad stop advanced base abandoned yesterday stop awaiting improvement" — Anybody happen to know who sent that cable and what it really meant? A clue: the year was 1953. It was special correspondent James (now Jan) Morris's coded message, sent by cleft stick from Everest Base Camp to Namche Bazar and radioed on to the British Embassy in Kathmandu and thence to *The Times* in London to inform them that Everest had been climbed on 29 May by Hillary and Tenzing.

9

It was coded to protect *The Times* from being scooped by assorted rival hacks lurking among the leaches and rhododendrons lower down the hill. And it worked apparently. They were all fooled.

I can remember exactly where I was and what I was doing when I heard Everest had been climbed for the first time. But for someone in Britain that isn't too remarkable a claim to make because the news was stage-managed to break in the UK on the morning of Queen Elizabeth II's coronation day—2nd June 1953. Which found me, aged 15, with my best friend Ruth, standing in the crowd at the Buckingham Palace end of the Mall—we were all little monarchists then. But we were very young. Ruth and I were about nine rows back and just able to see the tops of the helmets of the mounted policemen. It was dawn and had been pelting rain for hours and we were wondering when something was going to happen. What happened was someone brought the first morning newspapers into our part of the crowd and there it was, Everest Climbed, and there was Sherpa Tenzing with the ear to ear grin and Ed Hillary in that curious hat of his with its rear-action sunflap, looking like he's just stepping out of the chorus line of "A Desert Song." And I remember thinking it was all too much, too much drama for one day. It couldn't be true. How could it all happen at the same time like that. I didn't know about the Snow conditions bad stop advanced base abandoned yesterday and so forth. In fact, of course, the first ascent of Everest was about the only piece of news which wouldn't have got upstaged in England that day by the Coronation.

Eight years later, when I heard I had an interview for a job at the London book publishing firm of Hodder & Stoughton, I naturally rummaged round my parents' house to see which of Hodder's books we had at home. There were only two. One was the Moffat modern translation of the Bible. Hodders was always a good religious house. The other was John Hunt's *The Ascent of Everest* which we had all been given at our school back in Coronation year, along with royal blue propelling pencil with ER2 and the date on it in gilt. Well, the propelling pencil lost any ambition towards propulsion a very long time ago. ER2, she's still going—after her fashion. *The Ascent of Everest* however had an evergreen revival not long ago to mark its 40th anniversary (and again to celebrate 50th) and who would have thought in 1953 that so many people since would have climbed it by so many routes, skied down it, parapented off it, and package toured up it on a short rope as well. For a mountain that so many people keep telling us is so much less charismatic than so many others, Everest has held its allure by simply being the numero uno, the ultimate trophy peak.

The reason Hodder & Stoughton got to publish *The Ascent of Everest* was because they had served a prewar apprenticeship with Hugh Ruttledge and the book of the 1936 British Everest attempt. Not a bestseller. Hodders also put money into the abortive 1936 expedition and, as a consolation, (quite a good consolation) got to publish Eric Shipton; they also published the Chris Bonington of the thirties, a prolific writer and lecturer called Frank Smythe. So when, a world war later, the 1953 Everest expedition was being offered to the publishing scene by the worthies of the Mount Everest Committee, there was Hodders in the front row waving their check book. Some clubland wag was heard to say that it cost Hodder & Stoughton £10 a foot to get to the top of Everest. So you can work out the advance.

The actual publication was a famously rushed job for those days of hot metal presses.

They climbed the mountain, you will remember, at the end of May, and John Hunt didn't sit down to start writing the book until August (with the help of my first Hodder boss, a redoubtable chain-smoking Northumbrain called Elsie Herron), and the book was in the shops in November 1953, price 25 shillings. The first print was 80,000 copies, which was fairly plucky for 1953. But they ended up with 639,000 copies in circulation. So what by Krakauer standards, but remember this was postwar Britain and the publishers must have been pleased because the entire staff of Hodders received a one off Christmas bonus of £10 a head.

Incidentally, all the initial promotion material and jacket design, produced early to save time, was done with the title *The Conquest of Everest*, because, dammit, that's what we thought we'd done. But John Hunt, for all he was a serving colonel in the British army, was having none of this. You don't conquer mountains, he told his publishers severely and I've tried to make sure authors remember that ever since. So Hodders ground their teeth a bit and binned all the advance publicity and started again with *The Ascent of Everest*. The one thing they forgot to do was tell the American publisher. So the Americans went ahead and published it as *The Conquest of Everest* before anyone noticed. Same book, two titles.

The first hero of '53 who I myself met was Ed Hillary who, by the time I came to work with him, was into crossing Antarctica. I remember taking Ed to Cambridge once for a literary lunch. It was February and the week before his arrival the whole country was paralyzed by the sort of heavy snowfall everybody expects in February, everybody except the people who run the British train system and are famous for making excuses about there being too many leaves in the line in the autumn and the wrong sort of snow sticking to the track. Well, I thought, if I'm to be stuck in a snowdrift for twenty-four hours with an author, I couldn't have picked a better qualified one than Ed Hillary. For someone who had just beaten Bunny Fuchs to the South Pole there can't be such a thing as the wrong sort of snow. He'll know what to do.

I needn't have worried. The day we set out for Cambridge the thaw set in. I should explain we don't get winters like other places in the World. East Anglia, which is a flattish part of the world, was now flooded. We had arrived in Cambridge two hours early for the local TV station to interview Ed before the lunch began. But when push came to shove, the local floods were more compulsive viewing than the hero of Everest and the South Pole and all the cameras—all three of them were out photographing firemen carrying plucky fox terriers to safety through thigh-deep Saffron Walden High Street. That's when I discovered what a nice man Ed Hillary is and also that he had hollow legs, as we sat there drinking gin for two hours and waiting for his moment to earn his lunch.

There is no contest for the most venerable of all the Everest climbers I have ever met which was Captain John Noel. Captain Noel had been trying to find a way to Everest (never mind climbing the thing) before the first world war and went along as film-maker and photographer with the second Everest expedition in 1922 and the more famous Mallory and Irvine expedition in 1924, after which he blotted his copybook with Tibet by importing some dancing lamas to England as a warm up act to boost his film show. The Dalai Lama, like Queen Victoria, was not amused. But that's another story. I met Captain Noel when he was ninety-nine, stone deaf and addicted to the use of the telephone. "Is that Miss Body," he would boom down the phone to whoever picked it up on the Hodder switchboard.

I was trying to bring out a paperback reprint of his book, *Through Tibet to Everest* which I had discovered languishing on the backlist of another publisher's imprint which Hodders had just taken over. Doing business with Captain Noel was never easy. He had a famous long-running battle over picture rights with the Royal Geographical Society which went on for decades. He was always notoriously suspicious of anyone trying to do a deal with him. And now he was stone deaf as well. You might call it a bit of a challenge. I don't know how familiar you are with publishers' contracts, but English publishers' basic contracts are rather like British rural bus services, in that they try to cover every eventuality, every remote side turning, and only end up irritating those on the receiving end by their total obscurity of direction. For Captain Noel, aged 99, we felt that maybe a simplified one-off contract would be the thing. Yet he was insisting on a proper escalating royalty rate, as recognized by the Society of Authors, with all the assurance of someone who planned to live for ever. And he was retaining his film rights.

When we had more or less reached an understanding by bellowing at each other down the telephone, I decided I had better pay him a visit to get him to sign this much discussed document. He lived in the flattest part of Kent in an ancient bungalow with the debris of a lifetime silting up around him. He wore a woolly hat like a tea cosy, his eye sockets were sunken and red-rimmed, and he sat in a wheelchair, but he still had the massive shoulders of a man who in his youth had blacked up and forged his way across forbidden Tibetan passes disguised as "a Mahommedan from India."

As you know, everything in England stops for tea, even cricket matches, especially cricket matches, so after we'd done our business he wheeled himself into the kitchen where he had already set out some cheese sandwiches on a plate. Time for tea. "I'll put on the kettle, shall I?" said the editor brightly. To reach the sink to fill the kettle I had to step over a few cat bowls strewn about the really revolting kitchen floor and, trying to find an easy new topic to launch into with the stone deaf, and being a cat person myself, I gestured at the bowls and asked after the cat. A great grin crossed his face and he wheeled himself to the kitchen door, opened it, shouted something in what I took to be Tibetan, rattled his walking stick back and fouth across the door frame and in through the door and the open window hurtled no less than three very large cats who dived straight for the plate of sandwiches on the table, sending all flying.

"Oh cripes," said Captain Noel.

"Never mind," said the determined editor. And I knelt down and picked the constituent parts of those disintegrating door stoppers up off the filthy floor and blew on them gently and dusted them down and put them back together again and arranged them on the plate—and I ate two of them. But my reward was to have Captain Noel show me maps and photographs and paintings and say things like "As I said to Younghusband...." It's occasions like that that make the hair stand up on the back of the neck with a sense of history. It was certainly one of my most memorable author visits.

I mentioned Captain Noel had been on the second Everest expedition in 1922. The very first, in 1921, was led by a big game hunting Anglo-Irishman called Colonel Charles Howard Bury and late one winter Friday afternoon—the sort of afternoon you wonder whether there's anyone else still in the office—I received a call from the chief district librarian of Mullingar in County Westmeath in the center of Ireland who had inherited all the Howard Bury papers and wanted to know how to go about turning them into books. That was fun, finding someone who only ever merits a one-off mention in the climbing encyclopedias was a real person with a lively pen, and mercifully neat handwriting, who, when he wasn't chasing sheep in the Tien Shan had militarily disparaging things to say about Mallory's ability to pitch a tent or ride a pony uphill.

The Colonel adopted a bear cub on his Central Asian travels. It rode pillion behind him on his pony, in a complicated leather harness through which it periodically chewed to bite the pony's rump. It was as well the Colonel, an Irishman, was a good horseman. But Howard Bury persisted with this unaccommodating traveling companion and eventually brought it back to Ireland with his other hunting trophies. There are old people in Mullingar today who can still remember the bear, by their time full grown, and how the Colonel used to box with it for exercise in the grounds of his estate. The colonel died in 1965 and the bear went to his maker by way of Dublin Zoo but, being Ireland, that didn't stop us, 25 years on, having a very well lubricated publication party at his old home outside Mullingar. I like to think the Colonel and the bear were with us in spirit.

Proceeding chronologically, the next Everester I had to deal with was the man who everybody expected to be leading the successful 1953 expedition, Eric Shipton. How the vastly experienced and respected Shipton was removed, for perceived lack of commitment, in favor of the unknown John Hunt is now a matter of history and was long past when I came to work with Shipton in the early sixties. I hadn't been in the job long then and there's nothing quite like cutting your climbing publishing milk teeth on one of mountaineering's icons. I was given his maps to sort out. The Shipton title in question was *Land of Tempest* (1963) and the maps that exercised us, as well they might, were of the Patagonian Icecap. And from that experience I learned one basic fact of publishing climbers: they don't usually know where the hell they've been.

Working with Eric Shipton on *Land of Tempest* and later *That Untravelled World* was a somewhat unnerving experience. I was far too young to act the bossy old party, which the job soon turned me into, and he left a distinct impression that publishers' offices were not his natural habitat. So our encounters were vague, delightful but disconcerting. I remember him telling me just after it happened what became his famous story of how he'd borrowed Mallory's ice-axe (discovered on the 1933 expedition and enshrined ever since in the Alpine Club.) He'd borrowed it for some TV appearance, and in typical Shipton fashion had absentmindedly left it on the pavement in the street outside his London house when unloading his car; when he realized what he'd done it had gone. Visions of being drummed out of the Alpine Club, of which he was then president, ensued. Happily, a passerby had picked it up and handed it in at the police station and the very intelligent local constable, learning where it had been found, brought it round to Shipton's house because he knew he was a mountaineering gentleman. Working with Eric Shipton, I can't say I was on top of the job, but I, like every other lady he met, was so charmed by him that I hardly noticed.

And it is therefore especially enjoyable for me in my present quasi-retirement, to have had the chance last year to work on a splendid biography of Shipton by Peter Steele. Some climbers collect summits. Shipton didn't worry too much about summits, so long as he was enjoying the trip. Which was rather his problem with the Mount Everest Committee. But he did collect ladies and what was particularly clever about it was he managed to keep in continuing good order with all of them at the same time, leaving an ice axe under the occasional bed in his younger years as a love token. Because all their memories were pleasant ones, a few of these surviving ladies have been happy to reminisce, misty-eyed, to Peter Steele and, what's more, lend him Shipton's letters. So it's a very well rounded biography. It's called *Eric Shipton: Everest and Beyond* and well worth getting hold of.

Peter Steele, the author, is that odd thing, a doctor with stylish handwriting. He has also been to Everest. He was one of the two doctors on Norman Dyhrenfurth's strife-ridden international expedition of 1971. There were 30 members from 13 countries. It was supposed to be an experiment in international concord. Peter Steele wrote a book about the trip which started, I can still remember, with all the different nationalities digging their own separate latrines at Base Camp. A whiff, you might say, of the discord to come.

One of those who climbed the highest on that 1971 international expedition was the Scots climber, Dougal Haston, as charismatic a figure in his day as Eric Shipton had been between the wars. Dougal had been trying to find a route up the South-West Face and had reached the foot of the Rock Band, which made him a prime candidate for Chris Bonington's expedition on the same route the following year.

In best Hodder Everest tradition we first published the book about how Chris Bonington and his merry men didn't get up the South-West Face of Everest and then, three years later, we published the story of how they did it in 1975, cheekily called *Everest the Hard Way*. I remember I had some tricky explaining to do to John Hunt at that point. This was the end of an era, almost the last major siege-style assault on Everest mounted from the UK. Chapter 14 was the problem for Bonington. This was the summit push, the most important chapter in the book. Chris couldn't write it at first hand because of course he wasn't on the summit push, so he had asked the first two summiters, Dougal Haston and Doug Scott, to write their accounts for inclusion in the expedition book. Without any colluding they each separately wrote exactly nine pages of typescript about how we got to the top and dutifully despatched them to their leader. Chris took one horrified look and posted the two versions straight on to me, saying I was to choose which one to use and then he could blame me when apologizing to the other illustrious climber. Holding the shitty end of the stick you learn early on is all part of the editorial function.

This seemed to be a spread out on the kitchen table job to compare, contrast and discuss, as they say in exam papers. When I did this, I realized a very simple fact, they had each described their own lead, rope-length by rope-length, so all I needed to do was scissors and paste them alternately and it all fit perfectly. This, please note, was long before we were all equipped with cut and paste menus on our computer screens. This was heavy duty all action version. We got our fingers sticky in those days. Well, I sent the new chapter off to Dougal and Doug who by now just happened to be climbing together in Washington State. Doug wrote back at length with his opinions on the expedition and life and whither mountaineering, but generously approving what I'd done with the material. Dougal was always a bit of a trappist, totally useless for commentary on live outside broadcasts Hamish MacInnes always maintained, because while he could look quite spectacular, you could never get him to he say anything while doing this. Elliptical as ever, he scrawled one sentence around the edge of Doug's epistle: "Please reinstate the third rope-length of the traverse about the Rock Band." Of course, I did.

In those dying days of UK siege-style expeditioning everything was much more structured than it is today. There was a leader—who led. The team members had to sign an expedition contract and part of the deal was first access to the teams' diaries for use in the expedition book written by the expedition leader or designated other. One of the better diarists on Everest in 1975 proved to be the youngest climbing member of the party who also got to the top and who observed: "For a mountaineer surely a Bonington Everest Expedition is one of the last great imperial experiences that life can offer." This was the opinion of Peter Boardman whom we signed up soon afterwards, largely on the strength of that sentence.

Hodders published both his books *The Shining Mountain and Sacred Summits* and I think perhaps the best moment in my publishing career was when I learnt that Pete had won the John Llewelyn Rhys Prize for Literature for his first book. This is a prize which is not limited to climbing literature, and is given for British and Commonwealth writers of promise in any literary field under the age of thirty. I remember the novelist Bernice Rubens who was chair of the judges that year saying in her adjudication that they had given the prize to Pete because he had written a very good book and he probably didn't know it. Rubbish. He knew all right. He took his writing very seriously. He was into sustained metaphors in a big way and liked to model himself on George B. Schaller. He could have become the Noyce, the Shipton of our time, had he lived.

Pete got to the top of the SW Face of Everest in the second push in 1975. In 1982 he was back attempting the NE Ridge on another Bonington expedition, but one slightly less imperial in scale this time, and it was then that he and his regular climbing partner Joe Tasker disappeared between the First and Second Pinnacles. Their partnership and their writing are commemorated in the Boardman Tasker Prize for Mountain Literature which is the UK's response to the Banff book prizes. After Everest 75 there was the avalanche of expedition books. Expeditions were no longer siege-style, so they didn't need so much start-up money. The days were past when an international bank saw Bonington up Everest, or Jardine Matheson, the original Hong Kong Noble House, saw him into China, or an ill-fated K2 expedition was launched with colored balloons in the press pack which rather bemused everybody because the sponsors were the London Rubber Company whose prime output, perhaps I should explain, was and still is condoms.

What usually happened now with wannabe expeditions was they started with the extravagantly headed notepaper, then if they were really keen, they got on to the expedition tee-shirt, and the expedition postcard. And somewhere along the line they wrote to Hodders. That's the way I acquired Stephen Venables who climbed the Kangshung Face of Everest and is the only person I know who can hobble with one foot in plaster and three and a half gangrenous toes faster than I can walk. And there was Alison Hargreaves, impressively single-minded, who used to come in to the office with her two very self-possessed small children who would draw mountains on the back of spare printout paper with Mummy waving from the top of every one. And Kurt Diemberger, always with enough rainbow-hued hand baggage for an octopus, who had an entirely idiosyncratic view of book presentation and could find his way round the backside of K2 but was incapable of getting off the train from London to Bristol at the right stop.

But of all of them it was with Chris Bonington that I have had the longest working relationship and, eventually, the most uncomplicated, in that Chris, while very demanding on the design and photographic front, has always had a professional journalist's attitude to the fine-tuning of his prose and is perfectly happy to churn it out and see me scribbling all over it. At the crux of each book, I would go up and stay at his house on the northern edge of the English Lake District and we'd work a shift system. Chris is best first thing in the morning, I'm decidedly not. So he'd get up and start work at five or six but knock off by three. I'd start by nine, but get into my stride in the early evening and work late. Everything, however, would stop midday for the walk in my case, run in his, up High Pike. That's the hill at the back of his house with a view north over the Solway Firth to Scotland and Lockerbie. The Bonington dogs would come too and Chris's wonderful PA, Louse, and Frances, his picture librarian and her dog and Alison who did his accounts and her dog, and we'd all work up an appetite for one of Wendy Bonington's special vegetarian bean salads. Though if Wendy was off in Keswick for the day, we just might nip down to the pub in Caldbeck and have Cumberland sausages on the quiet. When not under the influence of a good woman, I have to tell you Chris is not a fully paid up vegetarian.

Margaret Body

Once I was asked to take Chris on a book tour. They were thin on the ground in the promotion department and editors had to chip in. Being Welsh, I drew the West of England and South Wales leg of the trip. "You can take Bonington to Bristol, Cardiff and Swansea," said my managing director, "and then you can go home and see your aunties for the weekend afterwards."

"Right ho," I said.

We started off in Bristol where we called into the best bookshop for Chris to sign stock, which was a fairly underwhelming experience, and then Chris was interviewed over lunch by the original freeloading journalist who had everything on the menu, ending up with a liqueur. I had to keep an eye on the time because at 3 pm Chris had an appointment with the local intrepid female reporter to take her climbing on the famous local cliff which is called the Avon Gorge. The week before she'd gone parachute jumping with the SAS or something. This week she was going climbing with Bonington. So I had ordered a taxi to pick us up at the restaurant at ten to three.

The taxi arrived. "The Avon Gorge," I said, and off we went corkscrewing round the one-way traffic system of the posh end of Bristol and we ended up outside a very discreet private hotel-- called the Avon Gorge. What did he think we wanted to do there at three o'clock in the afternoon? "No, no," I said. "He wants to climb it." So back down the one-way corkscrew we swooped and out to the grass at the foot of the Gorge where the intrepid female reporter and her film crew were awaiting us.

I passed Chris the day sack which I had been nursing all the while so that he didn't leave it on the train, or in the bookshop, or in the restaurant or in the taxi. And Chris tipped the contents out on the grass. Out fell his mothy old red longjohns, his boots, a large quantity of climbing irons. But no rope. And he was leading a beginner. "Oh gosh," he said. "Wendy packed the sack. Never mind, I'll just borrow one." And off he loped with an ingratiating grin plastered between his whiskers. He was back in less than five minutes with a rope which he'd borrowed off some innocent lads along the Gorge "for just half an hour." I expressed amazement. After all, he's just ruined their afternoon's climbing. "Oh, the camaraderie of the crags," he explained airily. What a splendid phrase.

So Chris and the intrepid female reporter roped up and put on their mikes and set off up the climb with the cameraman and sound recordist in attendance at a respectful distance, and I settled down to wait at the bottom. After a while the two climbers disappeared up into some bushes and then the rope stopped twitching and, even to my untutored eye, it looked less than riveting television. And the sound recordist was muttering that they'd dislodged their chest mikes so he couldn't hear what they were saying anyway.

"Is there a road at the top?" the cameraman asked me. I said he was the local tv team, but I supposed so. So we piled all the surplus gear and Chris's going for interviews suit into two cars and corkscrewed up to the top, but not before I had had this fleeting vision of two little lads setting off to the police station and reporting this chap who was passing himself off as Chris Bonington and then had it away with their rope. But no time to worry about them yet and anyway I didn't know who they were.

To a non-practitioner it is disconcerting how different a climb looks from the top looking down, compared with from the bottom looking up. Picture the scene on that nice polite grass in the genteel residential suburb of Bristol which lies at the top of the Avon Gorge: the cameraman, the sound recordist and the editor, tiptoeing along the rim peering over and calling "Chris, Chris, are you there." Is there anybody there—?" Rather like trainee mediums at their first seance. Eventually, we found them, sitting just under the lip of the gorge interviewing each other. The camera rolled. The intrepid female reporter climbed up over the edge. Everybody kissed everybody. Well nearly everybody. And Chris gave the dog-walking ladies a cheap thrill by changing out of his climbing longjohns and back into his suit there on the grass. The suit was because we were scheduled to do an interview in Cardiff, across the Bristol Channel, in an hour's time.

"Just time to catch the train," he said, throwing me a pacifying glance.

"What about the rope," I said.

"Oh, gosh," he said.

So back down the one way system we corkscrewed and there by the gents loo at the bottom of the Gorge, looking distinctly foolish by now, and not talking to each other, were young lads of whom he'd conned the rope over two hours earlier. We restored their rope. We took them to the nearest pub. We plied them with pints and while Chris signed them copies of the latest book, I phoned Cardiff and rearranged the publicity schedule.

Some ladies when they get to their mid-fifties go in for something called HRT, Hormone Replacement Therapy. I had my own special treatment prescribed for me which was AWK, Amalgamating With Ken. Ken is Ken Wilson, the prime shaker and mover in the UK climbing publishing scene, certainly the one with the most opinions, and now, under the imprint of Baton Wicks, carrying forward the torch he lit with such flair as Diadem Books, and as the editor of *Mountain Magazine*. For a brief heady time after Hodders took over Diadem, and before Headline took over Hodders, in the London publishing jungle of the early nineties, Ken and I worked in harness very well. Ken did his thing, I did mine, we batted ideas between us. He would make the occasional raid on London from his home in the north of England and he'd always take in an obscure art exhibition at the same time. "Have you seen the so and so Exhibition yet, Maggie?" he's say. "Ah, you must go, it finishes next week. There's a loan Van Gogh there and it's shit hot." Occasionally, when not discussing fine art, we collaborated, as for a Bonington picture autobiography called *Mountaineer* and the Doug Scott equivalent, *Himalayan Climber*. What would Ken and I have done all those years without mountaineers to boost our print runs. With the picture-led autobiographies the idea in each case was of course Ken's, and the execution and the design. My job in proceedings was to knock the text into shape to fit the spaces Ken had occasionally left for it. As far as Ken is concerned text is the black fuzzy stuff that stops the pictures colliding.

Working with Chris Bonington on this sort of magazine format book was fine. He could produce the words easily and didn't mind them being massacred to fit the length. Working with Doug Scott was a different rack of tools. Words on paper do not come easily with Doug and when they come he has weighed each one and understandably grown partial to it. We did not make progress. Doug's three expeditions a year schedule didn't help. As the deadline approached, we congregated at Ken Wilson's home in the north of England to beat the last chapters out of our author. Desperate times called for desperate measures. The only snag is that Doug and Ken are two people equally convinced of the rightness of their own thinking. Which of them was the irresistible force and which the irremovable object I, from my position below the parapet, wasn't always too certain.

Doug is the only person I know who buys king-size duty frees at the many airports he travels through during his jet-setting year, and then unravels them and makes them up into twice as many roll-ups. By day three the strain was telling and there were fragments of ex-Rothman roll-up all over the various boilings down of the text. But while Doug was prepared to stand up to Ken he was properly in awe of Ken's wife Gloria, who wouldn't have smoking in the house. So he had to smoke these things with his head stuck out of the French windows of the room in which he and I worked on the text in the lulls between the editorial storms. And so I have always been able to claim that, like some sort of lady veterinarian, I edited *Himalayan Climber* through the Scott's backside, which seemed to work just as well as addressing the more usual end.

When I first started editing climbing books there were two kinds. There were those written by the grand old men, mostly of private means, who had distilled the fruits of many expeditions over many years to the same area—Shipton on Patagonia for example—or they had written volumes of memoirs. Gentlemanly restraint was their hallmark. When Tilman got to the top of Nanda Devi with Noel Odell he records: "I believe we so far forgot ourselves as to shake hands on it." Wow! They were sahibs. Climbers like that would never dream of explaining the best way to take a shit on a crowded portaledge. And then there were the siege-style expedition books, written mostly by Chris Bonington who was the only one in the UK at least with enough organization and method to raise the finance to set them all in motion. He took with him a team who often muttered in the background about the lottery of whether or not they'd get a crack at the summit, for in siege-style climbing, as you know, many are called but few are chosen. But they were still sahibs, even if the team felt embarrassed by the title.

But what they also felt was that they should be climbing alpine-style and soon they all were in varying degrees. In spirit at least, if not always in the purest technical sense every inch of the way. All very commendable. But this presented a problem for the book writing contingent. A siege-style expedition, lasting a few months, cast of hundreds, with multiple appendices about everything from oxygen equipment to logistics to film stock filled out a 256 or 288 page book very nicely. Alpine-style is ecologically friendly, aesthetically acceptable, but it is also fast. You nip up and you nip back down. There's usually not enough going on in one alpine-style expedition to make a book, unless it is a real early epic, like Boardman and Tasker on Changabang and they called their ascent capsule-style anyway. So alpine-style climber writers have to string a few expeditions together to make a book of contrasts or similarities, deploying their climbs for the reader like a Japanese flower arrangement. Getting away from the fixed rope also loosens up their view of what goes, and now you find them baring not just their backsides for the hapless reader's inspection on the portaledge, but their souls and their climbing relationships as well. They are sure they are no longer sahibs, though as long as their cook-boy brings them bed tea at base camp I reckon they still are, whether they like it or not.

There's a new element in the picture now, the trekkers, who may even get as far as base camp and, bless them, have often bought all the books. The market for climbing books widens to embrace the camp followers. And where you get the crowd you get those increasingly anxious about the deleterious effect of the crowd—Ed Douglas on what it does to the villagers around the major mountains, and higher up, Joe Simpson searingly exposing the inhumanity bred on an overcrowded South Col. Books of tangential passion and concern join the climbing literature. I've yet to see a literature growing up for sprint climbing and competition climbing. But while people travel to mountains, up mountains and around mountains, we'll still get some wonderful stuff to read. And I feel very lucky to have spent thirty-five years being paid to read it. And very privileged to be allowed, in this essay, to name drop quite so shamelessly.

In Spite of Difficulty:
The Alps

Sir Leslie Stephen (1832-1904) was a leading nineteenth century British literary critic and biographer. He was son-in-law to William Makepeace Thackery and father of novelist Virginia Woolf. Stephen was also one of Britain's leading alpinists of the "Golden Age" having made numerous first ascents in the European Alps. He was president of the Alpine Club from 1866 to 1868 and authored the classic *The Playground of Europe.*

SIR LESLIE STEPHEN: THE REGRETS OF A MOUNTAINEER

From *The Playground of Europe*

I have often felt a sympathy, which almost rises to the pathetic when looking on at a cricket-match or boat-race. Something of the emotion with which Gray regarded the "distant spires and antique towers" rises within me. It is not, indeed, that I feel very deeply for the fine ingenuous lads, who, as somebody says, are about to be degraded into tricky, selfish Members of Parliament. I have seen too much of them. They are very fine animals; but they are rather too exclusively animal. The soul is apt to be in too embryonic a state within these cases of well-strung bone and muscle. It is impossible for a mere athletic machine, however finely constructed, to appeal very deeply to one's finer sentiments. I can scarcely look forward with even an affectation of sorrow for the time when, if more sophisticated, it will at least have made a nearer approach to the dignity of an intellectual being. It is not the boys who make me feel a touch of sadness; their approaching elevation to the dignity of manhood will raise them on the whole in the scale of humanity; it is the older spectators whose aspect has in it something affecting. The shaky old gentleman, who played in the days when it was decidedly less dangerous to stand up to bowling than to a cannonball, and who now hobbles about on rheumatic joints, by the help of a stick; the corpulent elder, who rowed when boats had gangways down their middle, and did not require as delicate a balance as an acrobat's at the top of a living pyramid. These are the persons whom I cannot see without an occasional sigh. They are really conscious that they have lost something which they can never regain; or, if they momentarily forget it, it is even more forcibly impressed upon the spectators. To see a respectable old gentleman of sixty, weighing some fifteen stone, suddenly attempt to forget a third of his weight and two-thirds of his years, and attempt to caper like a boy, is indeed a startling phenomenon. To the thoughtless, it may be simply comic; but without being a Jaques, one may contrive also to suck some melancholy out of it.

Now, I have never caught a cricket-ball, and, on the contrary, have caught numerous crabs in my life, the sympathy which I feel for these declining athletes is not due to any great personal interest in the matter. But I have long anticipated that a similar day would come for me, when I should no longer be able to pursue my favorite sport of mountaineering. Some day I should find that the ascent of a zigzag was as bad as a performance on the treadmill; that I could not look over a precipice without a swimming in the head; and that I could no more jump a crevasse than the Thames at Westminster.

None of these things have come to pass. So far as I know, my physical powers are still equal to the ascent of Mont Blanc or the Jungfrau. But I am no less effectually debarred it matters not how-from mountaineering. I wander at the foot of the gigantic Alps, and look up longingly to the summits, which are apparently so near, and yet know that they are divided from me by an impassable gulf. In some missionary work I have read that certain South Sea Islanders believed in a future paradise where the good should go on eating forever with insatiable appetites at an inexhaustible banquet. They were to continue their eternal dinner in a house with open wickerwork sides; and it was to be the punishment of the damned to crawl outside in perpetual hunger and look in through the chinks as little boys look in through the windows of a London cookshop. With similar feelings I lately watched through a telescope the small black dots, which were really men, creeping up the high flanks of Mont Blanc or Monte Rosa. The eternal snows represented for me the Elysian fields, into which entrance was sternly forbidden, and I lingered about the spot with a mixture of pleasure and pain, in the envious contemplation of my more fortunate companions.

Sir Leslie Stephen

I know there are those who will receive these assertions with civil incredulity. Some persons assume that every pleasure with which they cannot sympathize is necessarily affectation, and hold as a particular case of that doctrine, that Alpine travelers risk their lives merely from fashion or desire for notoriety. Others are kind enough to admit that there is something genuine in the passion, but put it on a level with the passion for climbing greased poles. They think it derogatory to the due dignity of Mont Blanc that he should be used as a greased pole, and assure us that the true pleasures of the Alps are those which are within reach of the old and the invalids who can only creep about village and along highroads. I cannot well argue with such detractors from what I consider a noble sport.

As for the first class, it is reduced almost to a question of veracity. I say that I enjoy being on the top of a mountain, or, indeed, halfway up a mountain; that climbing is a pleasure to me, and would be so if no one else climbed and no one ever heard of my climbing. They reply that they don't believe it. No more argument is possible than if I were to say that I liked eating olives, and some one asserted that I really eat them only out of affectation. My reply would be simply to go on eating olives; and I hope the reply of mountaineers will be to go on climbing Alps. The other assault is more intelligible. Our critics admit that we have a pleasure; but assert that it is a puerile pleasure-that it leads to an irreverent view of mountain beauty, and to oversight of that which would really most impress a refined and noble mind. To this I shall only make such an indirect reply as may result from a frank confession of my own regrets at giving up the climbing business-perhaps for ever.

I am sinking, so to speak, from the butterfly to the caterpillar stage, and, if the creeping thing is really the highest of the two, it will appear that there is something in the substance of my lamentations unworthy of an intellectual being. Let me try. By way of preface, however, I admit that mountaineering, in my sense of the word, is a sport. It is a sport which, like fishing or shooting, brings one into contact with the sublimest aspects of nature; and, without setting their enjoyment before one as an ultimate end or aim, helps one indirectly to absorb—and be penetrated by their influence. Still it is strictly a sport as—strictly as cricket, or rowing, or knurl and spell—and I have no wish to place it on a different footing. The game is won when a mountain top is reached in spite of difficulties; it is lost when one is forced to retreat; and, whether won or lost, it calls into play a great variety of physical and intellectual energies, of our faculties. Still it suffers in some degree from this undeniable characteristic, and especially from the tinge which has consequently been communicated to narratives of mountain adventures.

There are two ways which have been appropriated to the description of all sporting exploits. One is to indulge in fine writing about them, to burst out in sentences which swell to paragraphs, and in paragraphs which spread over pages; to plunge into ecstasies about infinite abysses and overpowering splendors, to compare mountains to archangels lying down in eternal winding-sheets of snow, and to convert them into allegories about man's highest destinies and aspirations. This is good when it is well done. Mr. Ruskin has covered the Matterhorn, for example, with a whole web of poetical associations, in language. Which, to a severe taste, is perhaps a trifle too fine, though he has done it with an eloquence which his bitterest antagonists must freely acknowledge. Yet most humble writers will feel that if they try to imitate Mr. Ruskin's eloquence they will pay the penalty of becoming ridiculous. It is not everyone who can with impunity compare Alps to archangels.

Tall talk is luckily an object of suspicion to Englishmen, and, consequently most writers, and especially those who frankly adopt the sporting view of the mountains, adopt the opposite scheme: they with allusions to fleas or to bitter beer; they shrink with the prevailing dread of Englishmen from the danger of overstepping the limits of the sublime into its proverbial opposite; and they humbly try to amuse us because they can't strike us with awe. This, too, if I may venture to say so, is good in its way and place; and it seems rather hard to these luckless writers when people assume that, because they make jokes on a mountain, they are necessarily insensible to its awful sublimities. A sense of humor is not incompatible with imaginative sensibility; and even Wordsworth might have been an equally powerful prophet of nature if he could sometimes have descended from his stilts. In shorts, a man may worship mountains, and yet have a quiet joke with them when he is wandering all day in their tremendous solitudes.

Joking, however, is, it must be admitted, a dangerous habit. I freely avow that, in my humble contributions to Alpine literature I have myself made some very poor and very unseasonable witticisms. I confess my error, and only wish that I had no worse errors to confess. Still I think that the poor little jokes in which we mountaineers sometimes indulge have been made liable to rather harsh constructions. We are accused, in downright earnest, not merely of being flippant but of an arrogant contempt

Sir Leslie Stephen

for all persons whose legs are not as strong as our own. We are supposed seriously to wrap ourselves in our own conceit, and to brag intolerably of our exploits. Now I will not say that no mountaineer ever swaggers; the quality called by the vulgar "bounce" is unluckily confined to no profession. Certainly I have seen a man intolerably vain because he could raise a hundredweight with his little finger; and I daresay that the "champion bill-poster," whose name is advertised on the walls of this metropolis, thinks excellence in bill-posting the highest virtue of a citizen. So some men may be silly enough to brag in all seriousness about mountain exploits. However, most lads of twenty learn that it is silly to give themselves airs about mere muscular eminence; and especially is this true of Alpine exploits—first, because they required less physical prowess than almost any other sport, and secondly, because a good amateur still feels himself the hopeless inferior of half the Alpine peasants whom he sees. You cannot be very conceited about a game in which the first clodhopper you meet can give you ten minutes' start in an hour. Still a man writing in a humorous vein naturally adopts a certain bumptious tone, just as our friend Punch ostentatiously declares himself to be omniscient and infallible. Nobody takes him at his word, or supposes that the editor of Punch is really the most conceited man in all England.

But we poor mountaineers are occasionally fixed with our own careless talk by some outsider who is not in on the secret. We know ourselves to be a small sect, and to be often laughed at; we reply by assuming that we are the slat of the earth, and that our amusement is the first and noblest of all amusements. Our only retort to the good-humored ridicule with which we are occasionally treated is to adopt an affected strut, and to carry it off as if we were the finest fellows in the world. We make a boast of our shame, and say, if you laugh we must crow. But we don't really mean anything: if we did, the only word which the English language would afford wherewith to describe us would be the very unpleasant antithesis to wise men, and certainly I hold that we have the average amount of common sense. When, therefore, I see us taken to task for swaggering, I think it a trifle hard that this merely playful affection of superiority should be made a serious fault. For the future I would promise to be careful, if it were worth avoiding misunderstanding of men who won't take a joke. Meanwhile, I can only state that when Alpine travelers indulge in a little swagger about their own performances and other people's incapacity, they don't mean more than an infinitesimal fraction of what they say, and that they know perfectly well that when history comes to renounce a final judgment upon the men of the time, it won't put mountain-climbing on a level with patriotism, or even with excellence in the fine arts.

The reproach of real bona fide with arrogance is, so far as I know, very little true of Alpine travelers. With the exception of the necessary fringe hanging on to every set of human beings—consisting of persons whose heads are weaker than their legs—the mountaineer, so far as my experience has gone, is generally modest enough. Perhaps he sometimes flaunts his ice-axes and ropes a little too much before the public eye at Chamonix, as a yachtsman occasionally flourishes his nautical costume at Cowes; but the fault may be pardoned by those not inexorable to human weaknesses. This opinion, I know, cuts at the root of the most popular theory as to our ruling passion. If we do not climb the Alps to gain notoriety, for what purpose can we possibly climb them? The same unlucky trick of joking is taken to indicate that we don't care much about the scenery; for who, with a really susceptible soul, could be facetious under the cliffs of the Jungfrau or the ghastly precipices of the Matterhorn? Hence people who kindly excuse us from the blame of notoriety-hunting generally accept the "greased-pole" theory. We are, it seems, overgrown schoolboys, enjoy being in dirt, and danger, and mischief, and have as much sensibility for natural beauty as the mountain mules. And against this, as a more serious complaint, I wish to make my feeble protest, in order that my lamentations on quitting the profession may not seem unworthy of a thinking being.

Let me try to recall some of the impressions which mountaineering has left with me, and see whether they throw any light upon the subject. As I gaze at the huge cliffs where I may no longer wander, I find innumerable recollections arise-some of them dim, as though belonging to a past existence; and some so brilliant that I can scarcely realize my exclusion from the scenes to which they belong. I am standing at the foot of what, to my mind, is the most glorious of all Alpine wonders—the huge Oberland precipice, on the slopes of the Faulhorn or the Wengern Alp. Innumerable tourists have done all that tourists can do to cocknify (if that is the right derivative from cockney) the scenery; but, like the Pyramids or a Gothic cathedral, it throws off the taint of vulgarity by its imperishable majesty. Even on turf strewn with sandwich-papers and empty bottles, even in the presence of hideous peasant-women singing "Stand er auf' for five centimes, we cannot but feel the influence of Alpine beauty. When the sunlight is dying off the snows, or the full moon lighting them up with ethereal tints, even sandwich-papers and singing women may be forgotten. How does the memory of scramble along snow aretes, of plunges—luckily not too deep—into crevasses, of toil through long snowfields, towards a refuge that seemed to recede as we advanced—where, to quote Tennyson with due alteration, to the traveler toiling in immeasurable snow— "Sown in a wrinkle of the monstrous hill. The chalet sparkles like a grain of salt; how do such memories as these harmonize with the sense of superlative sublimity?"

One element of mountain beauty is, we shall all admit, their vast size and steepness. That a mountain is very big, and is faced by perpendicular walls of rock, is the first thing which strikes everybody, and is the whole essence and outcome of a vast quantity of poetical description. Hence the first condition towards a due appreciation of mountain scenery is that these qualities should be impressed upon the imagination. The mere dry statement that a mountain is so many feet in vertical height above the sea, and contains so many tons of granite, is nothing. Mont Blanc is about three miles high. What of that? Three miles is an hour's walk for a lady—an eighteen-penny cab-fare—the distance from Hyde Park Corner to the Bank—an express train could do it in three minutes, or a racehorse in five. It is a measure which we have learned to despise, looking at it from a horizontal point of view; and accordingly most persons, on seeing the Alps for the first time, guess them to be higher, as measured in feet, than they really are.

What, indeed, is the use of giving measures in feet to any but the scientific mind? Who cares whether the moon is 250,000 or 2,500,000 miles distant? Mathematicians try to impress upon us that the distance of the fixed stars is only expressible by a row of figures which stretches across a page; suppose it stretched across two or across a dozen pages, should we be any the wiser, or have, in the least degree, a clearer notion of the superlative distances? We civilly say, "Dear Me!" when the astronomer looks to us for the appropriate stare, but we only say it with the mouth; internally our remark is "You might as well have multiplied by a few more millions whilst you were about it." Even astronomers, though not a specially imaginative race, feel the impotence of figures, and try to give us some measure which the mind can grasp a little more conveniently. They tell us about the cannon-ball which might have been flying ever since the time of Adam, and not yet have reached the heavenly body, or about the stars which may not yet have become visible, though the light has been flying to us at a rate inconceivable by the mind for an inconceivable number of years; and they succeed in producing a bewildering and giddy sensation, although the numbers are too vast to admit of any accurate apprehension.

We feel a similar need in the case of mountains. Besides the bare statement of figures, it is necessary to have some means for grasping the meaning of the figures. The bare tens and thousands must be clothed with some concrete images. The statement that a mountain is 15,000 feet high is, by itself, little more impressive than that of a 3,000; we want something more before we can mentally compare Mont Blanc and Snowdon. Indeed, the same people who guess of a mountain's height at a number of feet much exceeding the reality, show, when they are cross-examined, that they fail to appreciate in any tolerable degree the real meaning of the figures. An old lady one day, about 11 a.m., proposed to walk from the Eggshorn to the Jungfraujock, and to return for luncheon—the distance being a good twelve hours' journey for trained mountaineers. Every detail of which the huge mass is composed is certain to be underestimated. A gentleman the other day pointed out to me a grand ice-cliff at the end of a hanging glacier, which must have been at least 100 feet high, and asked me whether that snow was three feet deep.

Nothing is more common than for tourists to mistake some huge pinnacle of rock, as big as a church tower, for a traveler. The rocks of the Grands Mulets, in one corner of which the chalet is hidden, are often identified with a party ascending Mont Blanc; and I have seen boulders as big as a house pointed out confidently as chamois. People who make these blunders must evidently see the mountains as mere toys, however many feet they may give them at a random guess. Huge overhanging cliffs are to them steps within the reach of human legs; yawning crevasses are ditches to be jumped; and foaming waterfalls are like streams from penny squirts. Everyone knows the avalanches on the Jungfrau, and the curiously disproportionate appearance of the little puffs of white smoke, which are said to be the cause of the thunder; but the disproportion ceases to an eye that has learned really to measure distance, and to know that these smoke-puffs represent a cataract of crashing blocks of ice.

Now the first merit of mountaineering is that it enables one to have what theologians would call an experimental faith in the size of mountains—to substitute a real living belief for a dead intellectual assent. It enables one, first, to assign something like its true magnitude to a rock or a snow-slope; and, secondly, to measure that magnitude in units. Suppose that we are standing upon the Wen gem Alp; between the Monch and the Eiger there stretches a round white bank with a curved outline, which we may roughly compare to the back of one of Sir E. Landseer's lions. The ordinary tourists—the old man, the woman, or the cripple, who are supposed to appreciate the real beauties of Alpine scenery—may look at it comfortably from their hotel. They may see its graceful curve, the long straight lines that are ruled in delicate shading down its sides, and the contrast of the blinding white snow with the dark blue sky above; but they will probably guess it to be a mere bank—a snowdrift, perhaps, which has been piled by the last storm. If you pointed out to them one of the great rocky teeth that projected from its summit, and said that it was a guide, they would probably remark that he looked very small, and would fancy that he could jump over the bank with an effort.

Now a mountaineer knows, to begin with, that it is a massive rocky rib, covered with snow, lying at a sharp angle, and varying perhaps from 500 to 1,000 feet in height. So far he might be accompanied by men of less soaring ambition; by an engineer who had been mapping the country, or an artist who had been carefully observing the mountains from their bases. They might learn in time to interpret correctly the real meaning of shapes at which the uninitiated guess at random. But the mountaineer can go a step further, and it is the next step which gives the real significance to those delicate curves and lines. He can translate the 500 or 1,000 feet of snow-slope into a more tangible unit of measurement. To him, perhaps, they recall the memory of a toilsome ascent, the sun beating on his head for five or six hours, the snow returning the glare with still more parching effect; a stalwart guide toiling all the weary time, cutting steps in hard blue ice, the fragments hissing and spinning down the long straight grooves in the frozen snow till they lost themselves in the yawning chasm below; and step after step taken along the slippery staircase, till at length he triumphantly sprang upon the summit of the tremendous wall that no human foot had scaled before. The little black knobs that rise above the edge represent for him huge impassable rocks, sinking on one side in scarped slippery surfaces towards the snowfield, and on the other stooping in one tremendous cliff to a distorted glacier thousands of feet below.

The faint blue line across the upper neve, scarcely distinguishable to the eye, represents to one observer nothing but a trifling undulation; a second, perhaps, knows that it means a crevasse; the mountaineer remembers that it is the top of a huge chasm, thirty feet across, and perhaps

The Regrets of A Mountaineer

ten times as deep, with perpendicular sides of glimmering blue ice, and fringed by thick rows of enormous pendent icicles. The marks that are scored in delicate lines, such as might be ruled by a diamond on glass, have been cut by innumerable streams trickling in hot weather from the everlasting snow, or ploughed by succeeding avalanches that have slipped from the huge upper snowfields above. In short, there is no insignificant line or mark that has not its memory or its indication of the strange phenomena of the upper world. True, the same picture is painted upon the retina of all classes of observers; and so Porson and a schoolboy and a peasant might receive the same physical impression from a set of black and white marks on the page of a Greek play; but to one they would be an incoherent conglomeration of unmeaning and capricious lines; to another they would represent certain sounds more or less corresponding to some English words; whilst to the scholar they would reveal some of the noblest poetry in the world, and all the associations of successful intellectual labor.

I do not say that the difference is quite so great in the case of the mountains; still I am certain that no one can decipher the natural writing on the face of a snow-slope or a precipice who has not wandered amongst their recesses, and learned by slow experience what is indicated by marks which an ignorant observer would scarcely notice. True, even one who sees a mountain for the first time may know that, as a matter of fact, a scar on the face of a cliff means, for example, a recent fall of a rock; but between the bare knowledge and the acquaintance with all which that knowledge implies-the thunder of the fall, the crash of the smaller fragments the bounding energy of the descending mass-there is almost as much difference as between hearing that a battle has been fought and being present at it yourself. We have all read descriptions of Waterloo till we are sick of the subject; but I imagine that our emotions on seeing the shattered wall of Hougoumont are very inferior to those of one of the Guard who should revisit the place where he held out for a long day against the assaults of the French Army.

Now to an old mountaineer the Oberland cliffs are full of memories; and, more than this, he has learned the language spoken by every crag and every glacier. It is strange if they do not affect him rather more powerfully than the casual visitor who has never been initiated by practical experience into their difficulties. To him, the huge buttress which runs down from the Monch is something more than an irregular pyramid, purple with white patches at the bottom and pure white at the top. He fills up the bare outline supplied by the senses with a thousand lively images. He sees tier above tier of rock, rising in a gradually ascending scale of difficulty, covered at first by long lines of the debris that have been splintered by frost from the higher wall, and afterwards rising bare and black and threatening. He knows instinctively which of the ledges has a dangerous look-where such a bold mountaineer as John Lauener might slip on the polished surface, or be in danger of an avalanche from above. He sees the little shell-like swelling at the foot of the glacier crawling down the steep slope above, and knows that it means an almost inaccessible wall of ice; and the steep snowfields that rise towards the summit are suggestive of something very different from the picture which might have existed in the mind of a German student, who once asked me whether it was possible to make the ascent on a mule.

Hence, if mountains owe their influence upon the imagination in a great degree to their size and steepness, and apparent inaccessible objects-the advantages of the mountaineer are obvious. He can measure those qualities on a different scale from the ordinary traveler. He measures the size, not by the vague abstract term of so many thousand feet, but the hours of labor, divided into minutes-each separately felt-of strenuous muscular exertion. The steepness is not expressed in degrees, but by the memory of the sensation produced when a snow-slope seems to be rising up and smiting you in the face; when, far away from all human help, you are clinging like a fly to the slippery side of a mighty pinnacle in mid-air. And as for the inaccessibility, no one can measure the difficulty of climbing a hill who has not wearied his muscles and brain in struggling against the opposing obstacles. Alpine travelers, it is said, have removed the romance from the mountains by climbing them. What they have really done is to prove that there exists a narrow line by which a way may be found to the top of any given mountain; but the clue leads through innumerable inacessabilities, true, you can follow one path, but to right and left are cliffs which no human foot will ever tread, and whose terrors can only be realized when you are in their immediate neighborhood. The cliffs of the Matterhorn do not bar the way to the top effectually, but it is only by forcing a passage through them that you can really appreciate their terrible significance.

Hence I say that the qualities which strike every sensitive observer are impressed upon the mountaineer with tenfold force and intensity. If he is as accessible to poetical influences as his neighbors—and I don't know why he should be less so—he has opened new avenues of access between the scenery and his mind. He has learned a language which is but partially revealed to ordinary men. An artist is superior to an unlearned picture-seer, not merely because he has greater natural sensibility, but because he has improved it by methodical experience; because his senses have been sharpened by constant practice, till he can catch finer shades of coloring, and more delicate inflexions of line; because, also, the lines and colors have acquired new significance, and been associated with a thousand thoughts with which the mass of mankind has never cared to connect them. The mountaineer is improved by a similar process. But I know some skeptical critics will ask, does not the way which he is accustomed to regard mountains rather deaden their poetical influence? Doesn't he come to look at them as mere instruments of sport, and overlook their more spiritual teaching? Does not all the excitement of personal adventure and the noisy apparatus of guides, and ropes, and axes, and tobacco, and the fun of climbing, rather dull his perceptions and incapacitate him from perceiving.

"The silence that is in the starry sky,
The sleep that is among the lonely hills?"

Well, I have known some stupid and unpoetical mountaineers; and, since I have been dismounted from my favorite hobby, I think I have met some similar specimens amoung the humbler class of tourists. There are persons, I fancy, who "do" the Alps; who look upon the Lake of Lucerne as one more task ticked off from their memorandum book, and count up the list of summits visible from the Gornergrat without being penetrated with any keen sense of sublimity. And there are mountaineers who are capable of making a pun on the top of Mont Blanc-and capable of nothing more. Still I venture to deny that even punning is incompatible with poetry, or that those who make the pun can have no deeper feeling in their bosoms which they are perhaps too shamefaced to utter.

The fact is that that which gives its inexpressible charm to mountaineering is the incessant series of exquisite natural scenes, which are for the most part enjoyed by the mountaineer alone. This is, I am aware, a round assertion; but I will try to support it by a few of the visions which are recalled to me by these Oberland cliffs, and which I have seen profoundly enjoyed by men who, perhaps never mentioned them again, and probably in describing their adventures scrupulously avoided the danger of being sentimental.

Thus every traveler has occasionally done a sunrise, and a more lamentable proceeding than the ordinary view of a sunrise can hardly be imagined. You are cold, miserable, breakfastless; have risen shivering from a warm bed, and in your heart long only to creep into bed again. To the mountaineer all this is changed. He is beginning a day full of the anticipation of a pleasant excitement. He has, perhaps, been waiting anxiously for fine weather, to try conclusions with some huge giant not yet scaled. He moves out with something of the feeling with which a solider goes to the assault of a fortress, but without the same probability of coming home in fragments; the danger is trifling enough to be merely exhilatory, and to give a pleasant tension to the nerves; his muscles feel firm and springy, and his stomach—no small advantage to the enjoyment of scenery—is in excellent order. He looks at the sparkling stars with keen satisfaction, prepared to enjoy a fine sunrise with all his faculties at their best, and with the added pleasure of a good omen for his day's work. Then a huge dark mass begins to form a background of deep purple, against which the outline becomes gradually more definite as one by one, the peaks catch the exquisite Alpine glow, lighting up in rapid succession, like a vast illumination; and when at last the steady sunlight settles upon them, and shows every rock and glacier, without even a delicate film of mist to obscure them, he feels his heart bound, and steps out gaily to the assault-just as the people on the Rigi are giving thanks that the show is over and that they may go to bed.

Still grander is the sight when the mountaineer has already reached some lofty ridge, and as the sun rises, stands between the day and the night—the valley still in deep sleep, with the mists lying between the folds of the hills, and the snow-peaks, standing out clear and pale white just before the sun reaches them, whilst a broad band of orange light runs all round the vast horizon. The glory of sunsets is equally increased in the thin upper air. The grandest of all such sights that live in my memory is that of a sunset from the Aiguille du Gouter. The snow at our feet was glowing with rich light, and the shadows in our footsteps a vivid green by the contrast. Beneath us was a vast horizontal floor of thin level mists suspended in midair, spread like a canopy over the whole boundless landscape, and tinged with every hue of sunset. Through its rents and gaps we could see the lower mountains, the distant plains, and a fragment of the Lake of Geneva lying in a more sober purple. Above us rose the solemn mass of Mont Blanc in the richest glow of an Alpine sunset. The sense of lonely sublimity was almost oppressive, and although half our party was suffering from sickness, I believe even the guides were moved to a sense of solemn beauty.

The Regrets of A Mountaineer

These grand scenic effects are occasionally seen by ordinary travelers, though the ordinary traveler is for the most part out of temper at a.m. The mountaineer can enjoy them, both because his frame of mind is properly trained to receive the natural beauty, and because he alone sees them with their best accessories, amidst the silence of the eternal snow, and the vast panoramas visible from the loftier summits. And he has a similar advantage in most of the great natural phenomena of the cloud and the sunshine. No sight in the Alps is more impressive than the huge rocks of a black precipice suddenly frowning out through the chasms of a storm-cloud. But grand as such a sight may be from the safe verandahs of the inn at Grindelwald, it is far grander in the silence of the Central Alps amongst the savage wilderness of rock and snow.

Another characteristic effect of the High Alps often presents itself when one has been climbing for two or three hours, with nothing in sight but the varying wreaths of mist that chased each other monotonously along the rocky ribs up whose snow-covered backbone we were laboriously fighting our way. Suddenly there is a puff of wind, and looking round we find that we have in an instant pierced the clouds, and emerged, as it were, on the surface of the ocean of vapor. Beneath us stretches for hundreds of miles the level fleecy floor, and above us shines out clear in the eternal sunshine every mountain, from Mount Blanc to Monte Rosa and the Jungfrau. What, again, in the lower regions, can equal the mysterious charm of gazing from the edge of a torn rocky parapet into an apparently fathomless abyss, where nothing but what an Alpine traveler calls a "strange formless wreathing of vapor" indicates the storm-wind that is raging below us?

I might go on indefinitely recalling the strangely impressive scenes that frequently startle the traveler in the waste upper world; but language is feeble indeed to convey even a glimmering of what is to be seen to those who have not seen it for themselves, whilst to them it can be little more than a peg upon which to hang their own recollections. These glories, in which the mountain spirit reveals himself to his true worshippers, are only to be gained by the appropriate service of climbing—at some risk, though a very trifling risk, if he is approached with due form and ceremony—into the furthest recesses of his shrines. And without seeing them, I maintain that no man has really seen the Alps.

The difference between the exoteric and the esoteric school of mountaineers may be indicated by their different view of glaciers. At Grindelwald, for example, it is the fashion to go and "see the glaciers"—heaven save the mark! Ladies in costume, heavy German professors, Americans doing the Alps at a gallop, cook's tourists and other varieties of a well-known genus, go off in shoals and see-what? A gigantic mass of ice, strangely torn with a few of the exquisite blue crevasses, but defiled and prostrate in dirt and ruins. A stream foul with mud oozes out from the base; the whole mass seems to be melting fast away; the summer sun has evidently got the best of it in these lower regions, and nothing can resist him but the great mounds of decaying rock that strew the surface in confused lumps. It is as much like the glacier of the upper regions as the melting fragments of snow in a London street are like the surface of the fresh snow that has just fallen in a country field. And by way of improving its attractions a perpetual picnic is going on, and the ingenious natives have hewed a tunnel into the ice, for admission to which they charge certain centimes.

The unlucky glacier reminds me at his latter end of a wretched whale stranded on a beach, dissolving into masses of blubber, and hacked by remorseless fishermen, instead of plunging at his ease in the deep blue water. Far above, where the glacier begins his course, he is seen only by the true mountaineer. There are vast amphitheaters of pure snow, of which the glacier known to tourists is merely the insignificant drainage, but whose very existence they do not generally suspect. They are utterly ignorant that from the top of the icefall which they visit you may walk for hours on the eternal ice. After a long climb you come to the region where the glacier is truly at its noblest; where the surface is a spotless white; where the crevasses are enormous rents sinking to profound depths, with walls of the purest blue; where the glacier is torn and shattered by the energetic forces which mound it, but has an expression of superabundant power, like a full stream fretting against its banks and plunging through the vast gorges that it has hewn for itself in the course of centuries. The bases of the mountains are immersed in a deluge of cockneyism—fortunately a shallow deluge—whilst their summits rise high into the bracing air, where everything is pure and poetical.

The difference which I have thus endeavored to indicate is more or less traceable in a wider sense. The mountains are exquisitely beautiful, indeed, from whatever points of view we contemplate them; and the mountaineer would lose much if he never saw the beauties of the lower valleys, of pasturages deep in flowers, and dark pine-forests with the summits shining from far off between the stems. Only, as it seems to me, he has the exclusive perogative of thoroughly enjoying one—and that the most characteristic, though by no means only, element of the scenery. There may be a very good dinner spread before twenty people; but if nineteen of them were teetotalers, and the twentieth drank his wine like a man, he would be the only one to do it full justice; the others might praise the meat or the fruits, but he would alone enjoy the champagne; and in the great feast which nature spreads before us (a stock metaphor, which emboldens me to make the comparison), the high mountain scenery acts the part of the champagne. Unluckily, too, the teetotalers are very apt, in this case also, to sit in judgment upon their more adventurous neighbors. Especially are they pleased to carp at the views from high summits. I have been constantly asked, with a covert sneer, "Did it repay you?"—a question which involves the assumption that one wants to be repaid, as though the labor were not itself part of the pleasure, and which implies a doubt that the view is really enjoyable.

People are always demonstrating that the lower views are the most beautiful; and at the same time complaining that mountaineers frequently turn back without looking at the view from the top, as though that would necessarily imply that they cared nothing for scenery. In opposition to which I must first remark, that, as a rule, every step of an ascent has a beauty of its own, which one is quietly absorbing even when one is not directly making it a subject of contemplation, and that the view from the top is generally the crowning glory of the whole.

It will be enough if I conclude with an attempt to illustrate this last assertion; and I will do it by still referring to the Oberland. Every visitor with a soul for the beautiful admires the noble form of the Wetterhorn—the lofty snow-crowned pyramid rising in such light and yet massive lines from its huge basement of perpendicular cliffs. The Wetterhorn has, however, a further merit. To my mind—and I believe most connoisseurs of mountain tops agree with me—it is one of the most impressive summits in the Alps. It is not a sharp pinnacle like the Weisshorn, or a cupola like Mont Blanc, or a grand rocky tooth like Monte Rosa, but a long and nearly horizontal knife-edge, which, as seen from either end, has of course the appearance of a sharp-pointed cone. It is when balanced upon this ridge—sitting a stride of the knife-edge on which one can hardly stand without giddiness that one fully appreciates an Alpine precipice. Mr. Justice Wills has admirably described the first ascent, and the impression it made upon him, in a paper which has become classical for succeeding adventurers. Behind you the snow-slope sinks with perilous steepness towards the wilderness of glacier and rock through which

Sir Leslie Stephen

the ascent has lain. But in front the ice sinks with even greater steepness for a few feet or yards. Then it curves over and disappears, and the next thing that the eye catches is the meadowland of Grindelwald, some 9,000 feet below.

I have looked down many precipices, where the eye can trace the course of every pebble that bounds down the awful slopes, and where I have shuddered as some dislodged fragment of rock showed the course which, in case of accident, fragments of my own body would follow. A precipice is always, for obvious reasons, far more terrible from above than from below. The creeping, tingling sensation which passes through one's limbs even when one knows oneself to be in perfect safety, testifies to the thrilling influence of the sight. But I have never so realized the terrors of a terrific cliff as when I could not see it. The awful gulf which intervened between me and the green meadows struck the imagination by its invisibility. It was like the view which may be seen from the ridge of a cathedral roof, where the eaves have for their immediate background the pavement of the streets below; only this cathedral was 9,000 feet high. Now, anyone standing at the foot of the Wetterhorn may admire their stupendous massiveness and steepness; but, to feel their influence enter into the very marrow of one's bones, it is necessary to stand at the summit, and to fancy the one little slide down the short ice-slope, to be followed apparently by a bound into clear air and a fall down to the houses, from heights where only the eagle ventures to soar.

This is one of the alpine beauties, which, of course, is beyond the power of art to imitate, and which people are therefore apt to ignore. But it is not the only one to be seen on the high summits. It is often said that these views are not "beautiful"—apparently because they won't go into a picture, or, to put it more fairly, because no picture can in the faintest degree imitate them. But without quarreling about words, I think that, even if "beautiful" is not the correct epithet, they have a marvelously stimulating effect upon the imagination. Let us look round from this wonderful pinnacle in mid-air, and note one or two of the most striking elements of the scenery.

You are, in first place, perched on a cliff, whose presence is the more felt because it is unseen. Then you are in a region over which eternal silence is brooding. Not a sound ever comes from there, except the occasional fall of a splintered fragment of rock, or a layer of snow; no stream is heard trickling, and the sounds of animal life are left thousands of feet below. The most that you can hear is some mysterious noise made by the wind eddying round the gigantic rocks; sometimes a strange flapping sound, as if an unearthly flag was shaking its invisible folds in the air. The enormous tract of country over which your view extends—most of it dim and almost dissolved into air by distance—intensifies the strange influence of the silence. You feel the force of the line I have quoted from Wordsworth.

"The sleep that is among the lonely hills."

None of the travelers whom you can see crawling at your feet has the least conception of what is meant by the silent solitudes of the High Alps. To you, it is like a return to the stir of active life, when, after hours of lonely wandering, you return to hear the tinkling of the cowbells below; to them the same sound is the ultimate limit of the habitable world.

Whilst your mind is properly toned by these influences, you become conscious of another fact, to which the common variety of tourists is necessarily insensible. You begin to find out for the first time what the mountains really are. On one side, you look back upon the huge reservoirs from which the Oberland glaciers descend. You see the vast stores from which the great rivers of Europe are replenished, the monstrous crawling masses that are carving the mountains into shape, and the gigantic bulwarks that separate two great quarters of the world. From below these wild regions are half invisible; they are masked by the outer line of mountains; and it is not till you are able to command them from some lofty point that you can appreciate the grandeur of the huge barriers, and the snow that is piled within their folds.

There is another half of the view equally striking. Looking towards the north, the whole of Switzerland is couched at your feet, the Jura and the Black Forest lie on the far horizon. And then you know what is the nature of a really mountainous country. From below everything is seen in a kind of distorted perspective. The people of the valley naturally think that the valley is everything—that the country resembles old-fashioned maps, where a few sporadic lumps are distributed amongst towns and plains. The true proportions reveal themselves as you ascend. The valleys, you can now see, are nothing but narrow trenches scooped out amidst a tossing waste of mountain, just to carry off the drainage. The great ridges run hither and thither, having it all their own way, wild and untamable regions of rock or open grass or forest, at whose feet the valleys exist on sufferance. Creeping about amongst the roots of the hills, you half miss the hills themselves; you quite fail to understand the massiveness of the mountain chains, and, therefore, the wonderful energy of the forces that have heaved the surface of the world into these distorted shapes. And it is to a half-conscious sense of the powers that must have been at work that a great part of the influence of mountain scenery is due.

Geologists tell us that a theory of catastrophes is unphilosophical; but, whatever may be the scientific truth, our minds are impressed as though we were witnessing the results of some incredible convulsion. At Stonehenge we ask what human beings could have erected these strange grey monuments and in the mountains we instinctively ask what force can have carved out the Matterhorn, and placed the Wetterhorn on its gigantic pedestal. Now, it is not till we reach some commanding point that we realize the amazing extent of country over which the solid ground has been shaking and heaving itself in irresistible tumult.

Something, it is true, of this last effect may be seen from such mountains as the Rigi or the Faulhorn. There, too, one seems to be at the center of a vast sphere, the earth bending up in a cup-like form to meet the sky, and the blue vault above stretching in an arch majestical by its enormous extent. There you seem to see a sensible fraction of the world at your feet. But the effect is far less striking when other mountains obviously look down upon you; when, as it were, you are looking at the waves of the great ocean of hills merely from the crest of one of the waves themselves, and not from some lighthouse that rises far over their heads; for the Wetterhorn, like the Eiger, Monch, and Jungfrau, owes one great beauty to the fact that it is on the edge of the lower country, and stands between the real giants and the crowd of inferior, though still enormous, masses in attendance upon them. And, in the next place, your mind is far better adapted to receive impressions of sublimity when you are alone, in a silent region, with a black sky above and giant cliffs all round; with a sense still in your mind, if not of actual danger, still of danger that would become real with the slightest relaxation of caution, and with the world divided from you by hours of snow and rock.

I will go no further, not because I have no more to say, but because descriptions of scenery soon become wearisome, and because I have, I hope, said enough to show that the mountaineer may boast of some intellectual pleasures; that he is not a mere scrambler, but that he looks for poetical impressions, as well as for such small glory as his achievements may gain in a very small circle.

Something of what he gains fortunately sticks by him: he does not quite forget the mountain language; his eye still recognises the space and the height and the glory of the lofty mountains. And yet there is some pain in wandering ghostlike among the scenes of his earlier pleasures. For my part, I try in vain to hug myself in a sense of comfort. I turn over in bed when I hear the stamping of heavily nailed shoes along the passage of an inn about 2 a.m. I feel the skin of my nose complacently when I see others returning with a glistening tight aspect about that unluckily prominent feature, and know that in a day or two it will be raw and blistered and burning. I think, in a comfortable inn at night, of the miseries of those who are trying to sleep in damp hay, or on hard boards of chalets, at once cold and stuffy and haunted by innumerable fleas. I congratulate myself on having a whole skin and unfractured bones, and on the small danger of ever breaking them over an Alpine precipice. But yet I secretly know that these consolations are feeble. It is little use to avoid early rising and discomfort, and even fleas, if one also loses the pleasures to which they were the sauce—rather too piquant a sauce occasionally, it must be admitted.

The philosophy is all very well which recommends moderate enjoyment, regular exercise, and a careful avoidance of risk and overexcitement. That is, it is all very well so long as risk and excitement and immoderate enjoyment are out of your power; but it does not stand the test of looking on and seeing them just beyond your reach. In time, no doubt, a man may grow calm; he may learn to enjoy the pleasures and the exquisite beauties of the lower regions—though they, too, are most fully enjoyed when they have a contrast with beauties of a different, and pleasures of a keener excitement. When first debarred, at any rate, one feels like a balloon full of gas, and fixed by immovable ropes to the prosaic ground. It is pleasant to lie on one's back in a bed of rhododendrons, and look up to a mountain top peering at one from above a bank of cloud; but it is pleasantest when one has qualified oneself for repose by climbing the peak the day before and becoming familiar with its terrors and its beauties.

In time, doubtless, one may get reconciled to anything; one may settle down to be a caterpillar, even after one has known the pleasures of being a butterfly; one may become philosophical, and have one's clothes let out; and even in time, perhaps—though it is almost too terrible to contemplate—be content with a mule or a carriage, or that lowest depth to which human beings can sink, and for which the English language happily affords no name, a chaise a porteurs: and even in such degradation the memory of better times may be pleasant; for I doubt much whether it is truth the poet sings.

Sir Leslie Stephen

"That a sorrow's crown of sorrow is remembering happier things." —*Tennyson*

Certainly, to a philosophical mind, the sentiment is doubtful. For my part, the fate which has cut me off, if I may use the expression, in the flower of my youth, and doomed me to be a non-climbing animal in the future, is one which ought to exclude grumbling. I cannot indicate it more plainly, for I might so make even the grumbling in which I have already indulged look like a sin. I can only say that there are some very delightful things in which it is possible to discover an infinitesimal drop of bitterness, and that the mountaineer who undertakes to cut himself off from his favorite pastime, even for reasons which he will admit in his wildest moods to be more than amply sufficient must expect at times to feel certain pangs of regret, however quickly they may be smothered.

Edward Whymper (1840-1911), a writer and illustrator, is responsible for the first ascent of the Matterhorn that ended in what has become the most famous tragedy in mountaineering history. Whymper made extensive visits to the Alps, Andes, Greenland, the Rocky Mountains, and the mountains of Mexico. He is the author of *Scrambles Amoungst the Alps and Travels Among the Great Andes of the Equator.*

EDWARD WHYMPER: "DESCENT OF THE MATTERHORN"

from Scrambles Amongst the Alps

Hudson and I again consulted as to the best and safest arrangement of the party. We agreed that it would be best for Croz to go first, and Hadow second; Hudson, who was almost equal to a guide in sureness of foot, wished to be third; Lord F. Douglas was placed next, and old Peter, the strongest of the remainder, after him. I suggested to Hudson that we should attach a rope to the rocks on our arrival at the difficult bit, and hold it as we descended, as an additional protection. He approved the idea, but it was not definitely settled that it should be done. The party was being arranged in the above order whilst I was sketching the summit, and they had finished,and were waiting for me to be tied in line, when some one remembered that our names had not been left in a bottle. They requested me to write them down,and moved off while it was being done.

A few minutes afterward I tied myself to young Peter, ran down after the others, and caught them just as they were commencing the descent of the difficult part. Great care was being taken only one man was moving at a time: when he was firmly planted, the next advanced, and so on. They had not, however, attached the additional rope to rocks, and nothing was said about it. The suggestion was not made for my own sake, and I am not sure that it even occurred to me again. For some little distance we followed the others, detached from them, and should have continued

49

so had not Lord F. Douglas asked me, about 3 p.m., to tie on to old Peter, as he feared, he said, that Taugwalder would not be able to hold his ground if a slip occurred.

A few minutes later a sharp-eyed lad ran into the Monte Rosa hotel to Seiler, saying that he had seen an avalanche fall from the summit of the Matterhorn onto the Matterhorngletscher. The boy was reproved for telling idle stories: he was right, nevertheless, and this was what he saw.

Michel Croz had laid aside his axe, and in order to give Mr. Hadow greater security was absolutely taking hold of his legs and putting his feet, one by one, into their proper positions As far as I know, no one was actually descending. I cannot speak with certainty, because the two leading men were partially hidden from my sight by an intervening mass of rock, but it is my belief, from the movements of their shoulders, that Croz, having done as I hadsaid, was in the act of turning round to go down a step or two himself: at this moment Mr. Hadow slipped, fell against him and knocked him over. I heard one startled exclamation from Croz, then saw him and Mr. Hadow flying downward: in another moment Hudson was dragged from his steps, and Lord F. Douglas immediately after him. Immediately we heard Croz's exclamation, old Peter and I planted ourselves as firmly as the rocks would permit: the rope was taut between us, and the jerk came on us both as on one man, We held, but the rope broke midway between Taugwalder and Lord Francis Douglas. For a few seconds we saw our unfortunate companions sliding downward on their backs, and spreading out their hands, endeavoring to save themselves. They passed from our sight uninjured, disappeared one by one, and fell from precipice to precipice on to the Matterhorngletscher below, a distance of nearly four thousand feet in height. From the moment the rope broke it was impossible to help them.

So perished our comrades! For the space of half an hour we remained on the spot without moving a single step. The two men, paralyzed by terror, cried like infants, and trembled in such a manner as to threaten us with the fate of the others. Old Peter rent the air with exclamations of "Chamonix! Oh, what will Chamonix say?" He meant, who would believe that Croz could fall?

The young man did nothing but scream or sob, "We are lost! we are lost!" Fixed between the two, I could move neither up nor down. I begged young Peter to descend, but he dared not. Unless he did, we could not advance. Old Peter became alive to the danger, and swelled the cry, "We are lost! we are lost!" The father's fear was natural—he trembled for his son.

Edward Whymper

The young man's fear was cowardly—he thought of self alone. At last Old Peter summoned up courage, and changed his position to a rock to which he could fix the rope: the young man then descended, and we all stood together. Immediately we did so, I asked for the rope which had given way, and found, to my surprise-indeed, to my horror-that it was the weakest of the three ropes. It was not brought, and should not have been employed, for the purpose for which it was used. It was old rope, and, compared with the others, was feeble. It was intended as a reserve, in case we had to leave much rope behind attached to rocks. I saw at once that a serious question was involved, and made them give me the end. It had broken in mid-air, and it did not appear to have sustained previous injury.

For more than two hours afterward I thought almost every moment that the next would be my last, for the Taugwalders, utterly unnerved, were not only incapable of giving assistance, but were in such a state that a slip might have been expected from them at any moment. After a time we were able to do that which should have been done at first, and fixed rope to firm rocks, in addition to being tied together. These ropes were cut from time to time, and were left behind. Even with their assurance the men were afraid to proceed, and several times old Peter turned with ashy face and faltering limbs, and said with terrible emphasis, "I cannot!"

About 6 p.m. we arrived at the snow upon the ridge descending toward Zermatt, and all peril was over. We frequently looked, but in vain, for traces of our unfortunate companions: we bent over the ridge and cried to them, but no sound returned. Convinced at last that they were within neither sight nor hearing, we ceased from our useless efforts, and, too cast down for speech, silently gathered up our things and the little effects of those who were lost, prepare tory to continuing the descent. When lo! a mighty arch appeared, rising above the lyskamm high into the sky. Pale, Colorless and noiseless, but perfectly sharp and defined, except where it was lost in the clouds, this unearthly apparition seemed like a vision from another world, and almost appalled we watched with amazement the gradual development of two vast crosses, one on either side. If the Taugwalders had not been the first to perceive it, I should have doubted my senses. They thought it had some connection with the accident, and, after a while, that it might bear some relation to ourselves. But our movements had no effect upon it. The spectral forms remained motionless. It was a fearful and wonderful sight, unique in my experience, and impressive beyond description, coming at such a moment.

Decent of the Matterhorn

I was ready to leave, and waiting for the others. They had recovered
their appetites and the use of their tongues. They spoke in patois, which I
did not understand. At length the son said in French, "Monsieur." "Yes."
"We are poor men; we have lost our Herr; we shall not get paid; we can ill
afford this." "Stop!" I said, interrupting him—" that is nonsense: I shall
pay you, of course, just as if your Herr were here." They talked together
in their patois for a short time, and then the son spoke again: We don't
wish you to pay us. We wish you to write in the hotel-book at Zermatt
and to your journals that we have not been paid." "What nonsense are
you talking? I don't understand you. What do you mean?" He proceeded:
"Why, next year there will be many travelers at Zermatt, and we shall
get more voyageurs."

Who would answer such a proposition? I made them no reply in
words, but they knew very well the indignation that I felt. They filled the
cup of bitterness to overflowing, and I tore down the cliff madly and recklessly, in a way that caused them, more than once, to inquire if I wished
to kill them. Night fell, and for an hour the descent was continued in
the darkness. At half-past nine a resting-place was found, and upon a
wretched slab, barely large enough to hold the three, we passed six miserable hours. At daybreak the descent was resumed, and from the Hornli
ridge we ran down to the chalets of Buhl and on to Zermatt. Seizer met
me at his door, and followed in silence to my room: "What is the matter
?" "The Taugwalders and I have returned." He did not need more, and
burst into tears, but lost no time in useless lamentations, and set to work
to arouse the village. Ere long a score of men had started to ascend the
Hohlicht heights, above Kalbermatt and Z'Mutt, which commanded the
plateau of the Matterhorngletscher. They returned after six hours, and
reported that they had seen the bodies lying motionless on the snow. This
was on Saturday, and they proposed that we should leave on Sunday evening, so as to arrive upon the plateau at daybreak on Monday. Unwilling
to lose the slightest chance, the Rev. J. M'Cormick and I resolved to start
on Sunday morning. The Zermattmen, threatened with excommunica-
tion by their priests if they failed to attend the early mass, were unable
to accompany us. To several of them, at least, this was a severe trial, and
Peter Perm declared with tears that nothing else would have prevented
him from joining in the search for his old comrades, Englishmen came to
our aid. The Rev. J. Robertson and Mr. J. Phillpotts offered themselves

and their guide, Franz Andermatten: another Englishman lent us Joseph Marie and Alexandre Lochmatter. Frederic Payot and Jean Tairraz of Chamonix also volunteered.

We started at 2 a.m. on Sunday the 16th, and followed the route that we had taken on the previous Thursday as far as the Hornli. From thence we went down to the right of the ridge, and mounted through the seracs of the Matterhorngletscher. By 8:30 we had gotten to the plateau at the top of the glacier, and within sight of the corner in which we knew my companions must be. As we saw one weather-beaten man after another raise the telescope, turn deadly pale and pass it on without a word to the next, we knew that all hope was gone. We approached. They had fallen below as they had fallen above Croz a little in advance, Hadow near him, and Hudson some distance behind, but of Lord F. Douglas we could see nothing. We left them where they fell, buried in snow at the base of the grandest cliff of the most majestic mountain of the Alps.

All those who had fallen had been tied with the Manila, or with the second and equally strong rope, and consequently there had been only one link-that between old Peter and Lord F. Douglas, here the weaker rope had been used. This had a very ugly look for Taugwalder, for it was not possible to suppose that the others would have sanctioned the employment of a rope so greatly inferior in strength when there were more than two hundred and fifty feet of the better qualities still out of use. For the sake of the old guide (who bore a good reputation), and upon all other accounts, it was desirable that this matter should be cleared up; and after my examination before the court of inquiry which was instituted by the government was over, I handed in a number of questions which were framed so as to afford old Peter an opportunity of exculpating himself from the grave suspicions which at once fell upon him. The questions, I was told, were put and answered, but the answers, although promised, have never reached me.

Meanwhile, the administration sent strict injunctions to recover the bodies, and upon the 19th of July twenty-one men of Zermatt accomplished that sad and dangerous task. Of the body of Lord Francis Douglas they too saw nothing; it is probably still arrested on the rocks above. The remains of Hudson and Hadow were interred upon the north side of the Zermatt church, in the presence of a reverent crowd of sympathizing friends. The body of Michel Croz lies upon the other side, under a simpler tomb, whose inscription bears honorable testimony to his rectitude, to his courage and to his devotion.

Decent of the Matterhorn

So the traditional inaccessibility of the Matterhorn was vanquished, and was replaced by legends of a more real character. Others will essay to scale its proud cliffs, but to none will it be the mountain that it was to its early explorers. Others may tread its summit snows, but none will ever know the feelings of those who first gazed upon its marvelous panorama, and none, I trust, will ever be compelled to tell of joy turned into grief, and of laughter into mourning. It proved to be a stubborn foe; it resisted long and gave many a hard blow; it was defeated at last with an ease that none could have anticipated, but, like a relentless enemy conquered but not crushed, it took terrible vengeance. The time may come when the Matterhorn shall have passed away, and nothing save a heap of shapeless fragments will mark the spot where the great moutain stood, for, atom by atom, inch by inch, and yard by yard, it yields to forces which nothing can withstand. That time is far distant, and ages hence generations unborn will gaze upon its awful precipices and wonder at its unique form. However exalted may be their ideas and however exaggerated their expectations, none will come to return disappointed!

The play is over, and the curtain is, about to fall. Before we part, a word upon the graver teachings of the mountains. See yonder height! 'Tis far away-unbidden comes the word "Impossible!" "Not so, "says the mountaineer. "The way is long, I know; it's difficult—it may be dangerous. It's possible, I'm sure: I'll seek the way, take counsel of my brother mountaineers, and find how they have gained similar heights and learned to avoid the dangers." He starts (all slumbering down below): the path is slippery, maybe laborious too. Caution and perseverance gain the day— the height is reached! and those beneath cry, "Incredible! 'tis superhuman !"

We who go mountain-scrambling have constantly set before us the superiority of fixed purpose or perseverance to brute force. We know that each height, each step must be gained by patient, laborious toil, and that wishing cannot take the place of working: we know the benefits of mutual aid-that many a difficulty must be encountered, and many an obstacle must be grappled with or turned; but we know that where there's a will there's a way; and we come back to our daily occupations better fitted to fight the battle of life and to overcome the impediments which obstruct our paths, strengthened and cheered by the recollection of past labors and by the memories of victories gained in other fields.

I have not made myself an advocate or an apologist for mountaineering, nor do I now intend to usurp the functions of a moralist, but my task would have been ill performed if it had been concluded without one reference to the more serious lessons of the mountaineer. We glory in the physical regeneration which is the product of our exertions; we exult over the grandeur of the scenes that are brought before our eyes, the splendors of sunrise and sunset, and the beauties of hill, dale, lake, wood and waterfall; but we value more highly the development of manliness, and the evolution, under combat with difficulties, of those noble qualities of human nature—courage, patience, endurance and fortitude.

Some hold these virtues in less estimation, and assign base and contemptible motives to those who indulge in our innocent sport. "Be thou chaste as ice, as pure as snow, thou shalt not escape calumny." Others, again, who are not detractors, find mountaineering, as a sport, to be wholly unintelligible. It is not greatly to be wondered at-we are not all constituted alike. Mountaineering is a pursuit essentially adapted to the young or vigorous, and not to the old or feeble. To the latter toil may be no pleasure, and it is often said by such persons, "This man is making a toil of pleasure." Toil he must who goes mountaineering, but out of the toil comes strength (not merely muscular energy—more than that, an awakening of all the faculties), and from the strength arises pleasure. Then, again, it is often asked, in tones, which seem to imply that the answer must at least be doubtful, "But does it repay you?" Well, we cannot estimate our enjoyment as you measure your wine or weigh your lead: it is real, nevertheless. If I could blot out every reminiscence or erase every memory, still I should say that my scrambles amongst the Alps have repaid me, for they have given me two of the best things a man can possess—health and friends.

The recollections of past pleasures cannot be erased. Even now as I write they crowd up before me. First comes an endless series of pictures, magnificent in form, effect and color. I see the great peaks with clouded tops, seeming to mount up forever and ever; I hear the music of the distant herds, the peasant's yodel and the solemn church-bells and I scent the fragrant breath of the pines; and after these have passed away another train of thoughts succeeds—of those who have been upright, brave and true; of kind hearts and bold deeds; and of courtesies received at stranger hands, trifles in themselves, but expressive of that good-will toward men which is the essence of charity.

Still, the last sad memory hovers round, and sometimes drifts across like floating mist, cutting off sunshine and chilling the remembrance of happier times. There have been joys too great to be described in words,

Decent of the Matterhorn

and there have been griefs upon which I have not dared to dwell; and with these in mind I say; "Climb if you will, but remember that courage and strength are naught without prudence, and that a momentary negligence may destroy the happiness of a lifetime. Do nothing in haste, look well to each step, and from the beginning think what may be the end."

Heinrich Harrer (b. 1921) gained recognition as one of four climbers to make the first ascent of the North Face of the Eiger in 1938. He later was selected as a member of 1939 German Nanga Parbat expedition and was interned in India by the British because of the outbreak of WWII. He escaped and spent the next seven years in Tibet where he became a friend of and tutor to the Dalai Lama. He is the author of *The White Spider and Seven Years in Tibet.*

HEINRICH HARRER:
THE TRAGEDY OF TONI KURZ
From the White Spider

As is often the case with mountain folk, whose features have been carved by wind and storm so that they look older in their youth, younger in their old age, Albert von Allmen's face is ageless. He might be in his middle thirties or his middle fifties.

The mountains have been von Allmen's strict teachers and loyal friends, even if his profession leads him more into than onto the peaks. For Albert is a Sector-Guard on the Jungfrau Railway. He is responsible for everything along the line inside the Eiger, and sees to it that nothing goes wrong in that long tunneled section; but his are kindly eyes. They are surrounded by many little creases which record not only cares and the hard life of the mountains, but also the joy of laughter.

At noon on July 21st 1936 Albert was standing outside the gallery entrance at Kilometre 3-8, after opening the heavy wooden door.

It was a Tuesday. Ever since Saturday the 18th there had been four climbers on the Face; two Austrians, Edi Rainer and Willy Angerer, and two Bavarians, Anderl Hinterstoisser and Toni Kurz. Everyone had fallen for the fresh-faced, clean-limbed Toni Kurz, not only because he was himself a professional guide, but because of his laugh. When Toni laughed, it was as if life itself were laughing. All young men, these; Angerer, the eldest, was twenty-seven, Kurz and Hinterstoisser just twenty-three. They had already climbed almost as high on the Face as Sedlmayer and Mehringer the year before, on their ill-fated attempt from which they did not return. But these four would come back safely, what had been seen of them during the last few days gave solid grounds for hope that this time there would be no disaster.

None of those present had seen such magnificent climbing. True, one of the climbers, apparently Angerer, seemed to have been struck by a stone. That was why the party had been moving so slowly for the last two days, and that was probably why they had decided to turn back. The descent over ice-fields and rock cliffs swept by falling stones and avalanches looked ghastly enough; but the four men were moving steadily, if very slowly, downwards towards the safety of the easier ground below, in obvious good heart and without a moment's hesitation. The three fit ones were continually attending to the one who had clearly been hurt. They couldn't be bad, these lads who looked after each other so well. They must be fine fellows, even if a bit crack-pot.

Albert von Allmen thought of the Sunday tourists and excursionists, the blase men and the ladies in high heels who went to the tunnel-window at Eigerwand Station and uttered their "ah's" and "oh's" as they gazed at what seemed to them the terrifying gulfs and immeasurable heights of the Eiger's precipice. It was people like those, hungering for sensation, who were now crowding round the telescopes at Grindelwald and Kleine Scheidegg. And then too there were the pronunciamentos of the know-it-all's busy weighing up the chances of another catastrophe or of the safe return of four living men to the valley.

They must get back safely, thought Albert. His sympathy lay with youth, youth generally, but particularly these four youngsters on the Face. It would be a good idea to take a look at them and hear for himself how they were getting on. Allmen pushed back the bolts of the heavy wooden doors and stepped out into the open, as he had done a hundred times before. He was used to the grim aspect of the Face; but that day, perhaps because there were people on it, it seemed particularly horrific. A layer of glassy ice overlaid the rock; here and there a stone came clattering down; many of those lethal bullets went humming menacingly down for thousands of feet quite clear of the Face. Then, too, there was the hissing of snow-avalanches as they slid down, whole cascades of snow and ice. The very thought that there were living men somewhere up in that vertical Hell was oppressive. Could they still be alive?

Heinrich Harrer

Von Allmen shouted, listened, shouted again.

Then the answer reached him. A cheery, gay answer. The voices of four young people shouting, yodeling. Albert couldn't see them, but, judging by the sound, they couldn't be more than three or four hundred feet above him. It seemed incredible to him that anyone could climb down those icy, perpendicular or even overhanging rocks, continually swept by falling stones; but these crazy kids had so often shown how possible it is to climb impossible things. And, above all, there was that cheery shout coming down from above:

"We're climbing straight down. All's well!"

All well with all of them. The Sector-Guard's heart beat faster for joy.

"I'll brew you some hot tea," he shouted back.

Smiling with pleasure, Albert von Allmen went back through the gallery door to his shelter inside the mountain and put a huge kettle on for tea. He could already see, in his mind's eye, the arrival of the four lads, exhausted, injured perhaps by stones, maybe seriously frost-bitten, but alive and happy. He would meet them with his steaming tea. There was no better drink than hot tea for frost-bitten, exhausted men. He was slightly cross at the time it was taking the water to start bubbling; the lads would be here in a minute or two.

But the lads didn't come in a minute or two.

Long after the tea was ready, they hadn't come. Albert set the golden-brown drink on a low flame, just enough to keep it hot without getting stewed.

Still the lads didn't come; and the Sector-Guard, this man whose age it was impossible to guess, had time for second thoughts. . .

In truth, one could not hold it against a public avid for sensation that it should be thronging inquisitively about the telescopes. These climbs on the Eiger's Face had been worked up into a publicity feature. The Press and the Radio had taken charge of the "Eiger Drama." Some of the reports were sound enough, informed by the heart and mind of true mountain folk behind them, others displayed a woeful lack of knowledge of the subject.

1936 had started badly. The first to arrive had been the Munich pair, Albert Herbst and Hans Teufel, who were already at Kleine Scheidegg before the end of May. Had they come to look for last year's victims? The thought may have been there, but their secret aim was certainly the ascent of the Face. They were splendid climbers, to be sure, but perhaps lacking in that calm and relaxation which is the hall-mark of the accomplished master-climber.

They did not come to grieve on the Eiger's Face. They knew that to start up that gigantic wall so early in the year, in almost wintry conditions, would be nothing short of suicide; but the waiting about became unbearable. According to the calendar it was summer by now, but storms and snow didn't seem to mind about that. So Teufel and Herbst decided as part of their training to climb the as yet unclimbed North Face of the Schneehorn. This was purely an ice and snow-slope. Conditions were far from favorable. The heavy falls of new snow had as yet failed to cohere firmly with the old snow beneath. In spite of this, the pair tackled the ice-slope on July 1st and succeeded in reaching the summit cornice, beneath which they were forced to bivouac. They suffered no harm from their night in the open and, next morning, reached and traversed the summit. Everything seemed to be going well; but on the descent, while they were crossing a snow-slope, an avalanche broke away, carrying them with it for some six hundred feet. Teufel struck the lip of a crevasse, breaking his neck. Herbst got away with his life.

That was a bad enough beginning. . . .

A few days later two Austrians, Angerer and Rainer, arrived and put up a tent near the Scheidegg, both proven climbers, especially good on rock. As such, they were particularly outstanding at route-finding on vertical cliffs. They remembered how difficult the great rock-step below the First Ice-field had proved, and how Sedlmayer and Mehringer had taken it out of themselves on it. They felt sure there must be a direct route over to the right-up what later came to be known as the "First Pillar" and the "Shattered Pillar"—towards the smooth, perpendicular, unclimbable wall of the Rote Fluh (the Red Crag, a long-established feature of the Eiger's base). Below it, there must be some means of traversing across to the First Ice-field. Would such a traverse be possible?

On Monday, July 6th Angerer and Rainer started up the Face by their newly conceived route.

What did the wall look like at that particular moment?

The late Othmar Gurtner, the great Swiss climber and well-known writer on Alpine matters, wrote the following on July 8th in a Zurich paper, *Sport.*

An unusually changeable period of weather has hampered the progress of glaciation during the last few weeks. Heavy falls of snow and cold, raw days have preserved powder-snow down as far as 8,000 feet. . . . If one examines the North Face of the Eiger thoroughly for its conditions, one is led to the following possibly deceptive conclusion: on account of the heavy covering of snow the lower parts of the Face, and also the two great shields of ice above Eigerwand Station, invite climbing in the cold hours of early morning, when the snow ruined by the evening sunshine has become crusty again. It is possible to kick safe steps without use of the axe and to move forward very quickly in such snow; at the same time it lacks solid glaciation, i.e. firm consolidation with the old snow beneath. Because of the slight amount of sun on the Eiger's North Face it behaves like typical winter snow. Higher up on the Face and especially on the almost vertical summit-structure itself, the powder-snow is plastered on the rocks like sweepings from a broom. And, in between, there is the glitter of water-ice. . . this ice has its origin in the melting water which runs down from the mighty snow-roof of the mountain. So long as there is water-ice hanging from the summit structure, the whole Face is seriously threatened by falls of ice. Then one can actually see whole torrents coming down and craters made by them very closely situated in the snow. The Face is at the moment in the terrifying conditions which persist between winter and summer . . . .

As we write this report, the Rainer-Angerer rope is moving "according to plan" up the death-dealing wall on whose actual conditions we have reported above . . . .

The warning expressed in that report was written by a very great expert.

But Angerer and Rainer were no suicide squad; they, too, were well aware of the great danger, transcending all human strength and courage. They succeeded in opening a new route up the lower part of the Face to just below the Rote Fluh, where they bivouacked; next morning, July 7th, they climbed down again, and reached their tent wet through and tired, but safe and sound "We shall go up again," they said, "as soon as conditions improve."

The papers scented a corning sensation. Now that climbing attempts have been focused in the limelight of public interest, their readers had a right to be kept informed in detail about proceedings on the Face of the Eiger. The reports were almost like communiques of the General Staff during a war, even down to the constantly repeated titles: "The Battle with the Eiger Wall," "The Acrobatic Contest on the Eiger's Face," "New

Life on the Face," "Lull in the Eiger Battle," "The all-out Investment," "First Assault Repulsed." And sometimes they even went to the length of puns, such as Mordwand for Nordwand.

The ill-fortune of Herbst and Teufel appeared in many papers under the common headline of "Accidents and Crimes." Many sarcastic comments appeared on the subject of "extreme" climbers and the public, avid for a show. But was it really surprising that people who knew nothing of mountains should make pilgrimages in their thousands to savor a shiver of horror while standing in perfect safety at the eyepiece of a telescope? The Eiger's Face had become a magnificent natural stage.

The newspapers of July 7th and 8th certainly carried widespread expressions of delight at the safe return of Rainer and Angerer. All the same, every word and movement of the two men was recorded, and interpreted however it suited best (for gladiators must needs bow to the wishes of their public); yet the climbers themselves wanted only to be left in peace and, finding they were not, defended themselves after their own fashion. Many high-sounding phrases were uttered and accorded more weight than is normally given to the pronouncements of V.I.P.s "We are having another go!" they said. What presumption, after the grim bivouac, which many papers had described as a life-and-death battle, while Angerer and Rainer laugh it off scornfully with: "Grim? No, only just a trifle wet!"

And since these were no men of worldly affairs, but just ordinary lads, who did not weigh every word in the balance, and certainly didn't suspect that under the tension of the moment it would be given undue emphasis or be wrongly reported, they gave this answer to the barrage of questions as to why they came here bent on such a venture: "We have to climb your Wall for you, if you won't do it yourselves!" Or, still more in keeping with their pathetic youthfulness and the age in which they lived: "We must have the Wall or it must have us!"

That sparked off a new storm.

In this context, an article in the Berner Bund, which read: "Everyone who has come to know these charming, good-natured lads heartily wishes them a successful outcome to their venture," did much to pour balm on wounds.

Yet neither ridicule nor solemnity could influence events. On Saturday July 18th 1936, the two ropes Angerer-Rainer and Hinterstoisser-Kurz started up the Face. At first they moved independently; at the level of the bivouac previously occupied by the two Austrians they roped up as a foursome. The rope joining them was no longer a dead length of hemp for them but, as it were, a living artery, seeming to say: "for better or for worse, we belong together." This was an uncommonly daring, but in no sense a feather-brained undertaking.

They climbed the exceptionally severe crack below the Rote Fluh successfully. Above it, Andreas Hinterstoisser was the first to achieve the traverse to the First Ice-field, climbing in text-book fashion with the help of the rope. This technique of the "rope-traverse" had already been discovered and developed before the First World War by that master of rock-climbing, Hans Dulfer, during his first ascents of the East Face of the Fleischbank and the West Wall of the Totenkirchl in the Kaisergebirge. In this way Dulfer showed how to line climbable pitches by the use of a diagonal "lift" from the rope on unclimbable ones. The current joke about the Dulfer technique ran: "You go as long as it goes, and when it doesn't go any more, you just do a traverse and go on."

It was this kind of traverse which Hinterstoisser did on the Eiger Face. He had discovered the key to the climb. When they had all completed the traverse, he retrieved the traversing rope. In doing so he threw away the key. If it came to a retreat, the door to the way back was now locked behind them. . . but who was thinking of a retreat?

Many were watching the four men through field-glasses. And the spectators forgot their criticisms in admiration, even astonishment, at the speed and assurance with which the two ropes crossed the First Ice field, climbed up beyond it and reached the barrier between it and the Second the greater Iee slope. Since the Sedlmayer-Mehringer attempt, everyone knew how difficult those rocks must be.

But what had happened? Suddenly the second pair, Rainer and Angerer, were seen to be following the leaders slowly and hesitantly. Hinterstoisser and Kurz were already moving up to the rocks above the Rote Fluh. The other two remained motionless for a long time. Then it could be seen that one was supporting the other. Had there been an accident?

It will never be known exactly what happened, but it seems almost certain that Angerer was struck by a stone and Rainer was busy tending him. Presently Hinterstoisser and Kurz could be seen letting a rope down from their stance, which was plainly safe from bombardment by stones. Their joint efforts succeeded in bringing Angerer up to them. Then Rainer followed quickly, without making use of the emergency rope.

The tiny nest in the rocks above the Rote Fluh thus became the first bivouac-place for this party of four. They had reached an incredibly high level on their first day—more than halfway up the Face.

On the morning of Sunday the 19th there were more crowds around the telescopes. They saw the four men leave the bivouac at about seven o'clock. And how was the injured man? Obviously better, for instead of retreating, they were climbing on, across the huge slope of the Second Ice-field. All the same, they were moving more slowly than on the first day. Were they all tired, then, or was it all because of the injured man? Why didn't they turn back?

One fact stands out for certain; the four men were a united, indissoluble party. Kurz and Hinterstoisser, climbing in the lead again, never thought of leaving Rainer behind with the injured man. The Austrians didn't want to rob the other two of their chance of reaching the top. And so they all stayed together, though the leaders had frequently to wait for quite a time.

The weather was neither fine nor definitely bad. In the context of the Eiger, conditions were bearable. By the end of this Sunday the party had reached the Third ice-field; a little below the bivouac which had proved fatal to Sedlmayer and Mehringer, the four men made ready to spend their second night in the open. It had been a good day's work, but they had not gained enough height to make sure of a successful push forward to the top on the following day. What kind of a night would it be? In what condition is Angerer and how are the other three? The spectators down in the valley don't know any of the answers. They withdraw for the night, rubbernecks, reporters, guides and mountaineers. Tomorrow will show. . . .

The next day was Monday, July 20th. Once again no movement could be seen in the bivouac till seven o'clock. It was a tiny place, with hardly room to sit down. Once again Kurz and Hinterstoisser began to climb the steep ice-slope leading to the "Death Bivouac," After about half an hour they stopped. The others were not following them. Nobody knows what the four men said to each other. Whatever it was, the decision taken was crucial and bitter for the leaders, a matter of life and death for the other two. It was clear that Angerer was no longer in a condition to climb any further.

All of a sudden the Hinterstoisser party could be seen climbing down to the bivouac, where they remained for some time; then they all began the descent together. A human being was more important than the mere ascent of a mountain-face. Perhaps the united strength of the whole party would succeed in bringing the injured man down?

They crossed the great slope of the Second ice-field comparatively quickly; but the descent of the rock-step, on the doubled rope, to the First took several hours to accomplish. Once again the watchers were amazed at the care and assurance with which the ropes were handled. But night fell just as the men reached the lower ice-field. Close to where Sedlmayer and Mehringer's second bivouac had been, they camped for their third night on the Face. There could not be a stitch of dry clothing on their bodies and this third bivouac must needs sap their strength; yet three must now have enough strength for the fourth. They had only managed to come down about 1,000 feet during the whole day; fully another 3,000 of the Face still gaped below them. Still, once the Traverse and the Difficult Crack were behind them, the safety of the valley would not be so far away. They knew that part of the Wall from having climbed down it once already.

Yes, but that Traverse. . . .

It would be the crux of this new day, Tuesday, July 21st. All four seemed to have stood the bivouac quite well, for they came down the ice-slope to the start of the Traverse at a good pace; but at that point those watching could suddenly only see three men at work. Had one of them fallen?"

Mists wreathed about the Face, the wind rose, the rattle of falling stones grew sharper, avalanches of powder-snow swept the track of yesterday's descent. The worst danger from falling stones would be over as soon as the four men were safely across the Traverse. But where had the fourth got to?

When the cloud curtain parted again, the men at the telescopes could see all four climbers again, but Angerer, apparently hors de combat, was taking no part in the attempts to master the Traverse. One man seemed to be taking the lead in these efforts—surely it must be Hinterstoisser, the man who first dealt with this key point on the way up. But now there is no traversing-rope fixed to the rock. And the rock doesn't seem to be climbable without artificial aids.

The weather was worsening; it had in fact already broken. The water which had all along been pouring down the rocks must have hardened into ice. All the experts with field-glasses could sense the fearsome tragedy to come. Retreat was cut off; nobody could move over the glassy film overlaying the rock, not even an Andreas Hinterstoisser. The precious hours of the entire morning were consumed by vain, frustrating, incredibly exhausting and dangerous attempts. And then came the last desperate decision: to climb straight down the vertical rock-face, some 600 or 700 feet high, which at some points bulges far out even beyond the vertical.

The only way led through the line of fire from stones and avalanches. Sedlmayer and Mehringer had taken a whole day to climb that pitch, and that in fine weather on dry rock. Now all Hell had broken loose on the mountain. But it was the only chance.

They began to get the ropes ready for the descent through thin air.

It was at this moment that they heard Albert von Allmen's shouts coming up from below.

Someone shouting, so close at hand? Then things could not go wrong! A man's voice, giving strength and courage and the certainty that the bridge back to the living world was still there. And in spite of the dangers and their awareness of the seriousness of their situation, they all joined in yodeling back: "All's well!" Not a single cry for help, not even an admission of their terrifying peril.

All well. . . .

Albert von Allmen was getting cross. How long was he expected to keep their tea warm? Presently his irritation changed to apprehension. Two whole hours had gone by since he spoke to the climbers, and still no movement at the entrance to the gallery. Could they have climbed down past it? Could they have missed the ledge, which runs across the window?

The Sector-Guard went back to the door. The Face was looking grim and ghastly now; visibility was very restricted; mists were steaming up everywhere. Stones and avalanches were singing their pitiless song. Albert shouted.

And back came an answer.

This time no cheery yodel, but a shocking answer coming now from one man, the last lone survivor, crying for help. . . Toni Kurz.

The voice of a brave, unbelievably tough young guide, cradled in Bavaria in the shadow of the Watzmann; a man who had rescued many in distress on the mountains, but who had never yet shouted for help. But now he was shouting, shouting desperately for his very life.

"Help! Help! The others are all dead. I am the only one alive. Help!" The wind, the avalanches and the whistling stones forbade a more exact exchange of information. In any case, Albert von Allmen by himself could bring no aid. He shouted "We'll be coming" and hurried back into the gallery to telephone.

Eigergletscher Station, down below, answered his call.

"Allmen speaking. There's been a fearful disaster on the Face. There's only one survivor. We must fetch him in. Have you any guides with you?"

Yes, there were guides down there—Hans Schlunegger, with Christian and Adolf Rubi, all from Wengen. Yes, they would come up, of their own accord, even in face of instructions. It was a case of humanity triumphing over the regulations.

For Bohren, the chief guide of Grindelwald, in his concern for the guides under him had issued a communication to the Guides' Commission in Berne, and to the Central Committee of the Swiss Alpine Club, which had also been repeated in the Grindelwald Echo.

One cannot help regarding the contemplated climbing attempts on the North Face of the Eiger with serious misgivings. They are a plain indication of the great change which has taken place in the conception of the sport of mountaineering. We must accept that the visitors who take part in such attempts are aware of the dangers they are themselves risking; but no one can expect the despatch of guides, in unfavorable conditions, on a rescue operation, in case of any further accidents on the Eiger's North Face. . . . We should find it impossible to force our guides to take a compulsory part in the kind of acrobatics which others are undertaking voluntarily.

That was the Chief Guide's stated position. Nobody could have held it against the guides at Eigergletscher Station if they had refused to take a single step on to the Face when they heard of the accident. But there was one man still alive. They were all determined to rescue him, to snatch him if possible, from the clutches of that fatal wall.

The railway provided a train, which immediately took them to the gallery window at Kilometre 3-8; through it they stepped on to the Face, glistening under its coat of ice. Clouds of snow-dust blew into their faces, as they quietly traversed diagonally upwards on the slippery, treacherous ledges, till they reached a point about 300 feet below where Toni Kurz was hanging from the rope in a sling.

There was mixed despair and relief in his voice-still astonishingly strong as he heard his rescuers and answered them.

The Tragedy of Toni Kurz

"I'm the only one alive. Hinterstoisser came off and fell the whole way down. The rope pulled Rainer up against a snap-link. He froze to death there. And Angerer's dead too, hanging below me, strangled by the rope when he fell. . . ."

"All right, pal. We've come to help you?"

"I know," shouted Toni. "But you've got to come from above, to the right, up through the crack where we left some pitons on the way up. Then you could reach me by three descents on the doubled rope."

"That's impossible, pal. Nobody could climb it with this ice about."

"You can't rescue me from below," Kurz shouted back.

Day was drawing to its close. The guides would have to hurry if they were to get back safely to the gallery window before dark. They shouted up the wall: "Can you stick it for one more night, pal?"

"No! No! No!"

The words cut the guides to the quick. They were never to forget them. But any aid was out of the question in the dark, on this Face, in this weather.

"Stick it, pal!" they shouted. "We'll be back first thing in the morning!"

They could hear Toni's shouts for a long time, as they climbed down.

The young Berchtesgaden guide must have despaired of seeing the night through. But life had a strong hold on him; in spite of the gale, the volleys of stones, the fearsome cold, he survived the night, swinging backwards and forwards in his rope sling. It was so cold that the water thawed by the warmth of his body froze again immediately. Icicles eight inches long formed on the points of the crampons strapped to his boots. Toni lost the mitten from his left hand; his fingers, his hand, then his arm, froze into shapeless immovable lumps. But when dawn came, life was still awake in his agonized body. His voice too was strong and clear, when the guides got in touch with him again.

Arnold Glatthard had by now joined Schlunegger and the Rubi brothers. The four guides together were ready to fight this merciless wall for the life of their young colleague from Bavaria. The rocks were covered with an appalling glaze of ice. It seemed almost impossible to climb at all. And there was Toni pleading again: "You can only rescue me from above. You must climb the crack. . . ."

It was impossible. Even Kurz and Hinterstoisser in their full and unimpaired strength could not have climbed the crack in such conditions. It

Heinrich Harrer

was a pitch which even in fine weather would have seriously tested these four men, first-class guides, brought up in a great tradition, master-climbers all, but little versed in the technique of modern, artificial climbing. It would have called for just that kind of "acrobatics" against which Chief Guide Bohren had taken such a strong stand.

However, the four guides succeeded in reaching a point only about 130 feet below where Toni Kurz was hanging on the rope. So far did the overhang beetle out over the abyss that they could no longer see him from there. If Kurz had another rope on which to rope himself down, he would be saved. But how to get one to him? Attempts with rockets failed. The rope went shooting past Kurz, far out from the Face. There was only one thing left.

"Can you let a line down," they asked him, "so that we can attach a rope, rock-pitons and anything else you need?"

"I have no line," came the reply.

"Climb down as far as you can, then, and cut away Angerer's body. Then climb up again and cut the rope above you. Then untwist the strands of the piece of rope you have gained, join them and let the resulting line down."

The answer was a groan: "I'll try."

A little while later they heard the strokes of an axe. It seemed incredible that Kurz could hold on with one frozen hand and swing the axe with the other. Yet he managed to cut the rope away; only, Angerer's body didn't fall, for it was frozen solid to the rock. Almost in a trance, answering the last dictates of the will to live, Kurz climbed up again, cut away the rope there. The manoeuver had won him twenty-five feet of rope, frozen stiff And then began the unbelievable work of untwisting the strands. Every climber knows how difficult that is, even on firm ground, with two sound hands. But Toni Kurz was suspended between heaven and earth, on an ice-glazed cliff, threatened by falling stones, sometimes swept by snowslides. He worked with one hand and his teeth. . . for five hours. . .

A great avalanche fell, narrowly missing the guides. A huge block whizzed close by Schlunegger's head. And then a body came hurtling past. Toni's? No it wasn't Toni's, but Angerer's, freed from the imprisoning ice. Those were hours of agony for Toni, fighting for his life, agonizing too for the guides, who could do nothing to help, and could only wait for the moment when Kurz might still achieve the incredible.

Presently the fabricated line came swinging down to the rescue party. They fastened a rope to it, with pitons, snap-links, a hammer. Slowly those objects disappeared from the view of the guides. Toni Kurz's strength was ebbing fast; he could hardly draw up the line, but somehow he managed it. Even now the rope wasn't long enough. The guides attached a second to it. The knot where the two ropes were spliced swung visible but unreachable out there under the great overhang.

Another hour passed. Then, at last, Toni Kurz was able to start roping down, sitting in a sling attached to the rope by a snap-link. Inch by inch he worked his way downwards. Thirty, forty, fifty feet down. . . a hundred feet, a hundred and twenty. Now his legs could be seen dangling below the overhang.

At that moment the junction-knot jammed in the snap-link of the sling in which Toni was sitting as he roped down. The knot was too thick and Toni could not force it through the link. They could hear him groaning.

"Try, lad, try!" the frustrated rescuers tried to encourage the exhausted man. Toni, mumbling to himself, made one more effort with all his remaining strength, but he had little left; his incredible efforts had used it almost all up. His will to live had been keyed to the extreme so long as he was active; now, the downward journey in the safety of the rope-sling had eased the tension. He was nearing his rescuers now; now the battle was nearly over, now there were others close at hand to help. . .

And now this knot. . . just a single knot. . . but it won't go through. . . "Just one more try, pal. It'll go!"

There was a note of desperation in the guides' appeal. One last revolt against fate; one last call on the last reserves of strength against this last and only obstacle. Toni bent forwards, trying to use his teeth just once more. His frozen left arm with its useless hand stuck out stiff and helpless from his body. His last reserves were gone.

Toni mumbled unintelligibly, his handsome young face dyed purple with frost-bite and exhaustion, his lips just moving. Was he still trying to say something, or had his spirit already passed over to the beyond?

Then he spoke again, quite clearly. "I'm finished," he said.

His body tipped forward. The sling, almost within reaching distance of the rescuing guides, hung swinging gently far out over the gulf. The man sitting in it was dead.

It will never be known exactly how the whole disaster built up or what precisely happened while Sector-Guard and humanitarian Albert von Allmen was getting his tea ready. The very fact that Andreas Hinterstoisser was off the rope at the moment of his fall leads to the conclusion that he—

probably the best technician of the four— was trying to find a specially safe place for pitons to secure the descent on the rope. It was impossible to establish from Toni Kurz's fragmentary and incoherent sentences whether they all fell owing to a fall of stone, or whether the others were trying to catch Andreas as he fell and so were all pulled off their holds. The guide from Berchtesgaden needed all his strength for his own preservation, nor could he spare thoughts or words for reports. It is quite clear that all three were on the same rope, and that it ran through a snap-link attached to a piton. The fall jammed Rainer against the piton so that he could not move. Tatters of bandage found on Angerer's skull, when his body was recovered much later, proved that he had been the injured member of the party, seen on the Face by those who watched.

It was one of the grimmest tricks of fate which left Toni Kurz uninjured at the outset, so that he was forced to endure his agony to its uttermost end. He was like some messenger from the beyond, finding his way back to earth simply because he loved life so well.

The tragedy of Sedlmayer and Mehringer had been enacted behind the curtains of the mountain mists. Men could only guess at it. But Toni Kurz ended his brave and vigorous life before the eyes of his rescuers. It was this that made the tragedy of 1936 so impressive and so shattering that it will never be forgotten.

Arnold Glatthard, that reserved and silent guide, said: "It was the saddest moment of my life."

Unfortunately, not everybody showed that respect and reserve which death—and particularly death in such a manner—commands.

One newspaper wrote of Toni Kurz's death: "Kurz spent his fourth night complaining. When the search for notoriety and obstinate will-power conspire to bring a man to grief, one cannot really register regret. . . ."

Another, dated July 24th 1936, produced the following remarkable description of the men who climb the Eiger's Face and the motives that impel them:

Perhaps these young men have nothing more to loose. . . what is to become of a generation to which Society offers no social existence and which has only one thing left to look to, a single day's glory, the swiftly tarnishing highlight of a single hour? To be a bit of a hero, a bit of a soldier, sportsman or record-breaker, a gladiator, victorious one day, defeated the next. . . . The four recent victims of the Eiger's North Face were poor creatures. When some kindly folk in Grindelwald invited them to dinner, they tucked in to the proffered meal like true warriors; afterwards, they said they hadn't had such a good meal for three years. When asked what was the purpose of their risky venture, they replied that its main object was to improve their positions. They believed that such an exceptional feat would bring them honor and glory, and make people take notice of them. . . .

Another article bearing the same date and headlined "Climbing under Orders" gives the matter a bizarre twist in the opposite direction.

Kleine Scheidegg, July 24th. A report is current here that the four climbers had been ordered to make the ascent. It has been said that they were very excited on Friday evening; that they would never have taken such a grave risk as free agents. Perhaps their records will reveal this or that secret which did not pass their lips, now numbed and frozen into silence.

This was, of course, the direct reverse of the truth. Kurz and Hinterstoisser were at this time on the strength of the Mountain-Ranger (Jager) Regiment No. 100 and on leave from Bad Reichenhall. When their commanding officer Col. R. Konrad, who had experience of climbing in the Bernese Oberland, learned of their plans he telephoned Grindelwald and, in the strictest terms, vetoed any attempt on the Eiger. That was on the Friday evening. The message reached the tents on the Kleine Scheidegg too late. Kurz and Hinterstoisser had started up the Face a few hours earlier. . . .

In the context of previous tragedies on the Eiger's North Face a great many things were invented and written-up at various desks, which served to poison the atmosphere and made mutual understanding more difficult. Genuine mountaineers in Germany, Austria or Switzerland wrote on common lines, irrespective of whether they were for or against "Operation Eigerwand." They used the language of understanding, humanity and respect for the dead. While various papers were trying to drive a permanent wedge between German climbers and Swiss Guides, Gunther Lange was writing in *Bergsteiger*, the official organ of the German and Austrian Alpine Club: "I know the Swiss guides, who have shown typical mountaineering qualities in such an outstanding manner. I spent several weeks last year with Arnold Glatthard on difficult rock; a man carved from the best and hardest wood, with enough pluck for three. The Eigerwand guides deserve the recognition and gratitude of all climbers for what they did!" And as a postscript, Gunther Langes published a letter form Glatthard, which summarized the judgment of all the guides on the four men who died on the Face in 1936: "I watched them climbing and can only praise the lads. The North Face dealt harshly with our comrades. . ."

Heinrich Harrer

It is safe to say that guides, of whatever nationality, are fine men. It is nothing against them that they often exhibit a rugged exterior and don't speak in the smooth phraseology of diplomats.

On the fly-leaf of his guide's record-book Toni Kurz, when only nineteen, had written a little poem, the fruit of his fine, serious nature. It told of his love for the mountains, of the sober approach to every climb, and of the sacred obligation— "never to give one's life away to death."

To round off my report on the tragedy of 1936 I propose to quote the words of Sir Arnold Lunn, an enemy of unhealthy pathos and all forms of false heroics. This is what he wrote about Toni Kurz's death in his book *A Century of Mountaineering*:

His valiant heart had resisted the terrors of storm and solitude and misery such as mountaineers have seldom been called on to endure. He had hung in his rope-sling buffeted by the storm, but determined not to surrender. And he did not surrender. He died. In the annals of mountaineering there is no record of a more heroic endurance.

Giusto Gervasutti (1909-1946) was the premier Italian Alpinist of the pre-World War II era. His climbing achievements include the Matterhorn solo in winter, the North Face of the Grandes Jorasses, the Freney Pillar, and Mont Blanc. He published two books, *Gervasutti's Climbs and Alpinismo*, the latter with his climbing partner Rene Chabod.

GIUSTO GERVASUTTI: CONCLUSION

The little train ambled along and at every curve I felt it might leave the rails and take a rest beneath the fir-trees; the ascent was too steep for its worn-out pistons, and it gasped and spluttered its way up the valley. Sitting in a corner of the practically empty coach, I turned over in my mind the impulses which had brought me to the hills, and I dreamed of climbs to come.

I had set out alone, as I often did that particular year. The popular view of solitary climbing is that it is simply a form of suicidal mania; and that the individual has no right to devote himself of his own free will to a sport involving such excessive risks. But it seemed to me that a solitary wanderer like Lammer had found in mountaineering a practical application of his Nietzschean philosophy, and, urged on by his inner demon, climbed mountains in search of difficulties and dangers for their own sake. Or there was Preuss, who went as a conqueror from summit to summit, from victory to victory, disdaining all means of protection, sometimes linking another climber to his destiny, more often alone as he was when he won his most brilliant victory, as he was when, betrayed by a treacherous hold, he fell to his death. My aim was more modest than theirs: it was to lose, on the heights, all those evil humors accumulated during the long monotonous hours of city life; to find serenity and calm in the freedom and exhilaration of climbing on difficult rock, in the long silent communion with the sun, the wind, the blue sky, in the nostalgic sweetness of the sunset. And no softer or more passive view of life could make me change my mind. Such were my thoughts as the train puffed its way up.

I reached the little station in darkness. The storm which had been raging throughout the journey had only just abated, water was still pouring off the houses and trees, and the paths were muddy streams. Above the blackness of the mountains, clouds scudded across the sky before a driving wind, and the stars were beginning to come out. I had never climbed here before, though I had once driven through the valley; as I wanted to reach the hut that same night I looked on the list of paths for the distinctive mark to follow. A boy passed by, so I asked him where the mule-track started up.

"Do you want to go up now?" he asked.

"Yes, I want to do a climb, and I have to be back tomorrow evening."

"The path isn't well-marked; it's difficult to follow in the woods, and there is no moon. It will be quite a business finding the hut."

"Never mind, I've got an electric torch, I can look for the marks."

"All right: at the last house you turn right. To begin with there is a decent-sized mule-track, then, on the edge of the wood, you will find the path."

"Thanks very much; goodbye!"

He looked a bit dubious and stopped a minute to watch while I started slowly up. After wandering for awhile among the pines and on the higher pastures, taking twice the normal time, I knocked at the door of the hut at two in the morning, drank two steaming grogs, and then lay down fully dressed on one of the bunks to rest for a couple of hours.

Left the hut at dawn. As the slope grew steeper I made my way up lightly with the cool mountain air giving me that delicious sensation of floating. My body was tingling with a wonderful sense of well-being, and ready to rise to whatever demands I made on it.

The weather had not completely cleared: wisps of mist curled round the yellow towers, alternately masking and revealing them ghostly, distant, higher and bolder than in real life. I climbed up a grassy ridge, treading on a staircase of tufts, then on scree, slithery and exhausting like all Dolomite scree, but short, and so came to the foot of the climb where I changed my nailed boots for espadrilles. I took the rope from my sack and slung it round me, but I had neither pitons nor hammer, for I knew that on the descent I should find rappel loops already in position. Leaving sack and boots under a boulder, I approached the rock.

Giusto Gevarsutti

It began by a not very difficult vertical crack. I touched the rock with my hand, almost stroking it, as one strokes something one loves but has not seeing for some time. It was still cold, but when I looked up the sun, seeing it through the mist, a yellow disc with a halo round it had already appeared above a jagged ridge. Everything round me was quiet, with the rather startled silence of high places. I rubbed my foot two or three times on a polished bit of rock, as though to test its adherence, then I raised my arms in search of holds for my hands and, bracing my muscles, began to climb. I moved very slowly, without the least hurry, quietly looking for holds, studying each move so as to economize effort to the full. When a climber is on his own he can't afford to make the slightest mistake, for if he does, there is neither rope nor piton to save him. And if danger suddenly strikes, all he can do is to risk everything; but if he loses, it is his life that is forfeit.

All went well for about four hours, and the higher I climbed, the more impressive appeared the vertical wall beneath me. Down below, very far below, the last scattered fir-trees appeared as minute dots against the grassy ridge.

I had done about three-quarters of the climb, and was in a chimney blocked by an enormous chockstone which I had to get over. I went up with my legs wide apart, arrived beneath the chockstone, got round it by wriggling my body between it and the wall and then, raising my hands, I took hold of it. I now had to swing out under the overhang and mantelshelf up. Kicking off with my feet, I made the effort.

But I had miscalculated. My chin came only on a level with the edge and I looked about for other handholds, but higher up the chockstone was rounded, smooth and polished without the vestige of a crack. So I let myself down slowly, trying to get my feet back on to their holds, but as my face was right up against the rock, I could not see. Beneath the overhang was the chimney, dropping down into space. I tried in every direction; it was no good. Although my feet did come in contact with the rock, I couldn't find the holds. I realized then that if I did not get up at once, all was over: the drop to the scree was getting on for 1,000 feet. I gave a spring and pulled up again on my fingers, but I could not get beyond the point I'd already reached. A shiver ran down my spine. Again I made the effort, even using my teeth to get a hold, with no other result than a bloody mouth. I slipped back, still climbing with my finger-tips to the sloping edge, and stayed there, panting, for a few minutes; and while I tried unsuccessfully to find a reasonable way out of this fix, my strength began to ebb. My fingers were gradually slipping from the holds, and I could no longer see or think. Then, in a fury, I succeeded in giving a heave that brought my chest above the upper edge of the chockstone. For a fraction of a second I managed to hold myself in position with the help of my chin while I reversed one hand and got it palm downwards on the rock. I transferred my weight to it, holding on by friction, gradually pushed myself up and, with a final effort, got my body on to the chockstone and lay down, utterly exhausted. When the trembling caused by nervous reaction began to subside, I sat up and looked down into the valley. Everything was just as it had been before. In the stillness of the air there was nothing to give away my presence. The grey mountain was indifferent. The valley floor was green and peaceful. Even the wind had died down. It was I, and I alone, who had sought this moment of suspense, created it, compelled it. Everything round me was motionless and static, had played no active part. And again the question surged up: "Why?"

No answer came—perhaps it never would—but when I reached the sunflooded summit, with waves of floating mist beneath me, my heart sang for joy. The exaltation of that moment, out of the world, on the glory of the heights, would be justification enough for any rashness.

Reading through these lines, written many years ago about a venture of my younger days, I have often asked myself the same question: "Why" And I know now how impossibly difficult it would be to give any clear answer.

There are many people more competent than myself, at any rate in the art of writing, who have tried to give an answer, without much result beyond the controversies they have stimulated. I find it entirely natural that such attempts to define mountaineering should have produced no satisfactory result. For there is no such thing as objective mountaineering, there is only a form of activity, generically termed mountaineering, which enables certain people to express themselves, or gives them a means of satisfying an inner need, just as there are other forms of activity and other means by which other people may try to attain the same ends.

Of course, since the need is completely different for each individual, we have many forms of mountaineering. It may take the form of a need to live heroically, or to rebel against restraint and limitation: an escape from the restricting circle of daily life, a protest against being submerged in universal drabness, an affirmation of the freedom of the spirit in dangerous and splendid adventure. Or it may well be the pleasure of feeling strong and fit: of realizing, in one controlled harmony, physical fitness and moral energy, elegance of style and calculated daring; ordeals gaily

Giusto Gevarsutti

faced with friends themselves as firm as rock, the hard life of the high huts, the happy relaxation on remote pastures as one smokes a pipe or sings mountain songs. It may be the search for an intense aesthetic experience, for exquisite sensations, or for man's never satisfied desire for unknown country to explore, new paths to make. Best of all, it should be all these things together.

It follows that, at a certain moment one's personal preference for a particular line is bound to lead to the formation of a set of values. When a man, rising above the banality of his everyday existence, tries in one way or another to create for himself a higher mode of life, there are generally two possibilities open to him: either the way of pure imagination, or some mode which can be transformed into reality through action.

The first is generally considered the superior; but to be able to endow pure thought with a value, one must be a poet and an artist. Only those who have attained to poetry can allow themselves the luxury of giving a universal value to the creations of their imagination, while remaining comfortably in their armchairs. But the others, and among them mountaineers, if they do not wish to limit themselves to the pleasures of imagination, must seek the satisfaction of their spirit's needs in action, and this satisfaction will be greater, and more complete, in proportion to the intensity of the action.

In other words it seems to me that the contemplative side of mountaineering can only have an interpretative value, and that the ecstasy of creation can come from action alone.

Over and above all these academic analyses, one fact remains: the battle one fights on the mountain for hours on end, when life hangs by a thread above dizzy precipices, as one forces a route up the cold rock, or cuts an icy staircase to the sky, is work fit for men. Rocks that rise in a wondrous architecture, ice-couloirs that climb to the sky. The sky itself always the same, yet endlessly varied, sometimes a deep blue in which the soul melts and merges with the infinite, sometimes streaked with storm clouds that weigh like lead upon the spirit. What unforgettable moments give us!

To the young climber facing the harsh ordeals of the Alps for the first time, I would recall the words of a friend who fell on a great mountain: "Dare all, and you will be kin to the gods."

Sir Christian Bonington (b. 1934) is one of the most recognized mountaineers in history and is responsible for numerous first ascents is virtually every major mountain range in the world. He made the first British ascent of the North Face of the Eiger as well as many other important new routes in the Alps. He really established himself as an expedition leader having led the successful new routes on both Annapurna's Southeast Face and Everest's Southwest Face. He climbed Everest himself in 1985 at the age of 50 and is still climbing hard today at the age of 70. He is the last of the great "Golden Age" explorers. A prolific writer, he is the author of over a dozen books including *I Chose to Climb, Annapurna South Face, Everest the Hard Way, Mountaineer*, and *Tibet's Secret Mountain*. He has been awarded a CBE (Commander of the British Empire) and was knighted for his contributions to mountaineering and exploration.

Chris Bonington:
The Central Pillar
of Freney

The refuge bivouac on the Col de la Fourche is a tiny corrugated-iron Nissen hut designed to hold eight people; it clings to a small ledge just below the crest of the ridge and from its door you get a giddy view of the great Brenva Face of Mont Blanc. In early July of 1961 Walter Bonatti, with two companions, Andrea Oggioni and Roberto Gallieni, arrived at the hut. They were on their way to the Central Pillar of Freney, and unclimbed rock buttress high on the south face of Mont Blanc. At first glance this seems an unlikely approach, for the Central Pillar is at the head of the Freney Glacier, and from the Col de Fourche they would have to cross below the Brenva Face and then ascend the couloir leading up to the Col de Peuterey, a new route and major ascent in its own right. Only then would they be able to start climbing on the Pillar, the most remote and highest Grade VI Climb in Europe. The more direct approach up the Freney glacier was even more difficult, for the glacier is seamed by crevasses and threatened by tottering seracs.

To their surprise, the three Italians found the hut occupied by four Frenchmen. Bonatti recognized one of them as Robert Guillaume, a young climber who had already put up several important first ascents. The others were Pierre Mazeaud, an extremely experienced mountaineer, Antoine Vieille and Pierre Kohlman. There could be no doubt where they planned to go. Bonatti must have been bitterly disappointed to find them there: he had had his eye on the Central Pillar for nine years and had already made one attempt on it, but it is an indication of his character that he immediately offered to go on to another climb since the French were there first. They rejected this offer, however, insisting that the Italians should join them.

They set out in the middle of the night, and in cold, clear conditions crossed the head of the Brenva Glacier, over the Col Moore and up the Peuterey Couloir, reaching the Col de Peuterey just after dawn. That day they managed to climb about two-fifths of the way up the Pillar; so early in the season the cracks were still heavily iced, making progress slow.

The Central Pillar has a smooth rock obelisk about four hundred feet high, that rests on a 2,000-foot plinth of broken granite. They reached the foot of the obelisk on their second day, but during the afternoon, wisps of clouds had been forming, and suddenly the storm broke around their heads an inferno of snow, thunder and lightning. Kohlman was struck by one of the flashes and was badly shocked.

They settled down for the night, confident that a storm of such violence could last only a few hours and that they would then be able to scale the few hundred feet of steep rock that were between them and safety. But the next morning the storm was as furious as ever, and they resolved to stick it out. Retreat in those conditions didn't bear thinking about, especially down the icy chaos of the Freney Glacier.

They sat it out on the ledge for three days and nights, and still the storm showed no sign of letting up. In this type of bivouac it is impossible to stay dry—snow inevitably seeps into the bivouac tent, condensation from the breath soaks everything. They could eat only limited quantities for it was practically impossible to light their cooker in the storm. The French were even worse off than the Italians for they had no bivouac tent but relied on plastic sheets which they wrapped around themselves. Quite apart from the mutual warmth you gain in a tent, it is much easier to maintain morale when huddled close together, able to talk to each other.

Bonatti very quickly emerged as the natural leader of the party, closely supported by Pierre Mazeaud. On the fourth day, their fifth out from the Col de la Fourche, he decided that they must retreat, while they still had the strength to do so.

The snow was falling as thickly as ever, as they abseiled, rope length after rope length, down the Pillar the ropes must have been like hawsers, their clothes frozen into armour plating. Once off the Pillar, however; it was even worse; they were up to their chests in powdered snow and could only see a few feet in front. Bonatti, with an uncanny sense of direction, guided them to the Col de Peuterey, but by that time it was nearly dark, and they had to resign themselves to another bivouac in the bowels of a crevasse.

There was no question of getting back the way that they had come; the couloir leading down to the Brenva Glacier was a death trap, continuously swept by avalanches. They made for the Rochers Gruber, a rock rib running down into the lower basin of the Freney Glacier. Near the top of the rib, Vieille, the youngest member of the party, was unable to go any farther-they tried to haul him along, but he died in front of their eyes from exhaustion and exposure. Down on the glacier, Guillaume collapsed they were unable to carry him for they were all near the end of their tether; their only hope was to reach the Gamba Hut and send back a rescue party. Without Bonatti it is unlikely that they would ever have picked their way through the crevasses of the Freney Glacier, but eventually, when it was already getting dark, they reached the couloir leading up to the *Col de l'innominata*. Oggioni, who had taken up the hardest position of all throughout the retreat, at the rear of the column where he had retrieved all the abseil ropes and had helped on the others, was now able to go no farther. Mazeaud stayed with him at the foot of the couloir.

From the top of the Col de l'innominata they had 2,000 feet of steep descent to the Gamba Hut. Kohlman was now showing signs of delirium, threatening to take Bonatti and Gallieni, tied to him on the same rope, down with him. They tried to drag him along, but eventually, when he actually attacked them, were forced to untie from the rope and flee down to the Hut.

When the rescue party went out to pick up those who had been left behind only Mazeaud was left alive. So ended one of the most long drawn out and at the same time heroic tragedies in Alpine history. It was a miracle that anyone survived at all; this was largely a tribute to the determination and skill of Walter Bonatti.

Only a month later another party set out for the Pillar-Pierre Julien, an instructor at the Ecole Nationale in Chamnonix, and Ignazio Piussi, a leading Italian climber who was attending an international meet at the school. They caused some criticism by using a helicopter to reach the top of Mont Blanc and then just descending the Peuterey Ridge to the foot of the Pillar. That same day they climbed as far as the smooth section near the top, but dropped a rucksack containing their gear; as, anyway, the weather was beginning to look threatening, they made a quick retreat.

When we set out to try the Pillar for ourselves we knew no more than the bare outlines of the stories of the previous attempts and had only seen a photograph of it, taken from a distance. On reaching Chamonix, our first problem was to find a fourth member for our party-three is an awkward number on a long rock climb.

"How about asking Julien?" suggested Jan. "I know him quite well from a course at the Ecole I attended last year."

"Might as well ask him," agreed Don, "we might get a bit of information from him, if nothing else."

We walked over to the School that afternoon and asked for Julien. He wasn't much taller than Don, but was more heavily built-dark glasses, a smooth V-neck sweater and immaculate breeches; he oozed an aggressive, bouncy self-confidence.

After the preliminary introductions, Jan told him of our interest in the Central Pillar and asked if he would like to join us.

"It is impossible," he replied. "I have too much guiding to do, but I should be happy to give you any help I can."

"What is it like where you turned back?" asked Don.

"There are some cracks out to the left. You need plenty of big wedges," he told us.

On the way back to the camp site we met Ian Clough. He had just arrived from the Dolomites. Neither Don or I had climbed with him, but we knew him by reputation. Although only in his mid-twenties, he had done as much hard climbing in the Alps as anyone in Britain. He came from Baildon, in Yorkshire, had served three years in the R.A.F. Mountain rescue Team at Kinross, and had then decided to devote his entire time to climbing. For the last few years he had eked out a precarious living as an instructor for the Mountaineering Association. He had just climbed the North Face of the *Cima Ovest di Lavaredo* by the French *Direttissima* route. It was continuously overhanging for seven hundred feet and he had spent two nights sitting in his etriers—we decided that this was ample qualification for a place on our team.

A few days later, the weather seemed settled and we caught the last telepherique up to the top of the Aiguille du Midi. Just as the doors were about to close, three heavily laden climbers piled in. I immediately recognized Pierre Julien.

"The others are Rene Desmaison and Poulet Villard," Jan muttered to us. "I don't think there's any doubt where they're going," said Don.

For a few minutes we pretended to ignore each other, glancing across occasionally with lowered eyes; then Julien walked over to us.

"You go to Freney?" he asked.

"Perhaps, and you?"

"Perhaps."

At the top of the Midi the three Frenchmen took one of the tele-cabins going across to the Torino Hut. I couldn't understand this, for the obvious way to the Col de la Fourche is to walk down on to the Vallee Blanche, from the Midi.

"I was wonder what they are up to?" asked Ian.

"They probably got a helicopter waiting for them," suggested Don. "Anyway, there is nothing we can do about it. Let's get to the hut before its dark. We'll only have a couple of hours rest as it is."

From the Midi on the way across Midi Valley just below the dark spire of the Grand Capucin, we noticed a solitary tent, but at that stage were unaware of its significance. The hut, when we reached it, was crammed to bursting: there were already a dozen people packed on to the two-tiered bunk that almost entirely filled its interior. As we cooked our meal in the open doorway, I kept glancing across the expanse of the Brenva Glacier to the vast bulk of the Brenva Face and across it to the sheer silhouette of the Eckfeiler Buttress, climbed only a few years before by Walter Bonatti. You couldn't see the Pillar from here; it was hidden by the upper part of the face, but the sight of the ground we had to cover that night was frightening enough. Behind the Eckfeiler Buttress I could just see the Couloir leading up to the Col de Peuterey; it looked impossibly steep and long—a major climb in its own right and we had to get up it in the dark.

The Central Pillar of Freney

As I looked, my eye caught a puff of smoke high up on the face of the Eckfeiler Buttress; it quickly spread into a plunging torrent of swirling brown cloud that completely enveloped the face; almost at the same time came the noise, a deep pitched thunder then hammered at our ears, filling me with an instinctive fear. I have never seen such a rock-fall, it seemed to stretch into minutes, though in fact it could have only lasted a few seconds, but even when the sound had vanished into the stillness of the night a heavy sulphurous smell lingered on, though we were nearly a mile away from the Buttress. Later that night we intended to pass below the very same place.

To me it seemed an omen; before a big climb I have always felt some fear, but that night my imagination was working overtime as I thought of our prospects of survival should the weather break when we were high on the Pillar. There was little chance of sleep, anyway, for we were packed together like the inmates of a concentration-camp barracks; you couldn't possibly turn round, or even lie on your back, there was so little room.

But the evening's excitement was not over. At about eleven-thirty, the door swung open, and in strode a big, handsome looking man wearing a domed crash hat. He had an air of absolute self-confidence as if he owned, not only the hut, but the entire mountain. He went straight to the hut book, which we had filled in a few hours before (Freney Pillar with a big question mark), glanced at it, wrote his own entry and walked out. As the door closed we dived for the book—there it was—Walter Bonatti. He was with a client on his way to the Brenva Face.

"Well, at least he can't get up on the Pillar for a while," observed Ian.

"Put ye heads down. Let's get some kip," said Don. "We'll have to start in an hour."

I don't think any of us slept, we just lay and waited for the alarm. At last it was time to get up; the other occupants were also stirring. We had a quick brew of coffee, loaded our rucksacks and set out. A couple of parties had already left. We could see their lights slowly move across the glacier below. We put on crampons straight away, and scrambled down steep snow and rocky steps to the glacier. High up on the Brenva Face we could see tiny pinpoints of light-Walter Bonatti and his client.

The sky was a deep black, glistening with a myriad of stars; there wasn't a breath of wind and yet I felt there was something wrong; subconsciously, I think, wanting any excuse to avoid going on to the Pillar. I heard a trickle of water running down the rock.

Sir Chris Bonington

"You know, it can't be very cold. There's some running water over there. That could mean that the weather's changing. I wonder if we should just go up the Major."

"It's as settled as it ever will be," replied Don. "We've come this far, let's go on."

We crossed the Col Moore, and then left the beaten track to the Brenva Face and dropped down to the other fork of the Glacier. Now that we were committed, my fears seemed to vanish and I began to enjoy myself; we came to a bergshrund at the bottom of the slope. Don jumped across without hesitation, rolled a couple of times on the other side and stopped himself with his axe. I paused on the edge for a minute—I have always hated jumping—and then for fear of seeming a coward launched myself into the dark, bounced and rolled down the slope.

We roped up for fear of hidden crevasses, and were soon picking our way across the glacier. As we approached the dark bulk of the Eckfeiler Buttress we could still detect a heavy smell of sulphur in the air: we had to clamber over the debris of the rock-fall a full hundred yards out from the face.

The couloir now stretched above us. An awkward ice-bulge at the bottom fell to Don's axe, and we were then able to make our own way up the firm snow, climbing quickly and silently in pools of light from the head-torches. It was a good 2,000 feet long, but we reached the top well before dawn. For its last few feet it reared up steeply, a wall of mouldering rock held together by bonds of clear ice. It was my turn to lead; a boulder rattled away under my foot, narrowly missed Don fifty feet below, and bounded out of sight into the deep shadows of the couloir. I jerked my head, and my head-torch went out-I must have disconnected the battery. In complete darkness I felt my way up the rock-it was unpleasant, as dangerous as anything we were to find on the Central Pillar, but not unenjoyable. A few more feet and I was standing on the Col.

We had taken only four hours to reach the Col de Peuterey, and it was still dark. There was now no question of it being too warm-we were all chilled to the marrow.

"There's no point going to the foot of the Pillar before it's in the sun," decided Don. "Let's have a brew."

We crouched around the gas stove, trying to capture a little of its warmth, and stamped up and down the level plateau of the Col. We were there for over an hour before the line of dazzling sunlight slowly crept down the length of the Pillar to its foot. The rock, a rich brown in the sun, looked warm and inviting.

"Someone's coming up the couloir," shouted Ian.

"It must be the French," said Don. "How many of them are there?"

"Just two."

"That's odd, I wonder what's happened to the other. Anyway, we'd better get started before they arrive."

We quickly crossed the snow slope of the Upper Freney Glacier, found a way through the big bergschrund at the foot of the Pillar, and started up the rock. Don and I went first, followed by Ian and Jan. It was some of the best climbing I have ever done. The rock was superbly sound, warm to the touch, and we had all the excitement and interest of being on new ground. There were no signs of our predecessors and we just picked our own route, winding our way through thrutchy chimneys, up jamming cracks, over steep walls.

The shattered tooth of the Aiguille Noire had been far below us at the base of the Pillar; soon we could look over the corniced summit of the Aiguille Blanche to the haze-covered foothills of Italy. The couple we had seen in the couloir had now reached the Col; about an hour later another pair arrived. They made no move to follow us, but put up tents and seemed to be waiting to see how we fared. We assumed that these must be the French, and that somewhere they had picked up a fourth person. We were wrong, however. The first pair had been two Americans, Gary Hemming and John Harlin, complete outsiders to the Freney stakes, but formidable climbers. They had spent the previous night in the small tent we had seen below the Capucin. The second pair were Desmaison and Poulet Villard. They had had a hard time of it: they had climbed the couloir after the sun had come on to it, when the snow was dangerously soft, and they were constantly bombarded by stones dislodged by the two Americans.

The three French climbers had gone over to the Torino Hut the previous night, hoping to find there Ignatio Piussi who had been summoned by telegram to join the team. He had hired a car and raced across North Italy from his home near Trieste, but had been delayed on the way and missed the last telepherique up from the valley. Julien had therefore stayed behind while the other two pressed on. Piussi and he set out first thing that morning but only reached the couloir in the late afternoon. So, late that evening there were six camped on the Col de Peuterey.

Sir Chris Bonington

By that time we didn't worry about them; we were fifteen hundred feet up the climb, and it seemed a fair lead. At four o'clock we had reached the foot of the final tower. The Pillar now slimmed down from a board, crack-seamed buttress to a slender, monolithic candle of rock, girdled at half height with a belt of overhangs. There were few cracks up it, and what there were all petered out. Gazing up at it, we each had a twinge of doubt-we had no drills or expansion bolts with us—if there were no cracks, no holds, we should be defeated.

Resting against the Pillar was a rock pedestal some fifty feet high. Bonatti and his party had sat out the storm on top of it. There were a few sad relics of their ordeal, an empty gas cylinder, a cooking pot and some wooden wedges.

"We've time to have a look up there before it's dark," said Don. "Hold the rope."

The rock was smooth and sheer, but up to the line of overhangs there were some cracks, and Don made good progress, hammering in his own pegs and using a few left by our predecessors. On reaching the overhang, he edged his way to the left.

"I reckon this is as far as the others got," he shouted down. He disappeared out of sight and the rope lay still in my hand for nearly twenty minutes. At last he reappeared. "There's bugger all round here," he shouted.

"What about Julien's wide cracks?" I asked.

"Not a sign of them—the cracks are all blind and just vanish above the overhang-you'd never get up her without bolts. What's it like to the right-can you see round the corner?"

"Can't see much—there seems to be a chimney up through the roof and there's a corner leading up to it. There might be some cracks in it, but it looks as if it'd be bloody hard getting into it."

"I'll have a look."

Don worked his way back and was soon directly over me, spread eagled, crucified on an overhanging prow of rock. There were no cracks for pegs and he seemed to spend hours on end in the same position before inching forward imperceptibly. I longed for him to come down, so that we could put on duvets (Eiderdown jackets) and settle down for the night. The sun had dropped out of sight round the side of the Innominata Ridge and it was bitterly cold-we were now at a height of over 14,000 feet.

"I think it'll go," at last shouted Don.

"Well, come on down, I'm bloody freezing."

The Central Pillar of Freney

Ian and Jan had caught us up and were sorting out their equipment on a ledge to the side of ours. The gas stove was purring steadily. Don threaded a rope through his top piton and abseiled down in the fast-gathering dark.

We settled down for the night—Ian, as the youngest and most easy-going member of the party, was appointed chief brew-maker; every hour or so during the night he made us some tea or soup. None of us slept much, it was too cold for that—our legs, unprotected by down clothing, were numb. From time to time I had attacks of the shivers when my teeth chattered with the speed of castanets. I couldn't help thinking of the isolation of our position, of the difficulty of retreat if we should be unable to climb the sheer tower above our heads. I could imagine how Bonatti and his party, seated on this same ledge only a couple of months earlier, must have felt-with safety so near, and yet so unattainable.

After a bivouac you are so chilled that it is difficult to start moving before the sun warms your bones. Fortunately, high up on the south side of Mont Blanc, we caught the sun early.

This time I went up the first pitch, using the pegs Don had hammered in the night before. I took a stance on a small foothold just below the overhangs, sitting in a sling. I felt I was poised immediately above the great ice-falls of the Freney Glacier 3,000 feet below. Don moved up past me and was soon thrust out of balance on the overhanging prow. The time crept slowly by and it was all I could do to stay awake in the warmth of the morning sun. A hundred feet below, Jan and Ian basked on the bivouac ledge, while, on the Col de Peuterey, the campers were showing signs of life. Two tiny figures set off down towards the Rochers Grubers and the other four started out for the foot of the Pillar.

Don was now out of sight round the corner of the Pillar. I could hear the dull thud of his peg hammer—the cracks were all blind—and the hoarse pant of his breath. He was two hours on the prow: there was no-where on it to rest; nowhere was it less than vertical.

"Give me some tension."

My grasp tightened on the rope. Out of sight, poised, alone over the steep ice gully, he leant across the blank wall there was nothing for his hands or feet, no crack in which to hammer a peg. His fingers latched round a wrinkle; he was held in precarious balance by the tight rope stretched horizontally from round the corner. The farther he moved across, the more it tried to pull him back, to send him swinging, help-less, into mid-air far out from the overhanging wall. The corner, with

Sir Chris Bonington

a reassuring crack in it, was only six feet away, but it might just as well have been a hundred, the rock seemed utterly impregnable. He searched for a crack-relaxed, somehow, even though he had now been hanging on his fingers for nearly an hour. He found one low down to the right little more than a score on the surface of the granite. He probed it with a tiny ace-of-hearts peg, tried to make the point stick in, for he could only spare one hand; then, oh-so-carefully, reached for his hammer, just tapped at the head to lodge it in the crack. The peg skewed to one side and shot down out of sight-hands getting tired, muscles aching, Don patiently tried to place another peg. This time it stayed in the crack-went in a good half-inch. Holding it gingerly, he edged his way across the wall into the corner.

He had said nothing for over an hour, but I could feel the tension transmitted through the rope by the imperceptible slowness with which it had run through my hands. The pegs now had a good resonant ring to them. There was obviously a useful crack in the corner. Another hour crept by—you need a lot of patience to be a climber.

"You'd better come on up to me," came a muffled shout. "The rope's dragging and I think I'll have to do the next bit free. The crack's too wide for the channels and too narrow for wedges."

As I crossed the prow, I wondered how on earth Don had managed to lead it—it was all I could do to cling on. It was difficult to conceive how he had managed to place the pegs.

I found him ensconced half way up the corner, sitting in his etriers.

"You'd better stop down there. There's a bit of a ledge for you to stand on. There's sweet bugger all up here."

As soon as I was belayed, he started on the last stretch up to the roof. The crack in the corner was just wide enough for his fingers. The roof jutted out above him a good twelve feet, but in the corner of the roof the crack widened into a chimney actually cutting through its ceiling.

We were in heavy shade, and it was bitterly cold on the belay. The rope ran swiftly through my fingers—thank God he's nearly up—but then there was a long pause. I gripped the rope more firmly. He was now a good fifty feet above me—his shoulders jammed in the chimney, his feet pawing ineffectively on the smooth rock below. There was crack sufficiently small to take one of his pegs, right in front of his nose, but he was unable to let go with either hand to grab a peg and thrust it in. He struggled to get higher into the chimney, but could get no purchase with his boots.

The Central Pillar of Freney

"I'm coming off, Chris."

There was along pause not even a man as hard as Don resigns himself to falling. I hunched my belay, wondering what the impact would be, whether his pegs would stay in. A mass of flailing arms and legs shot down towards me, the rope came tight with a sudden, but not over-violent jerk and I found myself looking up into Don's face. He was hanging upside down a few feet above me, suspended from one of his pegs. He had fallen just over fifty feet.

"I've lose me 'at!" he stated.

"Are you all right?"

"Aye."

"Shall I have a go at it?" Quickly. I was tired of standing in the cold, anxious to seize the opportunity to get out in front while Don was still stunned.

We changed over that took a long time and I started up the crack. I had no illusions about it. If Don couldn't climb it free, I certainly couldn't, but I hope I might be able to engineer myself some kind of aid. There was nothing, however, as Don had said, the crack was too wide for our pegs, too narrow for the wedges.

I returned. "Let's see if the others have anything," I suggested, and shouted down to Ian and Jan. But it was no good, we had the entire stock of iron mongery with us.

Meanwhile, the other party had just arrived below the steep section, having climbed most of the way up the gully at the side.

"Ask the French if they have anything," I shouted.

There was a long pause. When the reply came I could only just hear it-we were a hundred and fifty feet from the others round the corner.

"They say we can have some gear in a minute. They want to look at the other side first," shouted Ian.

Another long pause, it was now late afternoon.

"Have they made up their bloody minds yet?" I asked.

"They say that we are on the wrong line, that it goes up the other side. They need all their gear for themselves."

"Well, bugger them in that case; we'll get up by our own means. Have you any slings down there?"

"Yes, what do you want them for?"

"I'll try chockstoning the crack show the Frogs some Welsh technique," I replied.

Sir Chris Bonington

It took us an hour to manoeuver the rope so that we could haul up the slings. I then collected some small stones from the back of the crack, jammed them into it, and, threading the slings behind them, clipped in my etriers and tentatively trusted my weight to them.

In this way I was able to reach the ceiling; standing in a sling, I hammered in a good peg. From there I had some of the most awe inspiring climbing I have ever experienced. Above my head the chimney narrowed down to a dark slit, while below there was nothing but space, dropping away to the Freney Glacier. If I had fallen I would have been dangling some ten feet out from the rock. At the end of the roof, the chimney thinned down to an ice-blocked crack; I had to arch myself out from its comforting confines and swing up on frighteningly small hand-holds. There was no time to pause, even to notice the fear that filled my body. I climbed those last few feet with a desperate speed, only conscious of the need to reach a resting place before my strength ran out.

I reached a ledge and let out a yell—we were over the main difficulties. Don followed me up quickly, and shot past round a ledge just above. It was now very nearly dark; we had climbed only two hundred feet in a complete day. Ian and Jan were still sitting on the ledge where we had spent the previous night. The French seemed to have made no progress round the corner and were preparing a bivouac site.

"You two had better prusik up," Don shouted down to the others. "It'll take too long if you try to climb. We'll drop a rope."

We dropped a single rope and Ian went first, spinning like a spider on the end of a thread, as he worked his way up on slings. Just as Jan prepared to follow him, Desmaison offered him some pegs and asked him to take their rope up, so that they could prusik up the next morning. Jan agreed to do this.

We found a small ledge on the other side of the Pillar. It was sloping and only just fitted the four of us, but that didn't matter-we were nearly up. Nothing could stop us now. My position was at the lower end of the ledge, and I spent most of the night fighting to maintain it as the others slowly slid on top of me-at any rate it helped to keep me warm.

Next morning we climbed the last two pitches. A couple of light planes were roaring round our heads, taking photographs. We all had a feeling of wild exhilaration and triumph, heightened by the struggle we had experienced the day before. The Pillar ended in a slender tower; thence a short abseil took us down to a snow slope leading to the top of the Brouillard Ridge of *Mont Blanc de Courmayeur*. Another hour's plod

The Central Pillar of Freney

and we were on the top of Mont Blanc. A French reporter, dropped there by helicopter, was waiting for us. More important than his congratulations was a flagon of red wine and tins of fruit juice. Slightly tipsy, we staggered to the Vallot Hut and then on down to *Chamonix*.

Sir Chris Bonington

Joe Brown (b. 1930) is by all accounts one of the best climbers of any age. His climbs in North Wales set the standards by which all modern rock climbing is judged. Teaming up with Don Whillans, he "knocked off" numerous standard setting climbs in Derbyshire, Scotland, the Lakes, and Snowdonia including Vector, Hardd, Cemetery Gates, and Cenotaph Corner. He also was responsible for successful ascents of Kanchenjunga and the Mustagh Tower. His autobiography, *The Hard Years*, appeared in 1967.

JOE BROWN:
"HARD DAYS IN THE ALPS"

We drove into the Chamonix valley at nine o'clock. It was dark and the shadows played tricks with the rain dancing on the ebony road. After a grueling journey across France we were groggy and wanted to sleep. I had already bashed my ankle on a roadside bollard and had nearly fainted and fallen off the pillion seat. A car edged out of a side-turning straight in front of us. The bike was traveling at fifty miles per hour. Jamming his brakes on, the car driver locked the wheels and failed to stop. We went into a long skid, were ejected from our seats as the bike toppled over, and shot along the slippery road in a sitting posture. In the helter-skelter situation I could see Don Cowan quite clearly. The bike spun round and he was silhouetted in the blazing headlight. He drifted into the bank at the side of the road at a terrific speed and vaulted over the top.

Picking myself up I made out the vague shape of Cowan splashing about in water. He had landed in the River Ane.

Although he was quite close to the bank he was wobbling in a daze, knee-deep in water, and uncertain which direction to take. Don had been sitting in a cramped driving position for eight hours and had been lulled to stupefaction by the motion of the bike. No bones were broken and the machine was undamaged. Bulging packages of equipment and belongings strapped to the bike had cushioned it.

We remounted the motorcycle and drove on to the Biolay sleeping quarters in Chamonix. The pair of us staggered across the threshold like two prisoners who had just escaped from Devil's Island and had swum to freedom. A member of a party of Cambridge students looked up from his supper and eyed us reproachfully.

"I say, old man, he drawled, "you look as if you have been in the rivet."

I had saved £20 to go to the Alps. I would have liked to have gone earlier but could not afford a visit before 1953 as I had spent most of my earnings on buying equipment and on climbing at home. Several members of the Rock and Ice had already been to the Alps. Don Cowan, whose motorcycle got us there (just), was the most experienced alpinist in the club and he had a number of excellent climbs to his credit.

Chamonix was much as I had pictured it—large, unlovely and swarming with tourists. In those days the Biolay was little more than a doss house suitable for climbers accustomed to rough quarters and not afraid of the occasional flea. The charge for staying in this converted barn was 2s. a night. An assortment of mattresses and bunk beds lay around in a loft and meals could be prepared on your own stoves. There was a yard outside the back door where trestle tables and benches could be set up on a fine day for meals al fresco. Unfortunately the pleasure of eating outside was spoiled by the unpleasant smell from the lavatory, which was simply a hole in the ground. We soon learned not to carry wallets in our back pockets when using this toilet. The barn was situated adjacent to a large camp-site and all sorts of unwelcome folk (or so climbers thought) crept in when the weather was inclement. No one was sure of the ownership; the French Alpine Club was said to have a stake in it but their name was not conspicuous. Various bodies, but usually an old lady called once a day to collect money. An inmate got the feeling that he was contributing to some charity. Needless to say les anglais made the Biolay their second home. I think it must have reminded them of living in road menders' huts and barns in the British mountains.

My first reaction to the mountains, foreshortened from the town, was that they were not particularly impressive of course in the bottom of many Alpine valleys all one can see is a deep forested corridor and the peaks are often screened behind it. Possibly I was unaware that Mont Blanc stands over 12,000 feet above the Chamonix valley, a height four times greater than any comparable situation in Snowdonia. Having read that the gigantic scale of Alpine peaks called for retraining in values of planning, method, and both physical and mental effort, I looked forward to judging these matters for myself.

Don Whillans arrived on his motorcycle looking suitably fit and confident. Our first climb was just about the smallest and most accessible peak in the neighbourhood, Pointe Albert. Short as the climb was it had the highest technical grading given in the Alps. The West Face is a sheer wall of granite, not a lot higher than Cloggy; the difference is that the bottom of the wall is 5,000 feet above the Biolay, through pine forest and over grass, scree and moraine. This was our first taste of the famous Chamonix granite, which is a hard red rock with plenty of cracks suitable for jamming techniques. We also resorted to some artificial climbing, using pegs and slings for standing in and pulling on to make progress. On the other hand there was nothing on Pointe Albert to match the technical standards on the artificial routes that we had been doing on the Derbyshire limestone.

For advice and guidance in choosing climbs we relied on Don Cowan. He suggested trying the East Ridge of the Crocodile. This was a longer and more serious route on a rock tower nearly 12,000 feet above sea level. It would give us a good introduction to the difficulties of a long glacier approach.

With my first taste of aching shoulders we tramped along the Mer de Glace to the Envers hut. On a hot day walking up these huge glaciers with a large rucksack on your back is really uncomfortable, and when you are unfit your entire body aches. The only compensation is the magnificent scenery. We found the Envers hut still in course of construction, and in the rather bare and unfinished building we had to fend for ourselves. The hut is perched on a rocky spine projecting from the base of the Aiguilles and commands a wonderful view across the glacier basin of the Mer de Glace. We gazed at some of the finest scenery in the Alps, a ragged tapestry of rock and ice, and retired to our bunks buoyant with anticipation.

Getting out of bed at 2 a.m. is one of the most unpleasant aspects of Alpine climbing. Rising early is necessary to cross the approach glaciers before sunrise and to ensure full use of all the daylight available to avoid a bivouac one reads about other people feeling exhilarated by getting up at this unearthly hour and being excited with the day's prospects. I tend to feel the opposite way, and hope that the weather is doubtful enough for us to go back to bed, for a few more hours sleep. In fact I found early starts so repulsive that it eventually became my practice to wander up to the foot of a climb on the previous day, make a comfortable bivouac and start climbing at first light next morning. Our approach to the foot of the Crocodile was made easier by the steps of a previous party leading most of the way up the steep icy glacier. By daybreak we were standing below the ice gully that marks the start of the difficult climbing. I was I leading and drove my axe into the upper lip of the big crevasse defending the entrance to the gully. As I pulled on it the shaft broke (ex-W.D. equipment of course!) and I fell back among my companions.

"That's a very good start, I must say," remarked Whillans dryly. The other Don said that the embedded piece of axe should be good enough for hauling ourselves across the gap; it was. Chopping steps in the gully ice, Cowan began a recitation hardly calculated to steady our nerves. He had been in the gully the year before when he was going up to do the Ryan-Lochmatter route on the Aiguille du Plan. On that occasion a block estimated as weighing half a ton had bounded down the X gully and grazed his head.

"You make me sick," said Whillans, looking round apprehensively and expecting to run for his life at any moment. Anyhow, this cautionary tale spurred us to scurry up some rocks and traverse out of the danger area to the foot of the East Ridge. All went well until we arrived at the hardest section of the climb. This involved climbing on pegs driven upside down into the rock. The two Dons were standing on a huge flat-topped rock flake about 50 feet high. A deep subterranean crevice went behind it while the top supplied a first-class stance. I led across the artificial pitch above the flake, finding little difficulty, and entered a groove. Then the rope stopped coming. "Hang on, the rope's jammed," shouted Cowan. Ten minutes later they still hadn't freed it so I climbed down to lend a hand.

The rope had slipped down the crevice behind the flake. We could see it hanging down inside but could not get it out. No amount of tugging and shaking would free it. Nearly three hours were lost climbing up and down the cracks on both sides of the flake, poking the rope with axes and trying to undo the tangle. Eventually we managed to pull out to one side most of the rope and we chopped it off into several long pieces. I could have cried; our beautiful 300 feet rope had been reduced to four 60-foot pieces. Tying them together the knots caught on bits of rock all over the ridge and made it impossible to use running belays. It was very late when we reached the summit. We left almost immediately, descending on the doubled rope. The knots interfered with the descent quite seriously, slowing us down and wearing us out. Rummaging for food in a rucksack, a torch was dropped, reducing us to two axes and one torch between three.

After an eternity we got down on the glacier. It was dark and the slopes now seemed twice as steep. After twenty hours or so of continuous climbing fatigue must take its toll. We had attached crampons (steel spikes) to our boots for gripping the icy surface. Stumbling down the glacier Don Whillans caught the crampon spikes in his flapping trousers and fell over. Within seconds he had knocked me over and both of us went flying down the slope. I braked to a standstill, trying to gather in the rope between myself and Whillans, but when the shock load came on the rope I could not contain it. I was jerked off my feet again. Having slowed the slide to some extent Cowan checked us with his rope at the expense of ripping two fingernails. Unluckily I collided with Whillans and punctured him in the thigh with my crampons; his bruised leg looked like the nozzle of a watering can.

Reorganized, we proceeded at a slower pace and reached the hut at 3.30 a.m., some twenty-five hours after setting out. During the last fifteen minutes I sank into an hallucination. I was convinced that we were in Scotland; we were hemmed in by dark forests, and as we dragged our heavy feet up the last leg of the track to the hut I saw myself approaching a castle. I must have been asleep on my feet and dreaming—a condition I that other mountaineers have suffered—after a trying day.

There was no question that Cowan had been the strong man of the party. He had kept us going. Now he sat down and fell asleep in a chair. Whillans and I tottered about making a brew and soon followed his example. I awoke at three in the afternoon. Still drugged with fatigue we ambled back to Chamonix. I had accomplished my first major Alpine route and reflecting on it over a glass of red wine in the Café National the effort had been worth it.

Browsing through the guidebook to the Mont Blanc range, we noticed that a crack on the Allain-Fix route on the West Face of the Blaitiere was graded VIb. This is the hardest grade given to any rock pitch in the range and was in fact the only pitch of this grade in the guidebook. Although we hadn't climbed a pitch even of Grade VI at this time we all agreed to go and have a look at it. At the Biolay we met Geoff Sutton, who spoke fluent French and who probably knew as much; about the Chamonix area as any Englishman. He pointed out that there had been a huge rockfall on the face and that it was now doubtful if the route was possible.

"I wouldn't mind joining you." he said, "then you could climb more rapidly a two pairs." We readily agreed, for Sutton and had convinced us that and inspection of the face was a worthwhile proposition.

At the foot of the Blaitiere it was obvious that something had radically changed. A great scar about 1,000 feet high discoloured the rocks, where a huge pillar had fallen down.

We scrambled up the easy lower part of the face to the foot of the scar. A crack reminiscent of Curving Crack on Cloggy led to a good ledge at the foot of a vertical wall. This was split by a huge bulging crack leaning to the left. The crack looked deceptively easy and I set off up it with my rucksack. It was not long before I realized that the pitch was liable to be as hard as some of the big cracks on gritstone. It was completely holdless and had to be climbed by wedging one arm and leg inside it. The climbing was strenuous but straightforward up to a bulge, where I managed to fix an upside down peg behind a poor flake. Overcoming the bulge was even more strenuous and all of us tore the skin off our knees.

Another long and difficult crack brought us to a terrace about one-third of the way up the face. Here we rested and had some food. Don Cowan and I prospected to the left for a line through the vertical walls above. This sortie side tracked us on to the pale-coloured scar marking the scene of the rockfall. The rock was brittle and unpleasant to handle. As an underlying skin, freshly exposed to the elements, it was completely unweathered. Whillans and Sutton pushed directly upwards from the terrace. They returned to report that the rocks looked exceedingly difficult. It was now too late to find the solution. The retreat was sounded and we roped down the cracks to the lower terrace. Darkness trapped us and we had to bivouac on a ledge overlooking the carnival of lights in the valley 6,000 feet below.

Ten days in the Alps flashed by and bad weather brought the holiday to an abrupt close. The experience of Alpine climbing haunted me. Back in Manchester I told myself that I might as well go back the following year for the whole of the season; three months. one would then stand a really good chance of making a number of major climbs. I would have to resign my job and look for something else when it was all over. Whillans, Moseley, Ray Greenall and others supported the idea although not all of us would be in the Alps at the same time.

In preparation for the event Moseley and I made a resolution: our general expenses must not exceed one shilling a week until we had saved about £100 each to pay for a long holiday. We dedicated ourselves to the cause. I gave up smoking and we cycled everywhere on weekend trips in Derbyshire.

The shilling was usually spent in a café. Our friends tucked into big meals with a loud smacking of lips while we watched in silence. We used to ride away in disgust or because we couldn't trust ourselves. I was saving about £5 a week and Ron, after deducting his fares to work, was putting by a similar amount. Week after week we persevered, denying ourselves the pleasures and most of the necessities of life. The target was reached, but not before we had transgressed a little!

After many months of scraping, saving and waiting the summer arrived. Ten of us rode or walked into Chamonix only to be tied to the town by atrocious weather for several weeks. We pottered about on the practice climbs of the Brevent and did one or two short routes on the Aiguilles.

Among other things, the East Face of the Grand Capucin loomed large in our ultimate plans. Girdled by overhangs and roofs this magnificent wall had been finally scaled by the brilliant Italian climber, Walter Bonatti, in 1951. Bonatti and a companion had toiled on the precipice for four days, finishing in a storm.

To reconnoitre the approach we had been up to the foot of the wall, quite a long way from Chamonix, on several occasions. Cautious with our hard-won savings we walked to the Montenvers Hotel, where the glacier trudge began, rather than use the railway. Expenses were also cut by avoiding staying in huts. Huge loads and sleeping gear were carried up the long glacier into the Geant Basin where an igloo was built below the mountain. We might sit inside for two days, melting snow and making endless brews of tea while the snow fell outside. During one attempt to find the climb the party was lost in a white-out. As far as we knew we had marched across the glacier in a straight line. When the cloud lifted for a moment we were high enough to see our tracks cutting in an arc away from the Capucin. The only good thing to be said for the long siege was that it kept us fit. We used to race down to Chamonix for fresh supplies and in descent the Montenvers train was regularly beaten on foot.

I had commuted up the glacier three or four times before or our luck changed. Whillans, Moseley and I were lying in the igloo when the roof collapsed. The top melted, leaving the walls with ominous cracks splitting them. In this condition we spent another night in the shelter but it couldn't last more than another day. Early next morning some voices woke us. It was still dark but the weather was fine. The voices receded, we got up, and thinking we had the Capucin to ourselves, prepared breakfast leisurely as dawn stole across the greywhite glacier.

When it became light enough to see the East Face clearly, we noticed two figures already on the traverse about 700 feet up the face. By the time we had sorted out our gear the leader was just starting on the third difficult pitch. As we climbed on to the face ourselves over an hour later we were very surprised to find the second man still in the same place. In this time the party which had got in front of us had hardly moved at all.

The sun was blazing and the rock was fit to fry an egg. With sacks weighing 50 pounds our pace slowed. Don kept shouting to Moseley to climb faster because he was taking longer to climb each pitch with all the pegs in place than the time I spent putting them in and climbing, and the time Don spent climbing and removing the pegs. The East Face was mainly sensational artificial climbing through and over some of the most improbable overhangs I had ever seen and it was important to recover the pegs progressively for use higher up. For some unaccountable reason I was sack-hauling without assistance and getting browned off. I was leading and hauling three sacks.

When I reached the first decent ledge on the face I was already thinking that we would have to bivouac much sooner than we intended. The appeal of the Grand Capucin was beginning to wane, even after waiting so long to get on the climb. I learnt that enthusiasm was more likely to fade under the mental stresses of Alpine climbing than at home. our progress might have been better if a party had not been climbing immediately above. By our standards the Frenchmen were slow, yet they were not the real cause of our delay. Our morale was drooping and we voted to go down. To descend, however, was easier said than done.

Owing to the fact that I had just made a long traverse through some overhangs, it was impossible to rope straight down the face from where I was standing. Moseley, who was half-way across the pitch between Don and me, decided it: would make our maneuver easier if he took a stance in slings at the other end of the traverse. I sent the three sacks across to Moseley and then reversed the traverse to join him. There I found that both of us and the three sacks were hanging on the same peg. We hurriedly sent the sacks down to Don and started roping down ourselves. Approaching the edge of the couloir near the bottom of the face we found a good ledge and decided to bivouac there. Ron had been practising bivouacking all winter in hard conditions, so no one raised any objections.

While Ron was making soup Don and I fell asleep and he must have felt that we were not being cooperative. In spite of his intensive training Ron remained awake all night, thinking to himself what a rotten pair of companions we made.

Later in Chamonix I commented to some Parisians on the slowness of the two Frenchmen who had been climbing the Capucin ahead of us. They insisted that I must be mistaken. The pair in question, they said, were two of the fastest climbers in France. A week later their argument was reinforced when the same Frenchmen made the second ascent of the West Face of the Dru in three and a half days. This climb ranked as a milestone in modern climbing in the Western Alps. The first ascent had taken seven days and a book had been written about it. Still we told ourselves that if the speed of the Frenchmen on the Capucin was better than normal, then we ought to be fairly capable of reducing their time on the Dru by half.

"What about having a look at the Dru?" I suggested to Whillans. "Well, there doesn't seem anything better to do, so let's go." With a vague description of the climb in my pocket he and I set off at midday with packs that dwarfed our figures. The granite thumb of the Dru presented its West Face in full view of the drinking terrace of the Montenvers Hotel. Turning our backs on all that, we crossed the glacier and made our way to the gully that led to the bottom of the face. The gully contained several hundred feet of clean ice. Each axe blow broke off large jagged chunks of the brittle stuff

"Hey, mate, watch it!" shouted Whillans, who was below and unable to dodge the cannonade. "Chop it into smaller pieces." Perhaps he thought that one could be artistic in cutting like the figures illustrating a textbook on climbing.

We bedded down for the night on the terraces at the bottom of the West Face. We were tremendously impressed by the wall of rock soaring above us. It was nearly 3,000 feet high. It rained off and on and neither of us slept much. our bivouac equipment consisted of a cagoule—a sheath-like anorak—which I had borrowed from Geoff Sutton, and a pacamac that Don had borrowed from me. The pacamac was more waterproof than the cagoule, but not as windproof, so by morning we were both very cold and damp.

Hard Day in the Alps

As soon as it was light we started moving. With just the right amount of exercise to loosen stiffened limbs we stepped from terrace to terrace with an odd Grade III wall between them. Before long the weight of the sacks became purgatory. The serious climbing was just starting.

"This is useless," I declared, throwing my pack down. "Yes," said Don, "let's wear ourselves out the other way." After that we hauled the packs up the face on ropes.

The first Grade VI pitch was the Vignes fissure. We had been warned about its difficulty. Bar room gossip in Chamonix was tinged with bated breath when the famous crack was mentioned. Don went up in splendid style, giving a running commentary on its merits. Calling out scornfully, the general drift of his remarks noted "big holds here, large holds there, jug holds above, piece of cake," and so on. Why the pitch should daunt so many ace French climbers baffled us. We thought that if this was the crux, then we were in for an easy climb.

A new power flowed in our veins. We really bombed up the face, pitch after pitch, without faltering. Sharing the leads I got the 40 metre crack which splits an incredibly smooth and overhanging wall. The start of this pitch is a traverse, so that the exposure on the broken wooden wedges that set my nerves on edge. The wedges had to be treated very carefully, but Don just laybacked straight up the crack, using them as footholds.

We had a snack at the foot of the remarkable 90-metre corner, the most conspicuous feature of the face, which opens below a barrier of tri-angular roofs outlined darkly against the sky. The sky was darker now, the rock colder and a woolly cloud-cuff had begun to grip the peak. I put on my down jacket half way up one of the pitches.This was distinctly awkward, sitting in slings and with no room to maneuver. We were told afterwards that telescope watchers at the Montenvers now lost sight of us for good as the peak was smothered in cloud. Shut off from the world and with vast blank walls on all sides, our loneliness was heightened by the snow falling and the uncanny presence of a rope hanging down the face a short distance above. It had been placed there by the first explorers as an escape route on to the easier North Face. We had to find another rope up to the right, which was used to make a pendulum descent to a ledge in the middle of the face.

"My turn, I think," said Don, who was full of beans. He went up a blind crack that—just as it became hopeless—revealed a rotten-looking fixed rope trailing down a rock curtain into the mist.

Joe Brown

"Come up now," he called. The stance at the top of the fixed rope was very insecure. "I'll test it," he said, yanking fiercely on the rope. He pronounced it good. Relying on me to guard two unsatisfactory pegs holding the rope, he jumped into space. Don and the rope vanished from sight. I was left in a fit suspense of waiting. If it doesn't work out, I thought, he'll have a hell of a job getting back up.

Presently a cheery shout rent the stillness. I went down to a big flake crack that we soon climbed to a little nest of a ledge that no self-respecting eagle would call its own.

"This will have to do for the night," Don announced. "Which side would you like to sleep on?" As if it mattered.

Neither of us could relax or stretch out. The ledge permitted only crouching in a variety of restless positions. Snow fell all night. I kept looking at Don, hour after hour, praying for daybreak. Don slept soundly through it all—I know not how—a hooded bundle huddled against the precipice. We were soon covered with a thick layer of snow. In the morning ropes and sacks were buried under snow; snow was melting everywhere and running water showered the rocks. With the equipment stiffened and weighted with water we started up a series of chimneys and cracks; before long we made our first error in route finding.

The estimated length of pitches we had climbed so far corresponded with the poor translation of a description of the route that we had procured in Chamonix. On the upper part of the face we realized too late that the description applied to sections as short as ten or fifteen feet. We had climbed too far up several slabs and cracks and were caught in difficulties more serious than anything else on the climb. Having regained our bearings, we discovered a caving ladder hanging in space. In his usual daring manner Don coolly bounced up and down on the lower rung and declared it safe. We learnt later that this curious and helpful piece of equipment had been removed from the Vignes fissure by the previous party and carried up to the overhang which it now adorned.

The top section of the climb goes on to the North Face. When we looked down the face it was all ice. The prospect upwards was quite the reverse—good clean rock. An explanation for this illogical condition on the mountain came to hand at the top of the first section. From below the landing appeared to be a flat ledge; when I got there it was banked up at 45 degrees with ice. The downward view had shown us similar ledges optically linked to represent an icy face. The top of every pitch was the same. You had to chip hand and foot holds before a standing position could be attained. Even then each stance was delicate and uncomfortable to stand on and we found no relief from the climbing effort.

About 200 feet below the summit a chimney was blocked by icy overhangs which Don avoided by traversing to the right. This was not the correct route and the traverse was the hardest pitch that we did on the West Face. The chimney was the correct route—a traverse line, not at all evident from below—went off to the left below the overhangs. As it was we searched for an exit to the summit. Bit by bit we girdled the top of the mountain, about 300 degrees of a circle. No breach could be found. Several hours were wasted looking for an escape before we hauled ourselves, dogtired, on to the summit.

This was the lower of the two summits of the Dru and we did not know the way down. The question of descending from this point was debated. Don was clearly in favour of pressing on to the higher summit, albeit farther away, from where we had a sketchy description of another way down. So we climbed the upper rock bastion, another short climb in itself on a very exposed wall. At the top, an interminable series of walls and chimneys swept down to the Charpoua glacier. Dusk had fallen when we reached the last rocks beside the glacier. Don had just leapt into space across the crevasse between the rock wall and the glacier.

"Come on," he yelled up. "It's all right." Not until I was dropping stone-like through the air did I realize that the jump to the glacier was a good 30 feet. One would probably never pluck up courage to jump down a place like this if it could be examined first from below.

The Charpoua glacier was a jumble of crevasses and ice walls, and never less than 40 degrees steep. We had neither torch nor crampons and had to cope with one broken axe between us. Our descent might be described as a controlled fall of 1,000 feet, taken in stages of one yard at a time—slip and stop, slip and stop.

We missed the hut on a rocky peninsula in the lower part of the glacier and spent our third night in the open. We wandered into a crevasse-maze and it was too dark to extricate ourselves. We cut a ledge in the ice, spread out the gear and sat down dejectedly. In saturated clothes, and with nothing to eat or drink, severe cramp in the back and legs tortured us all night. Sleeping was an invitation to succumb to the penetrating cold. We exercised our legs by stretching out and then drawing them up to our chins with arms wrapped tightly round the knees to keep our backs away from the ice. This rhythmic movement kept the blood circulating. Overhead the sky was filled with stars as cold and remote as wandering for ever in space.

A light came on in the Charpoua Hut, Later a party crossed the glacier barely 200 yards below us. We couldn't move immediately; we had to thaw out and force ourselves to stand up. Two frost-white figures, we finally got moving and trundled to the hut in ten minutes. The building was empty. We ransacked the place for matches to make a brew; there were none. After forty hours on the mountain, with not more than six hours sleep, I pointed to the valley that was still some hours away. "Let's go, Don." He nodded without speaking.

On the way down we met Hamish Nicol, who congratulated us on achieving something for the "old country." With Tom Bourdillon, he had made the first British ascent of the North Face of the Dru in 1950. His welcome might have forewarned us of the reception awaiting us in Chamonix, but it didn't. In the valley we were hailed as heroes. We had no inkling that our ascent of the West Face of the Dru would have this effect on people.

Back at the campsite we went into our tents and passed out. A violent storm broke loose during the night. Don's tent was flooded. He was lying in water with his head just above the surface. Far from waking up, he didn't stir and the salvage workers left him in peace. In another tent I was in much the same condition. Water was trickling over my face but I refused to wake up. Two friends dragged me to higher ground, saying afterwards that I was whimpering, and went away to attend to more urgent matters. In the morning Don and I felt deathly. The storm had wrought havoc in the campsite. Potato peelings, tea leaves and other rubbish had been washed among belongings and the whole place looked like a disaster zone after a hurricane. Louis Lachenal, one of France's foremost guides, came to pay his respects. He was dressed immaculately and was escorting a gorgeous girl. He found the party lounging on the ground in filth and squalor, like a band of brigands. Goodness knows what he thought of us. Homage from one so exalted in the mountaineering elite was indeed a surprise. After this the Chamonix guides came up to us in the street to shake our hands.

A fall I took while climbing the Menegaux route on the Aiguille de i'M could be attributed to over-confidence. By now I was feeling superbly fit and had unwisely dispensed with the normal procedures for overcoming an artificial pitch on the route. In result a boot slipped off a peg thatch was standing on. Falling free after 20 feet, I flashed past a runner that carried some slack rope leading down to the second man. That is my rope, I thought. I grabbed it together with the end tied to my waist and stopped myself. The second man was unaware that anything had happened. I broke the fall and saved myself by a fluke, otherwise it could have been very serious.

Bad weather prevented any further attempts to climb the Capucin. My thoughts turned to the Blaitiere. The job was unfinished. Could it be finished? The only way to answer that question was to go back on the face.

One afternoon Don and I strolled up to the West Face and bivouacked on the luxurious platform lit the bottom of the cracks that we had climbed the year before (now known as the Fissure Brown). We had a most comfortable night and next morning we romped up the cracks with hardly any effort to the ledges near the rock-fall scar. I traversed on to the rotten rock again and spied a delightful crack running up through much better rock to an overhang. Putting in a peg below the bulge, I swung out to one side and lodged myself in an even nicer groove that broke through the beetling rocks. The climbing was hard but unbelievably straightforward. Don came up remarking on the simplicity of the key that unlocked the door to the rest of the face. Instinctively I felt that nothing could stop us now. Cracks, walls and ledges guided me to the foot of a truly massive wall. It was split by the most gigantic crack that I had ever seen. The wall was either vertical or overhanging for some 400 feet and the crack zoomed up to the heavens.

Two pitches up I was stopped by an overhanging portion, the like of which I had not met before. Even brought to ground level in gritstone surroundings, I doubt whether I could have climbed it. It was dripping with black water, greasy, hold less and devoid of cracks for driving in pegs. After 20 feet of desperately insecure climbing I came down feeling rather shattered. Changing places, Don's attempt was repelled with the same result. We descended to the bottom of the wall to look for an alternative. Only a minute or two away we discovered a short wall leading to a thin unbroken crack that rose to a dizzy height. This was the noted Fissure Fix, climbed before the landslip by the first ascensionists. It is two inches wide and goes straight up—more or less vertically for 100 feet—to a ridge. Fingers and toes were pressed inside as jamming or pressure holds; every upward movement was identical and really enjoyable. I could not remember when a pitch had given me so much pleasure.

Joe Brown

Beyond the top of the ridge I slipped in a corner where the landing was on a ledge covered with stones. I fell a few feet, managed to jam a hand into the corner-crack and stopped myself. Soon it was dark and we moved cautiously on the last part of the wall below the summit. The ground was broken by dozens of little ledges, yet none of them would allow us to sit comfortably. We played about under the summit pinnacle for a while, more bemused by the revelation of having made a new and major route than putting our heads together on a course of action. A fresh breeze was blowing, we chatted, the lights came on in Chamonix far below and we forgot the time. Very much later, or so it seemed, a pale light stole across the horizon.

"Stir yourself, Don," I said, "dawn is breaking—let's get down."

"Oh, all right," he grumbled, "I was just getting comfortable and ready for a bit of shut-eye."

We packed the rucksacks and uncoiled the rope, ready to move off when the light was stronger. Suddenly Whillans growled: "What the hell's that?" I looked up and saw the moon rising above a dark ridge. The time was only about 11 p.m.

This made both of us so fed up that we couldn't stop talking about it for hours. Came the real dawn, we crossed to the head of the Spencer Couloir, which was in very good condition, and went down by the normal route. We reentered the campsite at seven-thirty, before anyone was up.

One of the worst post-war seasons in the Alps was 1954, a year that was remembered long afterwards for continuously bad weather. We had been lucky to snatch the climbing that we did before the season went completely sour. Six weeks of cat-and-mouse games with storms and gales blunted my patience, and Don and I agreed to return home to spend the rest of the summer in Wales. As it happened when we got back we were rewarded with three fine days in six weeks.

With money to spare I bought a lot of superlative French equipment. I carted my purchases home in a colossal suitcase, which was also stuffed with piles of dirty washing belonging to other people. The case was so heavy that two of us had to carry it with an ice axe pushed through the handle. In the customs shed at Folkestone the examining officer frowned suspiciously.

"Open this case, please," he said. He deliberately ignored our grubby-looking rucksacks. The counter was sagging under the weight.

I flicked open the catches. He can lift the lid himself, I thought.

"What have we here," he said in a flat tone, prising up the top. The lid sprang back and a mass of sticky rags that we called clothes billowed up.

The most distasteful smell imaginable rose from the case. The officers's face screwed up in horror and he stepped back a foot or two, poked a stick inside, lifted up a corner and let it drop. He chalked the case at arm's length, he said: "Yes, that will be all."

Dougal Haston (1940—1977) was instrumental in making the first
direct ascent of the North Face of the Eiger in winter 1966. In 1970,
on the Bonington-led Annapurna expedition, he teamed with Don
Whillans as the first summit team and made the first ascent of the
giant Southeast Face. Again on Bonington's successful 1975 Everest
Southwest Face expedition, he reached the summit with Doug Scott.
His autobiography, *High Places*, was published in 1972.

DOUGAL HASTON:
EIGER DIRECT

Most of the parties who climb the Eiger come down saying, "A
magnificent experience, but never again." I could not quite understand
this. To be sure, it is unusual for climber to repeat a major route; it is a
thing completed and there are so many new things to do. But the statement
was not relating only to this feeling. It was saying something about the
whole North Face of the Eiger itself. Climbers seemed to experience a great
sense of relief when finishing the North Face. The psychological impact
of that great wall and its history has been so great that potential climbers
seemed to be conditioned to the idea that they were going into a disaster
area. This is not an unreasonable feeling: the wall is dangerous. But there
again, accepting danger and trying to minimize it with one's experience is
an essential part of climbing.

On reaching Kleine Scheidegg after our ascent, I did not find this
sense of relief. I felt really happy at the completion of the climb, but there
was also another feeling concerning the progression in climbing that I
have tried to explain. The Eiger was 6,000 feet high and three-quarters
of a mile wide at the base. It seemed a lot of rock to have only one route.
Ideas for a new route began to form.

It was not until I met John Harlin that I found someone who was interested in such a project. He was more than interested; he had already
taken part in two attempts to establish a new line up the Face, once in

winter 1964 and again in June of that year. The high point had been the Second Icefield. What they were trying in fact was an old start, with a direct finish from the Death Bivouac upwards. They did not use the start of the usual Heckmair route but climbed directly up the rock buttress taken by the first pair to try the face, Sedlmayer and Mehringer in 1935. But ideas were developing for a more ambitious project. I have already explained how the direttissima concept had gained great momentum in the Dolomites. Harlin had tried to apply it on attempts at the West Face of the Dru direct. So why not a direct route on the Eiger?

We quickly realized that a project such as this would have to be tackled in winter. Any direct route would come in direct line of Spider fire. Only in winter is the stone fall frozen.

In February 1965 John and I decided to make a close reconnaissance of the face. The main barrier to a direct route seemed to be a cliff barrier about 300 feet high which stretched at the level of Eigerwand Station all the way from the North-West Ridge to the Hinterstoisser Traverse. It had been climbed on its extreme right by Sedlmayer and Mehringer, but this was too far over for a direct route. We wanted to examine the possibilities in the region of Eigerwand Station.

Telescope study is never satisfactory, so we decided to go on to the wall proper. As it was only a reece, a little cheating seemed to be in order.

We could not go out of the window at Eigerwand Station without being discovered. To be in the tunnel at all was strictly forbidden unless in emergency, and punishable by a large fine. By careful study of old plans, John had found that there was an old refuse opening just short of Eigerwand Station. This seemed to be for us. Chris Patterson, a British climber working in Leysin, and Bob Boucher came along to help carry equipment. We caught the last train up to Eigergletscher Station, and tried to be as inconspicuous as four laden climbers can be in a ski resort. To baffle the station authorities, we ploughed off round a corner in the direction of the Monch and sat out of sight waiting for darkness to fall. Soon we were tramping up the tunnel and after about two hours found the shaft we were looking for. This looked particularly good for staying unnoticed. There was an initial room with some tools in it, then another with a window opening out onto the Face. It was a weird experience the next day, slipping out of the window onto the wall. From our comfortable bivouac hole straight into the Eiger winter.

Dougal Haston

It was as I was to find it on many future wintery days. Shadowy, very cold, with a slight wind blowing spindrift in all directions. Up to our waists in powder, we ploughed leftwards towards Eigerwand Station. A very impressive wall, this first band. A few lines of weakness, but none that could by any stretch be called easy. Pensively, we returned to our cave at nightfall. Having effected that part of our recce, the next day John and I climbed most of the Sedlmayer-Mehringer buttress for training. I led and found it hard. Certainly it was winter and covered in powder and this made it very difficult, but one could see that even in dry conditions it was a formidable piece of climbing. Abseiling back down, I felt a lot of respect for those two who had tackled the cliff on sight on their first visit to the Western Alps.

As we climbed through the window, a train drew up outside and loud knocks began at the door. We had made a barrier of wood but it seemed as if we were discovered anyway, so we let in the railway officials. We were prepared for the worst, police and fines, but for once the officials seemed friendly. Amused by our wanderings, they said we had been spotted on the first day but it had taken them two days to find our whereabouts. Their initial thinking was that we were on a full-scale attempt and had started from the bottom. But when extensive telescope inspection failed to reveal tracks, they had come to the conclusion that we were either supernatural or using the tunnel. They did not even put us on a train but allowed us to walk out. This was unheard of, penniless climbers in the past had often been forced onto the train and charged a first-class fare which they could ill afford.

One thing remained in our minds after this recce a direct route would be a formidable problem. We planned to make an attempt the next winter.

During that summer John and I had a temporary altercation and split up. But as I was languishing back in Scotland he had been planning carefully, and had organized newspaper support for the climb which meant that a team could be equipped with the best equipment. After being turned down by various climbers, he eventually decided to patch up the quarrel and rang me up at Christmas. Not being proud where a new route on the Eiger was concerned, I quickly accepted. A further telegram brought me rushing straight from Ben Nevis to Leysin to find John and Layton Kor, one of America's best climbers. Old feelings were quickly lost in enthusiasm for the new project.

Our plan was to go onto the wall and hope to climb through in ten days. This was based on John's and my own previous knowledge of the Face, a helicopter reconnaissance in February just after my arrival in Leysin, and extensive study of photographs taken at that time. The only essential, but a very elusive one, was ten days of good weather.

There is a great weight problem in putting equipment and food for ten days on the backs of three people and still being able to climb upwards. Everything has to be selected with a view to weight. Ounces count. Even with the climbing equipment slung round our bodies the sacks would weigh around thirty pounds. This is too heavy for actual climbing and necessitates sack hauling. As for food, we could only budget minimally for ten days. Some dried meat, bacon, nuts, chocolate and a few hot drinks per man-day. In a period of ten days with extreme cold thrown in this means that your performance level is always decreasing slightly. One bad storm can put you close to the edge.

Knowing these problems we sat for three weeks in Kleine Scheidegg, monitoring weather forecasts twice a day. We really worked on the system. Phone-calls to Geneva, Zurich and London. There were occasional good days, but no sign of the settled period we wanted. Ten days is a lot of fine weather to ask for, but we had good precedents; in the previous two winters there had been even longer spells.

Towards the end of February, we decided to go back to Leysin for a couple of days, the weather still being unsettled. No sooner had we arrived than a panic-stricken phone-calls came from Chris Bonington at Kleine Scheidegg saying that eight Germans had started up our route using fixed rope tactics. Shattered, we turned right around and shot back.

Chris and Peter Gillman were covering the story for the *Daily Telegraph*, Chris to come some way with us on the wall and Peter to write the basic story. Looking for pictures, Chris had followed the Germans to the foot of the wall. At that time they hadn't been too friendly, throwing snowballs as he approached with cameras at the ready. But he had seen enough to find out their plan of campaign. Their intention was to use expedition tactics; that is, fixing ropes and establishing camps with four lead climbers and four behind carrying supplies. Though not as pure as our concept this technique had the advantage that it could be used in bad weather. It was slow, but on most days progress could be made and if really bad weather came in retreat could always be made down the fixed ropes.

A dilemma for us. Do we still wait for good weather and try the single push? If good weather didn't come then the Germans would be pushing steadily up the wall while we waited at the bottom, an almost intolerable state of affairs for our climbing minds. Also, if a push attempt was turned back by bad weather then we'd really be far behind. The weather forecasts were still mediocre, so the only solution seemed to be to resort to expedition tactics as well. This we did.

The conflict is fierce. Two separate parts of time and space are fighting their respective battles. I, a free being, am existing, but the fact of my existence has long ceased to give me trouble. It is where I am at present that is causing mental turmoil. The time late March 1966; the place, the Eiger Nordwand.

The second conflict is certain parts of Nature having private battles of their own. Though of late there seems to be some form of unison, in that everything seems to be determined to wipe this minute thinking object from the huge inanimate wall, where many think he has no right to be.

I am sitting with part of my right leg on the ice; the left one swings in a sling on the steep slope. A sodden, then frozen, sleeping-bag stirs memories of warmth from forgotten corners of the senses. The storm has been going on for two days; two of the many of striving to make this direct route exist. Our seeking to make a new line on this, the greatest north wall, has brought us to our present position.

The "us" are myself and four Germans. Two, Roland Votteler and Sigi Hupfauer are ten feet to my right, crouching crampon-held under a red tent sack. The others, Jorg Lehne and Gunter Strobel, are somewhere above, minute, sling-held spots in this morass of Nature's purgatory. I have just descended from above to find some sleeping gear. There would have been no survival without. We had been a bewildered three up above, lost in the storm, seeking the elusive Summit Icefield but unable to find it and wearied by the unrelenting difficulty. Sleep is not possible as my position is directly in an avalanche chute, and every so often I have to heave as much as I dare to disturb a huge mass of powder snow. Slowly I drift into a dream state and begin to reconsider the four weeks of effort that have led me to this position.

A February day and we were four at Scheidegg. John Harlin, Layton Kor and I, with Chris Bonington as photographer, a role which was to change. Thoughts of having hallucinations when eight figures appeared on "our" direct line. But a confirmation by many pairs of eyes affirmed reality. They retreated that day, and we found out that they were eight

Germans from Stuttgart: Jorg Lehne, Peter Haag, Gunter Strobel, Sigi Hupfauer, Roland Votteler, Karl Golkow, Gunter Schnaidt, Rolf Rosenzopf.

An interruption by an avalanche destroys my recall. Slowly I wriggle the snow into space and settle down once again to my dreaming. When sleep is not possible, dreaming is a great way of time passing on bad bivouacs. Recalling worrying moments that have been overcome often makes the present bad seem better. All is not clear in my mind at the moment, only certain incidents keep flashing back.

The difficult ice climbing, where we had thought it would be easy, leading up to the first band. Two days of sitting in slings above Eigerwand Station window, admiring the superb piton artistry of Layton Kor as the rope went out and out through pitons that seldom went in over an inch; a web of blind cracks that would have had most people fumbling. The day we finished the band there was an abseil for me that almost ended in disaster. A 300-foot free drop and an upside-down flip in the middle as I tangled with the climbing rope. Fortunate extraction by a knife from below.

The days above, leading to the second band, are a blur of crampon-strained calves and aching axe-arms overcoming seventy to eighty degree thin ice-plated slabs. Climbing parallel with the Germans to the top of the second band, then on over varying types of ground with one thing in common, seldom easy, to the Second Icefield and up to the crest of the Flatiron in a storm. A glorious day, with Layton on the Third Icefield. Then six days in a snow hole on the Death Bivouac with John. These six days of confinement are still vivid in my mind. There were immense problems in just staying alive. The constant battle to keep spindrift off our down clothing; freezing hands fumbling with petrol stoves which would not light; long periods during the day when nothing would ease the aching cold in one's limbs; functional problems; psychological problems; trying not to quarrel over petty things; talking to pass the long hours on almost every conceivable subject; sleep which was often disturbed by insidious spindrift, when one had to emerge from deep stupor to brush it off, only to find half an hour later that the same thing had happened again: food running out on the fourth day and eventual defeat on the sixth, as we were forced to go down just as the weather turned reasonable again.

Then the struggle of Layton and Chris as they gradually solved the problems beneath the Spider and Layton's amalgamation with the Germans to reach the Spider as Chris came down.

John and I were by then fit and reascended to the Death Bivouac to be greeted by a fresh bad-weather forecast. Layton went down and no sooner had he disappeared that we heard by radio that the Germans were in the Fly and we set off for the summit. I had left the Death Bivouac with a cheerful "see you in the Spider" to John. I never saw him again. A broken fixed rope ended the life of one who belonged to the finest of men. The whole climb had lain in the balance, but the thought of establishing the direct route as a memorial to John had overcome our urge to flee as we were rocking in the throes of bitter defeat. We five had been left to go for the summit. All below went down and stripped the face of fixed ropes.

The day after the accident the forecast storm had broken. It was savage, but we were determined. The achievement of the climb of our dreams was at hand and the storm gradually became the norm. After two days of fighting upward in it, clear days seemed to belong to memory. Gunter and Jorg had pushed up the summit cliffs and then descended to a communal bivouac in the Fly under the impression that the major difficulties were over. Jorg and I had set out today to finish the climb and had ended up in our present position. The difficulties were still all too painfully obvious. My reflections put me in a euphoric state. This was slowly but systematically shattered as a grayish light began to assert itself over the. black of the night. Dawn was here and all was not ended, so there had to be movement.

I unbend, creaking from the tent sack, and start to put on crampons. No need to describe the painfulness of this task. A thorough physical and mental check is then made. Both pass. I feel capable of days of struggle physically. My mind is now in a strange state of blank acceptance. It does not seem as if anything can get worse. The avalanches are pouring down the cracks. The nightmare wind whirls round in the bowl of the face, whipping snow in all directions. My eyelashes, nose and mouth are quickly plastered by a huge ice crust. I can hardly see Sigi and Roland ten feet to my left. The only link with those above is the ghostly line of the fixed rope that I had to come down the night before: an inanimate umbilical cord linking us to a mountain that seems only to want to reject those gathered on its flanks. I quickly move up this rope to try and catch Jorg and Gunter. But there is no sign of them at the Bivouac site, only a forty-foot gap in the fixed ropes. The immediate impulse is to try it alone, but I decided to wait on my two companions. There is a long period of reflection on the stance before they arrive. They look fantastic: completely white, with great long icicles hanging like fangs from nose and mouth. The gap is overcome and we three progress. A gap in the cloud suddenly reveals Jorg and Gunter just disappearing out of sight. We are on the Summit Icefield. Jubilation, then worry. I can't see a continuance of the fixed rope. We are on blank sixty-degree water ice. I eventually see rope 150 feet above. We have no ice-axes, no hammers, only one ice-piton. I fill in the gap. It is the nearest I have gone to the limit.

I was in a position to look out over the edge of all things as I at last grasped the fixed line. An hour later it was done. The memorial to John exists. The Eiger has lost its toughest battle.

The descent down the West Flank was wonderful. I was met on the summit by Chris Bonington, who showed the way to a snow-hole about a thousand feet down. An Amazing place—a four-man cave with twelve people crammed into it. As well as the German team and myself, there were Chris, Mick Burke and Toni Hiebeler. The whole trip nearly ended in suffocation due to the excess of Gauloise smoke. There was so much snow on the West Flank that it was one long glissade down to the tumult at Eigergletscher. Press, television, the whole place was in an uproar. My fingers were frostbitten. I only wanted to rest and talk quietly to friends. But it was not possible—Press conferences, telephone calls, telegrams, and parties in the evening. Mick and I nearly got lost coming from the German Pension to Scheidegg Hotel in a blizzard; that would have been a great piece of news.

Three days later I was in hospital in London. My fingers looked bad. Mike Ward, the Everest doctor, recommended an experimental treatment—hyperbaric oxygen. I spent ten days in the London hospital, joined half-way through by Chris who had frostbitten feet. Thanks to the treatment and the incredible care of the staff, I walked out after the ten days with no fingernails, badly withered fingers, but no amputations. I'll never forget stepping outside. It had been a worrying period. Life could go on. What use is a fingerless mountaineer? Chris also came out unscathed. I wish I could say the same for my German friends. Of the four who climbed out with me, three, Lehne, Strobel and Votteler, went into hospital for frostbite. A few weeks later I received a letter from Jorg Lehne: "I have had my right big toe amputated, Gunter and Roland have both lost all their toes but are bearing up very well." A shattering letter. But a climber can recover from lost toes, even though it is a long painful process. I wondered what could have happened if I hadn't come back to Britain. It had been a costly climb in human values-one life, twenty-one toes, and weeks in hospital.

Controversy raged for a long time after. The use of fixed ropes was condemned. Many climbers entered the issue with sweeping statements about the ethics of the route. The moment something new and controversial is done, some climbers seem only too willing to get up and shout about the wrongness of it all. What causes this? We had just established the hardest route in the Alps. Our tactics were new. But the environment was new. We had envisaged using classical methods, but at the time they proved impossible. But these people who had not dared were now coming out of their holes to criticize. Was it envy? Insecurity? I'll never know, but it left a sad impression on me that people could be so petty.

For most of the German team, the Eiger was the high point of their climbing careers. Layton Kor retired to become a Jehovah's Witness. For myself, I felt as if I had just come at last out of the darkness into the light, and the exploration of that light offered so many bewildering possibilities that my mind could scarcely cope with the contemplation of it all.

The only cloud was that another friend was gone. John Harlin was a complex person. Talented in certain fields, he wanted to be good at everything: a dreamer who sometimes believed his dreams were reality. He died while fulfilling his greatest ambition, a direct route on the Eiger. Could that not be the best time to die? My relationship with him was brief and stormy. On the mountain everything worked well. He was like a general in a mountaineering hierarchy, planning, directing, conceiving new ideas. I often fulfilled the straight practical part of leading, doing the most difficult parts. Disliked by many, John hated people who were less strong than he was. He was used to holding court and having people listen to his every opinion. I often quarrelled violently with him. Perhaps the basis of our relationship was mutual respect rather than close friendship, yet in our six days of surviving on the Death Bivouac we had become very close. Basically both withdrawn people, it seemed as if we'd both been holding back. With the shutters down we began to find out a lot which would have made for a different future relationship if he'd survived.

I began to wonder about partnerships in climbing. A mountaineering relationship, at least in the highest climbing levels, is a very strong thing. Everything is laid bare. You know your partner's strengths and weaknesses, most of his hopes and ideals. You are both working at levels often close to the limit. It's a big responsibility to have another's life in your hand, or to trust yours completely to someone. Life on the mountain is basically unemotional, you are too used to seeing the other person in strict control. That is perhaps why, in the emotional free-for-all of normal living you act as, or in fact are, different persons.

Steve Roper (b.1941) is an American rock climber, historian, and author who has his name attached to over 400 climbs in Yosemite Valley. His literary contributions include a long time partnership with Allen Steck as editors of the journal *Ascent*. He is the author of *The Climber's Guide to the High Sierra*, as well as *The Climber's Guide to Yosemite Valley, and Camp Four*. He is the co-author of *Fifty Classic Climbs of North America*.

STEVE ROPER:
DRESDEN

I had slowed down, no doubt about it. Climbing less than once a month, and nothing very demanding at that had mad my muscles flaccid, my brain porous. Other (read safer) interests, coupled with far too much wine, had interfered with a solemn promise made to myself fifteen years previously: I love climbing, it is the best of all possible activities, and I will climb, climb for the rest of my natural life. So I had to smile a wry smile when I was asked along on a climbing trip to East Germany by a man who for over forty years had actually obeyed this credo. Fritz Wiessner, before I was even born, had climbed in Asia (reaching 27,500 feet on K2), made numerous short forays into the Alps, and put up about fifty new routes in North America, among them Waddington and Devil's Tower. But of all the places Fritz had been, there was only one he loved above all others: Saxton Switzerland, a hundred-square mile area along the banks of the Elba River near Dresden. He was born in this incredibly lovely place in 1900 and by the age of 18 was already leading some of the hardest climbs in the region.

The name Saxon Switzerland is misleading. It does, in fact, lie in the state of Saxony, but whoever bestowed the rest of the name must never have seen Switzerland, for there is no permanent snow, and the highest point fails to attain even 2,000 feet. The German name for the area, Elb-sandsteingebirge, seemed too hard to say, so I began to refer to the region simply as Dresden. It is hilly country and the river makes very lazy turns through forests and fields. Occasionally a ridge of sandstone has been eroded by the Elba and it is here that the climber pauses. The rock is a dense and non-crumbly variety of sandstone, much more akin to the of El Dorado Canyon in Colorado that to the towers of the American Southwest. About 5,000 routes have been established on the 900-odd pinnacles. Through the climbs nowhere exceed eighty meters in length, there is great exposure, and, as I was to find out shortly, great continuity. Steep and continuous. Intimidating. Scary.

Over the years I had known him, Fritz had intimated that the Dresden climbers were equal to the best free climbers in the world. A startling Dresden climbing movie he showed at the annual American Alpine Club dinner in 1967 left the audience wiping palms on pants and me feeling that Fritz might well be right. By this time I was literally off big wall climbing, preferring short free climbs in new areas. So to me the movie offered a fascinating glimpse into what easily could become my personal mode of climbing: head to a strange area, get into shape on the old classics. Then split. No pressures, no aid climbing, no bivouacs. An easy way to climb, you say, but it would be my own way.

In the winter of '68-'69 I received a letter from old Fritz: Come with me to Dresden in May. I met him in Interlaken; we gravitated south, climbing in small areas, getting into shape. Then, halfway up a 200-meter wall in the south of France, Fritz began striking his chest, cursing in his gentlemanly style, proclaiming "indigestion." Unfortunately, it was a bit more serious than that: his heart was beginning to crap out. A few months of rest and Fritz was completely recovered, but in the meantime our 1969 expedition to Saxony had met its end on the Riviera.

My next chance came in the spring of—Fritz was—I felt like —(a winter of nose-to-the-grindstone hedonism had taken its toll); it seemed an inauspicious time and a team of which no one could have said—as I did in my early Valley days, in mock seriousness—"This is the finest team ever assembled." A third member was Fritz's daughter Polly, who, during those frequent interludes when Fritz would rattle along in German to his old and new cronies, became a valued friend. Already used to climbing barefooted, Polly would fit into the Dresden climbing scene with ease.

Paranoia is not usual state, but I had begun to have a nagging fear that on this trip I was to be exhibited as the Yosemite Fanatic, fresh from wild cracks and thousand-meter walls. So we drove down the deserted Autobahn toward our destiny, I began my final harangue: Fritz, old chap,

I'm in foul shape, you know, haven't even been in the Valley for a year, and I do not wish to be portrayed as the American Star, I do not want to get hurt, not badly, anyway, a sprained ankle would be quite nice, we could motor over to Prague and sightsee, you realize, Fritz, that I've never been in this part of the world and I'd sure hate to miss Prague, indeed, why don't we spend a few days over there when the weather goes bad as I hope. . . ah, I mean as it's sure to do sometime and there's no point in sticking around in a drizzle, right, Fritz, and by the way there's also no point in jumping right into the tiger climbs; we'll be here sixteen days, after all, and I don't really want to get hurt this far from home, Christ, I don't even speak the language, imagine a hospital stay, Jesus, they're asking me for my identity card and here I am lying here with a. . . . Then Fritz breaks in, saying, don't worry, Steve, we can climb in the rain, it's done all the time, not the sevens of course, but the sixes, he assures me, will be in fine shape. Then I recover, seeking my manhood, saying, boy it's sure nice to be headed for a new climbing area, what are we doing tomorrow?

Tomorrow. Overcast, visibility mile in rain and fog. I am introduced to two climbers, old types in their thirties. Gunther and Friedrich give crushing handshakes while their eyes seek the secrets of Yosemite. But they're not mine to give, fellows, not any more. I'm just here because. . . because God, Roper, get a grip, quit whining. Calm your brain.

A few easy climbs lull me into rainy day torpor. Then, at the base of a giant overhanging pinnacle, I see a confab. I know no German, but I get the idea pretty quick. I follow their looks upward, I watch Fritz making some sort of apology (I'm not paranoid, I reiterate!) and I see an agreement reached. Perhaps this agreement has doomed me, but I have no choice. So must an unwilling bride see as the dowry is discussed. With downcast eyes I follow Gunther to the rock. Then my savior, Fritz, speaks. At first you would like to follow, yes? To get used to the rock, which is much different than in your Valley.

And so the first days go by and I get into a bit of shape. I love the rock, even though Fritz thinks I prefer Valley granite. Actually I think I climb better on almost all other kinds, and the Dresden rock is a super-rock, solid, with edges, offset cracks, flakes; beautiful. Often just Fritz, Polly and I climb together. It is often pure joy to watch the septuagenarian climb, a half-century of technique behind him, every move precise and thoughtful, but then I feel sad when I watch once-powerful arms quiver with the strain of a pull-up. But, god, if I could climb like that in 2014. . . .

The grading system used in the area is just about as inconsistent, illogical and provincial as most other systems. Roman numerals from I to VII are used to indicate free climbing difficulty. At some point they ran into that problem faced in so many areas: when harder climbs are done, what do you call them? Rather than go to VIm, they have subdivided the VII category into a. b. and c. Yet, it seemed to me, each letter represented a palpable step upwards: VIIa is to VIIb as V is to VI. They can no more jump up to an VIII and a IX than the NCCS can head toward a 12. Only the Australians seem to have solved this particular problem; they have an open-ended system with no magic top number. Thus, when a climb recognized as harder than their present hardest a 21, is done, it becomes, without controversy, a 22.

Late in the first week Fritz tells me that the breaking-in period is over; tomorrow we meet Herbert Richter, an Ex-Master of Sport, and now a physicist. He will climb with us for a week. With trepidation I shake hands with Herbert. He looks amenable, is a bit of a clown, and speaks English to a degree. Later, Polly teaches him the phrase; so-and-so is lewd, crude and socially unacceptable. He loves this, and soon I hear him muttering, in the midst of a 5.10 move, "this rock is lewd, crude. . ." A fine chap. I liked him immediately. But, he was an Ex-Master of Sport and he was serious as hell about climbing. To be a Master of Sport (a phrase I like to roll around on my tongue much like Herbert with his lewd, crude). . . one must climb, per year, a set number of fearsome death routes. Apparently Herbert hadn't done enough of these, or had had a falling out with the people in charge of Sports, for he was an Ex.

Unlike the U.S. State Department, the East German regime recognizes that their hot climbers are an asset and they send them to various places within the Eastern bloc for climbing competitions and expeditions. But unlike their Polish, Czech or Russian counterparts, they are never allowed to cross into Western Europe, and I sensed that Herbert must mourn this, that he must often have thought: My whole climbing life will be spent on these rocks, no wonder I am an expert here, but what of the Alps? I dream of the Eigerwand, the great Chamonix Aiguilles; perhaps I would fail there, but how do I know? I read what I can, but we get few books here, and I have a family and cannot flee. And perhaps it is not that good outside? Herbert, I would gladly have told you of the rotten, insane and corrupt form of government our democracy provides us with. But I'm not sure I would have liked to tell you this: We're free, man, we can travel thousands of miles with no controls whatsoever; we can climb any place on earth.

And so the Ex-Master and I trotted over to one of the new classics, the Hollenhund (the Hound of Hell), an eighty-meter wall averaging about ninety degrees. Sieben C (VIIc) he told me. A fine route. It was a different kind of rock from what I had already become accustomed to: it was full of small holes, tiny jugs, stalactites. It didn't look too bad. Polly and Fritz stationed themselves in relaxed positions to watch the debacle. Herbert took off, climbing flawlessly, reminding me instantly of Robbins, not particularly graceful, but super cool, super competent, almost arrogant in his control. And very safe. He threaded runners through holes so tiny that a 7mm rope would not fit doubled. He would hover above me, clinging to pinch holds, untie a length of rope, thread it through a hole, then retie and jerk. Yeah, it didn't look too bad. I think one reason I hate to climb with guys like Robbins and Herbert is that they make it look so easy that I relax and lose the fine psychological edge which I have built up to on the approach march.

I think I could have done better if I hadn't had to stop and untie twelve jerked-taut runners. My arms ballooned and I swelled overly long on Robin Smith's phrase, "Then my fingers turned to butter." Mine went buttery just as I lunged for his hanging belay. Jesus, I told him, good lead dad, what's it like above? The same, eh? Well, Herbert, be a good fellow and lead on, I'm wiped out, you know, jet lag and bad food, no, not bad, Herbert, just different. Actually, you Germans sure know how to cook, yes siree, those giant liver dumplings are out of sight, as we say, yes sir. And so Herbert danced on, savoring his role, assuaging my inferiority complex with kind words. God, I thought, we have another week of this and my arms will be horrible tomorrow; how can I talk Fritz into Prague?

Luckily there were a few rainy days, and Fritz took us around Dresden and reminisced: Here was where our school was, here there was a marvelous square with a fine view toward the museum. It was all was, for on my fourth birthday, as I was mindlessly devouring a cake, the Allies were mindlessly bombing this most beautiful of cities. The war had only eighty days to run; Dresden was an acknowledged non-military target, a cultural landmark. Nevertheless, a hundred thousand people and a city among cities no longer exist. So it goes. The damage has, of course, been swept away, but the reconstructed buildings are cheap and efficient; aesthetics have received a low priority under the present regime.

Fritz had insisted that I buy a pair of EB's for this trip and I had rebelled, of course, for one doesn't like to be ordered about, especially by a father-figure, and anyway I had a beautiful pair of RR's, perfect fit, no complaints, and here I had to buy a pair of weird expensive shoes. I bought them as instructed, but I hated the idea. From the first day, however, the EB's were magical; it was a case of the shoe fitting the place, or however the cliche goes. I could put my foot anywhere and it would stick. So imagine my anxiety at the base of the Hollenhund when I saw Herbert strip his wretched hiking boots and strap on bizarre gauntlets of leather which covered only half his foot, leaving vulnerable the (to me) crucial part, the toes, Christ, I can't even walk barefoot along a street, and here this dude, strapping on a device best left to a porno flick, was preparing for 5.10. But East Germans have prehensile toes, it seems, and I would slack off belaying to watch entranced as those toes would seek sensuously for a hold, and then I would glance down at my beautifully encumbered feet and curse, knowing that once again I'd been had. And sure enough, the magical EB's can't compare with the great toe when it comes down to a one inch by one inch hole in the rock.

One day I was informed that a new climber would join us. Herbert, with just the barest trace of envy, said, "It is our Star, Berndt Arnold." Your Ubermensch? I asked and Herbert had to laugh. Not quite the exact translation, perhaps, but we laughed a lot and it became a trip phrase. When you're among friends the language barrier is not what it's made out to be. We met Arnold at dawn at the printing shop which he runs, an inconspicuous place in a village 20 miles out of Dresden; and they told me of the Star leaving work at five and trotting a few miles to the rocks and bouldering until he was exhausted, and then the weekend would arrive and with it his comrades from the city, and he would shine and shine and was surely fated for the National Team. I must say that he was an intense climber, a Master, a true Ubermensch. I watched from below while he and Herbert climbed a fearsome wall, a Master climb. I had begged off, so Fritz and I lay down in classically comfortable postures and watched the drama above, Fritz thinking how a few years ago he would have been first on the rope and poor humbled Roper thinking how glad he had made his feeble mark and was no longer compelled to get up there and prove his worth and, more importantly, risk his balls. But I loved watching the climbers move, and it showed me at last what Fritz had been implying all along: these fellows around Dresden are among the best free climbers on the planet.

I had been worried about the lack of protection ever since I had seen Fritz's movie. I can't say my fears were exactly groundless, but most of the climbs which I did were reasonably safe; even the hard ones I was shown looked no worse than some of the renowned modern climbs in Yosemite. A death route is, after all, a death route. In Dresden pitons are absolutely verboten and nuts are unknown. Thus, the only form of protection (outside of infrequent horns and holes) is the bolt. They really go in for the large, safe variety over there, I'll say that for them. Over half an inch in diameter and placed about five inches into the rock, they have huge rings into which a carabineer will barely fit. These bolts, called Ringen in German, rings by me, are rarely used for protection. I must explain this anomaly. Dresden climbing often consists of short but desperate class 4 pitches. Class 4 as in 5.7 through 5.11. (Ortenburger will smile ironically if he reads this.). Each ring is a belay station, often a hanging station, for the rings are installed not so much near ledges as just before hard moves. Therefore, it can be seen that the hard moves are reasonably well protected. Sometimes the pitches are less than 10 feet in length, and rarely are they more than 50 feet.

I recall once approaching a ring, relaxing as it got closer. I became horrified to find that I couldn't let go to clip in. I really couldn't let go. Briefly I thought of continuing, but the moves above definitely appeared to justify the ring. Finally I balanced and leaned and cavorted about and lunged for the mother. As I sat in my belay seat, it came to me that it would have been impossible for anyone to have placed the thing while leading. Fritz was watching from a nearby parapet, so I asked him about this seeming paradox. In fact, I opened my mouth too quickly, as usual, and stated in unequivocal terms that it was pretty low class to place bolts on rappel. "No, no, no!" he shouted instantly, "We don't do that, it was placed on the lead." But, Fritz, I couldn't let go to clip in. No one could let go with both hands, for Christ's sake, it's vertical. The shouting match didn't resolve itself at the time, but later in the beer parlor it turned out that these amazing chaps really had put them in on the lead, drilling the holes by hand-no hammers were used. The rock is fairly soft and a strong person can cling onto pinch holds while the drill is turned with the other hand. Upon getting tired, the driller will climb down to a retiring stance. Sometimes the work is so strenuous that he must come back day after day to work on his hole. When the drill gets far enough into the rock, he will rest in a seat sling from the drill itself. But after such a rest, which one gathers is not terribly long for these Ubermenschen, it's off the seat, back to pinch holds and more grinding away.

Belaying is another strange story. Pictures of Europeans belaying have. always amused me, and once in the Dolomites I saw a man belaying his entire family up a class 4 pitch; he wasn't anchored, he had the rope over his shoulder, he was leaning over the void to give advice, and I fled lest I see blood splashed on limestone. I had, just the day before, watched a blind climber, and I was beginning to think that European climbing was really quite bizarre. Anyway, back to Dresden belaying. Because most of the falls are steep drops with no intervening protection, the locals have developed their own peculiar belay habits. It is difficult to recall the actual technique, let alone describe it here, but somehow the rope is placed around the waist, then twisted a few times to induce friction. It is devilishly hard to learn how to payout rope quickly, and I was all thumbs at first. Although I was trying to adhere to the old "when in Rome etc." philosophy, I was a bit put off when I couldn't use my own belaying style. I knew that I would never try to force a foreigner to adopt my own belay habits, feeling that however odd his system might be, it was at least safer to let him have the obvious advantage of familiarity. Sometimes, when Herbert couldn't see me, I reverted to my California belay.

So far I have not mentioned the history of the area, primarily because I am intimidated by J. M. Thorington's excellent article in the 1964 *American Alpine Journal*. Briefly, though, it seems that by 1914 the hardest rockclimbs in the world were to be found in this area. Curiously, an American, Oliver Perry-Smith, was probably the best climber during the Golden Age of Dresden climbing, 1900-1914. I did only a few of Perry-Smith's routes—a bold 5.7 jamcrack flashes into my mind, but this was by no means his hardest route. My feeling is that there could easily be a 5.9 route somewhere among his thirty-two first ascents. The other great figure of these early days was Rudolf Fehrmann. He was not only a superb climber, but a visionary as well. He realized that by using artificial aids any tower could be overcome, so by means of lectures and articles he soon established the basic ground rule of Dresden climbing which has persisted to this day: no aid climbing whatsoever. Another stringent rule was developed in those early days and that is that only the first ascent party can place rings; subsequent ascents do it the original way or come back. Or fall. As Thorington comments,". . .the death rate has always been high, mainly due to rope breakage and because the climber was not equal to the task."

Accidents are a regular occurrence; ropes don't snap much anymore, but arms do give out on strenuous sections and competition for the coveted Master Rating takes its toll. One day while walking along a dirt road we noticed a commotion: first aid people gesturing effusively, revealing that orgiastic look common to ambulance drivers and rescue freaks the world over-blood, excitement, heroics. A youth had just smashed his spine on a climb we had done the preceding day. It was an unprotected 5.7 overhang with the chance of a thirty-foot drop onto a wide, hard ledge. I had been truly gripped on the thing; it hadn't looked bad, but my arms started to go at the crux move. With no finesse I adrenalined my way through, cursing Fritz, East Germany and climbing. And the next day we had done a wonderful climb, and on top Fritz casually mentioned that his cousin had taken a 250-foot groundfall here in the early 1920s. It seems the chap lost his balance on top of the slender pinnacle. You can bet I cowered low on that summit.

But I never got hurt; in fact I never even fell while leading. It seems that a lot of my fears are only in my head, as Dylan so sardonically puts it. Except for a few nightmarish armbusters that I had to do with Herbert (because they were such fine classics, I suppose), I actually enjoyed the climbing, just like I've heard can be done. It's entirely possible that I got into the best shape of my life. And as the trip came to a close, I almost wished it wouldn't. There was so much left to do. I figure I did only about 30 routes, and out of a total of 5,000 there must be about 1,000 that are really worth doing. So: 970 left, 30 per trip, Jesus, I might make it to the year 2014 yet.

Back of Beyond:
Mountain Exploration

Maurice Herzog (b.1919), French alpinist and politician who led the successful 1950 ascent of Annapurna, the first 8,000 meter (26,493 feet) peak to be climbed. He suffered severe frostbite of both hands and feet that led to amputations. He later held several important government offices and was a member of the International Olympic Committee. He is the author of several books including, the *Annapurna: Heroic Conquest of the Highest Mountain Ever Climbed by Man, The Mountain,* and *The Great Adventures of the Himalayas.*

MAURICE HERZOG: THE RETREAT

E veryone was now off the mountain and assembled at Camp II. But in what a state! It was Oudot's turn to take the initiative, and he made a rapid tour of inspection. Faced with the appalling sight that we presented, his countenance reflected, now the consternation of the friend, now the surgeon's impersonal severity.

He examined me first. My limbs were numb up to well beyond the ankles and wrists. My hands were in a frightful condition; there was practically no skin left, the little that remained was black, and long strips dangled down. My fingers were both swollen and distorted. My feet were scarcely any better: the entire soles were brown and violet, and completely without feeling. The arm which was hurting me, and which I was afraid might be broken, did not appear to be seriously injured, and my neck was all right.

I was anxious to have Oudot's first impression.

"What do you think of it all" I asked him, ready to hear the worst.

"It's pretty serious. You'll probably lose part of your feet and hands. At present I can't say more than that."

"Do you think you'll be able to save something?"

"Yes, I'm sure of it. I'll do all I can."

This was not encouraging, and I was convinced that my feet and hands would have to be amputated.

Oudot took my blood pressure and seemed rather concerned. There was no pressure in the right arm, and the needle did not respond at all on my left arm. On my legs the needle oscillated slightly, indicating a restricted flow of blood. After putting a dressing over my eyes to prevent the onset of ophthalmia, he said:

"I'm going to see Lachenal. I'll come back in a moment and give you some injections. I used them during the war and it's the only treatment that's any use with frost-bite. See you presently."

Lachenal's condition was slightly less serious. His hands were not affected, and the black discoloration of his feet did not extend beyond the toes, but the sinister color reappeared on his heels. He would probably lose his toes, but that would probably not prevent him from climbing, and from continuing to practice his profession as a guide.

Rebuffat's condition was much less serious. His feet were pink except for two small gray patches on his toes. Ichac massaged him with Dolpyc for two hours and this appeared to relieve him; his eyes were still painful, but that was only a mater of two or three days. Terray was unscathed: like Rebuffat he was suffering from ophthalmia-most painful, but only a temporary affliction. Couzy was very weak, and would have to be considered out of action. That was the balance sheet.

Night fell gradually. Oudot made his preparations, requisitioned Ichac and Schatz as nurses, and Camp II was turned into a hospital. In cold and discomfort, and to the accompaniment of continual avalanches, these men fought late in the night to save their friends. Armed with torches they passed from tent to tent, bending over the wounded and giving them emergency treatment, at this minute camp, perched 20,000 feet up on the flanks of one of the highest mountains in the world.

Oudot made ready to give me arterial injections. The lamp shone feebly and in the semi-darkness Ichac sterilized the syringes as best he could with ether. Before starting operations, Oudot explained:

"I am going to inject Novocain into your femoral and brachial arteries."

As I could not see a thing with the bandage over my eyes, he touched with his finger the places where he would insert the needle: both groins and in the bends of my elbow.

"It's going to hurt. Perhaps I shan't get the right place first shot. But in any case you mustn't move, particularly when I have got into the artery."

Maurice Herzog

I was not at all reassured by these preparations; I had always had a horror of injections. But it would have to be done, it was the only thing possible.

"Go ahead," I said to Oudot, "but warn me when you are going to stab."

Anyhow, perhaps it would not hurt all that much in my present condition. I heard the murmur of voices—Oudot asking if something was ready, and Ichac answering:

"Here you are. Got it?"

Oudot ran his fingers over my skin. I felt an acute pain in the groin and my legs began to tremble; I tried to control myself. He had to try again, for the artery rolled away from the needle. Another stab, and my whole body was seized with convulsions; I stiffened when I should have relaxed, and felt all my nerves in revolt.

"Gently!" I could not help myself.

Oudot began again: my blood was extremely thick and clotted in the needle.

"Your blood is black—it's like black pudding," he said in amazement.

"That's got it!" this time he had succeeded in spite of my howls which, I knew very well, made the operation all the more difficult to perform. The needle was now in position:

"Don't move! Oudot shouted at me. Then to Ichac:

"Hand it over!"

Ichac passed him the syringe; I felt the needle moving in my flesh and the liquid began to flow into the artery. I should never, until then, have believed so much pain to be possible. I tried to brace myself to the utmost to keep myself from trembling: it simply had to be successful! The liquid went on flowing in.

"Can you feel any warmth?" Asked Oudot, brusquely, while he was changing the syringe. Again the liquid went in; I gritted my teeth.

"Does it feel warm?"

Oudot was insistent—the point was evidently crucial; yet still I felt nothing. Several times the syringe was emptied, filled up, and emptied again:

"Now, do you feel anything?"

"I seem to feel a little warmth, but it's not very definite."

Was it auto-suggestion? The needle was withdrawn abruptly, and while Ichac sterilized the instruments, I had a few moments respite.

The Retreat

"It's excruciating, the way it hurts," I said, just as if Oudot needed telling!

"Yes, I know, but we must go on."

The performance was repeated on the other leg. My nerves were all to pieces, and to brace myself like this took all of my strength. In went the needle and I howled and sobbed miserably, but tried in vain to keep still. I could see nothing because of the bandage. If only I could have seen the faces of my friends it might perhaps have helped me. But I was in the dark—a terrible darkness—with nowhere to look for consolation but within myself. It was late and we had all had more than enough. Then, for that day it was over and the first-aid party moved on to Lachenal's tent. He perhaps, would have more courage in face of physical pain.

It seemed to me, when I vaguely became aware of the end of the session, that the treatment had gone more quickly for him. Terray slept in Lachenal's tent and Couzy and Ichac slept beside Rebuffat who was delirious and moaned about his feet all night. Oudot came and lay down next to me. If anything were to happen, he would be there.

Next day plans were completed for the evacuation of the entire camp: the three injured men would be taken down on sledges, two would be able to walk, with assistance, and four were all right. There were miles of glacier to cover, rock barriers to get down, interminable moraines and scree slopes to skirt around or to traverse, a river to cross, and a pass of over 13,000 feet to get over-and all this in the monsoon!

It was now June 6 and Ichac was worried, for he remembered the Tilman expedition to Nanda Devi, which was held up for three weeks by rivers swollen by the torrential monsoon rains. Should we have time to reach to Gandaki valley where the easier gradient would put fewer obstacles in our way? In a week's time we must be clear of the mountains. Soon Couzy would be fit again, Terray cured of his ophthalmia and Rebuffat able to walk. But there were two serious casualties who would have to be carried on the porters backs under the most appalling conditions, as far as the main valley.

"It's unbelievable," remarked Ichac, "it's actually fine today."

The medical supplies urgently demanded by Oudot had arrived from Camp I. He began his rounds with me, and was pleased because the injections had been effective and warmth had returned as far as my insteps. He put fresh dressings on my hands, and though I felt no real pain, there was, nevertheless, some sort of feeling in my fingers. Again I put my question:

Maurice Herzog

"What shall I have left?'

"I can't exactly say. Things have not completely settled down yet and I hope to be able to gain an inch or so. I think you'll be able to use your hands. Of course," and he hesitated for a moment, "you'll lose one or two joints of each finger, but if there's enough of the thumbs left, you'll have a pinch hold, and that's of prime importance."

It was grim news, but still, only yesterday I had feared that the consequences would be far worse. For me this meant goodbye to a great many plans, and it also implied a new kind of life, perhaps even a new conception of existence. But I had neither the strength nor the wish to look into the future.

I appreciated Oudot's courage and was grateful to him for not being afraid to tell me the extent of the amputations which he foresaw would be necessary. He treated me as a man and as a friend, with courage and frankness, which I shall never forget.

The injections, which had already done so much good, had to be repeated. This time the session would be even worse and I was terrified at the prospect. I am ashamed to say that the thought of this treatment daunted me, and yet so many people have had to endure it. This time it was to be an injection, not of novocain but acetylcholine, of which a few ampules had been brought up from Camp I. Terray joined me in the tent and stood close beside me. He, too could see nothing under his bandage, and he had to be guided if he wanted to move about at all. I pictured his face and touched his features with my forearms while Ichac and Oudot prepared the needles, ether, and ampoules. I whispered to Lionel what a fearful ordeal I found it and begged him to stay close.

"Oudot will warn me before inserting the needle; I mustn't budge then, and you must hold me as tight as you can in your arms."

I hoped that Terray's presence would help me bear the agony. Oudot began with my legs; like the day before, it was too awful for words. I howled and cried and sobbed in Terray's arms while he held me tight with all his strength. I felt as if my foot was burning-as if it had been suddenly plunged into boiling oil. Professionally Oudot was in seventh heaven and everybody showed his delight in my suffering, which was proof of the success of the treatment. This gave me new courage and at last, after the fourth syringeful, the necessary 100 cc had been injected.

"Now for the arms," announced Oudot.

This session seemed to go on for ever and I was utterly worn out, but there was distinctly more feeling in my right arm. Oudot stormed away-the needles were either too thick or too small, too thin or too long: never just right, and each time it meant a fresh stab. I began to howl like a dog again.

"Hold me tighter," I gasped between sobs to Terray, who was already holding me as tightly as he could. I tried hard not to tremble, but Oudot was still not satisfied:

"Don't move, nom d'une pipe! We'll go on as long as we must. It's got to succeed."

"Sorry, I'm doing all I can; I'll stay with it."

I held out my arm for a fresh attempt. When Oudot did find the artery, then it was the needle that got blocked-the too-thick blood clotted inside. From the bend of the elbow Oudot gradually tried higher and higher up towards the shoulder so as not to stab in the same place. Twice he touched a nerve: I did not cry but sobbed spasmodically. What an eternity of suffering! I could do nothing. Oudot stopped for a moment. "We'll manage all right," Ichac assured me.

"Stick with it, Maurice!" Terray whispered. "It'll soon be over; it's dreadful, I know, but I'm here beside you."

Yes, he was there. Without him I could never have borne it all. This man whom we thought hard because he was strong, who made himself out to be a tough peasant, showed a tenderness and affection towards me that I have never seen equaled. I hid my face against him and he put his arms around my neck.

"Come on! Get on with it!"

"Too small and too fine," shouted Oudot.

He began to lose patience. All this fuss with the instruments exasperated me, and I wondered if they would have succeeded the first attempt in a hospital.

After several hours, and goodness knows how many attempts, the injection was successfully made. In spite of frightful pain I remained immobile as the syringe was emptied. Deftly Oudot replaced it with another without removing the needle from the artery. With the second syringeful, I felt the warmth spreading, and Oudot was exultant. But this warmth became unbearable. I howled and clung to Terray in desperation, holding my arm out stiff, without, so I hoped, moving it a fraction of an inch. Then I felt the needle being withdrawn and cotton applied.

"Right arm finished! Now for the left!"

Oudot could not find the artery, and this puzzled him. I told him that when I was young I had seriously damaged this arm, and that explained everything: that was why there had been no blood pressure, and why he could feel no pulse. The position of the artery was not normal, and it was not possible to make an injection in the bend of the elbow; it would have to be done at the shoulder-much more difficult. I thought of what it had been like for the right arm! Suddenly, at the fifth or sixth attempt, Oudot shouted:

"I've got it!"

I kept absolutely still: syringeful after syringeful went in.

"I'll have to do a stellaire."

I had no idea what this was and Oudot explained that it meant injecting novocain into the nerve ganglion to dilate the arteries and make them easier to find, and improve the blood supply. A long needle was necessary, to be stuck into the neck in the region of the pleura. I was in despair. It was just too much. For hours and hours I had endured this agony—I should never have the strength for more. But Oudot lost no time, the needle was ready, and he began to explore my neck:

"This is a tricky business: You have to insert the needle in a certain direction, then, when you come up against an obstacle you have to push to the left, and you're bound to be in the right spot!"

"Warn me before you stick it in."

In the silence that followed I heard things being moved around. "I'm going to insert the needle," Oudot announced.

I braced myself immediately, and resolved to keep perfectly still. The needle went in—it must have been a tremendous length; it touched a very sensitive part and the pain made me cry out in Terray's arms. Oudot was now maneuvering to get the needle into the ganglion and I could feel it moving deep down. It was in! First shot! The liquid must have started flowing in, but I could not feel it.

"Will it take long?" I asked faintly.

"It's almost finished," he replied holding his breath. "Only another 20 cc to go in."

I felt the awful needle being pulled out. It was over, and now I could relax. Oudot was very pleased: it had been almost a whole day's work, but he had managed to do everything he wanted. Never had I suffered so much in my life; but if my feet and hands were to be saved it would be because of Oudot and his perseverance. Ichac helped him collect the instruments to take along to Lachenal's tent. For the time being he was satisfied with my general condition, but what effect this generalized frostbite would have on my body in the next few days remained to be seen. The camp was becoming more and more like a hospital: everybody's thoughts and actions hung on the surgeon's words.

That same day began the incredible work of transporting the injured, which ended only after a long and painful retreat, lasting five weeks, beneath torrential rain and over dangerously steep ground. This retreat, during which all the injured slowly recovered, will for ever remain an achievement of the highest order, and it reflects great honor upon all the members of the Expedition.

The sledge we had at our disposal was an extra-lightweight Dufour luge mounted on two skis for runners. Naturally, the Sherpas were not familiar with this contraption, so Oudot and Iehac decided to make the least injured of us, Rebuffat, the victim of the first try-out. Schatz took charge of operations, with four Sherpas whom he placed in V formation around the sledge, and the procession started off about two-thirty. Rebuffat was well wrapped up and firmly tied to the sledge in case it should tip over. As night fell the four Sherpas arrived back at camp, bringing a note from Schatz advising the use of six men for subsequent descents.

Meanwhile Oudot had given all his patients injections and the evening was spent in changing the dressings. Soon after nightfall the weather worsened, and again it snowed heavily. The others were alarmed, and decided to get the rest of the casualties down before it was too late. As luck would have it, next morning when we woke up, it was fine. I was to be taken down first, and before I left Oudot inspected my feet and hands and changed the dressings. He was very satisfied and described my progress as "spectacular!" I was dressed and put in a sleeping-bag and laid on the Dufour sledge, and Ang-Tharkey directed the team of Sherpas. I could see nothing under my bandage, but I felt the air was warm and so knew it must be fine; I hated the thought of being transported without being able to see what was going on. I was very glad to hear that Iehac would accompany me down so that I shouldn't be alone if I needed anything. In my heart I dreaded this descent, particularly the passage over the rock barriers. How would they manage? But the Sherpas were intelligent and never had to be shown anything twice. Afterwards, when we were in camp, Iehac told me how much he had admired them: "It would have been difficult to find a team like this in France," he said; "every one of them did his utmost and every move was perfectly coordinated."

With a few jerks the sledge started off. I was weak and slightly deaf but I recognized Oudot's voice in the climber's familiar "Bonne descente!" No doubt he was there behind us, waving a hand. Swaddled in all my clothes I began to sweat; I could feel the sun beating down. Now and then Iehac came close and said something, and it did me good to hear him and know he was there. Suddenly the slope steepened, and in spite of the straps holding me in position, I slipped forward. The Sherpas took up their positions in an inverted V in order to brake the sledge. We had reached the big rock band, and as far as I could remember, the angle here was steep. I guessed that Iehac had driven his axe in to keep me in balance.

I heard a hollow echo—seracs—and the pace had to be forced now for there was danger of their collapsing. We came to the rocks-and how these Sherpas managed, I shall never know. The wall was very steep yet I was carried on the sledge itself; Iehac told me later that if my eyes had not been blindfolded I should never have been able to stand the sight of such acrobatics, and of such impossible positions. I heard sighs of relief-we must have reached the glacier at last. The sledge reverted to a horizontal position, and I was on the snow. A few minutes rest, and on we went at what seemed to me a breakneck pace, and I pictured the Sherpas pulling on the ropes all around me and running in the snow, though no doubt this was only imagination. Then we slowed up, we had reached the moraine of Camp I.

I was left alone for a moment while the Sherpas put up a big valley tent into which they carried me a few minutes later. Ichac settled himself beside me, from now on we always shared the same tent and he watched over me, day and night, like a brother. The descent had taken two hours and twenty minutes, and the Sherpas had been marvelous. What should we have done without them?

Ichac briefly explained what was going on. Being blind was most demoralizing: I felt I was nothing but a chattel to be carted about. I knew my ophthalmia was less serious than that of the others and I kept asking for the bandage to be taken off. But since I was nothing but a chattel I had no right to speak.

Although it had clouded over and had begun to sleet, the Sherpas went up again to Camp II with Schatz and Noyelle to fetch Lachenal. About three o'clock snow started to fall. Time dragged as I lay in my tent alone with my thoughts. The silence was broken only by the persistent sound of ice cracking, which rather alarmed me. Where had they placed the tent? Suppose a crevasse suddenly opened? But I was ashamed of these childish fears surely a mountaineer of many years experience should know very well that a crevasse doesn't yawn open like that in a second!

Ichac, the only fit Sahib, supervised the organization of Camp I. Towards the end of the afternoon, at about five o'clock, he saw, to his great surprise, Noyelle and Lachenal's convoy emerge through the mist, covered with snow. This time the Sherpas had taken only an hour-and-three-quarters to come down-they had had a terrific day and were worn out. This resulted in some complaints: there was not enough food and part of their equipment had remained up at Camp III and Camp IV! This last point especially bothered them for on Himalayan expeditions the normal practice is for the Sherpas to keep their personal equipment as a prerequisite. They bitterly regretted these clothes, which had to be considered as lost, and Ang-Tharkey even declared his intention of going up to Camp III again.

I summoned Ang-Tharkey and warned him that I expressly forbade anyone to return higher than Camp II to fetch anything whatsoever. But at the same time I told him of my very great satisfaction at the magnificent behavior of the Sherpas under his orders, and assured him that they were not to worry about the clothes, for they would all receive generous compensation. Ang-Tharkey went off to give the others the good news.

There was tremendous activity all over the camp where Lachenal was being made as comfortable as possible. Tents seemed to have sprung up as if by magic, and a regular little village was formed at the foot of the great wall of ice.

The next day, after a fine start, the clouds collected again towards eleven o'clock, and it was not long before snow began to fall. Oudot had not yet come down from Camp II. I could hear the avalanches rumbling down in ever closer succession, making an appalling noise which wore my nerves thin. Ichac tried to joke about it.

"Here we are that's the three thirty-seven freight train. Now for the four o'clock express!" He succeeded in making me smile.

Through the telescope he saw, towards the end of the morning, the last tents of Camp II being taken down, and in the afternoon our doctor arrived with his Sherpas, laden like donkeys. Before even putting down his sack he asked about the condition of his patients: any developments since yesterday?

There was marked improvement: Rebuffat could now walk and his ophthalmia was nearly cured. As for Lachenal, circulation had been restored to his feet, and warmth had returned, except to his toes, though the black patches on his heels would probably leave scars. Improvement was visible on my limbs, too, and Oudot was well pleased. He spoke with a frankness that touched me far more than he will ever know.

"I think that the fingers of your left hand will have to be amputated, but I hope to be able to save the end joints of your right hand fingers. If all goes well, you'll have passable hands. As for your feet, I'm afraid that all your toes will have to go, but that won't prevent you from walking. Of course to begin with it'll be difficult, but you'll adapt yourself all right, you'll see."

I was aghast at the thought of what would have happened if Oudot had not given me the injections so promptly and efficiently. Perhaps they had not yet produced all their effect. More sessions would be necessary and I wondered whether I should be able to overcome the immense lassitude that came over me after all these painful ordeals. In any case I wanted to take every advantage of the respite, and celebrate our success with due ceremony. For the first time since our victory the whole expedition was assembled together and the condition of the casualties was now such as to warrant a little festivity. We gathered around the one and only tin of chicken in aspic and we uncorked the one bottle of Champagne. There was already a lot of us who wanted a drink of it but I was determined that the Sherpas should, somehow or other, join in the general rejoicing. I invited Ang-Tharkey and we drank with him to our victory. Ichac put our thoughts into words:

"You've taken a lot of punishment but our victory will remain."

In spite of the circumstances, the general atmosphere in the tent was remarkably cheerful. We wrote a telegram to be sent off to Devies by the next mail-runner:

"French Himalayan expedition 1950 successful stop Annapurna climbed June 3, 1950 Herzog."

Directly the festivities were over there were more injections-those in my legs were finished fairly quickly. Then Oudot tackled my arms and I knew by experience that these would be the most painful. For an hour all attempts were unsuccessful: the afternoon wore on and Oudot became exasperated.

"Don't move about like that!" he cried.

"Take no notice of the noise I make. . . do what's necessary."

Terray had come close to me. I was writhing in pain, and he held me tight.

"Stick with it! Don't move, don't move, Maurice."

"It's hopeless!" shouted Oudot. "When I do succeed in finding the artery, the blood clots. We'll never manage it!"

He sounded in despair, but his words belied him; he had not the slightest intention of giving up, and neither had I, in spite of the pain. The rest of them were appalled as they listened to the cries coming from the tent where Oudot was in action. The Sherpas were silent. Were they praying for their Bara Sahib? I sobbed so convulsively that I could not stop and was shaken by continual spasms.

Then, after a short rest, late in the evening, ten o'clock, the injection was successfully accomplished. Ichac passed syringes to Oudot in the dark. There was blood all over the tent. Ichac and Oudot went out while Terray soothed me with infinite gentleness. Never had I felt so wretched, I was utterly worn out with suffering and fatigue, incapable of resistance. Terray still held me in his arms. "It'll be all right, you'll see, later on."

"Oh but Lionel, everything's over for me, and I simply can't bear what they're doing to me any longer."

"Life's not over," he insisted, "you'll see France again, and Chamonix."

"Yes, Chamonix perhaps, but I'll never be able to climb again."

It was out at last, I had told him, and I let myself go in despair:

"I'll never be able to climb again—I'll never do the Eiger now, Lionel, and I wanted to so much."

Sobs choked me. My head was against Terray's and I felt his tears, for he was crying, too. He was the only one who could fully understand the tragedy that this represented for me, and I could see that to him, too, it appeared hopeless.

"No, of course, not the Eiger, but I'm sure you'll be able to go back to the mountains. . ." and then, very hesitantly, he added, "Not the same sort of climbs as before, of course."

"It will never be the same again. But, Lionel, even if I can't do the sort of climbs I used to, if I could still do easy things, that would be a great deal. The mountains meant everything to me—I spent the best days of my life among them—I don't want to do spectacular climbs, or famous ones, but I want to be able to enjoy myself in the mountains, even if it's only on the old standard routes.

"You'll go back all right, you'll see," said Lionel. "I feel just the same way."

"But mountains aren't the only thing: there are other things in life as well-what shall I do about all that?"

Maurice Herzog

"You'll manage somehow, Maurice."

There was a silence; then he said, "You ought to lie down now."

He settled me with such affectionate care that he accomplished the impossible and left me comforted and soothed. After a last look to see that I was comfortable, he went slowly out. What a friend I had found in Terray!

Next morning Oudot took off my bandage: it was wonderful to be able to see again. I noted that the weather was fine, and I asked the date: the last few days had been one long night.

"Friday, June 9," Ichac told me.

At the moment Lachenal was being made ready to go down to Base Camp. He would travel in a cacolet—an arrangement of canvas and webbing for carrying an injured man, who sits in it on a porter's back. It was an awkward and primitive contraption and had never liked the look of it. Lachenal, on the contrary. who was accustomed to the thing and had himself carried many casualties down by this method, was perfectly ready to descend this way, though later on he wasn't quite so enthusiastic. Soon he started off with his Sherpas, escorted by Couzy and Noyelle. His legs dangled down most uncomfortably and made him groan. In the afternoon the Sherpas came up again followed by Couzy: the descent had taken two hours, and Rebuffat and Lachenal were none the worse for the journey.

While I rested the others made up the loads. The next day, before going off, Oudot examined me and his favorable impression was confirmed: the injections of acetylcholine which had been abominably painful, had saved a part at least of my feet and hands. Adjiba, Sarki, Foutharkey and Pandy the Chinese were going to take turns at carrying me in the cacolet. The route was well marked, there were no stones and the going was straightforward. But I was crushed up against the porter and horribly jolted at every step. I was afraid of falling and clung desperately to his neck with both arms though I tried to do all in my power not to hinder his movements. Whenever his step faltered I was perfectly aware of it. Several times both Adjiba and Pandy slipped, and instinctively I tried to put my arm out without realizing that it was useless. I was less anxious in the couloirs than on the steep rock slabs where the porter might fall, and kept on being afraid that my hands or my feet might knock against the rock.

"Sarki! . . . Pay attention! . . ."Again and again I repeated this cry; which became an entreaty. At the awkward pitches they helped each other:

one placed the carrier's feet in position, and another would push from behind to maintain his balance. After many difficulties we got over the rocky section and arrived in view of Base Camp.

It felt as if we had been all day on this journey, but in fact it was only two hours and a half, and there had not been the slightest hitch. It was now the turn of the Base Camp to be the center of activity, which it had not hitherto known. Suddenly Ichac dashed into the tent where I had just been laid down and shouted:

"The coolies! The coolies are here!"

Lord John Henry Cecil Hunt (1910-1999) was a career military officer who led the 1953 Everest expedition that saw the mountain climbed for the first time by Sir Edmund Hillary and Sherpa Tenzing Norgay. Hunt was knighted for his leadership of the expedition, which coincided with the coronation of Queen Elizabeth II. He was president of the Alpine Club from 1956 to 1958 and is the author of *The Ascent of Everest, Our Everest Adventure, Life is Meaning,* and *Red Snows with Chris Basher.*

SIR JOHN HUNT:
FROM THE TWENTY-NINTH
TO THE THIRTIETH

It always seems to me right to bring lectures to a close soon, or not too long, after the summit. With its attainment, ambition has been fulfilled, the deed done. Some would say that a book's story should end here, too, at the climax of the year's hope and dream. But does the *Iliad* end with the victory of Achilles? Or any dramatic tale at the point of its highest emotional excitement? After the climax the detente. In the case of a personal narrative I would say that the most important remains, for me viewing the ascent as an individual. This was partly because the question of Everest's "personality" entered my thought after the climb far more than immediately before; partly for the childish reason that I had always wondered, from a boy, what it would "be like" after Everest had been climbed. Now I know.

Of course, at the time the whole achievement seemed laughably small, measured by the standards of some months later. We nestled into the tent, myself half-lying bulkily near the entrance. The conversation was often not far from the level of this:

"I bet old so-and-so will be bucked. He was pretty interested in the whole show from the start."

"Yes. The N.Z.A.C. and the Alpine Club ought to do us well, too."

147

"Wonder if they'll give us a dinner."

Such we accounted it. But first there were other things to think about. I left the Meade tent and wandered past Tenzing and Pasang Phutar in the "blister." I went on hap-hazard between these and the pyramid; wondered whether to unpack my rucksack; crawled in, very slowly, started and decided not to. All this time I was really trying to make up my mind whether to keep a promise to John. It had been my own suggestion, though it seemed now a silly one. All good expeditions that I had read of put out sleeping bags to signal to those above or below. The classic case was the 1924 expedition, when they gave the news of Mallory and Irvine. Well, just below the top of the Geneva Spur there appeared to be a convenient snow-patch upon which to lay sleeping bags so that they could be seen, through binoculars, from IV. I had suggested, therefore, that if they reached the top I should put two out in the shape of a T; John added that if it was the South Summit, one should be alongside the other; if nothing at all, then one sleeping-bag.

By the time I had decided, it was 5:0, nearly two hours after the descent. I stooped at the Meade entrance and looked in. I tried to shout.

"I promised John I'd take two bags up and put them on a slope. So that they can see from below."

"Wouldn't bother. Probably won't see them, anyway. What's wrong with tomorrow?"

"I don't know. Perhaps I'd better though."

Collecting Pasang was a harder job. I called three times going off between to do jobs that seemed very important at the time, but which I have completely forgotten. At last his broad face emerged at the "blister" door. Usually a gay face it was not grinning now. Very reasonably, Pasang had assumed that after a day with a 60-lb. load the sahib would leave him alone. And why the sleeping bag? He dragged off ahead up the crust

I followed slowly behind, but at last we had arrived at the boulders. They seemed in their turn to go on for ever. As an excuse for stopping, I stooped and put some small fragments in my pocket. They would like them back in England my son above all when he grew up. At last we were on snow. But meanwhile I was having uneasy doubts. As we topped the crest it seemed that there was cloud in the valley. Soon it could not be mistaken. Banks of afternoon mist hung over the floor of the Cwm. Above them the evening sun shone behind Nuptse, a dark paper silhouette traced against turquoise sky by the divinely delicate pencil of sun and wind. But in the Cwm, mist.

Sir John Hunt

We stopped at the first good snow-patch. The gusts, very strong on the Col, had dwindled here to a stiff breeze. "Down," I said, and we laid down our bags, in T position against the slope. To keep them there we lay upon them, myself the upright, Pasang the cross of the T. What was the poor man thinking of me? Hard things, I doubted not, and probably with reason, in view of this mist. We lay for ten minutes, myself hoping forlornly that some providence might have opened a small gap, allowed John a vignette of the two suffering figures. But after ten minutes with the wind flapping at us we had suffered enough. The evening cold was creeping up, through down suit and sleeping-bags, and Pasang was making fast tracks for home almost before I had started. That was all; until I was told, many days later, that there is now a pleasing legend in the valley, of the very mad Englishman who once wanted to sleep out in the snow above the South Col of Everest.

At the crest I halted, watching Pasang's strong figure moving down the frozen crust between the rocks, expressive in its every jolt of the conviction that all sahibs are off their head. I fancy that most Sherpas believe the sahibs to be harmless lunatics with plenty of money. Behind him the Col, above and beyond lurked the presence of Everest. Once again I remember thinking: Did the mountain feel an emotion, anger at the thought of "conquest"? That impression I certainly did not carry down as I thought about it. Everest is a mountain, by definition an emotionless mass of rock, snow and ice. If mountains move"between the eternal mode and mine," in Geoffrey Winthrop Young's phrase, then they are indifferent, caring neither one way or the other, to all our crawling. If there is any personification of Everest at all imaginable, it is for me in the impersonality of Swinburne's "Proserpine."

Pale, beyond porch and portal, Crowned with calm leaves, she stands.
. .

It is our human presumption, or so I thought, to sentimentalize the struggles that we endure upon these monstrous creatures into a struggle against them, rather than against our own feebleness which cannot face the magnitude of their ice cliffs and rock towers. In that huge loneliness of the Spur top it seemed a miracle of his own nature that man had been allowed to tread so high.

Returning I bent down again before the tent funnel.

"Do you mind if I do come in?" It had been George's original generous suggestion, and I fancied the pyramid to my self extremely little.

From the Twenty-Ninth to the Thirtieth

The two shifted to make space between, while I went over to collect my belongings. This simple operation took over twenty minutes, and meant two journeys across the fifty-odd feet separating the tents. In the little "blister" alongside our peace now seemed to reign. I looked in at the contented, recumbent forms of Tenzing and Pasang, to be cheered by the flashing smile. "Ji hazur. Thik hai." I crawled in, rammed belongings half-unpacked into the rucksack, climbed out and walked across, to put them in heaps outside the Meade door. It seemed a long time before I was sitting down, that being the easiest way, in bulky down clothing, of getting in through the Meade's sleeve entrance. A wriggle on the elbows, feet first, a hope that there was nothing precariously balanced just inside.

The far or windward door of the tent towards the Cwm was closed, the leeward door was not draughty. I could reach out to pull in rucksack, sleeping-bag and oddments, without endangering the Primus, in action at the other end. I found myself in a valley between two long New Zealand forms reposing on Li-Los. The ideal, of course, would be to get the sleeping-bag under me, but that involved raising on one elbow and wriggling it in by stages; a not easy feat up here. At last I was in a lying position, with sleeping-bag under or around me, reminiscent of the Romans (or was it the Carthaginians?) in Livy "Impedimentis obruti magis quam objecti." Overwhelmed I was, rather than protected, for the bits that would not go underneath I piled on top. But it was warm, George had the Primus going nicely. I tried to tie up the funnel door, but found myself bulging out into it.

We were now all settled for a cozy, fuggy evening, in the last light that lingered genially up here. Each of us was praying doubtless that nothing would occur to force him outside during the next twelve hours. Fortunately nothing did. Some expert concocting had been going on; I remember lemon with plenty of sugar, far the most refreshing drink high up, soup and fragments of food. For me it was raisins, a little chocolate, and, best of all, the scraping of a pot of Swiss honey found here. That honey I could have eaten in large quantity.

Ed was now talkative, and told more of the climb which would soon be a classic of mountaineering history. I heard for the first time of the two-hour job of digging, or at least levelling a platform for the tent yesterday, at 27,900 feet after George's party had left the loads; how Ed had to sit against the slope, to keep things in position, trying not to roll on top of Tenzing, while Tenzing lay below, doubtless trying not to be rolled on by Ed. They seemed to have made a lot of lemonade in the night,

Griffs teaching bearing fruit, and to have eaten biscuits and sardines, even tinned apricots. It was fortunate that Ed was enamoured of lemonade, for medical authority prescribed six pints a day of liquid. They had also had four hours' sleep on oxygen, in two batches, for when sleeping on oxygen, one woke as soon as the supply gave out and remained awake. At very first light they had looked out, over the sleeping black valleys that writhed like snakes among snow masses. In the east the dark sky lightened. They could pick out one patch, where must be the monastery of Thyangboche, far away and 16,000 feet below. Perhaps even then the monks were praying for our safety.

Tenzing was active very early with the cooker, and they started at 6:0, in comparatively windless conditions. Tenzing led the first stretch. The slope to the South Summit Ed did not like; it looked dangerous, nasty snow, a place to be left alone. But this was Everest, and others had been up before. He asked Tenzing, "What about it?" Tenzing, who is a perfect gentleman, replied, "As you wish," and they went on. The summit ridge from the South Summit looked formidable, a path narrow as virtue itself between the cornices on the right, overhanging the Kangshung Glacier 12,000 feet below, and the western precipice to the left. The snow was hard, steps could be chipped. At one point Tenzing had suffered. Something wrong. It was the ice blocking his outlet valve, easy to remove. But a nasty fright. So at last they had come to the forty-foot rock step in this final ridge. It must have been a fine piece of climbing at that height, a wriggle up the fissure between rock and snow, back against snow, hands against rock. We had looked at it time and again through glasses, a tiny vertical nick in the ridge, but it has been said that you cannot tell what a rock is going to be like till you have rubbed your nose on it. The whole climb from the South Summit took two and a half hours. (The rise in vertical height is, of course, no more than 400 feet.) "A good climb by New Zealand Alpine standards," thought Ed, who had been leading, and the top a perfect top, with a ridge dropping away in each direction. The blackness, bareness from snow, of the north side seemed to impress him specially and the steep drop there looked to be after the first few feet down on to the route which so many earlier parties had attempted. It is very easy, looking down, to misjudge the steepness of a ridge, for the eye leaps lightly to flatter ground beyond. But it looks certainly as if this north side, on the final pyramid, is steep indeed. For ten minutes Ed had his oxygen off, while he photographed in all directions. He felt no ill effects, but "I was quite glad to get it on again."

From the Twenty-Ninth to the Thirtieth

They had turned after a quarter of an hour, anxious about the descent and whether the oxygen would hold till they reached cylinders left by Tom and Charles. Ed had been doing mental arithmetic half way up, and calculated they should just make it. Where we saw them descending from the South Summit they had been extremely uncomfortable. The slope was steep, descent is always more nerve-wracking, and they looked straight down on to the Kangshung. The snow was rotten. It was a huge relief to be down, at the bottles left by Tom and Charles. Then back along the ridge, to the ridge tent which a modest wind had half-torn from its moorings. They had stopped here, to rest over the Primus and make drink. They came on down, very tired, not conscious of the greatness of the achievement. We knew the rest.

Even from that first, fragmentary account, full of mountaineering understatement, it was easy to judge that it had been a superb climb, by two companions worthy of it and climbing as a rope of two should. After this the conversation wandered a good deal, to scenes like that of Tom trying to get back, on his knees, up the Geneva Spur on the 27th. Sometimes he needed help. Greg had been all in, too, returning from the carry. Next day he had wanted oxygen for the Spur, but there had not been enough to spare. Both Ed and George generously said that it was now bad luck on me not to have the chance of a third shot, but I cannot recall any feeling of disappointment at all at the idea; nor later, when I wrote in my diary next day, "Ed and George very generous on me, say bad luck I can't do third assault and fittest to go high. But after it all I think my feeling is of great relief, the thing is done and I have had a good run." At the time all I knew about the third party was that I believed I would be on it. Only afterwards John confided his secret hope that he and I might make that last attempt.

The top layers of my mind were probably dormant up there, but it is very true that we all felt strongly that the team got to the top rather than the individuals, while the individuals chosen were worthy representatives of the team. Others had worked as hard. (George Lowe's performance, nine days work on the Lhotse Face, the ridge carry and four nights on the South Col, was as remarkable as any on the expedition.) This was the opinion expressed time and again, particularly since the ascent, by John, and one secret of his leadership; his too the conviction that the "team" included those who had gone before, over whose shoulders we climbed to the top. He said, suddenly and apropos of nothing (though he will have forgotten it), "Wouldn't Mallory be pleased if he knew about this?" Mallory forfeited his life on Everest, and I think we all felt the same: we were part of a greater company. Now the summit was reached, therefore all was well.

"Disappointment may creep in later," I wrote. Later, perhaps, I would feel, "Well, I was very fit. Given the oxygen I think I might have made it. A pity it wasn't me." No climber would be human if he went to Everest without the secret hope that he might be the man to find himself, those few minutes, on top. He would probably be the worse mountaineer if he did not allow that hope to promenade his day dreams. But if his fears are often dupes, hopes may be and are liars; he would be no mountaineer at all if he did not have a far wider hope for the wider unit involved in climbing the mountain. "Conquest" in connection with Everest suggests to me nothing but the conquest of rebellious bits of myself. Often on that mountain I must face and admit to my limitations, always curb the extravagance of desire.

We talked of Tenzing. What a good thing he had made of it. Good to have a Sherpa on top. John sent him, in the first place, because he had proved his fitness with Lambert, and this year too was "going like a bomb," in climbing parlance with Ed. But he was sent also, a far more important reason as it seemed to me, as a Sherpa to represent all the Sherpas who had worked, and in some cases died, upon Everest. Without the Sherpa the mountain could not have been climbed. Therefore it was fitting that one of the small, brown and smiling tribe should stand upon the top with a representative of ourselves: Tenzing, who had taken a leading part in the climb of last year, and before that carried a Sherpa load upon the norhtern flank. "Good for Tenzing," expressed the feelings of those that talked that night.

It was a curious night, when we finally settled for sleep. The valley between the two Li-Los proved to be on the short side, which meant for me the posture of a Michelin Man whose top half has been screwed sideways. My down hood was up, my head hard against the rucksack which itself was firmly against the now tied-up entrance. Half of me was at last in the sleeping-bag, but half, without violent movement of which I was incapable, I could not make enter. We had, however, achieved so rich an interior atmosphere that I hoped it would be thick enough to protect me. I had under my hip a good wad of sleeping-bag, but at some time in the night, with Ed's Li-Lo convenient against my buttock, I shifted my right hip on to it, and he, like a gentleman, moved over to make room. My toes were the greatest problem. They remained cold all night, despite bunching and stretching between sleeps. A very faint numbness lingered about them well after we were back home, and my toe-nails turned black.

The wind was with us all night, blustering across the level gap at the tents, pulling and pushing at the tent poles, squeezing in and then bellying out the fabric. There was no snow for the throwing, but occasional ice fragments tinkled against rocks or the poles. I must regret and apologise for being able to give no more dramatic wind scenes, but as I was not at the pitching of the tents on the 24th, undoubtedly our nastiest affair with wind, I can give no desperate descriptions to compare with those of the north side. I cannot remember wind being more than a very harassing nuisance, but nuisance it certainly was. It woke me at times, and I readjusted the buttock. But I must have slept, and soundly, for I heard only much later from Mike Ward that Ed and George had been sleeping on oxygen. I had not noticed, or did not remember, them putting it on. When the oxygen gave out, they talked. I certainly did not hear them. I remember nothing until the sun, striking into the symphony of wind, set the whole tent on fire. I opened the sleeve and looked out, to the east, where it lit up the white wavelets of ice all over the Col; where, just within reach to my left, the little red "blister" lay snugly streamlined against the blast.

At 6:00 I stretched out a hand for the cooker, which we had left outside to make room. This I did at the request of Tenzing, whose face had appeared, rather cold-looking, in the windward entrance of the "blister." I was exceptionally well placed for doing things outside, he exceptionally badly. I reached over the cooker without either of us having to leave his tent, and waited. Nobody minded waiting a long time before Tenzing's efficient hands produced tea, borne by a now broadly grinning Pasang Phutar. Poor Ed! He had never liked tea, even in the valleys, and had tested Thondup's resourcefulness by asking for coffee each time. However, we then went on to soup, at which we made some show but none of us a very good one. I took some raisins out of a sense of duty, some of our condensed milk (Lait Mont Blanc) and bits of saucisson, which, however, the others would not touch. Appetites were not now good. We had been above twenty thousand feet for just too long. It was an awkward business the saucisson; cutting off a round, peeling it and cutting up pieces. But I got some swallowed and even enjoyed it. I still think that if an omelette or a "nice bit of chicken" had appeared from a divine nowhere we could all have enjoyed it. I remembered Angtharkay's cooking, and was not Angtharkay reputed to have cooked a delicious three-course dinner at Camp VI on the north side of Everest?

The talk continued. I think we were now back with families and friends, how pleased they would be. My own thoughts were very vividly with my wife and family, and my year-old-son who would know nothing at all about it. But how happy everbody else would be that this was safely, successfully over! The idea of an accident now occurred to note of us. It was all very pleasant, but at last the harsh time came when there could be no excuse for lying longer. It was my painful duty, as janitor of the door, to be the first to leave the easeful horizontal position, kneel up, reach for boots, put both slowly on and climb into the vertical. It had seemed to me, lying down, that the wind was none so bad. Standing up disillusioned me. I reeled over to the pyramid, bent down and entered. The interior was bleaker and less inviting, if that were possible, than before. I felt doubly grateful for my night with the others, one of the most happy, least comfortable nights with the best of companions that I have ever had. I sat and did up my laces, put on my puttees, then out again and back to the Meade.

They were taking some time getting quite dressed and adjusting oxygen sets for Ed and Tenzing to use on the descent. A clutter of pots and cooking gear lay blocking the door. It seemed a pity to leave all this valuable equipment. At any rate I ought to take something, now that our Assault Rations would be lying here useless. I went back to the pyramid. On the ground, inside and out, 6-oz. packets of sugar were strewn. Sugar-that was very important, I slowly thought, and I picked some up and put them in my sack.

Everest is climbed. At times the astonishing thought penetrated even the sloth of a high camp. Now we must go down, must keep that story for another day. In the east the sun was warming. Over there, if one walked across, Kangchenjunga's huge bulk (28,150 feet) dominated the morning. Pasang and I, not having oxygen to worry about, set off the first at 9:0. We climbed slowly up the wind-crust towards our Spur. It was gratifying to find the handrail still in position, even more so that it was useful. I was reminded of the bottle of Benzedrine tablets still in my pocket. John's concern ahout this slope was strong enough to make him feel that the stimulant might be helpful. Suppose the Sherpas reached the Col and then had not strength to return up the initial climb? There had been a good deal of discussion about Benzedrine; Griff recounted the extraordinary things that it made men do in the War, when they thought themselves dead-beat. I always had the timid feeling that it was unsporting, though why it should be any more so than oxygen I could not tell. It was decided to experiment with Sherpas in the icefall, and this Charles Wylie had done, with most strange results. One man had found that it was excellent stuff, it cured his cough. Another said that it made him sleep extremely well! The truth is, perhaps, that the Sherpas have a toughness of fibre little affected, except psychologically, by drugs. They knew that it must be meant to have some effect, so did their best for the sahibs sake.

Going slowly, using the handrail, we had reached the snow crest; thence towards the rocks. I had some difficulty in finding the higher snow traverse into the wide snow gully, as it looks from here, that begins the Face of Lhotse. Crampons squeaked upon the flat stone as we cast about, found a doubtful line and descended ponderously. The wide, soft boots bent the unsupported ankle over at long steps down. At times feet slipped with a jolt through surface crust. Remember, there had been no serious snow for over a fortnight. Since then sun and wind had been playing with the remains. But I still blessed the warmth and comfort of the "H.A." boots. At the gully snow we halted, and I took off my down jacket. It was going to be hot, but I had not dared to take off anything on the Col. Here the other party, going strongly, caught us up. Ed and Tenzing were wearing their oxygen. The rock intrusions to which we now came were in fact two bands running across the Face, and at the lower of these Pasang had "crampon trouble." We suffered from this disease with the strapping of all three types of crampon. The strap had loosened, one crampon swung free of the ankle. While he was fastening it I went over to my oxygen set, still resting here from yesterday. With a delight pleasant at the time but which I regretted afterwards, for I would have liked the mask, I sent the whole thing sliding down towards the cum.

At the glacier top the others halted, and we sat with them in great heat. We took off remaining sweaters, but to take off down trousers, which meant removing boots, still demanded too iron a strength of purpose. This time there was almost a highway over the icefall: crampon marks, patches of dirt, silver paper reminiscent of the Todi in a fine July. Over the topmost crevasse we jumped without a thought. Down the fixed ropes we swung and turned with ease, while George took out his cine-camera for some shots. There was a holiday feeling about it all, as if this were the last day of term. The sun shone, the breathing came easier with descent, the down trousers grew hotter. Now we were on the last slope.

Sir John Hunt

Nobody had suspected that there would be anyone at VII. Charles Wylie would have gone down with my two. Already my thoughts were wandering to the time it would take to heat a drink, or should we go on without? Perhaps we ought. All of a sudden we saw a figure walking out between the tents: Charles himself without a doubt. What joy! A final trudge along the flat, sticky and uncomfortable between the legs, and we were there. Here was Charles, stayed up to see that everything was well, appearing like the god in the story with great beakers of lemonade! My first move was go get down into the shade of the tent which I had left, though it seemed quite incredible, yesterday morning. We drank and drank, sitting in the snow and pulling off down trousers. Charles, grinning hugely, heard the story and congratulated Ed and Tenzing. How good that he had stayed!

Ed's party was anxious to be away and down soon, to relieve John's anxieties and see once more the comfort of "civilized" life. Myself I was not sorry when Charles said he would have to stay and take the tents down, since all below the South Col were needed. I would have time, if I stayed with him, to cool out, collect my chattels, have another drink. My reaction from the excitement of yesterday was a feeling of happy relaxation. It did not matter, now, when we got down. Everything was settled, the weather looked fine, the golden ingots of the west had faded into a deep blue sky lightening at the horizon, above the frothy silver cloudlets of a Veronese canvas. Why hurry? Why not savour the last descent in its every detail, all the sensations evoked, at each step, by those words, "The last time. Everest has been climbed"? Even so, I might not have offered quite so gladly, had I known how much hard work would be awaiting us.

Ed, George and Tenzing were cramming their down clothing into rucksacks, roping up again, turning mugs upside down. They disappeared over the bend. We began to look at the tents. These had now been standing for nearly a fortnight. Each day the sun had melted the snow, then frozen it, melted and frozen, to rivet the pegs fast in ice and crease the tent floors into sagging hollows. Each peg we had laboriously to chip out with the ice-axe, with the help of Pasang Phutar and Phu Dorji, while Ang Dorji lay by the pyramid in the stupor of yesterday's weakness. It was a long job. Never had tents seemed to have so many pegs. Each hopeful pull at the canvas was frustrated by another, and the work started again. Outside, the whole scene was like a slovenly Bank Holiday. Now the tents were down, long stiff masses of them. They were being packed on to loads, smaller chattel, were entering rucksacks. A last look round, for in a few weeks this place would be its clean, cold self again. Everest would have forgotten us.

Now we were ready to move. It was early afternoon, the sun blazed upon us unclouded, although mist rose from the witches cauldron of the lower Cwm. As we at last prepared to step out, delaying the moment of fastening crampons making the odd adjustment to sacks, it was clear that Ang Dorji would have a hard time. His face, handsome in the Sherpa way, was dulled with the unseeing listlessness that I had seen already on Ang Temba. He fumbled weakly at his straps. I suggested to Charles that I might take him on one rope, Charles the other two on another. We started off. After a very few steps both Ang Dorji's crampons came off almost simultaneously. I leaned across in the steps to fasten them, but to do that service for another person is almost as hard as tying his bow-tie. He cannot sit down upon the slope, you cannot get right above him. I kept very close on the traverse, holding the rope tight. Then I let Charles's party through, saying that we would make our way, slowly. Ang Dorji moved on, like a sleep-walker. Often his foot caught and he stumbled, giving every indication that he was about to plunge into the Cwm. Once he stopped for some time, and I wondered why. He wanted to drink water from a dirty little puddle set in the pock-mark of a crevasse-edge. But he kept on, from sheer instinct.

Charles most thoughtfully waited at the empty ledge of Camp VI. Here we rested some time, watching the mist as it boiled up and reached webbed fingers between us and the sun. The slopes below, with their fixed ropes, went easily down to the last steep stretch some 250 feet below VI. Ang Dorji descended the last feet as a suspended lump. Now we were down through the lower ins and outs, now muddied with that icecream-carton appearance that snow can have after a dry spell. We were at the roping-up platform, looking at three solemn black cylinders reposing in the snow. I now felt glad that they had not come up; it was satisfying to have managed without them. Here we took off crampons and prepared to carry them in our hands. But the Sherpas asked to rest; could we go on and they come after? We untied and left them a rope, for no harm could now come to them; two strong men could support Ang Dorji if he needed it. But he looked like one who would go on.

I shall not forget the walk back to IV. The afternoon mist, battling at the lower buttresses of Nuptse, interposed wreathing veils that thickened, and dispersed, and thickened again between ourselves and the burning sun, which burned none the less fiercely. We walked in shirt-sleeves, crampons in hand, with a weight upon our backs. We walked down upon a trail now beaten by many feet: one trail through a white loneliness, and that too would soon be covered up. We reached V, now desolate, and paused only to admire for a moment the great slanting ice plunges of the West Shoulder, with their metallic shine as if a myriad jet aeroplanes were speeding down to destruction. I have never asked Charles what he felt here, but I sensed that he too was tired with the thought that it was "over," with the weight on his back and the looseness of muscle in descent. Tiredness took strange forms. We were going on together for ever, through this loneliness, among magical personalities around. One of them was friendly. The shapes of the hills, half-hidden and magnified by mist, were present watching us. And the mist, a diaphanous green through my sun goggles, laughed in and out of them and played with the outline of their faces. Mingma Dorji might any moment step out from his grave, over there on the right to greet us. The ghosts of Mallory and Irvine themselves were not far round the corner; it seemed even that the Swiss would climb up to meet us. Would anybody bother to come?

There, at last the smudge of tents showed over a bend. We were descending slowly towards it, but there seemed nobody there, only two figures making off down towards III. Perhaps ghosts were here, too. But there was John himself coming out and up to meet us. Even under the white smear of glacier cream, under a white hat and sun-glasses, it was clear that he was very moved. With the warmth of his pressed hand the spell of tiredness was broken.

From the Twenty-Ninth to the Thirtieth

Eric Shipton (1907—1977) was one of history's great mountain explorers and an early advocate of the lightweight expedition. He participated in expeditions to Everest in 1933, 1935, 1936, and 1938. He made the first ascent of Mount Kenya's Nelion summit and the second ascent of the Batain summit. He was president of the Alpine Club from 1965 to 1968. He is author of several books including *Nanda Devi, Blank on the Map, Upon That Mountain, Land of Tempest,* and *The Untraveled World.*

ERIC SHIPTON:
MOUNTAINS OF THE MOON

Whether Ruwenzory, Kenya, Kilimanjaro or the group of volcanoes of Kivu are Ptolemy's "Mountains of the Moon" is an open question. Nor is it of great importance, for the ancient tradition of the Nile rising in a system of lakes fed by snow mountains, though true, seems to have been more in the nature of a lucky guess than a result of actual geographical observation. However, as Rowenzori alone fulfils the ancient tradition, it has come to be labelled with that romantic title. Its mystery, invisibility and remoteness, surrounded by thousands of miles of tropical swamp and vegetation, and the fact that, unlike its rivals, it is a range of non-volcanic mountains, perhaps make it the more worthy of the distinction. The origin of the name Ruwenzori is very doubtful, and it is not used by any local natives in speaking of the mountain range.

Nevertheless, it is remarkable that the ancients should have believed in the existence of these snow mountains, as it was not until 1888, some thirty years after the discovery of the Victoria Nile by Speke, that Stanley discovered the existence of snow mountains in Central Africa; this despite the fact that many explorers had been travelling for a number of years in the neighbourhood of the range, and Stanley had himself camped for months at its foot without so much as suspecting the existence of vast glacier-covered mountains. To those who have experienced Ruwenzori weather this is not so surprising!

During the next eighteen years various attempts were made to penetrate to the glaciers, but it was not until 1906 that a large expedition led by H.R.H. the Duke of the Abruzzi explored the peaks and glaciers of the range and reached the summits of the highest peaks.

In 1926, G. N. Humphreys led two remarkable expeditions, during which he explored much new country to the north of the range, and carried out some very good work amongst the peaks. During the second expedition he reached the summits of Margherita and Alexandra for the first time since the Duke's expedition.

In spite of the opening of good motor roads through Uganda to Fort Portal and beyond to the foothills of Ruwenzori, very few Europeans ever penetrated far into the mountains, and, since 1926, the ascent of the high peaks had not been repeated. In recent years Humphreys had explored much of the country, but there was a great deal still to be discovered. Tilman and I had decided to go to Ruwenzori at the earliest opportunity. Our interest was centred mainly upon the high peaks, for we had not yet realised the fascination of unexplored valleys.

In 1931 I was invited to join Smythe's expedition to Kamet, and it was not until early in 1932 that we had the chance of further African ventures. We travelled the five hundred miles from Turbo in Kenya to the foot of the mountains in Tilman's car. We had no difficulty whatsoever in collecting porters to accompany us. Our requirements were very small, as we proposed to establish any high-level camps ourselves. We started with twelve porters, and one man cut a path through the forest. All porters' food had, of course, to be taken with us.

The porters were of the Bakonju tribe, who live on the lower slopes of the range. They were delightful people, with a ready grin, even in adverse circumstances, and they were generally cheerful and willing. One of their chief characteristics was the way they balanced up and down formidable slopes, or from one tree trunk to another, with 50-lb. loads on their heads, a feat to be envied by even the most practised mountaineer.

Three marches took us to the forest. It, was difficult going as the vegetation was everywhere dense and perpetually wet. Sometimes we went for half an hour at a time without touching the ground, walking over thickly-matted branches. The sides of the valley were steep and broken, and progress was infinitely laborious. We found rock shelters at frequent intervals; these were very useful as camping sites, for it was always raining. In the evening, sitting before a fire, sheltered from the rain, it was good to watch the clouds driven wildly about the craggy foothills of the range, or clinging to the gullies in the enormous rock precipices; to listen to the roar of a hundred torrents; and, after dark, to see the flickering of lightning towards the high peaks. One afternoon, while still in the forest, the weather cleared, and we saw the great ice peaks of Stanley and Speke—a startling sight indeed, seen from such very tropical surroundings. It is easy to realize with what excitement those early explorers first set eyes on these snow peaks after travelling for many months through the swamps of Central Africa.

At an altitude of about 10,000 feet we came to very strange country. A fantastic tangle of rotting vegetation—giant groundsel, lobelia and giant heath all thickly covered in moss. Moss was everywhere; we waded feet deep in it and walked through tunnels of it. The very air seemed to be tinged with an eerie green light. All the streams were hushed and a strange silence reigned.

Two more days were spent in reaching the Bujuku Lake, at the foot of the Scott-Elliott pass, where we made our base camp in a cave. Moving about in the high valleys was exasperating. We were either in swamp, groundsel forest, or struggling through a vile growth known as "Helichrysum," which is a sort of juniper growing to a height of about seven feet, and so dense as to be at times impenetrable. The giant groundsels found on Mount Kenya grow singly and far apart. In the Ruwenzori they grow close together in dense forests, their rotten trunks lying about in a thick tangle on the ground. These, though stout, were rarely strong enough to bear our full weight, so that when we stepped on them they snapped and down we went to be firmly wedged with our feet struggling helplessly in mid-air. Apart from the great labor needed to make any headway, it was almost impossible to go more than a few yards in any direction without getting wet to the hips even if it did not happen to be raining or snowing. Again, above the limit of the Helichrysum the rocks were covered with thick moss, which peeled off as soon as any weight was placed on it. This rendered any but the simplest approaches very dangerous.

But when all is said, Ruwenzori, like our Lakeland, would lose a great deal of its beauty, mystery and charm were it deprived of its continuous cloud and damp. Nor did we go there for comfort or freedom of movement.

We discharged two porters en route, and from the Bujuku camp we sent down another five. The remaining six were installed in a cave, and waited there with food and fires until we returned down the mountain. We went on alone with a light bivouac camp to the glaciers of Mount Stanley. All the time we were in thick mist and, with our heavy packs, our progress was slow, for we became involved in many difficulties by not being able to see more than a few yards ahead. Eventually, however, we reached the plateau of the Stanley glacier and, by accident rather than by design, camped right on the summit of the main divide. Though when we pitched the camp we had no idea where we were.

At sunset that evening the mists cleared, and we looked straight down to the Congo. In the foreground was a sheer precipice of broken glacier, from which angry clouds strove to detach themselves. Beyond, like a hazy map beneath us, stretched the plains of the Congo across which the Semliki river coiled like a silver snake. To the south was the huge expanse of Lake Edward. The whole scene was flooded in the deepest blue, a blue so vivid that it colored everything around us, becoming more and more intense the farther one gazed over the Congo, until swallowed up in a blazing sunset. For the next twenty-four hours it snowed almost continuously. The following morning we set out in the vain hope of finding our way about the glaciers, but we spent a fruitless day losing ourselves in snow flurries, as our tracks were immediately blotted out by the driving snow. However, late in the evening, we managed to reach the foot of the south ridge of Alexandra. The next day, January 19th, we climbed the ridge to the summit of that peak. There was one difficult cornice to be overcome and a fair amount of step cutting on the ridge. This, I believe, was the route taken by the Duke of the Abruzzi's party. We found a cairn on the summit. The mist cleared for a few moments while we were on the top, but we could see very little.

We were four and a half days on the glacier. There was a high wind most of the time, and snow fell all night and most of the day. But each evening at sunset the weather cleared for a moment and gave us superb views over the Congo. On the 20th we became hopelessly involved in a maze of crevasses while attempting to reach the east ridge of Margherita. At last, on the 21st, after repeated efforts, we managed to strike it at a point where the cornice was small, and could be cut through without great difficulty. From there we had little trouble in making the third ascent of the highest peak of Ruwenzori.

Eric Shipton

The snow and ice formations on these peaks are remarkable. Strong, cold winds, blowing newly-fallen snow against any irregularity, produce the most fantastic shapes and forms. Practically no melting seems to take place, and gigantic cornices are formed. The snow surfaces have a very curious feathery appearance which is most beautiful.

When our food was finished we started an undignified descent to our base. We slid and slithered on moss and lichen covered rocks, and spent most of the time sitting down heavily on the ground. Our packs were far heavier than they had been when we left our base camp, owing to the fact that tent, sleeping bags and all our kit were water-logged. But our real troubles began when we got amongst the helichrysum and rotting giant groundsel. At last, floundering through swamp and black mire, we reached the luxury of our cave by the Bujuku Lake.

We allowed ourselves a whole day to recuperate from this battering and to dry our sodden garments and bedding. It was a mystery to me how the porters continued to keep a fire going, still more to light it in that perpetual wet. But it did not seem to present any problem to them and two furnaces raged day and night at the mouth of the cave.

The Bakonjus of Ruwenzori have a remarkable method of carrying fire about with them. Straw thatched tightly in the shape of a cigar about 18 inches long, forms a receptacle in which the fire lies dormant. They carry these curious objects strapped to their shoulders and when they want a light they just take off the end of the cigar and blow. It is said that fire can be carried in this way for a month without renewal.

We set out for Mount Speke in thick weather on January 23rd, and after a further tussle with swamp and drenching vegetation, reached a glacier. A short clearing enabled us to see that we were almost directly above the Stuhlmann pass. We climbed to the crest of a ridge and followed it to the summit of Vittorio Emmanuele Peak without encountering any mountaineering difficulties. There was a biting wind and we were wet to the waist. We waited for three hours hoping for a view, stamping about in a vain attempt to keep the circulation moving in our legs. At about 1.30 p.m. the mists lifted for a short time. We raced along the long ridge to the north, and, after crossing three intervening peaks, reached the unnamed peak which was climbed by Humphreys in 1926. It is the highest point of Mount Speke.

One of our principal objects was to force a route direct from the Bujuku valley to the highest peaks of Mount Baker. With this in view, we left our camp at dawn on January 24th. We had hoped to make the attempt direct from the Scott-Elliott pass, but the ice-filled cracks and gullies of the ridge above the pass looked impossible, so we decided to attempt the face about half a mile farther down the valley. The lower part of the face was covered in thick moss and lichen, and required extreme care. Above this the steep rocks were covered with ice and snow which, together with the rottenness of the rock, produced an exasperatingly false appearance of simplicity. It was difficult in the thick mist to make a good choice of route. After some hours of this sort of climbing we were faced by a formidable line of overhangs guarding this side of the east ridge of Baker. But after several attempts we overcame these and gained the ridge at 11 a.m.

Turning to the west, we followed a long easy ridge leading over several minor peaks to Semple Peak, which we reached at about 1 p.m. From there we turned south and climbed to the summit of King Edward Peak, the highest point of Mount Baker.

Shortly before reaching the summit, the whole range of high peaks cleared and we had a superb view of Mount Stanley. Having been surrounded by impenetrable fog for many days, the effect of such a sudden and complete clearing was indescribably wonderful; it felt as though a great load had been removed from one's mind. Subjects of considerable speculation and heated argument suddenly became clear. Our flounderings amongst the glaciers of Mount Stanley were at once revealed, and it was difficult to understand why we should ever have been at a loss to know where to go; though no doubt we would have been in exactly the same state of perplexity had we found ourselves again on the Stanley glacier wrapped in cloud.

With the sudden clear weather we decided to complete the traverse of Baker, disregarding the painful prospect of the weary return to the Bujuku valley by way of the Scott-Elliott pass. We allowed ourselves about half an hour's rest on King Edward Peak, to examine our first real view of the range as a whole. Far below, the valleys, now bathed in sunlight, looked mild and beautiful, and we almost forgot our struggles amongst their vile vegetation and swamp. Their intense green contrasted superbly with the crags surrounding them. Here and there deep blue lakes nestled in emerald beds. The neighboring ice peaks, with the fantastic shapes of the twin peaks of Mount Stanley, completed this wonderful scene. Boiling masses of cloud still hung over the lower valleys.

The descent to the south towards Freshfield pass was easy, though we had to be careful as the snow was inclined to avalanche. About half-way down the ridge we turned west and descended the steep glacier, on which there was a layer of unstable snow covering the ice. Once off the glacier we again encountered rocks with a treacherous coating of moss. At first it was so sparse as to be hardly perceptible, which made it the more dangerous, as our feet were apt unaccountably to slip off the most secure ledges. This direct descent was something of a step in the dark, as we could not see what was below us. Lower down, when we reached the upper line of helichrysum, we became involved in a series of difficult crags. There the helichrysum in part atoned for its previous behaviour, as without its assistance the crags would have been impassable and a return to the summit ridge unavoidable—a matter of many hours toil. Even as it was, the descent of the line of crags, which we were lucky enough to strike in the only feasible place, proved a difficult struggle, during which Tilman lost his watch and I succeeded in spraining my right shoulder. We reached the valley close by a small lake, and then toiled wearily towards the Scott-Elliott pass. When at last we reached its foot, we were delighted to find that the vegetation gave place to scree, up which we could walk in a normal position. The clouds had long since enveloped us again, and we were fortunate in reaching the pass at a point from which a descent could be made on either side. Most of the way down was through a narrow gully, at the foot of which we were exasperated to find more giant groundsel and helichrysum. During the descent Tilman suffered the further loss of his camera. It was getting dark when we reached the Bujuku valley once more, and we spent a long time before reaching camp, floundering knee-deep in vilely smelling black mud by the lake.

Long into the night we sat before a blazing fire of groundsel wood in our cave and in turn forgave this plant some of its atrocities, taking back a few of the unmentionable names we had called it. Even when damp (which is always) it makes excellent firewood.

On the following day we started back. Progress was almost as bad as on the ascent, except that there was no cutting to be done. But the porters were anxious to reach their homes, and consented, with some persuasion, to a double march each day.

Climbing on Ruwenzori was a memorable experience, and well worth the discomfort and the exasperating toil. When at length we left the rainforest it felt as though we had emerged from a world of fantasy, where nothing was real but only a wild and lovely flight of imagination. I think perhaps the range is unique. It is well named "Mountains of the Moon."

Woodrow Wilson Sayre (1919—2002) occupies and unusual place in the history of mountaineering in that he is a twentieth century mountaineer with the hardihood and romantic vision of a "Golden Age" adventurer. In 1962 he led a very bold four man attempt on Mount Everest's North Wall that included a twenty-five mile traverse at over 20,000 feet with no Sherpa support and without the aid of oxygen. This effort almost led to an international incident, as he didn't have permission for the climb. He is the author of *Four Against Everest*.

WOODROW WILSON SAYRE: WHY DO MEN CLIMB?

Why do men climb? The question is asked so often one would think the answer was one of the great mysteries of all time on a par with the answer to such questions as "What is Beauty?" or "What is Truth?" At every one of my lectures or discussions somebody is sure to bring it up. Often they do so with an air of triumph. For however little they may know about mountain climbing they have somehow heard that this is the question to stump the experts. Actually, the question is not particularly difficult. It has seemed so mainly because of confusion over what the question is really about. Because of this confusion there is an equal confusion over what makes a satisfactory answer.

But first, let's look at Mallory's famous answer. When asked once at a lecture why he climbed Everest, he replied, "Because it is there." Many people have been tremendously impressed with this answer. I think it is a tribute to their vivid imaginations. For, as it stands, it really doesn't say anything. It is too ambiguous.

Does it imply a challenge? Does it imply some kind of inevitability? Or does it simply mean that there is no reason? And what does thereness have to do with it? Not far from my home is an impressive pile of junk which is called the town dump. It also is "there" and yet I have no desire at all to climb it. So something more than there-ness is needed as a reason for climbing.

Maybe it is the it-ness that counts. "Because it is there." The particular character of Everest itself is what attracts. This amounts to saying you climb it because you climb it. It is a reason, but not a very deep one.

Interpreting Mallory's answer to mean, "because it is a challenge," the question still remains: why is it a challenge? Why does it challenge that particular breed of men called mountaineers, whereas the vast majority couldn't care less?

My own guess would be that Mallory meant by his answer: "Please, dear questioner, ask me some other question. I am terribly tired of that one." For I am sure that all that Everest meant to him could hardly be put in a brief answer. And I suspect that setting forth all that he really felt was not something he would care to do again and again and again before a lecture audience. Wouldn't he, perhaps, be amused by the mystique built up around his actual reply?

For a long time I was puzzled why this question couldn't just be answered, "I climb mountains because I like to." Certainly this would be a perfectly good answer for most other activities. Why do I play tennis? I play tennis because I like to. Why do I ski or swim? Because I enjoy them. Now, why doesn't that kind of an answer satisfy anybody when it comes to mountain climbing? Why is a lecturer on mountain climbing asked again and again why he climbs, whereas a lecturer, say, on golf would almost never be asked why he played golf?

Eventually, I realized the root of the difference. The question about climbing is not a question about motivation at all. If it were, then the answer, "I climb because I like to," would be a perfectly appropriate answer. It is really a question about relative values. What the question is really asking is: "Look, this mountain climbing business is dangerous. It costs money. It is hard, exhausting work. You have to disrupt the family to do it. Now what values do you gain from climbing mountains that can possibly offset these obvious disvalues?"

Put this way it is a perfectly straightforward question which is capable of a perfectly straightforward answer. It is not particularly difficult to list the values which I derive from mountain climbing which do in fact for me offset the disvalues—if such they be—of cost, family disruption, unnecessary risk, and so forth. I will do this in the next part of this chapter. So the question, why do I personally climb mountains, is capable of a reasonably precise answer.

If the question is generalized to "Why do people climb mountains?" The answer will have to be much less precise. For there is no reason to suppose that what I get out of climbing mountains is exactly the same as what another climber gets out of it. His list of values may very well leave out a value that is on my list, and, of course, my list may leave out a value that is on his. Furthermore, the order of preference may be different. That is, my main value may only be a secondary one for him, or perhaps not even on his list at all.

I suppose one could make a combined list of all the values that anyone ever found in mountain climbing and present it as the answer to the general question of why people climb. But it would be rather bulky and not too significant. A better plan would be to try and find values that are common to everybody's, or nearly everybody's, list. This can be done, and as far as I can see that is about all that can be done in answering the general question. So, after I have listed the values that I derive from climbing I will indicate the values that are most commonly acknowledged by other climbers. Then, at the very end of the chapter I will give a brief justification of these values.

First on my list, but not necessarily first in importance, I would mention beauty. There are the colors: black rock and ultramarine shadows, pure white swell of snow, turquoise and amethyst crevasses, and the diamond glitter of sun on ice. In the afterglow of sunset the air itself becomes pink and gold. And there are the infinite clean shapes: windcarved snow, fluted ice, weathered stone, and cloud-brushed sky. Most of all, there are the great mountains themselves set in their rivers of ice, changing grandeur in every light and every weather. If a person will cross the ocean just to look at the beauty of a cathedral, why would he not do as much or more to see sights such as these?

Very closely associated with the beauty of the mountains are some special emotions which the highest and wildest peaks provoke. I feel a special excitement when I look out over thousands of square miles of untouched country. I feel it again when I walk where only a handful of men have walked in the history of the world, when I explore some hidden ridge or crag, or when I make the first track across a great unbroken snow field. I feel a special happiness to be alone in the high, silent places of the world tucked close under the sky. Such things are worth a little insecurity and sacrifice.

Speaking of "aloneness" this brings up two other important values which I find in mountain climbing: solitude and companionship. Paradoxically, the mountains provide both.

The companionship provided by climbing together is almost universally valued by mountaineers. The friendships established are lasting and irreplaceable. When you have walked the feather edge of danger with someone, when you have held his life at the end of a rope in your hand, and he has later held yours, you have an almost impregnable foundation for a friendship. For the deepest friendships spring from sharing failure as well as success, danger as well as safety. There is really no substitute.

Indeed, this is one of the regrettable trends in our present civilization. Real friendship is increasingly difficult. We hurry so much, we move, we change jobs, we juggle a hundred responsibilities. How often do we see even our best friends? Once we do see them, it is at a cocktail party or some occasion where the conversation remains superficial. If we hardly see them, how can we really share joy and tragedy with them? I think men are made for a deeper sort of friendship. Men are made for the close warmth of a friendship tested in danger and adversity. It is not impossible without this testing, but it is much more difficult.

In most primitive societies this testing is an established custom. There is the hunting party, the war party, or games and rituals involving danger and difficulty. But in our society testing depends on individual initiative or on accident. In war, of course, men find the closeness of shared danger—the men of a gun crew or an infantry patrol, for example—but where else is the opportunity? At any rate mountain climbing is one way of providing it.

As for solitude, that, too, is a great value and is something which the mountains can provide. It is a great value because it is just as essential as companionship. A man is unhappy unless he has both. He needs to be with his fellow man, and he needs to be apart from him. If he is forced to be completely apart, that is the torture which is called "solitary confinement." If he is forced to be completely with his fellow, that also is a torture. It has no name, but it is equally harrowing. When personnel were chosen for the early Antarctic expeditions they had to be specially screened because of the psychological strains of living so closely together. Each man was forever in the public view. In their winter quarters they were packed so tightly that a man couldn't walk across the hut without another man moving out of the way. According to prisoners the absence of all privacy is a torture that has often been used by the Communists.

Once again, going to the mountains is not the only way to get this essential solitude. But our civilization is making it more and more difficult to do it any other way. As a boy I used to know frog ponds and hidden glades where no one ever came. Now they are housing developments. I used to know streams where I could fish. Now you have to wait in line just to get to the bank. The national parks are more and more committed to hard living. Even the great empty deserts are filling. Increasingly they are cut up with jeep tracks and shacks and billboards and telephone wires. The largest untouched areas left are the oceans and the poles and the highest mountains. And the demographers assure us that in less than a century it will be "Standing Room Only" even there. The human race is almost like a mold that inhabits a glass jar. The mold multiplies and grows until it so crowds the jar that it poisons itself in its own wastes. People are wonderful, but an infinite number of them are not. A man must refill the inner springs of his being in solitude and reflection. I think there is a deep inner need for this. Without this refilling life becomes increasingly hurried, it becomes increasingly mechanical, and it becomes increasingly insensitive.

So this is a need which the mountains can fulfill. There are many hours, especially in a small expedition, when you walk the trails completely alone. And this aloneness depends in large part on unspoilt, untouched nature. I would say that there is need for alternation here too. We need to experience nature with the friendly marks upon it of human work and struggle and hope. But also we need to see nature apart from even the smallest sign of human interference. For this the high mountains are perfect.

If it is a bit of a paradox that the mountains should provide both solitude and deep companionship, it is also a bit of a paradox that society should not provide those values. That is, in spite of all the crowded "togetherness" increasingly required of us, real companionship is nevertheless hard to find. Arid on the other hand, in spite of all the solitude—in the sense of loneliness—that there is in society today, nevertheless, the solitude that I have been describing is absent. It involves being alone where no voice reaches and no foot falls, where there can be and is no other sign of a human. Only then does the person turn deeply inward. Loneliness is not enough.

Why Men Climb

Thus, mountain climbing tends to furnish an antidote to much that is wrong or overemphasized in society. The pendulum has swung much too far towards "togetherness" mountaineering redresses the balance. Society tends to make human relationships superficial; mountaineering deepens them. Other values can be added.

For instance, our society catches us up in a great hurry and rush of activity. Mountaineering returns one to the slower natural rhythms of the rising and setting sun, the changing weather, and the simple physical needs of the day. Headlines and frenetic concern for the universe fade away.

Again, our society imposes tighter and tighter routines on us. Mountaineering relaxes them.

Finally, I will mention that society tends to submerge our self-reliance and individuality in a great mass-handling of people treated almost as statistics. Mountaineering reverses this. It forces self-reliance. For instance, we were often weeks from help of any kind. If a piece of equipment broke or an accident occurred, we had to handle it entirely from our own resources. We did, and felt a good, proud feeling for having done so.

Thus, in one blow, as it were, many corrective values are achieved by climbing. Anyone of them could be achieved in other ways. But it is an especially valuable activity that can achieve them all at the same time.

I will set down only three more of the values on my list. First, there is the obvious value of adventure. It is exciting to discover new lands, new situations, new places. The thought of what may be just over the next ridge is intriguing. Many have been attracted by adventure, and I confess a weakness for it also.

Secondly, knowledge and understanding have a value. Certainly there is increased understanding of oneself, as well as of others, for on a trip of this nature one is stripped down to the basic. One sees relationships more realistically than ever before. Also there is increased understanding of many matters traditionally discussed in the classroom: courage, friendship, death, fear, even hunger and suffering. As a teacher of philosophy I think direct acquaintance with such subjects as these is not at all out of place. I cannot be satisfied with mere book learning.

Lastly, I think that there definitely is an element of challenge in any mountaineering. One cannot help dreaming of meeting some particular problem better than anyone else has met it. Indeed, there are no more provocative words for at least some of us than the phrase "It can't be done." Immediately you think of ways that it might be done. Toni Hiebeler describes how he first was attracted to the North Face of the Eiger by having the impossibilities pointed out to him when he was still a boy. How many hours have been spent by people trying to trisect an angle with straight-edge and compass just because they were told that it was impossible?

From the point of view of society it is good for men to meet their challenges. In fact, if man ever loses his attraction for the impossible all that is generally called "progress" would cease. From the point of view of the individual it is also good to pursue those goals which have caught one's imagination. It is exciting to try the impossible; it is even more exciting to accomplish it.

These, then, are the main values that I derive from climbing. For me they overbalance the expense, the risk, and all the rest. It is not a particularly unusual list of values, but it answers the question why I climb.

The question why climbers in general climb cannot be answered so precisely. As I said earlier, one can only list the most commonly shared values. Most of these are on my list, too. Most widespread, probably, is the pleasure of meeting, and if possible overcoming, some particular challenge. Next, and almost equally widespread, is the value and depth of the friendships made while climbing. Then usually at least one of the values derived from getting away from society, which I mentioned on my list, is also included on others lists. Also quite common is the value of beauty and adventure. Finally, there is a sense of communion with God. Those who experience it quite often feel it to be the most important value of all. I have not included it on my list, not because I do not think it has a very great value, but simply because it is not specifically one of the reasons why I climb.

This list of the most universally acknowledged values which climbers derive from climbing is imprecise in two respects. For one thing, the reason, or reasons why any particular climber climbs may not be on the list at all. He may climb for quite unusual reasons. Secondly, the list does not give one unambiguous answer to the question why men climb. I think that if it had been realized that the question was actually a question of relative values, then no one would ever have expected that there should be a single answer which was valid for all climbers. An approximate list, valid for most, but not all, would have been seen as the only significant answer to the question.

Some justification of the values on this list should probably be made. This can be done in two ways. I can show that these values are more important than most people realize, or I can try to show that the usual competing values are less valuable than is generally realized. To some extent I have already done the former. I argued that solitude and deep friendship and self-reliance were, in fact, very important and were more easily available on a mountain than in ordinary "civilized" society. It remains, then, to show that some of the competing values are less valuable. I shall confine myself to the chief one. This is the tremendous value that American society places on safety and security.

I think we have made a fetish of this value. Job interviewers report that the first question that they are asked by college graduates seeking jobs is what kind of a retirement program does the company have. Consider these diverse random examples. In the name of safety the Fourth of July is now only a spectator celebration. The ban on fireworks is justified, it is claimed, if the life of one child is saved thereby. In the name of safety every holiday weekend is publicized endlessly in advance as a death dealer. The exact death toll is predicted with gruesome futility. And there is obvious disappointment if a new record, one way or the other, is not achieved. Americans insure everything. Finally, a corollary of preoccupation with safety is the prevention of death, apparently forever. We will do anything to add one minute, or one hour, or one month to the life of some poor being who can never be anything more than a vegetable. The Christian doctrine of the infinite worth of every soul is perverted to the infinite worth of mere physical existence.

But it is not mere existence that counts. As Socrates said, any man can extend his life a little longer if he is willing to do or say anything. And as he also said, it is not how long you live, but how well that is important. Mere security is a barren ideal. We need to pay attention to what is done with that security. And we also need to ask whether security itself does not have its own dangers. Is a parent really better who tries to protect his child from every conceivable danger and difficulty? I think not. Neither, then, is a society better for trying to protect every one of its members from all danger and difficulties. They are not better off for being carefully wrapped in cotton batting. Deep within us I think we know that we need challenge and danger, and the risk and hurt that will sometimes follow. "Dangerous" sports would not be as popular as they are if this were not so.

Again, mountain climbing is not the only way of dealing with an over-organized, over-protective society. But it is one good way.

Woodrow Wilson Sayre

Contemplating all the values achieved by climbing mountains, I am tempted yet again to try the impossible and summarize it all in a single sentence. Men climb mountains because they are not satisfied to exist, they want to live climbing the heights is one way.

Jim Curran (b.1944) is an artist, film maker, and writer. He has
climbed extensively in Britain and the Himalaya. He is the recipient
of the Banff Mountain Literature Award and has, several times, been
short-listed for the Boardman-Tasker Mountain Literature Award.
His works include *K2: The Story of the Savage Mountain and Savage
Mountain*, *The Middle-Aged Mountaineer and High Achiever: The
Life of Chris Bonington*.

JIM CURRAN:
THE GREAT BEAST 666

While Conway reaped the plaudits after his return from India,
Eckenstein was ignored, returning to North Wales to climb on his
beloved Lliwedd, and quietly develop his theories of balance and technique.
His suspicions of the Alpine Club and all it stood for had been proved all
too true.

Then in 1898 he met the man who was to become an unlikely and
quite bizarre cult figure of the twentieth century. Climber, mystic, char-
latan, magician, Satanist, "sex fiend," Aleister Crowley was all of these
and more. He was born in 1875 in Leamington, Warwickshire. His father,
a brewer, was an active member of the Plymouth Brethren, a sect that
believed they were the only true Christians, took the Bible as the literal
truth and thought that the Second Coming was imminent.

Possibly as a result of extreme indoctrination, Crowley by the age of
eleven decided that the Devil was a far more interesting alternative and
from then on devoted most of his life to worshipping "the Beast 666."
But Crowley was not fool. Clever, articulate and widely read, he was
educated at Malvern and Tonbridge and then Cambridge University. He
clearly suffered or entertained delusions of grandeur from an early age,
leaving Cambridge without a degree and taking a flat in London under
the name of Count Vladimir Svaref and undertaking a "career" of magic
in the Outer Order of the Great White Brotherhood.

It would be tedious to delve too deeply here into Crowley's strange obsessions: suffice to say he gives them an extensive airing in what he called "an autohagiography"—*The Confessions of Aleister Crowley*. They are best summarised by his own Law of Mankind—"Do What Thou Wilt Shall Be the Whole of the Law." It has often been said that with this exhortation to "do your own thing," and his obsessions with sex, drugs and Eastern philosophy, Crowley would have passed unnoticed in the Californian hippy scene or in the flower-power streets of London, and his brooding face actually appears on the Beatles' Sergeant Pepper album, the cult icon of the "sixties." I am not so sure. Crowley was an arrogant and devious character who fell out with almost everyone he met—an extraordinary figure in any age, and not a particularly likeable one. Almost the only person he didn't end up despising was Oscar Eckenstein to who his *Confessions* are dedicated along with, amongst others, the explorer Richard Burton and the artist Augustus John.

One of Crowley's few redeeming features was his love of climbing and mountains generally. He was, in the words of Tom Longstaff, the great Himalayan pioneer, "a fine climber, if an unconventional one." He started climbing on the chalk cliffs of Beachy Head, which must have given him a refined eye for the safest line up what is still considered suicidally dangerous ground—only recently have any of the sea cliffs of the south of England been explored using ice-climbing gear in the soft rock.

He climbed in the Lakes and the Alps—again unconventionally. Longstaff saw his solo of the dangerous and difficult true right side of the Mer de Glace icefall below the Geant, a horribly risky and ill-advised escapade by any standards. Crowley despised guided climbing and it was this that probably attracted him to Eckenstein —and vice versa. In one scathing passage in *Confessions* he sums up his feelings for the climbing establishment of the late 1890s:

Mountaineering differs from other sports in one important aspect. A man cannot obtain a reputation at cricket or football by hiring professionals to play for him. His achievements are checked by averages. But hardly anyone in England at that time knew anything about mountaineering. Various old fogeys who could not have climbed the simplest rocks in Cumberland or led across an easy Alpine pass, had been personally conducted by peasants up a few mountains and written themselves into fame.

In some ways Crowley was indeed a climber ahead of his time, in attitude if not achievement. Hatred of guides, pitons and fixed ropes (which were already in use in the Alps) would strike chords with generations of climbers to come. But compared with the great British names of his day—Mummery, Collie, Raeburn and Eckenstein himself—Crowley was an erratic and occasional performer who, had it not been for the notoriety of his private and public life, would probably have only been a footnote in the history of Victorian climbing.

In 1901 he and Eckenstein joined forces for the first time and climbed together in Mexico. Eckenstein had his own typically forthright views on Crowley's obsessions with magic: "He openly jeered at me for wasting my time on such rubbish. . . . "He said, "Give up your Magick with all its romantic fascinations and deceitful thoughts. Promise to do this for a time and I will teach you how to master your mind." Yet somehow their unlikely friendship survived. They climbed Ixtaccihuatl, "the most beautiful mountain in Mexico," several times and Popocatapetl, Crowley claiming, incidentally, to have broken "several world records." On their return to civilization they were gently made aware of the terrible news that Queen Victoria was dead, at which they (or perhaps just Crowley?) Broke into "shouts of joy and an impromptu war dance." The successful expedition was a preparation for the following year, for Eckenstein had invited Crowley to go with him to the Karakoram to climb Chogo Ri, as Crowley invariably refers to K2.

The 1902 K2 expedition has the distinction of being the first actually to declare its intention to climb the mountain. Led by Eckenstein with Crowley his deputy, it included one other English-man, Guy Knowles, a twenty-two-year-old from Trinity College, Cambridge; two Austrians, Heinrich Pfannl and Victor Wesseley; and a Swiss doctor, Jules Jacot-Guillarmod. The Austrians were reputed to be the best rock climbers in their country, but neither Knowles nor Guillarmod had much mountain experience. It was not, therefore, a very strong team that met in Rawalpindi at the end of March.

They had drawn up formal conditions for the expedition, agreeing that each should contribute the then huge sum of £1,000. Guy Knowles later told John Symonds, author of *The Great Beast, the biography of Crowley*, that Crowley contributed nothing and he, Knowles, put up most of the money for the expedition. This would seem a likely scenario and would certainly explain his presence in the party. Other key passages in the contract stipulated absolute obedience to the leader, unless to obey an order meant the loss of life, permission to be obtained from Eckenstein before the purchase of anything, an order not to interfere in the beliefs and customs of the natives and to "leave the women alone."

No sooner had they set out than there occurred an incident that has been the source of conjecture and rumour ever since. A telegram arrived from the Governor of Rawalpindi recalling Eckenstein and forbidding him to enter Kashmir. The reason for this is far from clear. Crowley was convinced that Sir Martin Conway, by now President of the Alpine Club, had somehow managed to use his influence with Curzon, the Viceroy of India, to attempt to sabotage the expedition, inspired by jealousy and as revenge for his quarrel with Eckenstein in 1892. Guy Knowles seems to have agreed that this was the explanation but there is not other evidence to support it. Could Conway have perpetrated this rather squalid little plot? And to what purpose? True he could have been worried that his achievements on the Golden Throne and Pioneer Peak might be reassessed, and even eclipsed by Eckenstein's team, but he must have realized that sooner or later someone would return and that any record was there for the taking. Would he have risked his own reputation on such meager grounds? Exposure would surely have been a humiliation he dare not risk. Yet pride does take strange forms and there remains a small unanswered question mark over Conway's conduct. This argument can of course be crudely countered by the fact that as Crowley himself was the one to make the allegation against Conway it may well have been a fabrication designed to show the Alpine Club and its president in the worst possible light.

There are at least two other possible explanations. One quite likely scenario is that Eckenstein, with his German-Jewish name, was thought to be a Prussion spy. This, given the state of paranoia over the intentions of Russia, cannot be dismissed lightly. Any rumors surfacing from the presence of an expedition composed of (seemingly) a majority of "foreigners" would have to be investigated and the incident could simply have been the knee-jerk reaction of a nervous official.

The other possibility is equally plausible. Louis Baume in his authoritative book *Sivalaya—The 8,000-Metre Peaks of the Himalaya* reveals that a brief article appeared in the *Friend of India* on first of May reporting that Eckenstein's expedition was to climb Mount Everest! Though this is erroneous to the point of absurdity (Rawalpindi being about eight hundred miles away from the mountain in any case), it is possible that unfounded rumors of an illicit journey into Tibet or Nepal could have

reached the ear of Curzon who was at the time involved in the first dip-
lomatic moves to mount an official British expedition to Everest. Eckenstein's recall to explain himself would clearly be necessary before he
could continue.

Whether by conspiracy or cock-up, Eckenstein was delayed for three
weeks before persuading Curzon himself that his motives were innocent.
He managed to catch up with the others at Srinagar. Writing of the affair,
Crowley makes a wholehearted defence of his friend from real of imaginary injustice: "Eckenstein was the noblest man that I have ever known.
His integrity was absolute and his sympathetic understanding of the native character supreme."

After this first setback the expedition proceeded reasonably smoothly
to Askole, arriving on 26 May. Before they got there they had their first
introduction to a rope bridge, which gave Crowley an excuse for a gratu-
itously snide dig at Conway: "They are a little terrifying at first sight, it is
only fair to admit, but one cannot help thinking that Sir Martin Conway
was almost too considerate of the nervousness of others when he insisted
on roping Zurbriggen on one side of him and Bruce on the other before
pirouetting lightly across."

At Askole Crowley and Eckenstein had a brief but unpleasant altercation over how many books Crowley should be allowed to take in his
personal gear limit of forty pounds. Crowley threatened to leave the expedition if he couldn't take "Milton and the rest" and eventually won the
argument claiming he would rather risk physical than intellectual starvation. (Though I have never risked either, I do recall Alan Rouse in Skardu
in 1986 also getting quite upset at the number of paperbacks I thought
necessary to last our own K2 expedition. Like Crowley, I too got my own
way, but even so the books ran out long before my return.)

Before they left Askole the two Austrians, Wesseley and Pfannl, asked
for permission to take three day's provisions in their rucksacks and go
off and climb K2! Crowley was astonished that after so much travelling
they were still incapable of grasping the scale and distances involved in
climbing the Karakoram mountains. Whether their intentions were serious
or a try-on is debatable, for Crowley himself admits that they all found
Eckenstein's discipline difficult to accept. In any case they were refused
and, like so many expeditions to come, the team began developing the ir-
reconcilable differences that would make any remote chance of success on
the mountain even slimmer. Crowley in particular lost no opportunity to
disparage the Austrians and his comments are unpleasantly xenophobic.

Slowly they made their way up the Baltoro, finding as do most trekkers today that "the journey is morally tedious and physically wearisome beyond belief. The compensation is the majesty of the surrounding mountains." Urdokas, the last grassy oasis on the true left or southern bank of the Baltoro, and commanding superb views of the Trango Towers and Cathedrals, was "a veritable Beulah. . . the atmosphere of restfulness is paramount. There was here quite a lot of grass: even some flowers." Sadly, this is not the case today. Urdokas is now almost bare of vegetation and horribly polluted.

Three days later Crowley arrived at the head of the Baltoro Glacier, and with astounding cheek observed, "I was irresistibly reminded of Concordia Platz in the Oberland and named the plateau in affectionate remembrance." Conway had not only named Concordia in 1892 but recorded the fact in his book published in 1894! Crowley continues with a description of the view from Concordia that is first accurate, if incomplete, and then vitriolic and bordering on defamatory:

Once again the astounding variety of nature in this district impressed itself upon my mind. One would have said that it was theoretically impossible to combine so many different types of mountain. The only exception to the otherwise invariable rule of practical inaccessibility was the Golden Throne, a minor point of which Conway claims to have claimed. "I was very disgusted at the bad taste of some of the coolies who had been with him in saying that he had never been on the mountain at all, but turned back at the foot of the icefall. How could such common creatures presume to decide such a delicate scientific question of this sort?"

Ironically, Crowley was so keen to put the boot into Conway that he never really gave K2 the description it deserved. His memory, too, seems to be a little at fault in his account of his approach to K2. On 16 June he left ahead of the others to reconnoitre the best route and walked up the Godwin-Austen Glacier ("where man had never yet trodden"). He camped up roughly "the first of a subsidiary spur descending from the ridge of which Chogo Ri is the climax," in other words the site of all future Base Camps. Here he observed the mountain "all day and night," coming to the conclusion that "while the South Face, perhaps possible theoretically, meant a complicated climb with no halfway house, there should be no difficulty in walking up the snow slopes on the east-southeast to the snowy shoulder below the final rock pyramid." In order to see these slopes Crowley must have first viewed them from Concordia, for here, so close to the mountain, they are blocked by the rocky silhouette of the South-East Spur. It is true that from Concordia it does look as though it might be possible to climb to the Shoulder almost entirely on snow (though "walking up" is surely a tongue-in-check understatement), but this is, of course, an illusion, as history would prove.

Here it is appropriate to understand the layout of at least the south side of K2 as seen from Concordia by Conway's and Eckenstein's expeditions. From here K2 appears to be a not quite perfect four-sided pyramid—a classic yet erroneous illusion that would take a long time to dispel. The far left skyline ridge is the West Ridge; nearer, the South-West Ridge runs towards an obvious col joining K2 to an elegant satellite, the Angelus or Angel Peak, at the foot of which base camps are normally placed on the Godwin-Austen Glacier. Between the West and the South-West Ridges is the foreshortened and rocky West Race. To the right of the South-West Ridge is the vast amphitheatre of the South Face seen head on with its own hanging glacier, spurs, seracs and retaining walls. It is bounded by the South-East Ridge which forms the right profile. The South-East Spur drops from the Shoulder of K2 to the Godwin-Austen Glacier. The true South-East Ridge as such doesn't really exist below the Shoulder, as it consists of huge snowfields and various ribs that stretch to the North-East Ridge, out of sight from Concordia. The Godwin-Austen Glacier runs at first due north then north-east, around the base of the mountain to a wide basin and horseshoe of smaller peaks, of which Sky-ang Kangri (Staircase Peak) is the largest.

Crowley's assessment of the South Face is almost as wildly optimistic as Pfannl and Wesseley's intention of climbing K2 in three days from Askole, and it is questionable whether any credit given to him in being the first person to spot the feasibility of the South-East Spur is really justified, with or without the competing claim of Robert Lerco. He didn't appear to notice the barrier that would come to be known as House's Chimney and totally ignored the presence of the Black Pyramid, the large broken buttress below the Shoulder. As for the difficulties above it, over thirty years would elapse before anyone even realised that the last six hundred metres of the South-East Ridge would prove to be as hard, or harder, a way to the top, as any of the 8,000-metre peaks. But however unaware of the true problems posed by the Spur, Crowley did recognise that it was the most likely weakness, and this must be acknowledged.

He pushed on through the small and relatively innocuous icefall on the Godwin-Austen Glacier and camped below the South-East Spur. When Eckenstein caught him up he immediately poured cold water on Crowley's proposed route and his choice of camp, ignoring the latter's assertions that they would be unlikely ". . . to meet any conditions which would make Camp X other than a desirable country residence for a gentleman in failing health." Despite his misgivings, Crowley accepted Eckenstein's decision to send back the porters and abandon the South-East Spur. Yet "It was so obviously right to take them up the slopes of the shoulder and establish the camp at a point whence Chogo Ri could have been reached without question in one fine day." If only it was that simple! The porters were much relieved, for they had been convinced that Crowley had been planning to lead them to their deaths over a non-existent pass to Yarkand. (But did they know that there was no pass?) "Their delight at being reprieved was pathetically charming." Crowley, unlike many of his successors, did seem genuinely fond of the Balti people and treated them well and sympathetically throughout. (Or at least he claims to have done.)

On 19 and 20 July Pfannl, Wesseley, Knowles and Guillarmod arrived. So, too, did a blizzard a couple of days later, which pinned them down for three further days. Then it was decided to reconnoitre the long and complex North-East Ridge and also go up to what Crowley called Windy Gap, the col at the very end of the Godwin-Austen Glacier.

Here, with hindsight that is all too easy, Eckenstein would have been wise to change his objectives. Skyang Kangri (or Staircase Peak) might just have been within their abilities to climb. At 24,750 feet 7,544 m, it would have been a truly remarkable ascent for its time—a height record that would stand for many years. But it is easy to see that at this very early stage of Himalayan climbing almost every decision was made in ignorance of scale, technical difficulty and, above all, altitude. Here lack of knowledge was almost total. No one knew whether it was possible to live for any length of time above 6,000 metres, and the mechanics of acclimatisation were a closed book. Even so, Crowley, by luck or good judgement (or Satanic intervention?), stumbled upon an important insight when he asserted that the only way of getting up the really high mountains was to "lay in a stock of energy, get rid of all your fat at the exact moment when you have a chance to climb a mountain, and jump back out of its reach, so to speak, before it can take its revenge." This is an almost exact description of the alpine-style tactics developed and promulgated seventy years later by Reinhold Messner and others, but occasionally demonstrated earlier, notably by Tom Longstaff's ascent of Trisul 7,120, when he climbed the last 2,000 meters in just ten hours. Crowley, never losing a chance to criticize the Alpine Club, later poured scorn on the siege mentality of acclimatization shown in the early Everest expeditions.

Eckenstein's decision to attempt the North-East Ridge was a strange one. It is a very long and complex and quite obviously difficult. Presumably he chose it because it looked to be at an easier angle than the South-East Spur, and possibly because he thought it might prove to be safer. But the classic view from Windy Gap shows an interminable knife-edged ridge leading the featureless upper slopes of the mountain and a final steepening in the summit cone. The ridge was not to succumb until 1978 when it was climbed by a very strong American expedition who nevertheless took over two months to reach the summit. In 1902 Eckenstein's little team didn't stand a chance.

At first Pfannl and Wesseley made some progress and reached a high of around 21,000 feet 6,400 m. Then Pfannl fell ill and protracted rescue had to be undertaken, Crowley almost casually explaining that Pfannl had oedema of both lungs and had to be taken. Both high-altitude pulmonary and cerebral oedema have only comparatively recently begun to be understood and remedies developed to counteract their potentially fatal results. Amazingly Crowley appeared to know and understand the problem years before it was accepted that the illness wasn't simply pneumonia. Even the deaths on K2 in 1954 of the Italian Mario Puchoz, and on Masherbrum in 1957 of Bob Downes, were both misdiagnosed as pneumonia.

Pfannl's illness and complicated evacuation to Urdokas effectively put an end to any concerted attempt on the mountain. Both Eckenstein and Crowley fell ill, Crowley with a bout of malaria and, semi-delirious, he threatened Guy Knowles with a revolver. Knowles disarmed him with a blow to the stomach. Returning to Urdokas they found Pfannl much recovered. Wesseley had earlier irritated Crowley with his eating habits.

In order to eat he would bend his head over his plate, and, using his knife and fork like the blades of a paddle wheel, would churn the food into his mouth with a rapid rotatory motion. There was always some going up and some going down...It was the most disgusting sight I have ever seen...I admit my human weakness. All forms of genius should be admired and studied and Wesseley was a world champion.

Now they found Wesseley had "stolen" the bulk of the emergency rations. He was expelled from the expedition and Pfannl went with him.

And so for the first but certainly not the last time, a K2 expedition ended in disarray and petty feuding, a circumstance not unique in the annals of Himalayan climbing, but there does seem to be something in the very remoteness and savagery of K2 and its surroundings that undermines the unity of so many expeditions. The relentless strain of just living there is much greater than, for example, the Everest Base Camp, which has easy access to civilization in the form of tea houses, villages, and varied company.

Eckenstein's expedition was studiously ignored by the British establishment and there is no mention of it in the *Alpine Journal* of the time. Younghusband, whose book *Epic of Mount Everest* starts with a brief resume of Himalayan exploration in general only mentions that, "The Swiss, Fr. Jacot-Buillarmod, explored in the same region," which is not even damning with faint praise!

Given the results of the 1902 expedition it is almost unbelievable that any two members of it should ever contemplate another joint project, but in 1905 Crowley and Guillarmod teamed up for an attempt on Kangchenjunga. Eckenstein and Knowles wisely declined to accompany them and the expedition ended disastrously with the death of a Swiss climber, Alexis Pache, and three porters. Crowley was not directly involved but his behaviour throughout the expedition and particularly after the accident was irresponsible and callous in the extreme. Crowley was emphatically disowned by the Alpine Club who pointed out in the *Alpine Journal of 1906* that Crowley had never had any connection with the Club. From then on Crowley lost interest in climbing, and his life degenerated into the self-indulgent, self-deluding shambles that lasted until his death in 1947.

But it is hard not to feel sorry for Eckenstein. Two visits to the Karakoram had both ended in disappointment and though he doubtless didn't help his own cause by his own attitude, he must have felt he deserved a lot more credit, both for his explorations of K2 and his undoubted contribution to the techniques of climbing. Eckenstein died in 1921 a rather isolated eccentric. The man whom Longstaff described as a "rough diamond" would doubtless be amazed to see, seventy years later, the technical revolution of ice climbing with short, dropped head axes, rigid clip-on crampons, and plastic boots. Had he been born one hundred years later, he might have made a fortune designing, manufacturing and marketing his inventions.

Jim Curran

Greg Child (b. 1955) was born in Australia but resides in the United States. He is recognized as one of the world's best all around mountaineers. He is equally at home on extreme rock, ice, or climbing Himalayan giants. He is also a very accomplished writer and has written for a number of major magazines. His books include *Thin Air, Climbing: The Complete Reference*, and *Post Cards from the Ledge, Climbing Free, Over the Edge* and *Mixed Emotions*. He is the recipient of the American Alpine Club Literary Award.

GREG CHILD:
BALTORO!

Cr-a-a-a-ck! The shock wave surges through the ice, passing underfoot, announcing its release with a sharp snap a hundred yards down the Baltoro Glacier. With a sudden jolt, several million tons of ice and boulders creep an inch down the valley. Melon-sized rocks tumble from sun-sculpted pedestals of ice. They clatter about our feet and splash into water-filled crevasses. Hussein, the old Balti porter, carrying my load clucks his tongue in mimicry of the glacial chatter, beams his toothless smile at me, then shuffles on his way. I follow his steps, hopping from stone to shifting stone, marching ever deeper into the Karakoram Range of Northern Pakistan. A few minutes later, puffing in the rarified 14,000-foot air, I pause to rest beside a glacial pond. All around tower ice-clad peaks. Ahead, scudding clouds alternately obscure and reveal the sun, dappling the turbulent terrain with light and shadow, animating the rock-strewn pressure ridges into a pitching chiaroscuro sea. This world appears utterly lifeless till a bumblebee buzzes around me before departing into the emptiness ahead.

Rasul, the Balti cook, joins me. He points to a herd of ibex traversing the yellow cliffs of the Trango Towers beside us. With awakening senses, I notice tiny yellow and lilac flowers springing up at our feet. Looking more closely at the pond, I see that it too is alive, bustling with the frenetic movements of minute ground spiders and wriggling larvae rising to the sun-warmed surface.

This life on the glacier amazes me. Tonight, the pond will freeze solid. But somehow the larvae will survive, and, somewhere, the bumblebee will find another outpost of flowers, pollinate them, and help sustain a meadow that may germinate in time to fatten the roaming ibex. Above the glacier, though, near the summits that thrust into the jet stream, it is still a lifeless world. The solitude broken only when winds from the baking plains of the Punjab blow insects onto the snows, and when humans plod toward a frozen summit.

Suddenly, the sound of a Pakistan Army helicopter rends the air. Our caravan of porters halt to watch the barrel of a small howitzer swaying on a cable beneath the chopper. In a few days the gun will be lobbing shells onto Indian positions on the Siachen Glacier. Spooked by the din of whipping rotors, the ibex scatter. They would do well to learn even more fear of man.

This is the Baltoro Glacier.

Four expeditions, encompassing some two hundred days on this thirty-five mile river of ice, have left me with a strange affinity for this difficult tract of land and its people. One doesn't easily fall in love with Pakistan or the Baltoro, as one might with part of Nepal. If the words "lush" and "green" describe the Nepalese mountainscape, the Baltoro equivalents are "barren" and "ocher." No, an affinity for the Baltoro is an acquired taste.

The Baltoro's is a harsh environment. Once you leave the last little village on the approach up the Braldu River Valley, little grows that's worthy of being called a tree, save, perhaps, a few gnarled junipers clutching at the sandy hillsides. On the Baltoro, sub-zero blizzards can rage a week; the next day clear skies and scorching temperatures might melt the snowpack, etching sudden streams into the glacial surface. Mountains with mysterious names fringe the skyline, their 10,000-foot faces roaring with avalanches that billow across the. three-kilometer-wide glacier. The Baltoro patiently, relentlessly removes the debris like a natural conveyor belt.

Long before I ever dreamed I would visit this place, I read of the early expeditions that made the long walk here. Books like K2, The Savage Mountain, by Houston and Bates, and Karakoram, by Fosco Mariani, described an area so rugged it was barely known by the Pakistani government. Even the local Balti people, hired to carry supplies into the glacial wastes, feared entering its deeper corridors. These places loomed large in my imagination, places like Bardumal, the wind-swept plain whose name means "troublesome place;" Rdokas, the fairy-tale meadow; and Concordia, at the intersection of two great glaciers and humbled beneath towers K2, Broad Peak, and Gasherbrum IV. When an expedition to climb Lobsang Spire and Broad Peak finally, unexpectedly, delivered me to the Baltoro in 1983, I found a land no less fantastic than that described by the early expeditioners.

Something about this small spot on the map of Asia has fascinated Westerners for more than a century. Perhaps the fuss began in 1856 when Captain Montgomerie of the British Survey of India sighted his transit on the highest of the Baltoro peaks—K2, he named it—and declared to his Indian assistant, "Babu, we have shot the giant." From one hundred and twenty-eight miles away, Montgomerie: had triangulated K2 (K for Karakoram, 2 being second in his list of readings), the summit second in height to Everest by only a few lengths of a climber's rope, but as climbers would find in later years, a summit far more difficult to reach than Everest's. For the rest of the: century, a handful of explorers would try to penetrate: that distant cluster of massive peaks.

One of those explorers, Francis Younghusband, using his Balti guide Wali's unwound turban as a makeshift climbing rope, crested the icy 17,800-foot pass at the Baltoro's source. In so doing, Younghusband became the first Englishman to link the known world to the Baltoro Glacier and the still-medieval villages below: Askole, Chakpo, and Chongo. That was scarcely more than one hundred years ago.

Atop the Mustagh Pass, Younghusband, a Kiplingesque political agent of the British Raj of India-gazed over the jagged peaks of Masherbrum, the Gasherbrums, and K2. He was no stranger to Himalayan mountains, but the startling symmetry of the Baltoro skyline struck him in the same way that it would captivate subsequent generations of alpinists. So spectacular is the layout of the Baltoro that an element of design seems to be at work.

At first appearance, it seems little about the Baltoro experience or landscape has changed since Younghusband's travels in 1887. Yet today's Baltoro is no longer a solitary experience. With Pakistans embracing of tourism of the 1980s, the Baltoro became Pakistan's version of Nepal's popular Everest trek. Lured by the talismans of adventure and high altitude, trekkers today tour the valleys and villages, and climbers flock to the challenge of K2 and its massive neighbors.

But the booming tourist trade has overnight propelled the tribal people into the 20th Century. The sudden influx of visitors is squeezing the land

and its wildlife. An undeclared war between India and Pakistan—known as the Siachen Conflict—ravages the mountainous border just a few miles from the trekking routes. With the dawning of the 1990s, the Baltoro stands on the verge of great change.

In Younghusband's day, maps of the Himalayas were filled with blank spots. But few were blanker than this branch of the Karakoram. The nation of Pakistan didn't even exist; it was still part of Indian Kashmir, divided into numerous, often warring, tribal regions. Of these quarrelsome tribesmen, the front liners of the Raj though they are no less reliable a band of brigands, yet conversely no more loyal breed of man, than the Balti from the valleys around Askole and Skardu, where modern Baltoro treks begin.

Early explorers told tales of treachery, strikes, and desertion among Balti porters. The rugged terrain was difficult enough, but its inhabitants could make it hell. Today's Balti remain a tough, feisty bunch, molded by lifelong struggles with the seasons in an unyielding land, and by centuries of conquest by Buddhist Ladakh, Hindu India, perhaps even by the Greeks under Alexander and most recently, by conquering Kashmiri Muslims who converted the region to Islam several hundred years ago. The Balti are poor farmers, traditionally illiterate, since they have no written language. Their origins are vague, though their spoken language-an archaic Tibetan dialect-points to a Tibetan ancestry.

For Younghusband's trouble of crossing the Mustagh Pass into Askole, the explorer was run out of the valley. Villagers were enraged that a foreigner had discovered the secret of their isolation, for the trade routes to Ladakh and Hunza that converged on the Baltoro Glacier were closely guarded secrets. Today, the great-grandchildren of those villagers are the porters, cooks, guides, jeep drivers, shopkeepers, and hotel clerks who vie for the business of trekkers and mountaineers visiting Baltistan.

As progress creeps up their valley, this once reclusive people have become the measuring-sticks of change. In 1989, when I last entered the cobbled street of Askole, it seemed that half the village turned out to sell their wares. Women, working the wheat fields, have already halted us on the edge of town, shouting "Hello! Hello!" and waving jewelry and embroidered caps made from homespun cloth.

Just a few years before, village women had veiled their faces and fled at the sight of us; now they were driving hard bargains. I looked over a few of the trinkets. The caps were decorated with found objects, like zippers, battery caps, heads, and old coins. Among the jewelry—mostly composed of plastic beads—were a few bits of coral, turquoise, and Xi stones, all common in the Sherpa valleys of Nepal. The stones attested to a bygone trading era between Ladakh and the Braldu Valley, an era that only the grandparents of these Balti women would recall.

As I wondered if they would regret selling their family heirlooms, a young boy held up an empty shotgun shell. From it, he removed the biggest, fattest grasshopper I'd ever seen. "One rupee?" he asked, having learned from experience that foreigners are likely to buy anything.

In the village came the men's turn to market with us. In the house of Haji Medi, Askole's mayor, we drank tea and negotiated the price of a goat for our porters to eat. Haji spoke of the improvements to Askole since my last visit—a medical clinic across the river, a resident schoolteacher—and of future plans, a radio for emergencies, and, of course, the road, moving up the Braldu Valley only slightly faster than the glacier moves down.

"But do you think the road will really come this far?" I asked skeptically, thinking of the unstable gorge and the landslides that frequently erase the centuries-old path.

"Yes," Haji insisted, and to prove his point he took me into another room, where he proudly displayed an incongruous item for this village where yaks still plow the fields with wooden plowshares: a brand-new mountain bike.

"When the road comes," explained Haji, "I can ride to Skardu."

Sometime in the future, an archeological report on the approach to the Baltoro might read something like this: "The boulder-strewn valleys between Skardu and the Baltoro Glacier are littered with the rock peckings of Baltistan's earliest visitors. Chipping through the desert varnish covering the boulders, artists pre-dating the birth of Christ and through the second millennium A.D. left symbols of their daily lives: hunting scenes, Buddhist Stupas, Shivaite tridents, Chinese characters. By the mid-to-latter half of the 20th century, a different range of relics appears: the sardine tin, the empty stove-gas canister, the worn out plastic boots. These artifacts abound along the glacier and the summits of 8,000-meter peaks. The wheeled period began about 1987 A.D., with the first penetration of the glacier by a Swiss expedition on mountain bikes. Bicycle spokes and brake-grips from this period have been discovered near the Dunge Glacier, while automobile relics are common along the road to Askole."

Explorers of the 19th Century faced a months-long overland journey through India to Baltistan's capital, Skardu. From there, they could finally set out on foot for the Baltoro. Even by the 1950s, when aircraft delivered expeditions to Skardu, the walk to K2 took eighteen days and involved river crossings by rope bridge and zahk-rafts made from inflated goat-bellies. By the 1980s, bridges and jeep roads halved that time. By the mid-1990s, at least according to plan, the dangerous Braldu Gorge, once Askole's best defense against invasion, will be tamed by jackhammer and blasting powder, so expeditions can drive straight to Askole.

The people there eagerly await the road and the prosperity expected to follow in its wake. Villagers who have been to Skardu and have seen its thriving bazaar, its hospital, and the luxuries of electricity-lights, appliances, and, if they've peeked into the K2 Hotel, television-know how a road can change a village. They know that the jeep drivers and hotel and teahouse owners who cater to tourists are wealthy men.

Until the road's approach two years ago, the Balti shunned Western culture, in marked contrast to the mimicry of Western tastes that runs rampant in Nepal. Disinclined to embrace outside influences, and too poor to afford modern luxuries, places like Askole remained time capsules of a medieval lifestyle. The Balti sluggishness to cash in on the tourist trade stemmed largely from disdain for things foreign. The Balti, devout Muslims, had their Koranic sensibilities so shocked by Western brash behavior and dress that villagers were always relieved when foreigners left town. But now Haji Medi has given up politely asking trekkers passing through Askole to wear trousers rather than immodest shorts. These examples may seem small, but they forecast changes of glacial impact. Progress offers the Balti solutions to many problems. Health care will reduce the high infant mortality rate, and ensure that simple ills don't become life-threatening. Winters, when Askole is snowed in, need no longer be desperate and hungry, as jeeploads of food and kerosene can be easily stockpiled. But progress will also dilute their ancient culture. "Young men don't know the old songs anymore," our cook Rasul lamented one day, "They listen to radio instead."

Yet Askole is just one stop on this road of change; the real reason the highway is being built is to allow the Pakistani military better access to the strategic passes at the head of the Baltoro Glacier. The Siachen Conflict is the highest war in history. Though both sides keep their own casualty counts classified, they admit that as many soldiers have fallen to altitude maladies and Karakoram storms as have to bullets. Since 1984, the Baltoro experience includes army camps, daily helicopter sorties, and the distant thunder of artillery strikes.

The conflict erupted when Indian forces established bases on the vast Siachen Glacier, adjacent to the Baltoro, and placed outposts on several passes straddling the two glacier systems. The border hereabouts is vague, with both nations claiming the region. Pakistan sent troops to remove the intruders, but the Indians held fast to their high ground. Both armies dug in for a long siege under tortuous conditions.

It's a war where the skin on a soldier's finger freezes to his rifle trigger, and where long stays at 20,000 feet sap the strength and sanity of even the most disciplined trooper. Storms that ground helicopter or porter-support leave outposts starving. Opposing dugouts are sometimes separated by only a few hundred yards. Snipers fire on anything that moves. Artillery rounds often fail to explode on impact in soft snow, so fuses detonate the shells in mid-air, scattering a dead line rain of shrapnel. Assaults on foot at 20,000 feet degenerate into desperate uphill trudges where the gasping attackers make easy targets. Occasionally, mountain passes change hands, but usually who ever holds the high ground maintains. Trench warfare at its worst.

All this bloodshed over control of a few empty ice fields seems curious, until you look at the conflict's roots. Problems on the populous plains used to keep Indian and Pakistan preoccupied. At that time, neither cared much about shared borders in the fastness of the Karakoram, where boundaries ran along unreachable mountain ridgecrests and glacial valleys. Then Pakistan split from India in 1947, and fought again in 1965 and 1971 for control of areas along the length of their borders. In the end, the cease-fire lines drawn in the north left many Moslem-settled parts of Kashmir under Indian (Hindu) control. Meanwhile, Pakistan claimed valleys opening onto Indian territory.

Efforts to resolve boundary claims proved fruitless. Maps of the north drawn during the British rule of India were full of uncertainties. Entire areas were left unsurveyed; maps of some northern areas simply received a wash of color and the terse notation "undetermined."

Indian Army mountaineering expeditions ventured into the Siachen region for years before the current conflict erupted; they found no one to counter them. When Pakistan did finally challenge the Indians, neither side envisioned the long, costly war that would follow. But neither side will relinquish their claim over an inch of land, not even uninhabitable ice and snow. If any issue might close the Baltoro to tourism, as happened during previous wars with India, it is this struggle.

The road, the war, the tourists; sounds of jackhammers, smoke on the horizon, trash on the trail: Intrusions, yes, but I wonder just how much the Baltoro's stubborn spirit of wildness has really diminished. I suppose each of my Baltoro visits has attempted to find again that ephemeral state of being I've encountered when luck and weather have allowed me to reach high on a mountain. The very things that make high altitude climbing so dangerous, oxygen deprivation, and the short circuiting of body chemistry, also heighten your awareness of the mountain world and your place in it.

I remember scratching out a snowcave with two companions at 26,000 feet on Gasherbrum IV in 1986. Night was approaching, the temperature plummeting. The concept of surviving a bitter bivouac wearing nothing but the clothes on our backs seemed tenuous at best; the very thought released a switchblade of adrenalin inside me, and spurred feverish digging. Catching my breath between pawing handfuls of snow from our shelter, I looked down on the Baltoro. Alpenglow spilled over the west face of our mountain, setting our snowfield alight; a sudden calm settled in.

Here we stood, at the apex of all symmetries, or so it seemed. Eleven thousand feet below at Concordia, the glacier forked in a perfect "Y." Parallel lines of rubble ribbed the glacier's length, and waves of ice-blue mountains paralleled its flow. Distant monsoon thunderheads loomed over Indian Kashmir, but the Karakoram sky remained cloudless, divided into starpocked bands of cobalt and pink. To one side of me hung the ascending moon, to the other the setting sun.

The Chaos of colliding tectonic plates suddenly assumed a perfection of proportions. The mountains, I realized as never from below, defined the glacier, while the glacier, whittling away at the mountains, defined the architecture of the range. Radiating from this, all aspects of the mountainscape marched upward in equilibrium. So exact did this balance appear, it seemed there was neither one grain of sand too few nor one too many.

As expected, the bivouac was frigid. But we summited the next morning, and a week later I was back on the Baltoro Glacier, stumbling over scree, with only the recollection of those thoughts and sights from the mountain. As we hiked home, we caught up with a commercial trek, sharing the trail with them, enjoying their friendly company.

Greg Child

When the trekkers heard we were low on provisions after two months on the Baltoro, they generously shared their excellent imported food. I complimented the cooking, and they told me I'd missed the best of the eating, as they'd dined on ibex the previous week. "Delicious, if you know how to cook it," someone said. At first I thought they were joking, but then they informed me that their guide had shot an ibex for them on the meadow above the campsite called Lillego.

"Don't you know that all wildlife is protected here?" I asked one of them later, mentioning the sign by the bridge at Dassu proclaiming that very fact.

"I don't recall any sign. Anyway, the fellow wanted to shoot it as a gift for us. I didn't want to offend him by refusing," replied the trekker.

Speechless before the fundamental ignorance of his answer, I realized that the sight of an ibex and the paw print of the snow leopard, always present but so elusive as to be invisible, would soon be a thing of the past. I tried to fathom the mindset that would take such encounters and turn them into trophy hunts. One could argue that the villagers are entitled to take a few ibex during the year, as they are the real owners of the land; but for foreign trekkers to deplete the herds is inexcusable.

Growing human pressure is upsetting the natural balance on the Baltoro. When I first set foot on the glacier in 1983, I shared it with fourteen climbing expeditions and a handful of trekkers. On my next visit in 1986, nine expeditions were camped at the foot of K2 alone, while sixteen other climbing expeditions and a seemingly endless stream of trekkers dotted the Baltoro's length. Every year, the barren hillsides get scoured ever cleaner for firewood, while rubbish piles up in campsites, and wayside stops like Paiju have become giant, open-air latrines.

Though slightly bruised, the Baltoro still reigns magnificent. A full-blown Karakoram storm or the white chaos of an avalanche reminds us that nature still controls here; man's visitations are temporary stains easily buried in the ice. The threat isn't so much what we leave, as what we take away.

The Gasherbrum trek over, I re-enter civilization just in time for the video night in Skardu. In the lounge of the K2 Hotel, German, English, and American trekkers, freshly returned from or about to embark on forays into the Karakoram, gather around a television. They are watching an incredibly bad, American-made sci-fi flick.

Through the window beside the TV, I glimpse the waxing moon surmount the hills that flank Skardu and channel the mighty rivers that roar out of the Karakoram. Suddenly, below the hotel, the sprawling delta of the Shigar and Indus Rivers lights up bright as a pool of mercury. It's a beautiful last look at the Karakoram before I jet out on the morning flight. But somehow my eyes can't leave the trash on the television. All too soon, it seems I've re-entered the global village. My two months of wandering and climbing on the Baltoro Glacier suddenly seem distant.

Conversation among a group of trekkers catches my ear. A woman, just returned from the mountains, laments that the Balti will never be the same after the road is built. Isolation, she argues, has preserved them from the corruption that has turned Nepal into a land of rupee-sharks; progress will do the Balti no good. She would, it seems, prefer they remain pickled by poverty, culturally embalmed exhibits in a private museum. I wonder if she'd be so keen on living life without a doctor or raising her own children in a dirt-floored hut.

She looks to me for support; "If the road reaches Askole, will you help me blow it up?"

The trekker, so well-intentioned yet so naive with her fantasy of third World monkey wrenching; the Balti of the Braldu Valley, so eager for the good life: These people epitomize the double-reflection of the romantics and the aspirants, those who look back and those who look forward in history. She may envy the simplicity of a Balti way of life, but not as much as the Balti envy our prosperity. What the Balti dream, we live, and what the Balti live, we dream.

Arlene Blum (b.1945), has participated in more than twenty successful mountaineering expeditions, including climbs of Mt. Everest and Mt. McKinley. She led the first American and all women's climb of Annapurna, the world's tenth highest peak, as well as completed a 2,000 mile trek across the Himalayan regions of Bhutan, Nepal and India. She is the author of *Annapurna: A Woman's Place*, *Breaking Trail: A Climbing Life* and was awarded Gold Medal from the Society of Women Geographers.

ARLENE BLUM: THE MEMORIAL

The time had come to take down the colorful tents at Camp II that had sheltered us over these past weeks. Was it only weeks? it seemed as if we had lived up here for a very long time. Christy and I packed up huge loads—at least 70 pounds—and stumbled down the glacier in the hot sun. Now that the climb was over, the air was calm and the mountain looked sunny and benign. I could not help glancing up from time to time to the serac near Camp IV where I knew Alison and Vera were.

When we reached Camp I, we looked at the face through a 500-millimeter lens and could unmistakably see the red of Alison's jacket. This clear sight hit me hard, and I sat down heavily on a rock, full of grief. The Sherpas believe in reincarnation and have had much experience with death in the mountains, but they, too, were severely shaken by the tragedy. Lopsang sat near me, looking at the serac with binoculars and shaking his head. Then he came over, patted me on the shoulder and said, "Let them go. You have to let them go."

The mist came up from the Miristi Khola as we packed up what was left of Camp I and began to walk down toward Base Camp for the last time. Each step into the gray, muffling fog took us farther from Annapurna, from Vera and Alison. Each step brought us closer to the reality that they were not coming with us. Occasionally I felt waves of elation that we had actually succeeded, had reached the top of Annapurna, but mostly I was filled with despair. We stumbled through the moraine rocks and for the last time labored up the steep, rocky slope leading to the first grass. The green grass and the tiny flowers made me feel like crying, and I lay down in the meadow to rest. The slender grass blades were like velvet on my skin after all these weeks of ice and snow.

Down at Base, our friends gathered around, and tears ran down my face as I hugged Margi, Christy, and Irene. Margi, hobbling around in huge ensolite booties to protect her tender feet, tried to cheer me up.

"You did a good job, Arlene," she said. "You did a great job. Don't worry."

"You couldn't have done anything any differently."

I was greatful to her—truly, I felt close to all of these women. During the last months we had experienced so much together. Our hearts were full now, but there was very little to say.

"Have a bath," Irene suggested practically. "The one I had yesterday was wonderful. And the food down here is pretty good."

The bath was wonderful. Now that it was fall, the air was chill and the stream was smaller, as the glaciers that fed it were no longer melting. There was neither enough water to get totally immersed nor any desire to do so. I sat next to the stream, washing myself bit by bit; it was almost a surprise to see my body emerge from the layers of down, sweat, and salt that had encased it.

The porters Lopsang had sent for arrived from Choya to carry our gear down, and I dressed hurriedly. It would still take an enormous amount of organization and hard work to get us and our gear back to Kathmandu. I was grateful now for the need to make lists; it was much better to keep busy than to think about what had happened. I went through the motions of dealing with the porters and Sherpas and making our plans like an automaton.

Throughout the day the rest of the team members and Sherpas straggled down to Base Camp with enormous packs. Piro arrived with her finger still heavily bandaged, but she was confident it would heal and that she could continue to perform surgery. What an enormous difference such a small thing as a tear in a glove can make. Had it not been for that small hole, Piro would certainly have made the summit.

Joan came down last, after thoroughly cleaning up the Camp I site. I told her how much I appreciated her hard work for the expedition even though she had not been able to climb high; she responded by praising the job I had done leading the climb, saying she could not have done so well herself.

Soon the team was together again at Base Camp. Looking up at the remote summit, it was hard to believe that any of us had ever stood there, even harder to comprehend the great loss that accompanied our achievement. But we had gained something more than the summit. The years of planning and the months of climbing together had changed and strengthened us. We had survived the hardest physical and psychological stresses and found that as a team we could do great things. Each woman had contributed her abilities and effort in full measure, and each was rewarded with the knowledge that her contribution had helped us attain our goal. In addition, we had gained the friendship and warmth that now united us. The long-standing conflict between Joan and me had been amicably resolved, and no other lasting antagonisms had developed during the past stress-filled months. For me, this was as important as having reached the summit.

That evening I wrote letters to Alison's parents and husband, to Vera'a husband and friends, and to Liz, whose skills had so aided the climb and who cared so much about all of us. I wrote them the factual details of the last days and tried to find words of comfort, which always ended up sounding like platitudes: "She died doing what she loved best. . . Annapurna is a fitting place for them to rest. . . It was a quick and painless death." The words brought little comfort to me as I wrote them, and I doubted whether they would help Vera's and Alison's families and friends. But what else could I write? That they should be here with us still-that it wasn't fair the mountain had extracted so terrible a price?

Vera and Alison, like all high-altitude climbers, had taken risks in the mountains before. Vera had told us many stories of her solo climb of Aconcagua: of severe storms, hallucinations, the horror of finding a boot with a human leg bone in it. Still she had persevered, climbing all the way to the top and back down by herself. And Alison, while climbing Noshaq in 1972, had been part of a team that elected to continue onto the top in the late afternoon, even though they knew that the descent would be hazardous in the dark. Coming down, Alison lost her crampon, fell, and stopped herself just in time above a cliff. But this time neither she nor Vera had been so fortunate.

As I struggled with those letters, I heard the sounds of the Sherpas dancing and singing around the campfire near the kitchen. The other members were gathered around the fire watching them dance, but I stayed in the mess tent, feeling close to Vera and Alison and the people who loved them.

Early the next morning I walked over to the stone on which are engraved the names of seven other climbers who died on this side of Annapurna. Marie had lettered Vera's and Alison's names on a blank side of the rock facing the mountain. The sun had not risen, and the morning was chill as I began to chip out the letters on the stone, using a hammer and screwdriver. Their names in the rock would stay here forever, looking toward the summit they had so hoped to reach.

October 17, 1978
Vera Watson
Alison Chadwick

Suddenly I heard a clattering noise in the distance. "A helicopter," some one yelled.

"It must be Marquita!" I exclaimed. Marquita Maytag had been a friend since my 1976 trip to Everest, when she was the American ambassador to Nepal. She had told me that if we reached the summit of Annapurna, she would come to Base Camp to congratulate us, and apparently she was keeping her word.

As the helicopter approached, everyone rushed around the camp to secure things against the downblast from its rotors. The porters, many of whom had never seen a helicopter before, were astounded at this creature from the sky. Even we were shocked at this sudden apparition from the mechanized world after our months of isolation.

Marquita got out and formally congratulated us. "What a wonderful thing you have done for yourselves and for the women of the world."

I introduced her to the team. She looked around and asked, "Is this everyone?"

"No," I said. "The second summit team did not come back."

"What!"

"Vera Watson and Alison Chadwick fell to their deaths while making their summit attempt."

"Oh, no!" Marquita's face crumpled. "I can't believe it. How horrible."

I tried to comfort her. She had to face all at once the terrible fact that we had lived with for the last three days.

Arlene Blume

"Is there anything I can do? Should I get more Sherpas by helicopter to bring down the bodies?" She asked.

"No. It's no use. The bodies couldn't be brought down without risking many lives. Thank you, Marquita, but there's nothing anyone can do."

"What happened?"

"They fell a thousand feet from just below Camp V. Either one of them slipped, or they were swept down by a small avalanche or rockfall. The sherpas said the bodies were separated. If either had been alive, she would probably have gone over to the other, so they were presumably dead when they landed."

Marquita is a strong woman. She composed herself and went on with her congratulations, if somewhat mechanically.

She had brought us fried chicken, sandwiches, a case of California wine, and best of all, our mail. As we sat in the warm sun, reading our letters and feasting on the first fresh food and wine we had tasted in weeks, Marquita told us the welcome news that Wanda Rutkiewicz had just climbed to the top of Everest, making the summit in one eight-hour push all the way from the South Col—a remarkable achievement. Alison would have been happy to hear that.

During the course of the day we all took turns chipping the letters of Vera's and Alison's names in the memorial stone. We had planned to hold a memorial service that afternoon, but kept putting it off, fearing the finality of it. At last, when it was almost dark and the summit shrouded in fog, we could wait no longer; we would be breaking camp early the next day. We walked over to the rock in the somber twilight and stood there silently. Our minds and hearts were filled with thoughts of Vera and Alison, but we could not say anything.

Finally Christy started the service. "We are gathered to pay tribute to Vera and Alison, our dear friends. Does anyone have a memento of them to leave here?"

Christy held out a box that contained photos and mementos of the other climbers who had died on Annapurna. It had been placed in a hollow on top of the memorial stone. We added pictures of Vera and Alison, a rock from the summit of Annapurna, and I left a prayer scarf that had been given me by a monk from the monastery at Thyangboche. I had worn it on Everest to protect me from avalanches.

The Memorial

"I hope this will help keep their souls safe here on Annapurna," I murmured. Then Christy put the box back on the stone, and we piled heavy rocks on top of the monument to rebury the box.

"I miss Vera and Alison so much," Christy said. "I miss Vera's warmth and enthusiasm and how much she cared about all of us and this climb."

"Without Vera's drive from the beginning, we would have given up and never gotten approval for the expedition," I said. "When things looked bad, Vera Watson persevered, and so we were able to come here."

"I miss Alison's concern and her integrity and her idealism," Marie said. "She really believed in women's climbing and what women could attain."

We all locked arms and sang the Quaker song, "Tis the gift to be simple, 'tis the gift to be free, 'tis the gift to come down where we ought to be. . ." Then the Sherpas began to chant, "Om mani padme hum, om mani padme hum. . . The jewel is in the lotus, the spirit of humanity is in the universe"—the spirits of Vera and Alison stay with Annapurna. Members and Sherpas chanted together with arms linked.

The mountain did not reappear as we trooped back in the heavy fog to dinner. After dinner everyone went over to the campfire to dance and be together on our last night. I looked around at the faces, golden in the flickering light, thinking about what we had all shared and wondering what effects this experience would have on our lives.

Annie and Yeshi were sitting comfortably with their arms around each other. Annie would be staying in Nepal for a month, and the two planned to go trekking. Joan, Margi, and Vera K. also had plans to stay and trek in Nepal. Watching Vera K. dancing energetically with the Sherpas, you could not tell she had just climbed a high mountain. She looked strong and full of enthusiasm indeed, she was already thinking of organizing an expedition to climb Dhaulagiri. Christy would be going out early the next morning with Marquita's helicopter to telephone the tragic news to Vera's and Alison's families and friends.

The isolation and sensory deprivation that we had lived with so long was ending. As we descended the next day, we would first encounter shrubs, then trees, finally forests. We would see animals and meet local people. Only too soon our tight group—united by both our shared victory and our shared sorrow—would be intruded upon by the tourists from all over the world who trek up the Kali Gandaki in November. Then we would meet our friends and the press back in Kathmandu. Finally, we would all separate and try to resume our normal lives. But for the moment we simply relaxed and watched the Sherpas dancing.

When I had crossed the avalanche slope for the last time, I felt myself on a distinct edge: on one side was the abyss of falling snow, burial, death; on the other side was life and a renewed appreciation of its value. Those weeks spent under the threat of imminent death-followed by the loss of Vera and Alison had taught us to see the important things, to focus on essentials. We had risked our lives, and our reward was in part a reaffirmation of life.

The next morning we had to clean up the camp and burn the garbage. We made a huge bonfire of all the boxes. A kind of madness seized the Sherpas and porters, and they began throwing things helter-skelter into the fire. Aerosol cans exploded, bottles broke, even leftover food was thrown in. It was an amazing scene in a country where every conceivably useful item is valued and saved. Perhaps this frenzy of burning was some sort of exorcism. I watched with a fascination that verged on horror.

When everyone else had left, I went and sat by the memorial stone a last time. I touched Vera's and Alison's names and tried to focus on the happier times of the last months. I remembered Vera playing with the puppy on the trek, Alison's and Liz's delight when they established Camp I, the joy of the summit, the ethereal beauty of this world of rock, ice, and snow. And then I thought of the migrating geese, which had been flying back and forth between Tibet and India since before the Himalaya had been uplifted and would continue to do so long after we were all forgotten.

I stood up. My feet moved automatically, step by step, carrying me away from Annapurna.

An excerpt from the final entry in Annie Whitehouse's diary reads:

Flying back home over a blanket of clouds, the sun setting behind us leaving a rim of colors: pink, orange, yellow, fading into the deep blue sky. The expedition is over, and my life in Nepal is turning to memories. . . The end of my climbing with my dear companion, Vera Watson, but she will live forever in my mind. The end of my life as it was, as a result of my commitment to Yeshi . . . The clouds along the horizon have erupted into brilliant orange. It is good to know that every end is also a beginning. The end of this long day is the first flickering light of a star. One by one, the stars will show their light, glow brightly, then fade into the light of the rising sun.

There have been other endings and beginnings for the Annapurna team members since our return from Nepal. One February 16, 1980, Joan Firey died in Seattle, Washington, of a rare bone marrow disease. In her last months, she continued to inspire those who knew her with her courage, vitality, and warmth. We all will miss her.

For the rest of the Annapurna team the future holds plans for more climbs. In fall, 1980, Vera Komarkova will lead a women's team up "The Pear" on Dhaulagiri I, a technically demanding route that has been attempted many times but never successfully climbed. Alison would have been delighted.

Liz Klobusicky continues to do hard climbs in Europe with her husband, Nicko. Annie Whitehouse has a permit for 1982 to climb Ama Dablam in Nepal, which she and many others regard as the most beautiful mountain in the world. That team includes Vera K., Piro, and Annie's husband, Yeshi Tenzing (they were married in Wyoming in 1979). Both Annie and Margi Rusmore have been invited to go on a proposed expedition to Tibet in 1981.

Irene Miller (now going by her maiden name, Beardsley) and her daughter Teresa will trek together in Nepal during the summer of 1980. At about the same time, I will be leading a small Indian-American women's expedition to Brigupanth, a beautiful, unclimbed 22,000-foot ice peak on the Gangotri Glacier in the Indian Himalaya. Piro and Christy will be on the team, as will several young women who I hope will be able to use this experience to organize their own expeditions in the future.

Change is coming slowly, however. Besides the climbs just mentioned, very few women are included in the dozens of other expeditions approved by the AAC for the next few years.

We have established a memorial fund in Vera's and Alison's names to provide support for women's high-altitude climbing. When we first proposed the fund, we met resistance. "You've got to give money to men climbers too. There are just not that many women who climb," one vulnerable AAC member assured me. I protested that the money had been raised on the premise that it would go for women's climbing and should not be used for anything else. The response was that "women are good at things like raising money and supporting climbing. But if you're going to have a substantial fund, you should give a share of the money to the real climbers, to the men."

And that, unfortunately, is still the attitude of some in the "high and serene circles" of the climbing establishment. Nevertheless, our fund was established through the AAC to support women's expeditionary mountaineering, and Alison's family and friends have set up a similar fund in Britain. Last summer we sponsored the first of what has become an annual climbing meet in the Tetons to teach women climbers about expeditionary planning. Some forty women and men participated.

Annapurna itself remains unchanged—still beautiful, remote, indifferent to human concerns. A year after our climb an American eight-man expedition attempting to repeat the Dutch Route without Sherpas or oxygen was making excellent progress until the wind coming from an enormous avalanche down the Bobsled blew Camp III and its three occupants off the Dutch Rib.

Recently a Swedish team wrote to me for advice about their scheduled 1981 attempt on the north side of Annapurna. In my reply I warned that the mountain was extremely avalanche prone but did not try to discourage them. I could not tell them the risk was too great; they would have to make that decision for themselves. In mountaineering, the truism holds: the greatest rewards come only from the greatest commitment.

On Annapurna our entire team took the risk, made the commitment. Only time will reveal its full consequences. As Maurice Herzog declares at the end of his book: There are other Annapurnas in the lives of men."

And in the lives of women as well.

Jeff Long (b. 1951) is a veteran climber who has had experience in the mountains of Colorado and the Himalayas. He is a prodigious writer having published two non-fiction works, *Outlaw: The Story of Claude Dallas* and *Duel of Eagles: The Mexican and U.S. Fight for the Alamo*. He has also written novels with mountaineering as their central theme, *Angles of Light*, *The Ascent*, for which he became the first American to be awarded the Boardman-Tasker Mountain Literature Award, and his most recent works, *The Descent* and *Ground Zero*.

JEFF LONG:
CANNIBALS
(Fiction)

November 24, 1974

Kathmandu, Nepal (AP) One month after an international expedition of climbers was reported lost on 27,800-foot Makalu in the Nepalese Himalayas, a sole survivor has been found. Daniel Bogle of Eldorado Springs, Colorado, was recently led to civilization by a Tibetan yak herder.

Bogle claims avalanches trapped him and climbing companion Cameron Corder of Butte, Arkansas, high on the mountain for nearly ten days. The partially eaten remains of an unidentified man were found at the base of the mountain. Bogle denies accusations of cannibalism.

Yes, I survived, but not because I ate Corder. For one thing, raw meat doesn't digest at those altitudes. I'd have killed myself with constipation. Besides, there was food up there, though the amount varies each time I tell the story. Sometimes I detail the scene with a cornucopia of food. At other times the tent is bare of morsels, only bones. Over these past six years, sometimes I've told the truth; other times I've taken liberties. This time, the truth. It's not really my story, anyway. Corder was largely responsible.

I remember him in bits and pieces, not chronologically but in order of biological impact. He had massive hands, suitably enormous for his six and a half feet of muscle and thick bone. His face was furrowed by premature wrinkles. When his eyes chanced upon you, you reacted. Their deep blackness set the tone for the rest of his face, the dark simian brow, the beard and blacker mane of hair. Instinctively you felt that Corder was a creature of melancholy, a naked conscience.

I knew all about Cameron J. Corder, of course, there being no other climbers near his size and power who spoke with an Arkansas drawl. But I'd never actually met him before our introduction in Kathmandu, where the international expedition of British, Italians, French, and Americans was mustering rank. Corder and I were the American pair. When Corder first appeared on the brown cobblestones of an alley that reeked of curry and goat blood, my impression was one of a gigantic human animal built for labor and physical, not intellectual, ascent. He was dressed in gym shorts, sandals, and a white T-shirt, clothing that did not hide his numerous scars. Both his legs were scarred with slight pale lines and with deeper, wider purple stripes. His right arm was marked with a shiny dent where a bullet had passed through the triceps.

We shook hands and immediately found a tea shop that served cold Indian beer. Pulling out our photos of Makalu, we smeared our fingerprints up and down the routes, possible and impossible, on the west face of the mountain.

During the remainder of that week, Corder and I explored Katmandu's charming decadence. Dodging bicycles in alley ways where old women were laden with twisted firewood or rice, we ferreted out beer stalls and found black marketeers from whom, for the sheer gall of it, we bought Nepalese rupees and Afghan hash.

I was still young then. Twenty-two years old with not a worry. I owned $80 climbing boots, a bellyband of three-inch sling, and $60 worth of metal, enough chocks, pins, and biners. to ring like a Swiss cow when I walked with my rack on. No stereo, no car, not even a bed. My prized possession was 165 feet of prime European rope, a blue Perlon© line freckled with clean white diamonds. I lived to climb. With a bachelor's in philosophy, what else, I took spot jobs as a stonemason, a waiter, even a paperboy. If I went to the movies with a woman, she paid for herself. You see? Ascent was everything. And I was so innocent, with so little past.

I can't say when Vietnam took hold again of Corder's mind. Not once in the city had he mentioned that he was a vet. I had heard back in the States that he'd been on a helicopter crew during the war and that he'd endured some mysterious ordeals. But he didn't talk about them, not until long after we'd passed through the jungle and had reached the mountain. By that time he was possessed.

The longer I think about it, the more it seems Corder could have managed more sanctuary from his memories than he did at Makalu. The acid whiteness of the bleached mountain, its angles and lifelessness, couldn't possibly have been more alien to his memories of Vietnam; and yet he was stricken. I think he may have been reminded, initially, by that jungle we had to pass through in getting to the mountain. Down there among the rotted Hindi shrines, among the ghostly herds of monkeys, Corder must have begun remembering. The jungle, like other jungles, was lukewarm. Every 15 minutes it had us genuflecting with knives to scrape away the monsoon leeches. Down there, I'm quite sure, Corder's Vietnam loomed up, though he kept it to himself like an embarrassing souvenir until those final ten days of avalanches.

Through September and early October, the climb progressed with talented vigor. All of us in the expedition were proud of ourselves for being so gentlemanly and industrious. Rope stitched the route together, an 8,000-foot thread of polypropylene that snaked toward the summit. On October 23 Corder and I occupied the highest camp, Camp VI at 26,5000 feet, and were prepared to force the line another 500 feet higher so the British pair could leapfrog and go on to the top. Early the next morning, on October 24, a blizzard set in.

That afternoon the first avalanche struck, taking the two Italians at Camp II with it. The avalanching effectively marooned two French climbers, an Englishman, a Scot, Corder, and me on the upper regions of Makalu's west face, all of us at camps above 23,000 feet. The crackle of walkie-talkies was fierce and prolonged that evening as each pair of us debated our alternatives. There were only two really, though it seemed the universe depended on our choice: We could go down or we could stay put. The high altitude had us stunned and delirious, so our decision that night was a poor one. We chose to stay put the two French in Camp III, the two British in Camp V, and we two Americans in Camp VI.

Cannibals

Tipped at a forbidding 70-degree angle, the face was composed of very hard blue ice. Our tents were pitched precariously on platforms carved from the snow or stolen from brief ledges of rock. Just above Corder and me, dangling with erotic menace, hung a wide bosom poised to avalanche. We talked about it, willed it to either freeze solid or fall to the north, and hoped that by waiting a few more days we could outwit it. But on October 25 a second slide hurtled past Camp II, knocking the French and their tents into the abyss. We knew we were doomed, too. In medieval times travelers swore that avalanches were giant snowballs, triggered by the flapping of a solitary swallow's wings. Our avalanches were inspired by something even quieter than that—Corder. Or, to be more precise, Corder's sin. So Corder thought.

"Yes... yes," he murmured as we lay in our sleeping bags, hesitating as much to breathe the thin air as to sort his thoughts. With our crampons and axes, our jumars, helmets, and ropes, all our tools for both ascent and descent useless in the tent with us, Corder began to talk about Vietnam.

I'd never heard of soldiers hunting animals in Vietnam, though more than a few American soldiers were killed by wild animals in the surreal jungles of Indochina. As Corder said at the start of his rhapsody, "Grunts ate monkeys, tigers ate grunts."

"King Bees," Corder drawled softly. "They done it most. Fire up a tiger, go down, gut it, and sell the hide and teeth back in the cities." Gradually, almost somnolently, I learned Corder's slang. King Bees were CH-34 helicopters that had been manufactured in Korea and were flown by Vietnamese pilots. The term King Bee applied collectively to the craft and its crew. "They were 90 pounds of person and 500 pounds of balls. They weren't always lucky, but they were always right there, you know. I remember one King Bee, a gunner, he took off into the jungle to fetch the carcass and never came out again. The cat must have got him."

When the blizzard paused, and when Corder slowed down with his storytelling, I could hear the ropes outside fluttering in the rarefied wind. Individual snowflakes clattered dryly against the nylon tent wall. I half expected the sullen hiss of an avalanche to sweep our tent and us away at any moment. But Corder had started; he kept right on going. At first I was sure he was talking to suppress the avalanche; then, slowly, I realized he was trying to come up with a reason for our predicament.

"American crews couldn't go hunting any old time like King Bees." He startled me. Hours had passed since his last words. "We had a whole lot of laws on us. There was trouble for firing things up. But we done it anyway." Spindrift, driven by the wind, formed a silent dune by a rip in the far corner. The bigger glass tent poles bowed overhead like the ribs of a whale.

"But sometimes it was legitimate, like once. . ." He drew at the thin air. "Viet Cong used to use elephants for transport, and this one time we spotted a big gray all rigged out with .51 caliber machine guns, one on each side for antiaircraft. We only had five rockets left, but we went down on it anyway and missed with everything except a white phosphorous. You can believe we burned that beast. It took off like hell, knocking trees down every which way, and it's sure they never got their guns back."

I was paralyzed by the avalanches that were still to come, stock still and afraid; but somehow Corder's little sketches of Vietnam seemed vitally relevant. He was building to something, and that progression was more dynamic than my own concerns. Already Corder had begun to take possession of our tent. There were two of us listening to the walkie-talkie morning and night at seven o'clock, two of us drinking tea, two of us gasping for air 24 hours a day; but more and more there was only one real presence in that tent, and it was Corder's.

"I was gunner on a Huey," he took up again. "There was Huey slicks and there was Huey guns. Slicks carried troops, and guns rode shotgun for the slicks. There was all kinds of guns, Cobras and Bravo models. And then there was November models—the best." I felt he was comparing himself to me. "They had every killing thing. Twin miniguns, 20-millimeter Vulcan cannons, chunkers. And fast, man, 160 knots. When we came along with those November guns, we had the power." His story was not meant for me, though once or twice he remembered me with a glance. He was addressing an image, and in speaking aloud he drew it nearer.

"Roger, Roger, you know. Like, keep your heads down; we're coming in with spook," he explained. "Then they'd go 'Roger, Roger' and duck their asses down for the fireworks. Those guns was so goddam fast they didn't go bang-bang or rat-Hat. Just this low grunt for 10 or 20 seconds, and that's all she wrote. Even the grass was mowed." Corder touched the tip of his tongue to each wide split in his weathered lips. Suddenly he looked at me. "Don't worry," he winked. "I'm not crazy, brother."

A day passed, nearly as cold and dark as night. The wind and snow continued to rattle against the bellowing tent wall. At seven the British called, their voices pinched by the radio's static, their fear, and, no doubt, bronchitis. Our position was the same: Wait out the storm. It would let up in a day or two. So we hoped, but it didn't.

I've been asked if I felt despair in that violent region so far above the earth. It wasn't that I trusted Corder's sanity or our decision to wait, nor that I believed the weather would suddenly spare us. There was just so little sense of urgency, how could there be despair?

On the morning of October 28, for no particular reason, Corder and I shared a nearly empty yellow bottle of oxygen. Five minutes for him, five for me. In those five-minute gulps of pure air, the world turned richer, fuller, and focused into smells, sights, and sounds. We had a painful sense of what we had missed. I watched Corder's face suddenly fatten with some vast, oxygenated memory and, with it, distress. Then it was my turn again, and while I stared at him and inhaled the thick air, Corder's exhaustion lines and sunburn and dandruff overwhelmed me.

"You're dying, Corder," I whispered through the mask, and he nodded back in terror. "We're. . . ."

The oxygen ran out. The mask's rubber bladder collapsed, and we were again stupefied.

Corder's face returned to its side of the tent; his eyes clouded over. The urgency evaporated. I lay back with the cold snow outside and the tired desire to sleep and escape the tedious dream of wind and nylon that surrounded me.

We weren't without certain tasks. Snow had to be knocked from the sagging walls. The walkie-talkie, though it was becoming silent, had to be kept warm with body heat. Water had to be melted for drinking. I made a habit of reaching through the north door to fill cook pots with snow, a special ritual that Corder fouled when he emptied his piss-bottle all over the drinking-water snow.

"Damn it Corder," I snapped. He'd violated one of my only taboos, making my presence in the tent even more transparent and unreal. "Drop Vietnam. Take a look where you are."

The giant pushed one big bare hand out of the top of his sleeping bag and wiped his eyes. "I can't," he insisted in a soft voice. "It's eating at me." I didn't retort, though I wanted to. Restraint was all-important; I couldn't afford to have Corder annoyed at me. "Believe me," he pleaded, second-guessing my silence. "It's on me. I got to."

Afterward Corder was quiet for half a day before resuming his tales. At last, five days into his imagery of Vietnam, Corder began to actually weave a bona fide story, not just piecemeal anecdotes.

Not often, but now and then, Corder's November gun would stray on its return from missions in order to hunt tigers and elephants. They always hunted from the air. From up there, Corder told me, the tigers were fluid orange and red lights that glowed through the overgrowth. Elephants were black shadows. Once driven from the trees by rocket fire, the orange lights and black shadows turned into miniature animals. As Corder snaked his miniguns down, the pilot tipped the craft to broaden the field. Excitement mounted. Everyone wanted to reach out to touch the animals and, like magicians, to drop them in their tracks. While I listened for the hiss of incipient avalanches, Corder told me how slow roses of blood would blossom when the rockets hit an elephant's rib cage. He gestured with his hands to show how the tigers would hatefully dodge the November's quick shadow.

To pass the time while Corder unwound his story, I kept a veiled eye on our food. It wasn't promising. There was a small, freeze-dried slab of beef, four fresh tea bags, two packets of Quaker Oats, a cube of cheese, and three marbled Hershey bars. I rationed the food, apportioning equal shares until the fifth night, when I decided Corder had gone crazy. His gentle, twangy voice had begun to accelerate the tale, and he'd even let his tea freeze in its cup while he rambled.

The food was scarce, but I wasn't worried. I believed that, like me, Corder had brought provisions. We'd make it.

"Let me have the food." I thought I said it aloud. Perhaps I didn't really say anything. When Corder didn't move, I watched myself reach across and pull the man's pack onto my legs. Although it felt light, there was some weight to it, some food anyway. I watched myself upend the pack.

A book landed on my sleeping bag. Nothing more. Corder had brought a Bible.

The afternoon was a vacuum, not a sound except for snowflakes on nylon and Corder breathing.

"We're out of food," I told him when he awoke. "Here. . . tea," and I handed him a cup, then half of a candy bar. "That's it."

"Where's my gear?" Corder demanded.

I didn't answer. I watched myself not answer. Corder knew I knew.

"Where's my Bible?"

I handed it to him. "You screwed up," I said, but without an ominous tone. Corder might have suspected.

He grabbed at the book. It should have been two pounds of food—bread and fish, so to speak—not paper. I lay down, thinking there was a chance Corder had killed both of us. But it was a sure thing that Corder had killed himself. He wouldn't last long at that altitude. Over the next two days, sleep and imagination were the antagonists. Every time I closed my eyes, I could see the future: murder, then food.

So, I had made my choice. I started hiding bits of food for myself. If the storm continued, I knew we'd both be dead inside of three days anyway; on the other hand, if there was only one of us, the survivor might last as long as nine or ten days. I wanted to live, and all Corder could seem to think about was death and hunting wild animals.

One incident among the many animals slaughtered and people killed had affected Corder deeply, and that was the death of a white tiger. I think, after piecing together Corder's accounts, that I can understand some of his feeling of guilt. Up in their helicopter, from their vantage point of height and omnipotent fire power, the crew members had lost patience with the common and ordinary. The earth had become a topography for them, small and insipid. Animals and men were now nothing but targets, more to test the crew's indifference than its weaponry. One day, near the border of Cambodia, Corder's crew spied a watery white shape surging through the dark trees below. It was an albino tiger. The gunship dropped lower, hovering like an insect as the young soldiers fed their curiosity about the extraordinary animal. For such a long, long time they had seen nothing beautiful, uncommon.

Beneath the thunder of the rotor blades, the pilot suggested the tiger be spared, and over the headphones the copilot agreed. They would show mercy. But just as the gunship started to lift away, the act was spoiled. Corder shot the tiger with his miniguns. I suspect he did it out of fascination, or maybe because of a desire to be completely free of that impoverished landscape or to commit a crime where there was no law. The reason doesn't matter; it didn't matter as the gunship throbbed above the white carcass, and it didn't matter as Corder and I lay half-conscious at Camp VI. The tiger was dead.

On the morning of October 29, our sixth straight day of storm and solitude, we lost radio contact with the British at Camp V, 800 feet below us. We waited until seven o'clock that night, assuring each other that their batteries must have frozen or their antenna broken, but they were gone. An avalanche took them, of course, though to Corder and me they'd been bluntly erased. I accepted their nonexistence without a second thought. The world had become a very plain and simple finger painting for me. Sunset, had we been able to see it, would have been a few broad stripes of color. The ice would have been purple. The summit would have been an inky triangle. The deaths of six fellow climbers fit quite naturally into this matter-of-fact tableau.

Far from mourning the loss of the climbers at Camp V, Corder accepted it as unsophisticated destiny, part and parcel of his sin. I finally understood his sin was the murder of that white tiger. But guilt no longer interested me; I was too hungry and exhausted to share Corder's moods.

"It's happened like this before." He was glaring through me again, a glare I was learning to equate with further confession.

"Hey," I said soothingly, "it's okay."

Corder blinked and emitted a shy, repentant grin: white teeth in a black beard, black and white like a Durer etching. Death's-head. He lay back, quiet for a few minutes, then launched into his tale again.

After Corder "fired up" the white tiger, the gunship had hung above the jungle for a moment or two, then arched away from the isolated clearing. The pilot and copilot were disappointed in Corder, but no one ever mentioned the tiger again. A week later the gunship was shot down, killing everyone but Corder. Corder put one huge hand on my shoulder as I lay in my filthy sleeping bag and swore to God that, just before he died, the copilot had looked him straight in the eye and coldly whispered, "Don't blame yourself." At that point, and with enduring guilt, Corder had realized he alone was responsible for the deaths of his friends. It had been he, after all, who had tampered with a pattern of mercy.

Within five minutes a second and third gunship had tracked the distress signal from Corder's ship and had come snapping over the jungle's edge, laying down heavy veils of gunfire all around the craft. Two minutes later Corder was safely plucked from his burning gunship. But for seven minutes he was alone, surrounded by flames, gunfire, and his dead friends, one of whom had accused him with his last breath. For seven minutes Corder was tormented by the belief that an animistic force had pursued and destroyed everyone but him, because he was the guilty one.

After the crash of his gunship and the death of his crew, the giant gunner had encased himself in guilt and horror. He had a prostitute for a girlfriend who habitually dressed in white; she disappeared the same day Corder's Huey was shot down. Even more ominous, he confided to me, every now and then one of his dead crew members would quiver into view on the streets of Ban Me Thuot in central Vietnam.

"They wouldn't say nothing, just sort of look at me like I done. . . well, the tiger."

He was reassigned to another gunship, and it was shot down the next morning. Corder survived this catastrophe, too, only to be haunted by the ghosts of two gunship crews.

"So, now you know." He paused. "What do you think? Crazy, huh?" I knew what I thought, but didn't know what to say. It was a strange story, I cautiously admitted. A terrible story. I was afraid to say any more. He was huge, and I was more than a little convinced that Corder was out of his mind. Eight thousand vertical feet from the foot of the mountain, I was trapped in a tent with a madman.

There were a few edible odds and ends tucked deep inside my sleeping bag, but I felt justified in withholding them for myself. It had come down to that kind of deceit. We were dying. Lives had ceased to be, but as I said, the mountain made us all seem so insignificant.

"You aren't going to eat me, are you?" Corder joked, cocking a wasted grin at me. I looked long and hard at his face, at his black beard and his ragged mane of hair, at his nose scabbed with old sunburn. I thought he could survive on the flesh of his memories. Corder glanced at me. His eyes hungered for forgiveness. Utterly convinced of his sin, he was, in confessing to me, inviting death.

On October 31, my suspicions that Corder was deranged were confirmed when he began to repeat his stories of the white tiger, his helicopter crashes, and his young whore in immaculate clothing. I was lying beside him, my back pressed up against the great wall of his rib cage to absorb every possible bit of warmth.

For the eighth straight day he was talking when I woke from my nauseous doze. The blue and orange tent fabric was coated with our breath, which had turned to hoarfrost. His deep, gentle voice was repeating the story. At first I was groggy, ill from the long frozen night, and I was irritated that Corder was echoing himself. Then I noticed that his tale was more severe and cogent this second time around; it made a little more sense. As Corder droned on, I envisioned the floating gunship that had laced the humid skies. I could feel the miniguns shudder as the tiger leaped high and dropped. I understood the graceful white curve of his young whore's hip.

Throughout the day I lay against Corder's back, delirious from the high altitude, starvation, and his tale. I ached because the snow was hard and cold, and I couldn't move except to face Corder. The tent wall was sucked in and out as the storm respirated. Near dusk I stealthily chewed a piece of cheese, savoring the strength it would give. As quietly as possible, I sipped from the bottle of water I'd kept thawed inside my sleeping bag. Corder rambled on, crazy as a loon.

I had two hopes. One was that Corder would weaken enough so that, even if his madness turned physical, he couldn't hurt me. I was praying that his arms were already too heavy to move. With very little effort Corder could have pushed me through the side of the tent. The drop was a mile and a half. My other hope, so primal one might call it a drive, was that by nibbling at my hoarded food I could outlive the storm and descend to safety. Of course, if Corder had discovered my deception he probably would have killed me outright.

The end came as suddenly and innocently as the first avalanche ten days earlier. The tent wall turned dark blue at sunset. In tides the wind relaxed, then slapped at the mountain, then relaxed. Dropping off to sleep, I wondered again when the storm would stop, when Corder would be quiet. He had begun for the fourth time to retell his story of the white tiger. It was all like a dream: the storm and deaths, Corder's immaterial story, my deception with the food. That thought was still with me when I woke up in pitch darkness, unconsciously groaning to protest an absence, a blank spot.

The storm had stopped. There was silence.

"Corder," I rasped, my voice unfamiliar. "Corder, you can shut up now." But he kept talking even after I'd turned on my flashlight and clambered over his rib cage. His eyes were as motionless as his jaw. His powerful features were locked and blue, hollowed by the cold. Corder was dead.

In prying the giant's body from the tent floor that night, I realized I was going to have enough strength to descend. When I unzipped the door, I saw the stars were glittering. The storm had truly broken. There was a long, chilling moment as I hesitated, unsure whether the corpse in my hands was dead or just pretending to be while it continued talking about the white tiger and eternal guilt. Then, with one decisive shove, Corder was gone and I was left alone inside that bony, sagging tent.

I can still feel his heart in my ears, beating, his voice like mine. You should believe me when I say I am not the cannibal. But Corder is inside me.

Simon Yates (b. 1963) gained international recognition in 1985 with the first ascent of the West face of Siula Grande in the Andes Mountains followed by the now famous descent described in both Joe Simpson's book *Touching the Void* and the recently released feature film of the same name. Since then Simon had distinguished himself with numerous new routes in India, Pakistan, Nepal, Kazakhstan, Australia, and more in South America. Simon was a short-list finalist for the Boardman Tasker Mountain Literature Award with his first book *Against the Wall*. The essay in this collection comes from his second book, *The Flame of Adventure*. Simon now lives in Cumbria and makes his living as a lecturer and by running his commercial guiding business, Mountain Dream.

SIMON YATES: AT HOME ABROAD

I paced around the hospital room restlessly, before stopping at the window and staring outside. The sky was grey and drab, which matched the room and my mood. It was the last place I wanted to be.

I had been back from Pakistan only three days. I did not feel particularly ill and saw my continuing diarrhoea as more of an inconvenience than a serious problem. During the time away I had gradually lost weight, but viewed my emaciated body as being lean and fit. My parents, however, did not and insisted that I go to hospital. A doctor made a cursory examination of a stool sample, weighed me and promptly admitted me. I had arrived back in the country with just twenty-two pence to my name and now I had been incarcerated in hospital. All my fears about coming back to Britain seemed well founded.

My situation depressed me. I had been free, travelling and climbing in a far-away country just the week before and now I was trapped. The doctors had little idea of what was wrong with me or how to treat me, and simply said I should stay while they completed their tests. I was given a bedpan and every time I used it, I had to press an alarm. A nurse would come and inspect the contents and write the results on a form on the door. When my family and friends visited for the first time they had to wear paper clothes and face masks. It felt as if I was in prison.

On the second day a doctor appeared, whom I had not seen before.

"I'd just like to take a blood sample Mr. Yates," he said.

I looked away as he put a tourniquet around my upper left arm and began to probe at my veins lower down. He stabbed the needle in and pulled it out several times.

"Careful," I pleaded. "That hurts."

"Sorry, can't seem to find a vein."

I found his excuse hard to take. My body was covered in bulging veins. In addition to those normally visible, they were sticking out of my legs and even my stomach.

"Just try the other side," he said, after further probing.

All the poking with the needle started to make me feel faint. Eventually he withdrew the needle. The syringe had only a little blood inside.

"That"ll have to do," he said, taking the sample away.

Within half an hour bruises had run up and down both arms from my elbows and I could barely move them. The doctor returned and seemed undeterred by the damage he had done.

"We'll have to do some more tests," he announced. "You wouldn"t mind if we brought in some medical students, would you? They rarely get the chance to examine someone so thin."

Over the following two days I was subjected to a variety of painful, uncomfortable and degrading tests. Pipes were put into me from either end. Samples were removed from my intestine and my colon. I ate a slab of butter and blood samples were taken at half-hourly intervals to gauge my rate of fat absorption. The students visited, prodded me about and got very excited about feeling the outline of my heart under my rib-cage. I sat through the tests passively, although I did begin to feel increasingly hungry with the inadequate hospital food.

"Could I have some more?" I asked a nurse after the third evening meal.

"I'll see what I can do," she replied kindly.

A little later she returned with two spare portions of rhubarb crumble. I ate them greedily. They went straight through me and within two hours I was using the bedpan and ringing the alarm at regular intervals. It was a long and weary night and yet I still looked forward to the breakfast trolley arriving in the morning.

When breakfast did arrive, I was given a drink and nothing more. The trolley was taken away and after a while I realized I was not going to be fed. The same happened at lunch. I began to get incredibly hungry and yet still did not ask why I had been given no food.

At dinner the trolley passed me by yet again. I had had enough. I felt angry for willingly handing over responsibility for myself to the hospital staff, for slipping so easily and unquestionably into the role of the patient. Just a couple of weeks before I had been making life or death decisions for myself, and now I had happily surrendered to others the basic decision of whether to eat or not.

I stormed out of my room and up the ward wearing just a pair of pyjama bottoms. I spotted some staff through a window in a side room and burst in through the door.

"Look at me," I pleaded, pointing at my protruding ribs. `I'm a bag of bones, and for some reason you lot have decided to starve me."

The doctors and nurses looked stunned, but for a moment were speechless.

"Mr. Yates, we are in the middle of a meeting," a nurse finally said. "We will come and see you in a minute."

I returned to my room still fuming, wondering why we bow to authority and allow ourselves to become institutionalised so unquestioningly. It seemed ridiculous that the urge to herd, not to cause a fuss and not to stand out could at times be strong enough to override the basic need to eat.

After a short time the ward sister came into my room.

"We stopped feeding you because of your reaction to the extra puddings," she explained.

"It would have been nice to have been told," I pointed out.

`I'll see what I can do about getting you some food," she replied sympathetically, before leaving.

A little later the sister returned with some sandwiches, and for the rest of my stay I was given double helpings at mealtimes regardless of their effect.

In the morning the doctor proudly announced to me that the tests showed I had dysentery. It was information I had known for two months.

After five days I was discharged from hospital with a handful of antibiotics, the same I had been taking all summer with little effect. I had blindly followed the advice of those around me, been their guinea pig and undergone a variety of painful tests for nothing. It was over a year later before my digestive system returned to normal. As I left I realized that I could have bought the same tablets from a pharmacy in Rawalpindi a little over a week earlier for just a few rupees and prevented the nightmare of the previous few days.

I looked across the table at Mike, who seemed to be getting increasingly anxious as the meal went on. Mike Searle was a quietly spoken academic and it was rare to see him getting particularly bothered by anything. I had made my first trip to Pakistan with him two years previously. Having suggested that we return to try an unclimbed peak called Biale that he had found, he had taken it upon himself to organize much of the expedition. In addition to Sean, Mark Miller and myself he had invited along his longstanding friend Nick Groves and his partner Mary Rose Fowlie. At times I wondered if he ever doubted his choice of climbing companions.

"I'm beginning to get worried about Mark," he said. "He should have brought the jeep back over an hour ago." "The what?" spluttered Sean. "The jeep. I let him go to Islamabad in it."

Sean and I burst out laughing. "But he can't drive, Mike," Sean pointed out. "Well he can sort of, but he's never taken a test."

"Oh, dear," said Mike, now looking very worried. "He didn"t tell me he hadn"t got a licence."

"Well he wouldn't, would he?" Sean replied casually.

"I'm sure he'll be all right," I said trying to reassure him. "He's probably just gone to visit some friends."

We continued the meal in a tense silence and I tried to exude an air of confidence I did not have. Strange events had a habit of happening in Mark's vicinity.

Then suddenly Mark burst in through the restaurant door. He was red-faced, sweating heavily and covered in dirt and oil. He stormed up to our table.

"I've rolled the jeep," he announced, sitting down and grabbing the jug of water. He drank two glasses in succession, before adding, "But don't worry, I've had it fixed."

The color completely drained from Mike's face. I was not surprised. The precious jeep belonged to Leicester University, his employers, and had been specially shipped out to Pakistan for a geology project they were running in the country.

"Where is it now?" Mike asked feebly.

"Outside."

The pair went off to look at the damage, while we continued with the meal. Mike came back a little later.

"I'm sorry, but I'm going to have to take the jeep to a garage."

"I thought Mark had fixed it," Sean quipped.

"Well I think it needs looking over."

"We'd better go and check it out," I said, putting down my chappatti and heading for the door.

The jeep was parked across the main road down a side street, where there was no lighting. At first sight little seemed to be wrong, but Mike quickly started pointing out faults. There were scratches down one side, the bonnet was buckled and the doors protruded from their surrounds. Mark had obviously parked it in the gloom to try to hide the damage.

"Hey, look at this, guys," shouted Sean.

He was standing in front of the jeep looking at it head on. I saw the problem as soon as I joined him. The entire vehicle was lopsided. Sean and I began to giggle.

"So tell me again. What happened?" Mike demanded angrily.

I let most of Mark's story pass me by. The crux seemed to involve a thunderstorm and a bullock cart, but as it had been dry and sunny all day where we were, a mere twenty kilometres away, the story sounded implausible. I remembered an elaborate tale Mark had told me some months earlier back in Sheffield, concerning the loss of my cycle, which I had lent to him. I later learned a more truthful version of events. He had simply left it unlocked outside a shop and it had been stolen.

Fortunately, the jeep did start and Mike and Mark went off in search of a garage. We returned to the restaurant and finished the meal. When they arrived back at the hotel later that night, Mike said an additional problem had been discovered—the bolts holding the engine in place had all sheared in the accident. Had they not been replaced, the engine could have dropped out on to the road at any time.

We had hoped to leave for the mountains the following day, but it seemed as if events were conspiring against us. The jeep had to be taken for repairs and we were still short of a liaison officer. We had paid a peak fee for the mountain we wished to climb, and the Ministry of Tourism regulations stipulated that the expedition had to be accompanied by a liaison officer.

When we had arrived a few days before and met the officials in the Ministry, we were told they were expecting us a week later. Mike protested that he had written saying we were arriving early. They retrieved the expedition file from a dusty cabinet and soon found the letter. It was evident that nobody had even bothered to read it. However, despite their mistake, we were not allowed to leave for the mountains without the officer.

Mike and I stepped out of the taxi and into the manicured gardens outside the Ministry of Tourism offices in Islamabad. We walked into the now familiar office with its tatty pictures of K2 on the walls and a creaking fan on the ceiling, and sat down.

"Where's our liaison officer?" I demanded from the official behind the desk.

"He has been summoned from Lahore and should arrive presently."

"You said that yesterday. When is he going to arrive?" Maybe today, perhaps tomorrow."

"I'm getting pissed off with this," I said to Mike. "We want our liaison officer now," I shouted. "Do you understand?" "Do you have a wife, Mr Simon?"

"No," I replied puzzled.

"Well, this is why you are so anxious," the official explained. "If you were to get yourself a wife, then you would be much more content."

"But I don't want a wife," I replied trying to stop a smile from breaking across my face. It was difficult to counter his simple logic, and Mike was already laughing openly. "I just want a liaison officer."

A day later when we arrived at the Ministry we were greeted by a fresh-faced young army captain called Naveed. The official proudly announced that the government of Pakistan had allocated him to our expedition as liaison officer. We sat through the formality of a briefing and were then allowed to leave for the mountains. Sean cannily arranged a lift with Mike in the jeep, under the pretext that he would be able to take photographs on the way. We filled the back of the jeep with baggage.

"Well, I'm afraid the rest of you will have to get on the bus," Mike announced.

"Oh, right," Mark remarked, raising an eyebrow.

Simon Yates

"Well, Mike's hardly going to let you share the driving. Is he?" I said cynically.

"I suppose not," he was forced to admit.

Reluctantly, we took a taxi to the bus station and booked some seats for a night coach to Gilgit.

Three days later we sat in the gardens of the K2 Motel in Skardu, drinking tea. The setting could hardly have been grander. The town lay in the centre of a flood plain, where the Indus river spilled out of the mountains and meandered sluggishly, before pouring down into a gorge cutting into the foothills. The hotel itself stood on a terrace high above a broad bend in the river, overlooked by an old fort perched on a rocky hill. The views out across the river and into the distant Shigar valley were superb and it was just possible to make out tantalising outlines of snow-capped peaks on the horizon.

"I've been thinking," said Mark.

"Oh dear," replied Mike laughing.

"What do you think about Simon and I going on ahead and finding a spot to put the base camp?"

"That's not a bad idea. If we arrange a place to meet you can guide us to the site you have chosen."

Mark's suggestion was sensible as we had very little information about the approaches to the mountain. In fact our knowledge was limited to some distant photographs Mike had taken a few years earlier and a notoriously inaccurate map.

When two days later, Mark and I got out of the jeep beyond the small village of Dassu, it was something of a shock. It felt unnatural to be saying goodbye at the start of the trip, even if the parting was only temporary. I was looking forward to getting into the mountains though and getting some exercise after the days of cramped travel. Unlike the others we would be able to move quickly without the burden of dozens of porters and the associated starts, stops and continual negotiations.

"We'll see you in ten days time, at the junction of the Trango and Baltoro Glaciers," said Mike.

"Right," I replied, delighted by the vagueness of the meeting arrangements. We were talking about a vast area of glacier and yet I had no doubt that we would meet as planned. We simply had to, otherwise we would run out of food. We shook hands, shouldered our rucksacks and walked across the small landslide blocking the road towards a baked brown gorge.

When I reached the other side of the debris I looked back. Mike had already turned the jeep round and was driving away from us down the thin dirt road.

Walking over the jumble of large brown boulders required intense concentration. They had a slippery, shiny finish, as if the outer rock had been melted by the searing sunlight. To cross the large chasms between the stones often required a jump. A mistake could easily result in a leg-breaking fall.

I skipped across the rocks trying to catch glimpses of Mark's unmistakably large frame through the heat haze in front. It was difficult to keep up with his pace and the sun, dry air and warm wind was desiccating my body. I could feel the salt from dried sweat in my clothes chafing my skin. Our three days of walking had been much the same. A very early start followed by flat-out marching with minimal rests until the early afternoon. This way we could cover a good distance and then set up camp to escape the hottest part of the day.

Suddenly the boulder field ended. For hours we had been walking steadily uphill, now there was just a thin dusty path contouring across a scrubby hillside. Huge granite cliffs hung above, which made my neck ache when I tried to look at them.

I turned a corner and the view changed, but I kept walking until the picture was complete. About a kilometer further up the valley at the base of the cliffs a ribbon of radiant green ran down the hillside. Some large birch trees stuck into the air and their leaves shimmered silver in the wind. Locals called the place Paiju. Beyond the green the valley opened out. I could see the snout of the Baltoro Glacier and a highway of ice beyond it. Spectacular mountains stood on either side.

As I entered the oasis I could see that springs rising at the base of the cliffs provided the water, which ran downhill in small streams. Below the birch trees were more abundant willows and roses. The ground was covered in grass and flowers. Insects and butterflies filled the air. Bird song echoed all around and a rich smell of life hung about the place.

It was, however, a flawed paradise used as a campsite by many on their way to K2 or the other peaks along the Baltoro Glacier. Large terraces had been chopped into the earth for tent platforms, and many were covered in rubbish. Porters from many expeditions were tearing at the undergrowth for firewood and there was a distinct smell of excrement. Yet despite the faults Paiju was still a unique and special place.

Simon Yates

Mark had found a decent platform in the center of the site and was already setting up the tent. Anwar was busy with the stove nearby. It was the first time I had seen him for a few hours, as it had proved impossible to keep up with him. I had met Anwar Ali briefly the year before in Hushe and on the back of his wicked sense of humour had offered him work the next time I returned to Pakistan. We had hired him to act as both porter and cook for our reconnaissance. He was already proving to be exceptional at both.

"Lunch ready," he announced with a characteristic smile, handing Mark and me bowls of dhal and a plate full of freshly made chappattis.

"You're a star, Anwar," Mark said as he eagerly began to eat. It was impossible to disagree with him. Anwar was carrying a larger load than either of us, faster, and he still had enough energy to start cooking the moment he arrived in camp.

Anwar watched us eat and insisted that we finished all he had prepared.

"What will you have?" Mark asked.

"I will go and see my friends," Anwar replied.

He went and joined a group of about a dozen porters further down the hillside. Literally hundreds of people were at the campsite for the night and most were porters, who had split into groups for cooking and eating. People came from the whole of the north of Pakistan to work as porters on the Baltoro and usually formed clans based on which region or valley they came from.

A little later Anwar returned clutching something in his hands.

"Oh Anwar," Mark groaned. "That's gross."

He smiled broadly, holding what I now recognised as a goat's head. The head was blackened and smooth from being burnt to remove the hair.

"Now I make goat's head soup," Anwar proudly announced, putting the head into the pressure cooker. He added a little water and soon had the dish hissing over the stove. An hour later he opened the steaming pan and began eating the head. The neck and face went first, then Anwar gouged out the eyes, before cracking open the skull and starting on the brain.

"You're not a vegetarian then Anwar?" Mark asked jokingly, as he chewed away the gums from the jaw. Nothing was wasted and only bones and teeth remained.

The next morning we decided to have a rest day. The porters usually paused at Paiyu as it was the last camp before the glacier. I spent a lot of time watching them stock up with firewood and prepare bread, chappattis and parathas to cook higher up.

Anwar became friendly with a coach driver from Abbotabad, who had somehow ended up working as a cook for the liaison officer of a Yugoslav expedition that was going to K2. It turned out that he had never left the plains of Pakistan and had no idea about the place he now found himself. He was a lousy cook and was terrified by the prospect of going on to the glacier.

To me, his was a remarkable story, but in some ways just an extreme example of that of many of the men who were in Paiyu that day. Although most of those working as porters did come from mountain areas, many rarely left their small villages and most never ventured deep into the mountains themselves. Most would have endured days of travel by jeep, bus and foot to reach the villages where hiring took place. There was no guarantee of work at the end of their travels and competition for jobs was so fierce that men virtually fought over them. Nearly all the men would have left their villages with very limited supplies of food and money.

We had come to Pakistan to climb—a pastime that is considered in the western world to involve high levels of adventure and risk. Yet we had travelled in relative comfort and were bringing those comforts with us into the mountains. As I lay inside the tent in my warm down sleeping hag, reading before I went to sleep, I could see the porters settling down for the night under single blankets. They huddled together to keep warm. To me it seemed in many ways there was more uncertainty, risk and adventure in their work than in our mountaineering.

In the morning we left Paiyu. Once we were on to the glacier, the main track to Concordia and ultimately K2 Base Camp veered to the other side. For a while we followed a vague path on the north side of the glacier, but it quickly disappeared altogether, leaving us following Anwar as he picked his way through the rolling, rubble-covered ice. Eventually we reached the Trango glacier and crossed to its far side.

"This will do," I said, dumping my rucksack on a mud flat next to a large glacial pool.

"We'll call it dust camp," Mark joked. His face was already covered and as he stamped his feet clouds of the grey powder blew into the air.

In a bout of activity over two days, Mark and I explored the surrounding glacier systems, discovered a site for our Biale base camp and marvelled at the Trango Towers, some of the largest rock towers in the world. Then we returned to the camp to wait for the others. Mark gathered dust. Whatever he did he seemed to cover himself in more of the ash-like powder.

"You look like an aborigine doing one of those ceremonial dances," I observed, sniggering.

After a day of waiting we were awoken early the next morning. The arrival of the others with twenty-three porters took us by surprise. We had expected them at the end of a day. We hurriedly got dressed and broke camp while Anwar made some tea for everyone. There was a tense atmosphere among the porters.

"There's been some trouble," Sean explained. "The porters are not happy about walking on this side of the glacier and they stopped yesterday after what they considered a full day's walk. They say they will not walk long today."

There was one porter who seemed to be doing the talking.

"He's the guy who's been causing most of the trouble," Sean continued. "I nearly dobbed him yesterday."

"Right, We'll have to sort him out," I replied.

We set off at a blistering pace, but I was deeply worried about what the porters would do. We had limited funds and the porters were our largest expense by far. It looked as if they would stop short of the base camp we had chosen and demand more money to go on.

Sean and I isolated the ring-leader at the back of the group and tried to slow him down, while Mark continued at a relentless pace. Hours passed and the group got more spread out. After we crossed another side-glacier there were murmurings of discontent, and I noticed that Mike was beginning to march in front of the porters.

"What's Mike in a hurry for?" I asked Sean.

"He's got the money," he replied smiling.

Once the porters knew their wages had gone off in front, they realized there was no point in delaying tactics. Even if they abandoned their loads, they would still have to catch Mike to collect their money. Further protest would simply delay their return.

Finally, over a crest on the ridge we had been following, the small grassy ablation valley that we had chosen for our base camp came into view. It was a very dramatic place. A small triangle of grass defined by moraine ridges on two sides and sweeping granite slabs on the other. Mike was already paying off the crowd of gathered porters.

"It's some spot this," Mike remarked as the porters left.

Eventually the last man departed and there was silence. Our contact with the world outside was leaving. The remoteness of the place sank in immediately and the mountains seemed to gain in size. I felt exhilarated, but at the same time nervous. This was beyond anything I had experienced before. I hardly noticed the concern in Nick's voice as he helped our cook Haqeem sort out the loads.

"Shit," he shouted, "they've taken one load of flour and one load of rice."

We had not managed to outwit the porters after all.

"Right. Let's do it," said Mark dramatically.

Sean, Mark and myself were in a tent on a col between two of the Lobsang Spires. Having climbed up a couloir below in the night, we had paused for a brew and to let the coldest part of the night pass before starting the more technical climbing above. Now the sun was coming up, it was time to leave the tent.

There was little to do but put our plastic climbing boots back on again and get on with the climbing. As we expected to be back down later the same day, we could leave much of our kit behind in the tent.

"Have you seen my sunglasses?" Sean asked searching through his rucksack.

"No," we chorused in reply.

"Does anyone have a spare pair?"

"Sorry."

"I'm going to have to go down then."

As Mark and I moved away from the tent towards Lobsang II, Sean began down-climbing the couloir. He looked despondent. There was little else he could do. A day exposed to the light reflecting from the snow and ice could easily send him snow blind. It did not seem appropriate to shout down goodbye.

Before Sean was out of sight, Mark was already climbing above. I sat and belayed, marvelling at how elegantly he was moving his large, powerful body up thin runnels of ice lying over steep rock slabs. He was having to place his ice-axes very delicately to avoid knocking away the ice. Mark was not always so careful. On many occasions I had struggled to follow him up ice-climbs he had knocked away.

Climbing with Mark was always fun though, even when it was not going well. I remembered how when half way up a climb in Scotland we stopped to have a bite to eat and Mark clumsily pulled an apple out of the top pocket of his rucksack. As the apple flew out of his hands and down the face, I laughed. "I've got an orange I can lose later," he said casually. I forgot about the incident until he opened his rucksack again and the orange bounced out.

It was soon my turn to follow. The climbing was not overly difficult, but the position was sensational. Nearby the slabby face we were climbing ended in a ridge. The face beyond must have been very steep, because it was possible to look straight down to a glacier over a thousand metres below. The glacier led up to the shapely slopes of Mustagh Tower.

We climbed on until it seemed that Mark had arrived at the top.

"You're not going to believe this view," he said as I climbed up just below him.

I took a photo of him astride a pinnacle of rock before joining him. In all directions there was nothing but mountains and glaciers. I gazed at the Baltoro Glacier. From up there it looked like an amazing patchwork of rubble and differing shades of green and blue pools lying on the ice. In front of us were four of the world's fourteen 8,000-metre peaks. K2, Broad Peak and the Gasherbrums I and II stood above countless other peaks of slightly smaller stature. Biale, the mountain we had come to climb, was nearby. They all looked breathtaking.

"Hey, We're not on the summit," I pointed out.

"So what?" Mark replied.

I could see his point. A knife-edge ridge stretched out from where we were sitting for two hundred metres to a slightly higher pinnacle. It would have taken many hours to reach, besides it was nicer to just sit in the sun and take in the view.

We sat for far too long, simply staring.

"I'm getting addled," Mark announced.

"Me too."

Without another word we began setting up an abseil and then set off down.

By the time we arrived back at the col it was desperately hot. We simply dived into the tent with the others and sat in our underpants through the heat of the day.

Sean had met Mike and Nick coming up on his way down. Fortunately Mike had a spare pair of sunglasses, so Sean had been able to turn around and immediately come hack up again.

In the late afternoon it had cooled enough for us to leave the others and descend the couloir. We paused briefly on the glacier to look at Biale and stash some gear under a large boulder before walking slowly back to the camp. The others returned the following day, Sean and Nick having climbed to the same high point as Mark and I, while Mike opted to wait for them at the col. They too had come to the conclusion that following the ridge further to gain a slightly higher summit was not worth the effort. We had only intended to climb the peak as a means of acclimatising, and as such, although we had not reached the top, the outing had been completely successful. Now it was time to turn our attention to the main objective.

I awoke to the shrill tone of a small plastic alarm clock next to my head. I still felt very sleepy. Turning on my head torch, I soon saw why—the clock read 11 p.m. I had been asleep for just three hours. I stopped the alarm and let out a deep sigh. It was a strange time to be starting a day's climbing.

Five unproductive days had passed since the climb on Lobsang. It had taken us two days to figure out the correct way up the glacier and through an ice-fall. After a day's rest, it had then taken a further two days to reach the bottom of the face. Above, we would follow a line of snowy ramps across the left-hand side of the face to reach a ridge. The ridge offered an interesting and safe line to the summit. The waist-deep wet snow on the glacier had convinced us that it would be best to operate at night, at least on the lower part of the mountain.

Silently we began our day. Having recently had an evening meal there was little for us to do. We had one drink each and then packed everything into our rucksacks. Outside was cold and clear and the ground below us was frozen. We collapsed the tent and then started. It was a joy to be able to stand on the snow without sinking into it.

We walked slowly across the frosty, high plateau in our solitary patches of head-torch light. It was hard to imagine that the same place had been a furnace during the day. After crossing the bergschrund we started climbing.

"Let's get rid of this rope," Mark suggested, already untying from his end.

Now we were off the glacier there was little need for it. There was no danger of falling into a crevasse and we would move together up the gently angled snow slope above. Under such circumstances, if we all remained tied to the rope, there was the danger that if one fell they would pull the other two off as well. If there was going to be an accident, we all reasoned that one death was better than three.

Simon Yates

Already Mike and Nick had dropped behind and the entire group became more spread out as we climbed up the snow slope. Mark was setting a relentless pace. I tried to keep up with him, but also soon dropped behind. He was stronger, but I could not help feeling resentful of the fact that compared to Sean and me the load he was carrying was a smaller proportion of his body weight.

As the first light of dawn appeared, we caught Mark up waiting below where the ground steepened. A band of rock barred the way. It was going to be necessary to pitch the climbing. We emptied the ropes and climbing kit from our rucksacks and then I set off. The climbing, up ice-filled cracks between patches of snow, was difficult. It was tricky to find the best way within the limited scope of the head-torch beam and my hands got very cold when I had to remove my gloves to place pieces of equipment into the rock to safeguard my progress. By the time Mark and Sean joined me at the belay it was already light.

Sean led off above, as the chill went from the air. When we reached the next belay, both Mark and I were sweating heavily. It was nice to rest, to let my heavy breathing subside and to admire the views. We had cleared the rock band and snow slopes lay above again. It was hard to understand why it had taken so long to find a way through the ice-fall. It now looked obvious from above. Mike and Nick were just beginning the steeper section of climbing.

Suddenly, shouting shattered the silence,

"It's easy up here," echoed around.

Then almost immediately I heard a familiar hissing sound and looked up to see one of the ropes being dropped down. "What the hell's he playing at?" asked Sean.

"I don't know," I replied, moments before the second rope followed.

"I guess we're climbing without ropes now," Sean added sarcastically.

"That's all very well," I hissed. "But who's going to carry Mark's bloody rope?"

Mark was away now. I could see the outline of his arms and shoulders as he pounded his axes in before moving up the slope. We had divided the gear and food out equally before the climb and part of Mark's share had been one of the ropes he had dropped down. We would simply have to add the rope to everything else we were carrying.

We redistributed what we were carrying between us and set off. The sacks felt heavy, but got heavier still as it got warmer and we shed clothing. Then at about seven o'clock the sun hit and our progress slowed to a crawl, as snow on the slope turned to slush. I just wanted to get out of the sun and go to sleep. Mark had disappeared and there was nowhere to pitch a tent. We would have to carry on until we reached the ridge, where I suspected Mark was waiting for us. I quickly emptied my water bottle and my head began to throb. I dearly wanted to abandon my rucksack, but knew I would have to return for it. As time went by, I spent longer doing nothing, slumped over my axes. However I was not the only one suffering. I was slowly pulling away from Sean, and Mike and Nick were nowhere to be seen. It seemed ridiculous that a fine, sunny day that had passed without hitches was turning into such a struggle.

Finally the slope levelled out and I staggered along a shelf leading across to a notch in the ridge. Mark was lying on a foam mat in the snow, stripped to his vest.

"I've been here for two hours," he bragged.

I could have been as well without carrying the rope, I thought. Mark's disregard for convention was in varying degrees exciting, funny and charming. Sometimes he went too far and could seem a little arrogant. But usually his attitude and behavior meant he often ended up in strange situations doing unusual things and this generally made him great fun to be with. However, at times like these he was just plain annoying.

Without a word I threw my rucksack down and slumped on to it. The greatest concentration of high mountains in the world lay in front of me. To the east lay Mustagh Tower, K2, Broad Peak, the Gasherbrums and Chogolisa, clustered around the head of the Baltoro Glacier. If I looked in the other direction I could see the huge 1,500-metre face on the west side of the Greater Trango Tower one of the world's largest vertical rock faces. The Nameless Tower stood nearby and another rock spire—Uli Biaho—in the valley behind. The climbing had required such effort that I had hardly noticed them.

I lay on the snow and marvelled at the view. Then, as Sean arrived, I took out my camera and framed a series of pictures. I knew the photographs would be stunning the moment I took them and felt privileged and humble to be in such a place. It was remarkable to think no others had viewed what we were looking at.

After a while we pitched the tent and dived inside in our underwear to escape the heat and sun. It was incredibly uncomfortable. We lay around and panted. Mark managed to get the stove going and maked a brew. At midday Nick arrived.

"Mike's suffering with the heat and altitude," he said. Mike was not having a very good time and I felt sorry for him, stuck down on the face in the searing glare of the sun. Nick rested while we made him a drink. Then he surprised us all by starting off down again. "I'm going to help Mike," he announced.

Four hours later Mike crawled into camp. Nick was carrying his rucksack. The day had been demanding enough inside our tent, and I could only imagine how much they had suffered. We helped them put up their tent nearby. Then, as the sun mercifully began to set, we tried to grab some sleep.

At midnight we were up again, collapsing the tent. By the time we had finished, my hands were cold. We moved off and climbed the gently angled snow ridge above. It was tiring work sinking into the deep, powdery snow and soon my feet were cold as well.

I was leading the steepest section of the ridge when the dawn began. As the horizon to the east gradually brightened I saw lightning flickering inside a mass of thunder heads. The sky above turned amazing shades of blues, violets and purples. Beams of light cut through the gaps in the cloud and illuminated distant mountains. Then suddenly the sun popped up from behind the West Ridge of K2, bathing the mountains all around in a rich, orange light. Tears poured from my eyes and rolled down my cheeks. I wiped them away with my hands and they froze to my gloves. I looked down at the others and watched their heads darting one way then the other, trying to take everything in.

The light show did not last long. The sun climbed quickly and we reached a notch on the ridge as it began to get hot again. Above was a steep rocky buttress, which barred the way to the summit perhaps four hundred metres above.

"We could go to the top from here," Mark suggested as we dug out yet another platform for the tent.

"We'll wait and see what the weather does," I cautioned.

I lay in the tent, hoping that the spell of clear skies that had blessed our time in the mountains would continue, but the signs did not look good. The wind increased and high clouds gathered. Then as the tent heated up, I developed a splitting headache. After suffering all day, I took some aspirin and the pain went away, making me feel very stupid for not taking some earlier. As the light faded, the sky cleared and I hoped we would get the extra decent day we needed in order to summit.

I awoke suddenly. The tent was shaking violently and snow was hissing in through the entrance which we had left slightly unzipped to allow some air to circulate. I sat up, leaned across Mark and Sean and closed the zip. It looked as if we would not get a chance to go to the summit on this occasion. As the weather deteriorated, the others woke up. By six in the morning, we were all sat with our backs up against the end of the tent, bracing it against the wind.

"Let's clear off," Mark said, after a particularly severe gust, expressing what we had all been thinking for some time.

Outside, the driven snow stung our eyes. Visibility was less than ten metres and it was difficult to determine which was the slope below and which was sky. Our tracks from the previous day had all drifted over.

"Which way?" Mark yelled into my ear.

"This way," I replied, striding off down the slope.

There was no way of knowing for certain if I was going in the right direction. It felt right, but without any way of checking all I could do was trust my senses. I ploughed on down, occasionally pausing to squint into the wind and snow to see if I could find the horizon, any feature that was recognisable. Nothing appeared, and as time went on I began to imagine that I had made some terrible mistake. The big worry was straying too far from the ridge. Then we would be left stranded on a large, open face of snow and ice above enormous cliffs. However, I did not want to get too close to the ridge either, as in sections standing waves of snow formed huge cornices, which we had been careful to avoid on the way up. With the present visibility it would be easy for us to wander on to one of these features and only realize the error as it collapsed beneath our feet. The lower we descended the more paranoid I became.

Then surprisingly the sky brightened, and looking up through the cloud I could just make out the outline of the sun. Way off to our right the rolling outline of the ridge slowly came into focus. A tiny, radiant splash of yellow marked the site of Mike and Nick's tent. Without pausing, I turned and made straight for it. Then the sky darkened and the tent and ridge were once more engulfed in cloud. It no longer mattered, my bearings were set. Ten minutes later we arrived at the camp.

"We're going down," I shouted, shaking the tent.

Simon Yates

There was some movement inside, before the entrance was unzipped and Nick's head appeared.

"We're going to sit it out," he said, grimacing at the weather.

Being able to see the tent on the ridge had been a lucky break. It marked the point where we needed to descend straight down, to drop into the narrow ramp line that we had followed on the way up. We set off down without the intense, draining concentration of the first part of the descent. We no longer had to worry about getting lost.

After walking for a way, we down-climbed to the rock band. Three simple abseils brought us to the top of the slope that dropped on to the plateau. Mark was in a hurry to get off the mountain and galloped off down the snow slope, dragging Sean and me behind him with the rope. After the slow progress higher up it was exhilarating to be moving quickly again, and the deep, wet snow allowed us to stumble and slide without losing control. In a matter of minutes we had descended most of the slope and jumped the bergschrund.

We were some way short of the plateau when the snow finished and we walked on to ice. It was an extension of the main glacier running up the slope above. It was an unusual feature, which I would have expected to have been much steeper. I hardly gave it a second thought until Mark was about a hundred metres above the plateau. Suddenly he sat down and started bum-sliding. Moments later Sean was pulled from his feet by the rope. Already I could see they were sliding down the ice far too quickly for safety. A horrible fear welled up inside me. I took two large steps forward, and as the rope came taut sat down on the ice. I reasoned that it was better to slide on my backside, than to be pulled from my feet and possibly cartwheel. I lifted my feet to stop my crampons catching on the ice, then there was a sharp tug at my waist where the rope was tied to my harness and I was off.

The toboggan ride was short and brutal. I accelerated rapidly and a series of bone-jarring impacts passed through my backside and up my spine. I saw Mark and Sean spill out on to the snow at the base of the slope and for a moment thought I was going to escape unhurt. Then I bottomed out again. My vision blurred and I felt nauseous.

I came to a halt in the snow and lay groaning. Pain ran down my back and into my right leg. I could hear Mark laughing. Slowly my breathing calmed and I tried to sit upright. A surge of pain made me lie down again.

"Are you okay?" asked Sean, looking concerned.

"No," I replied angrily, annoyed by the pointless nature of my injury. Now none of us would get off the mountain quickly.

With Sean's help I managed to get to my feet, but I was in so much pain that it was difficult to move.

"It's no good," I said. "I'll have to take a Temgesic."

I found the packet of painkillers in my rucksack and slipped one under my tongue. A few minutes later, after the pill had dissolved I felt nauseous again. It did little to ease the pain.

There seemed little point in delaying what was going to be a long descent. I put my right arm around Sean's shoulders and we set off, trying to follow Mark's footprints. It was difficult because of the size of his stride and I often broke through into the soft, wet snow around his steps. As I sank up to my thighs, pain seared up my back. There was further agony as I struggled to extract myself.

Once we were off the plateau and we began to drop down through the ice-fall, it was more comfortable for Sean simply to tow me through the snow. However there were crevasses to cross. The only way was to jump, which caused a massive surge of pain and left me gasping. As we dropped height, the snow turned to rain. By about midday we were off the snowy upper reaches of the glacier and conditions under foot improved. I was able to hobble slowly on the surface of the ice and rocks.

"I'll see you back at the camp," Mark said, handing me his ski-poles before running off into the mist.

"You might as well leave me to it," I told Sean after he had been watching my painfully slow steps for thirty minutes. There was little he could do to help me, and as my movements were slow and deliberate it seemed unlikely that I would injure myself further in a fall.

I staggered down the glacier feeling sorry for myself. It looked like this was the end of my expedition. I had obviously done some serious damage to my lower back or pelvis. The pain was just about bearable, but I had to stop frequently to let it subside. Climbing the loose scree slope above the glacier to reach the ridge of moraine which ran down to the camp was agony. The darkening cloud, mist and driving rain seemed to match my mood. I could hardly remember such a miserable afternoon.

When I finally arrived in camp, it was nearly dark. All I wanted to do was sleep, hoping that when I woke my injury would have somehow disappeared. I ate a little under the kitchen shelter, but it was not an evening for sitting around. The rain was still falling heavily and I was pleased we had taken the decision to come down, despite what had happened during our retreat. I joined Mark in the tent. By lying on my left side and packing clothing around my backside I finally made myself comfortable. I had no intention of moving until the morning.

I had barely fallen asleep when I woke to the tent shaking. "Quick, much water coming," Haqeem was shouting.

"Go and sleep with Sean," I snapped, convinced that his tent must have been leaking. "We'll sort it out in the morning."

"No. No. Much water coming soon." There was panic in his voice.

"Shit," Mark groaned. "I'll go and see what he's going on about."

He slid out of his sleeping bag, put on a waterproof jacket, grabbed his head-torch and putting his feet into his boots stepped outside. I could hear him and Haqeem running around, their voices sounded very serious.

"Get up now!" Mark burst into the entrance of the tent. "There's a flood coming."

I began to pull myself upright. The pain was intense, as the muscles around the injured area had stiffened while I was asleep. Now I could hear the water. It sounded like a torrent.

"Get a move on," Mark shouted.

"Give me a hand then," I demanded.

Mark dived into the tent and stuffed equipment into rucksacks while I tried to put on a few clothes. Then he leapt out again and pulled me out of the tent and stood me upright. Sean was also up. I helped as best as I could as Mark ripped the tent pegs from the ground. A wave of water washed round my ankles.

"Pick this up," Mark screamed as the water hit the tent.

We grabbed each end and lifted the shelter above the encroaching flood. Suddenly it seemed everywhere was covered in water. As the water level rose above our boots, we ploughed uphill until finally Mark's head-torch beam picked out a raised dry spot next to Sean's tent. We made for it and dropped the tent down. The pain in my back returned and there was little I could do but stand and watch as the others tried to salvage the remaining tents and the kitchen.

Now I realized what had happened. After the prolonged rain, a river had started to flow along a narrow valley at the side of a moraine ridge which ran down into the camp. We were surrounded by a further moraine ridge and cliffs leaving nowhere for the water to escape. A lake had formed over the grassy meadow where we had pitched our tents.

After moving the kitchen the others returned, pitched my tent and insisted that I get some sleep. I was happy to oblige. I was beginning to think the day had no end. Finally, I rearranged my bedding and fell into a deep sleep.

In the morning the water had drained a little and I watched Mark, Sean and Haqeem building a dam to divert the main flow of water further down the valley. It was only partially successful, as sections kept breaking.

"Now I know what it was like to live in Holland in the eighteenth century," Mark joked.

At midday, Mike and Nick returned. Mike had suffered severe headaches for two days before they had decided to come down. Their retreat had been both terrifying and arduous, as they descended avalanche-prone slopes and then waded through nearly meter-deep snow on the plateau.

It seemed that with the flood some of our momentum and enthusiasm were washed away, along with much of the kitchen. Mike decided he would limit his further activities to collecting rock samples in the valley. Mary Rose returned a day later from a trip to K2 Base Camp with the liaison officer and she chose to start making her way home to New Zealand.

My back gradually healed, marked by an enormous purple, red and yellow bruise running from my buttock down the back of my right leg. I teamed up with Nick and along with Mark and Sean we made two further attempts on the mountain, but luck was not with us. Each time we reached the ridge, bad weather set in, forcing us back down.

On a bright beautiful morning a group of porters arrived and we packed up the camp. We had arranged our collection date with them and there was no realistic way of changing it and besides, the food we had brought in with us was also coming to an end. The time to leave had arrived. We crossed the Baltoro Glacier to Urdukas where we joined the main trail to K2. Sean and I stayed behind for a while as the others followed the porters down. It was a beautiful place high on a terrace above the glacier, looking straight across to the mountains we had been among in the previous weeks.

It was a little frustrating not to climb to the summit of Biale, but the uncertainty of our undertaking had been the main attraction for me. However the excitement involved in attempting an unclimbed peak in such a remarkable place more than outweighed any disappointment I was feeling.

Simon Yates

We had no intention of using the porters who had carried loads up to the base camp. After arriving we had been forced to take a visit to Urdukas to replace the flour and rice that had been taken during the walk-in. While we were there, we hired ten porters in advance for the walk-out. A week later two of the porters had arrived with fresh loads of flour and rice. The loads had been paid for in advance and so it was obvious the men were trustworthy. The men turned out to be of a completely different caliber to the ones who had carried for us on the way in. These porters were strong, fit and well organized. They simply wanted to get the job done as quickly and efficiently as possible. They had made five carries to K2 base camp already that summer. They told us they could complete the two week walk-up in eight days, and then ran down in three to obtain work with another expedition. For them, to get work on their way down was a bonus.

Walking down with our new employees was a pleasure. I warmed to the men immediately. They set off at a blistering pace and kept it up, although they did take regular breaks. At lunchtime they stopped and made tea on tiny fires of precious fire wood, carried up from Paiyu. We sat and shared thick, unleavened Balti bread and washed it down with the tea. Then one of the men marched off into a boulder field and returned clutching a bag. The bag was full of cigarettes. I laughed. As the only non-smoker in the group, he had stashed the cigarettes on the way up knowing the others would run out. Now he was selling them for a two rupee per packet profit.

When we reached Paiyu that evening I watched the men quietly organising themselves. Some made bread, while others collected wood. Then one man removed his boot to reveal a split a centimetre deep in the leathery skin of his heel. He pulled a strand of thread from one of the woven polypropylene bags in which we had packed the loads, threaded it through a rusty curved needle and sewed up the wound. These were hardy, honest people whom I felt the utmost respect for.

Despite being in such an alien environment and a long way from home, I felt content and relaxed. For me, it was starting to feel like my home.

Sean arrived late at the camp that night, having spent some time filming and taking photographs at Urdukas. He came straight over to where Mark and I were sitting. "You're never going to guess what I saw after you left?" he said seriously.

"No idea," I replied casually, not expecting anything important.

"Those ice-cliffs above the plateau on Biale fell down. They took out the whole fucking basin."

We laughed nervously, quite aware of how many nights we had spent camped below the cliffs, but made light of Sean's news. It was back in Sheffield over a year later that Sean showed us some film footage he had been taking when the avalanche had occurred. We sat open-mouthed, watching the cloud of ice and snow engulfing the entire plateau and many hundreds of metres further down the valley. There was no doubt that such an event would have killed us had we been there at the time. The film was unedited and immediately after the pictures of the avalanche it cut to three choughs pecking at rubbish around the campsite at Urdukas. We all laughed at the coincidence and symbolism, imagining that we would have been reincarnated as the birds.

For me this was the first time that I realized the arbitrary and random nature of the risks I took going to climb in big mountains. It showed me it was possible to get killed even if you were careful, took the right decisions and did not make mistakes. In subsequent years, I have seen more outrageous and unpredictable events that had the potential to be fatal. In each case, as on Biale, I would never have thought they were possible. Yet this knowledge has never bothered me sufficiently to stop returning to those places. I have learned to accept this arbitrary risk and view it in a similar way to the risk I take every time I get into a car, although obviously I realize the risks associated with being in big mountains are much higher.

Mikel Vause (b. 1952) has climbed extensively in the Teton and Wasatch Mountains and in England, Scotland, Wales, Norway, and the Himalayas. He is the author of *On Mountains and Mountaineers,* and *I Knew It Would Come to This,* editor of *Rock and Roses, The Peregrine Reader* and co-editor of *Wilderness Tapestry* with Sam Zeveloff and Bill McVaugh.

Mikel Vause: Mountaineering: The Heroic Expression of Our Age

However mechanized, or automatized, the conditions of human life may become, the same number of human beings will, I believe, continue to carry this inherited memory, reinforced for action by the new awareness of mountains and of mountaineering which has come with this last century

—*G. Winthrop Young*

In the past few years, with the influx of climbing parties in all the major mountain ranges, the number of accidents, many that end in death, the question of why humans climb has come to the forefront. For what purpose do people go into high, cold and extremely dangerous places. It is obvious the money to be made from such enterprises is minimal. Aside from airlines, a few expedition outfitters are making some profit from supplying equipment, food, guides, etc. The native economies such as in Nepal receive certain benefits, and occasionally a climber might sell a book or film. The reality is the commercial aspects of climbing mountains are limited.

For most mountaineers the pure physical enjoyment and the spiritual uplift that accompanies a body tired from the adventure to be had in wild nature is reason enough to climb mountains and materialism is, for most, at the bottom of the list. That as John Henry Newman argues, "knowledge [has] its end in itself," so also climbing mountains has "its end in itself." One ventures out only for the riches of building both a strong body and mind and in some cases to become rich in the spiritual sense. This argument could be fairly made until recently, but in the past decade or so there has developed an ever growing sense of commercialism in the world of mountaineering. The guiding business is nothing new to mountaineering. In fact climbing may never have evolved as it has were it not for the early shepherds and hunters leading European aristocracy through the Alps, Scottish Highlands, and England's Lake District. Climbing schools like The International Alpine School in Switzerland, Exum Guides in the Tetons, N.O.L.S., and Outward Bound, to name a few, have continued in this sport-old tradition of taking people out. One need only to look in the advertisement pages of outdoors and climbing magazines to find dozens of schools and services that offer the climbing experience. The fact that there are places people can go to get instruction on how to become mountaineers is a good thing, which was the overarching philosophy of guide services and instructional companies. Such companies, for the most part, continue to be useful when they focus on teaching mountaineering. But sadly, as with about every other aspect of our society, individuals start looking for ways to profit by providing shortcuts, ways to achieve desired ends by cutting corners. The television is replacing books and the telephone is replacing written correspondence. Why read a novel when one can watch a film based on a novel or write a letter when, in a matter of seconds, space and distance can be spanned with a phone call. There is very little in our world that technology has not affected. This coupled with the immediacy modern society attaches to all aspects of life paradoxically makes much of what we do, in the end, more complicated.

TECHNOLOGY VS. EXPERIENCE

Climbing is no different. As Broughton Coburn in *Everest: Mountain without Mercy* points out because of air support the trip from Kathmandu to Lukla that was once "a two week walk [has]...been reduced to a forty minute flight" (53). Air support now allows one relatively easy access to high, remote mountains and this is not the only high-tech advantage. One must also consider all the advances in equipment such as plastic boots, step-in crampons, high-tech ice axes, ever-dry ropes made from stronger and lighter nylon, and clothing that weighs nothing, and is not only waterproof, but breathable, light weight stoves, freeze-dried food, and the list goes on and on.

Yet with these many improvements intended to make the activity more safe, and certainly more comfortable, why are people climbing big mountains dying at such alarming rates? Part of the problem has to do with why they are on the mountain in the first place. Are they there for intrinsic reasons i.e. personal physical challenge and mental and spiritual elevation? Or are they climbing because high adventure is in vogue and that they have some disposable income? It is commonly held that one can do anything with money. When it comes to climbing, the idea that because one can hire an experienced guide and is able to purchase the latest Gore-Tex clothing and the most up to date climbing hardware, all the bases are covered; they will be safe. By taking on the role of client they have purchased protection without paying the "real" dues that comes from personal experience. According to Peter Athans, a professional Everest guide: "Occasionally you'll get a client who thinks he's bought a guaranteed ticket to the summit" (Krakauer 23). The truth is that no amount of expensive equipment or the fact that one is part of a guided party can substitute for experience. In order to perform in difficult situations one must be prepared and preparation comes from experience.

APPRENTICESHIP

In the climbing community I grew up in there was a core group of climbers who served as mentors to almost all the beginning climbers in the area. It was nearly impossible to start a climbing career without having some contact with members of that core group. It was a friendly time and new climbers were welcomed so long as they wanted to learn proper climbing techniques. One served an informal apprenticeship by climbing with more experienced climbers. After one had learned rope handling, proper belaying techniques, and how all the equipment worked, (admittedly it wasn't all that hard to figure how to drive and remove pitons, today's equipment is a bit more technical and takes more practice to use) on short top roped climbs, the new climber was ready to serve as a second and participate in multi-pitch climbs. After a period of participation as a second the opportunity to lead came. By today's standards this process seems long and drawn out, but looking back I remember very few accidents, and a fatality was extremely rare. Part of the problem today is

impatience. We live in a world that has come to expect immediate gratification on all fronts. Everything one wants in life must be immediately
available.

IMMEDIATE GRATIFICATION

In the 1990's it is almost unheard of for a young person to save money
to buy a car. Why should one have to wait when they can simply take out
a loan. One can hardly walk across a college campus in America without
being confronted by numerous opportunities to apply for various credit
cards. This "have it now" philosophy easily transfers to all other aspects
of society. There can be no question that in any way the amazing tech-
nological advances of the twentieth century has made life better, but in
some ways it has made life more dangerous as it provides opportunities
too easily and without requiring proper preparations.

The disasters on Everest in 1996 drives this point home. In an attempt to "unite vocation and avocation," climbing guides like Rob Hall
and Scott Fischer and there are others, somewhat unwittingly diminished
the dangers of climbing a mountain the size and immensity of Everest.

In an attempt to make a living doing what they loved to do they allowed people who had no business being on Everest due to lack of experience and preparation, who hadn't paid their dues so to speak, to not
only endanger themselves, but to put the lives of other climbers on the
mountain, the guides in particular, in jeopardy. According to Sir Edmund
Hillary, the first to successfully summit Everest in 1953, ventures such
as Hall's and Fischer's are "engendering disrespect for the mountain"
(Krakauer 66). Jon Krakauer, in his book *Into Thin Air*, provides a concerning illustration as he recounts a conversation with Scott Fisher:

A few weeks after Fischer returned victorious from Everest in 1994,
I encountered him in Seattle. I didn't know him well, but we had
some friends in common and often ran into each other at the crags
or at climber's parties. On this occasion he buttonholed me to talk
about the guided Everest expedition he was planning: I should come
along, he cajoled, and write an article about the climb for *Outside*.
When I replied that it would be crazy for someone with my limited
high-altitude experience to attempt Everest, he said, "Hey, experience is overrated. It's not the altitude that's important, it's your
attitude, bro. You'll do fine. You've done some pretty sick climbs—
stuff harder than Everest. We've got the big E figured out, we've got

it totally wired. These days, I'm telling you, we've built a yellow brick road to the summit. (66)

Statements such as those attributed to Scott Fischer are not only deceptive, but extremely dangerous. As all mountaineers know, the complection of a big mountain changes moment to moment. In a recent conversation with Doug Scott, who reached the summit of Everest via the Southwest Face in 1976, the point was made that if one signs on a guided expedition to Everest they should be sure they have purchased a round trip ticket. "...we've built a yellow brick road to the summit," but what about getting down from the summit alive? There were some in 1996 who unfortunately only had a one way ticket.

This essay is not meant to be an attack on Rob Hall, Steve Fisher, or any other mountain guide, but it does raise questions about the "materialistic premises" creeping into mountaineering which is the concern Walter Bonatti addresses in his essay *Mountaineering.*

In Bonatti's essay one finds one of the best examinations of why humans climb mountains. In the book *Great Days*, the essay *Mountaineering* is sandwiched between Bonatti's accounts of his many standard setting climbs and is a careful examination of the role of the mountaineer in the modern era that is dominated by technology and industry. Because mountaineering is basically a romantic (intrinsic) pursuit it seems to be at odds with the basic philosophies that govern a (extrinsic) techno-industrial society where material gain equates success. The article deals with the age old, archetypical conflict between the spiritual and the physical. Many mountaineers find the time spent in the mountains brings them to elevated inner-feelings, sometime revelatory, sometimes insightful or reflective, that comes as the result of varying periods of direct contact with wild nature, that is, nature in a relatively unmolested state—free from the harmful by-products of human over-involvement.

PHILOSOPHICAL CONSIDERATIONS

It is clear in romantic philosophy, whether it be the ancient eastern philosophers of Buddhism, Taoism, Hinduism or the more modern western philosophers such as the German romantics Goethe and Schiller, the English romantics Blake, Wordsworth, and Coleridge, or the Americans Emerson, Thoreau, and Whitman, that humans, if left to the influences of the unspoiled natural world will, in fact, elevate themselves to an almost divine state through repeated contact with the workings of the natural world. Humans learn best by first hand experience. In the words of Ann Zwinger, "there is no substitute for blisters and sunburn" (qtd in Trimble, *Words from the Land* 9). Bonatti's philosophy agrees with that of Zwinger as he explains that to venture into the mountains is a natural human desire. He, in fact, argues that testing oneself against the mountain is "a way of expressing man's ancestral dialogue of love with mother nature in terms of action" (71). Bonatti, the romantic, goes on to lament the loss of past values, particularly those placed on mystery and heros. He says:"Daily living has become a round of demands, provocations, and doubts. The intellect sweeps away spiritual values even before they are formed. Deprived of standards in a decadent society where nothing is fixed or defined, heroism has leaked away for sheer lack of purpose" (71-72). Edgar Allan Poe expresses the same concern in the poem *Sonnet—To Science:*

Science! True daughter of Old Time thou art!
Who altarist all things with thy peering eyes.
Why preyesy thou thus upon the poet's heart,
Vulture, whose wings are dull realities?
How should he love thee? Or how deem thee wise,
Who would not leave him in his wandering
To seek for treasure in the jeweled skies,
Albeit he soared with undaunted wing?
Hast thou not dragged Diana from her car?
And driven the Hamadryad from the wood
To seek a shelter in some happier star?
Hast thou not torn the Naiad from her flood,
The Elfin from the green grass, and from me
The summer dream beneath the tamarind tree? (771-772)

Bonatti sees the mountaineer as taking up the role of hero in a time when the human spirit needs a new champion who, through physical action and spiritual elevation, leads a rebellion against: "the frustrations of industrial civilization, rebellion against a collective society, a society almost happy to sink into a general mediocrity, and always content to seem rather than be. It is also a rebuttal of disillusion and ignobility and of that security offered as progress, which, when achieved, makes spiritual progress impossible"(72).

To the romantics a techno-society is evil as it entices, through the glorification of the material, people to divorce themselves from nature. There is an obvious danger in the invitation of industry for people to leave the pastoral settings such as small villages and farms where they are in constant contact with harmonious workings of nature, for the large industrial urban centers made up of row houses and factories. In the pastoral setting currency is much less important that in urban settings as much of what is necessary for existence is produced through an active partnership with nature i.e. tilling the land, planting the seed, tending the garden, and reaping the harvest. Where as in the urban setting of the industrial community one receives wages for working in the factories and it is necessary to purchase life's necessities from vendors thus eliminating the first-hand participation in the harmonious natural process. As William Wordsworth states in his poem "The Old Cumberland Beggar:"

May never HOUSE, misnamed INDUSTRY,

Make him captive!—for that pent up din,

Those life-consuming sounds that clog the air,

Be his natural silence of old age!

Let him be free of mountains solitudes;

And have around him, whether heard or not,

The pleasant melody of woodland birds...

As in the eye of Nature he has lived,

So in the eye of Nature let him die! (Lines 179-200)

Emerson states humans are the only animals not in harmony with the natural world and that human disharmony is learned, not innate. Such a philosophy is in direct conflict with the old puritan standards of the time which argued humans are born degenerate as a result of the fall of Adam. Emerson sees in most humans an innate goodness that gets replaced with learned disharmony and are therefore further removed from the natural world and its spiritual by-products. Emerson goes on to argue that humans can in fact, but only through frequent contact with wild nature, actually unite what he called the "ideal and the actual" and thus bring together the physical and spiritual to create a harmonious existence.

This same idea is paramount in Doug Scott's essay titled *On the Profundity Trail* in which he argues that going into remote places, places that take commitment to visit, that he is able to recharge his spiritual batteries and when he returns to the social world he is better prepared to contribute to its betterment. In recounting his ascent of the Salathe Wall Scott states: ". . . after the trip I did seem to know positively where to go next—and that was back into society, relaxed, but with a new zest and enthusiasm. . . ." He goes on to explain that the more commitment it takes to complete the journey that the reward is also greater:

If big wall climbing is pursued in a more hostile environment and for longer periods, if the big wall climber climbs alone, as Bonatti did on the Dru, then the doors of perception will be opened wide. The climber involved may experience a more lasting state of heightened awareness, and may even reach a truly visionary, if not mystical, state of being which transcends normal human comprehension.... The climber who is willing to extend himself to the limit of his technical skill and endurance on any long climb, is en route up the profundity trail.(Scott 17)

Who Should Be on Everest, and Why.

Returning to the idea of novice climbers on Mount Everest, it should be noted that even though both Bonatti and Scott speak of committing oneself to the "limits of technical skill and endurance" the point should also be made that one must know, and be realistic, about one's limitations. Spiritual and intellectual enlightenment does little good if one is dead and unable to share it with others.

So why climb? The argument has been made that to do so for material reasons can, in many cases, only lead to disaster as was the case with Everest in 1996. Ironically it was those with the most experience that were killed in an effort to meet their obligations to paying clients. Wilford Noyce, and member of the successful 1953 British Everest Expedition said: ". . . we go out because it is our nature to go out" (qtd. in Vause, *On Mountains and Mountaineers* 10). J.R.L. Anderson, in his work, *The Ulysses Factor*, states it is a natural human instinct to explore—to seek adventure.

The philosopher Woodrow Wilson Sayre led a four man expedition to the north side of Mount Everest in 1962 and recorded the adventure in the book *Four Against Everest*. In this most interesting expedition account he discusses several reasons humans climb: "the question about climbing is not a question about motivation at all. . . . It is really a question about relative values." One value is that of beauty: "If a person will cross the ocean just to look at the beauty of a cathedral, why would he not do as much or more to see sights such as these [speaking of the Himalayas]"(204). Sayre goes on to say that there is a reason greater than to view beauty, but that is directly connected to beauty:

Very closely assisted with the beauty of the mountains are some special emotions which the highest and wildest peaks provoke. I feel a special excitement when I look out over thousands of square miles of untouched country. I feel it again when I walk where only a handful of men have walked in the history of the world, when I explore some hidden ridge or crag, or when I make the first track across a great unbroken snow field. I feel a special happiness to be alone in the high, silent places of the world tucked close under the sky. Such things are worth a little insecurity and sacrifice. (205)

Just as Bonatti and Scott, Sayre loves his time in wild solitude, but he also recognizes the need for contact with others of his kind: "We need to experience nature with friendly marks upon it of human works and struggle and hope. But also we need to see nature apart from even the smallest sigh of human interference. For this Phil Bartlett, a mountaineer and author of *The Undiscovered Country*, sees the need for humans to return to their primitive roots and that going into the mountains is a means to that end. He points out: "A return to the primitive encourages a mental retrenchment in which the forgotten elements of life regain their rightful status. . . . The attraction of the primitive life is that it takes one away from these pressures [Bonatti's industrial, collective society] which make it impossible to feel psychologically free" (71). One of the ways this whole process comes about, according to Bonatti, is that mountaineering is a natural "next step" for the people who live around mountains. Referring to early mountaineers Bonatti states: After they had explored the valleys and passes they "felt the urge to conquer the summits" (71). As the routes to the summits became harder and more technical Bonatti states:

"Mountaineering really transcended its origins, assuming an almost philosophical significance. I would say that it acquired a soul, and from there went on to become an active and heroic expression of our age" (71). That expression is the escape from the doldrums of collective society and the freedom and elevation of the human spirit coming from contact with wild nature. Bonatti continues:

Knowledge and wisdom are both essential to human progress, but they are not the same thing, as philosophy has long reminded us. However, let us accept our so called social conquests; let us disembark on the moon and other planets in our insatiable pride; only let us not forget that the destiny of man is to become ever more human. That is what the wise, useless, "mad actions" of our present-day heroes are meant to remind us. (73)

What is the purpose of mountaineering? To gain in things material? No. The purpose is as stated by John Muir, the nineteenth century American mountaineer:

"Climb the mountains and get their good tidings. Nature's peace will flow into you as sunshine flows into trees. The winds will blow their own freshness into you, and the storms their energy, while cares will drop off like autumn leaves" (qtd. in *John of the Mountains: The Unpublished Journals of John Muir* ed. Linnie Marsh Wolfe 317).

Works Cited

Anderson, J.R.L. *The Ulysses Factor*. New York, N.Y., U.S.A.: Harcourt Brace Jovanovich, Inc. 1970.

Bartlett, Phil. *The Undiscovered Country*. London, England: The Ernest Press, 1993.

Bonatti, Walter. *The Great Days*. Tr. Geoffrey Sutton. London, England: Victor Gollancz Ltd, 1974.

Coburn, Broughton. Everest: Mountain Without Mercy. Washington D.C., U.S.A.: The National Geographic Society, 1997. Krakauer, Jon. Into Thin Air. New York, N.Y. U.S.A.: Villard, 1997.

Muir, John. *John of the Mountains: The Unpublished Journals of John Muir*. Ed. Linnie Marsh Wolfe. Madison, WI, U.S.A.: University of Wisconsin Press, 1979.

Poe. Edgar Allan. The Complete Stories and Poems of Edgar Allan Poe. New York N.Y., U.S.A.: Doubleday, 1966.

Sayre, Woodrow Wilson. *Four Against Everest*. Englewood Cliffs, NJ, U.S.A.: Prentice-Hall, 1964.

Scott, Doug. "On the Profundity Trail. " *Mountain 15* 1971:12-17.

Trimble, Stephen. *Words from the Land*. Layton, UT, U.S.A.: Gibbs M. Smith Books, 1989.

Vause, Mikel. *On Mountains and Mountaineers*. La Crescenta, CA, U.S.A.: Mountain N' Air Books, 1993.

Wordsworth, William. *Poetical Works*. New York, NY, U.S.A.: Oxford University Press, 1990.

Young, Geoffrey Winthrop. *The Effects of Mountains upon the Development of Human Intelligence*. Glasgow, Scotland: Jackson, Son & Company, 1957.

Nothing Ventured Nothing Gained: Vocation and Avocation United

Doug Robinson (b. 1945) is a native Californian who has spent most of his life skiing and climbing in the California mountains, although he has made forays into the greater ranges including the second ascent of Ama Dablam. He is one of the initiators of the "clean climbing movement" and was a member of the team that did the first "clean" ascent of Yosemite's Half Dome. He is founding member of the North American Guides Association and was the first president. He is the author of *A Night on the Ground, A Day in the Open.*

DOUG ROBINSON:
HALF DOME COMES CLEAN

By 1972, when "The Whole Natural Art" came out, I had climbed hammerless up grade IV and V walls in Yosemite. Then along came Galen Rowell's first assignment for *National Geographic* cover, a big wall climb in Yosemite. Galen invited Dennis Hennek and me to do the classic Northwest Face of Half Dome, and I said sure, as long as we could try to climb it clean. Dennis and I both knew that we were ready and the time had come for a hammerless ascent of a big wall. Galen, however, had a crucial assignment for his budding career to get in the can, so he suggested putting pins and hammer in the haul bag just in case.

Galen Rowell was a Chevy mechanic at the time, and the proprietor of a somewhat greasy dive of a shop down on San Pablo Avenue in Berkeley. Once when my Volkswagen blew up near Sacramento, Galen generously drove all the way up and towed my car back to his shop. There were limits, however, to his hospitality; I did my rebuild out back, where my foreign car couldn't offend any red-blooded customers. Every spare minute Galen slipped out of the shop into the office in back, pounding away on a well-lubricated typewriter. He wrote, for instance, about one of the many thousand-mile weekends when he would appear on my doorstep at Cardinal Village up Bishop Creek for a quick bivy on his way into the mountains.

We had done some fine routes together, including The Smokestick, the first modern route on the Wheeler Crest, which featured offwidth and flaring-chimney cruxes. Looking up at the thousand-foot buttress from Round Valley, it was dwarfed by the backdrop of the 7,000-foot escarpment it lived on; we underestimated it so badly as to wear mountain boots for our first attempt. Galen tilted his shot of the attempt a wee bit too much, but that didn't get us up the moves either and we had to come back to take it more seriously. The climb was so good that we soon did the buttress next door, Adam's Rib. Today there are dozens of fine routes on the Wheeler Crest, but the pace of development has stalled. It is ironic that the Owens River Gorge a few miles away draws international attention for good but short sport routes packed into a slot in the ground with no view. Every year now ten thousand climbers pull over the rim of the Gorge with the Wheeler Crest full in their faces and don't even see it. Nearly as much exposed rock as Yosemite Valley, with major lines awaiting even a first attempt, and climbing fashion has shifted so much that this vast mountainside draped with granite has become effectively invisible. But I digress.

I was thinking more about driving, about Galen behind the wheel of many a Chevy. He is like most climbers in that he knows the mountain roads well, has an adrenalized urge to get places in a hurry using them, and does it just for sport. But unlike the rest, he had that shop to rebuild and tune and tinker. The result was succession of powerful mountain cars. Add a dose of testosterone, and it's easy to see that everyone who has climbed with Galen for any length of time ends up with at least one epic tale of a badly stuck vehicle. Mine took place at 10,000 feet on the Rock Creek road. The snow was getting deeper as we climbed, and Galen had been suffering the usual beginners frustrations on skis. . . . Anyway, a lot of digging ensued. Dick Dorworth wrote some inspired words in *Mountain Gazette* around then about "Night Driving," and it was he who captured the archetypal image of Galen at the wheel of a Chevy hurtling through Nevada at ninety per and all the while carrying on an animated discussion full face with someone in the back seat. One of the best things about traveling with Galen was that those conversations kept spilling over from climbing into a much broader world of ideas, and ranged from the place of aggression in the evolution of man, to how climbing fit into the life of the satanist/magician Aleister Crowley, to–whoa, stop!–there's an eagle.

Doug Robinson

Sure enough, the eagle was standing on the edge of a gravel road in eastern Nevada. Galen reigned in the Chevy and backed up until we were staring at the great bird from ten feet away. It stared back, steadily. Magnificent being, it could easily have carried off a large marmot and it wasn't the least bit intimidated by a pack of humans in a big car. When it had had enough of us, it turned and stalked off, rather stufly, into the sage. We had been summarily dismissed.

Dennis Hennek had already made the second ascent of the North American Wall by the time we met. He loved the challenge of clean climbing. One of the early places we practiced it together was weekend forays from Ventura to Tahquitz Rock. There we made the first clean ascent of the Open Book, which had become the first 5.9 in the Americas when Royal Robbins freed it in 1952. My prototype Tube Chocks were handy in the offwidth crux. Later Dennis got the job of tearing down the movie set of Lago, which had been built near Mono Lake for a Clint Eastwood epic, "The Good, The Bad, and the Ugly." Dennis crafted together a fine little cabin from the salvaged wood. It sat in the first line of willows up from the waters edge, From the loft you could see the sunrise over the lake, then roll over and watch "baby cakes" and coffee underway on the wood range. One day we got completely skunked on the north pillar of Mount Goode. Almost worse than missing the climb was abandoning the name we had already picked out, Goodie Goodie, from a line in *"The Night Climbers of Cambridge,"* "This climber had the interesting habit of saying 'goodie goodie' after each successful ascent." Our consolation was a superb first ascent on Cardinal Pinnacle, clean all the way, and named after a cucumber we peeled on the summit.

August 1973: The biggest aluminum steamer trunk you could imagine arrived air freight from *National Geographic*, and it was just burstin with Nikons, lenses, and many cases of film. Galen went to work sorting and packing camera gear for Half Dome while Dennis and I racked the hardware. On the climb I could only manage to shoot three rolls of film, which was a lot for me, and Dennis did about the same. Galen, of course, rarely emerged from behind some lens or other. In the end a *Geographic* editor commented that this was the smallest lot of slides they had ever picked a story from: 10,000.

The climb went "vedy" clean, including anchors constructed of nuts and runners even when there were fixed pins and bolts right in our faces. The hardest part of the protection and aid was finding alternative placements to fixed pieces that were often lodged in the best parts of the crack.

Half Dome Clean

The crux was clearly Dennis' lead of pitch 23, an incipient crack sprouting rurps and bashies; it would not have gone clean without prototypes of Tom Frost's wild new Crack'n Ups. In the end we did use one fixed pin, though Galen remembers it being one Dennis clipped for the pendulum in the Robbins Traverse, while I thought it was one Galen clipped for aid up in the Zig Zags.

Three pitches up the face, far enough so we figured that it would be too much trouble to go back down for them, Dennis casually mentioned to Galen that he had been rummaging through the haul bag and couldn't seem to find the pitons anywhere. Galen's only comment was that Dennis wasn't a very convincing liar.

Seven pitches up is a ledge, sloping but good sized by wall standards, where we stopped for the day. We were getting comfortable and sorting gear when Galen suddenly decided we needed a shot of bivouacking in a hammock. In a flurry he dug one out, set it up, and hopped in. I snapped a photo, and no one could tell when it came out in the *Geographic* that Galen was hanging just above a big ledge. What I didn't realize until much later was that Dennis was behind me, documenting the whole process. Apparently an old-maid photo editor kept this shot in the lineup right up to the final edit, leading to speculation that I might become the first white male nude in *National Geographic*.

A highlight of the second day was the Robbins Chimney, and right after lunch I drew the lead. Quite recently a friend overheard in Boulder, Colorado, a modern nerve-center of climbing wisdom, the opinion that "nobody climbs the Robbins Chimney, you just go around to the left." I guess that news hadn't gotten to Yosemite twenty years earlier, because I was eager, for the notorious lead, though it was narrow, flaring and steepened inexorably to a runout crux. At that point I was eighty feet out with no chance of fitting any clean hardware into the flaring offwidth crack, and gulping down little waves of panic. The pitch was typical of Yosemite climbing of that era: awkwardly offwidth and completely unprotectable, with the climber making sweaty progress only inches at a time, his back against the wall and staring out over thousands of feet of lovely but quite empty space, all the while trying to maintain his cool and a few shreds of concentration, as carefree shouts from swimmers in the Merced River drifted upward on every meager puff of breeze.

Higher, another notorious offwidth was completely missing from the face. Psych Flake, as it had been called on the first ascent, was 80 feet tall, only eight inches thick at its base, and detached from the face along its bottom. The route followed an offwidth crack up one edge. Legend had it that the whole flake would vibrate if struck by the heel of the hand; and legend also made it out to be a spooky lead. Then one summer not long before our climb, the first party up there for the season found it missing, just completely gone. We stared at the downsloping ledge where Psych Flake had recently rested. It was still covered with some of the sand and gravel that had lubricated the great flake's passage. Fortunately, a straight-in crack in the wall behind made an easy alternate pitch. It even had a lieback edge not far inside, hinting at future exfoliation.

Thank God Ledge, with its dramatic position just under the Visor leering over the top of the face, was named for offering a timely escape from the prospect of climbing the Visor's stacked crockery. It is exfoliating too. In recent years the crack behind Thank God Ledge is twice as wide as when we tiptoed and then shamelessly crawled across. Perhaps it will become a horizontal chimney before disappearing completely.

Chuck Pratt, who was probably the first person to walk upright across Thank God Ledge, was once coiling his rope on the summit. He began to complain loudly to no one in particular or more likely addressing his monologue toward the heavens in general, commenting on the perversity of ropes, and the cheerful and seemingly willful way that they become caught under flakes, stuck in cracks at inconvenient times and distances, and generally make life miserable for the poor climber, who is minding his own business and just humbly trying to make a little vertical progress on the rocks of the world, thank you. All the while he was laying on the neat coils and shaking out kinds in his meticulous fashion. Having finished both his soliloquy and a textbook mountaineers coil, and having made perhaps too convincing and argument to the fates at large, he flung the coil with all his strength out over the dozens of acres of gently-rolling summit slabs. It sailed directly into a deep crack parallel to and not far back from the Northwest Face, never to be seen again. Someday, in the geological equivalent of a glacier spitting out a climber swallowed by its bergschrund centuries before, Chuck's rope will fall out of the sky into the forest that replaces the meadow that in the next hundred years will replace Mirror Lake.

Which reminds me of a geological interest sign along the Tioga Road that announces "Exfoliating Granite." That makes the process sound so immediate, that every time I see it I'm tempted to screech to a stop and watch for it to happen. On the other hand, after a few decades of seeing the walls in the Valley change, after hiking over freshly deposited talus beneath Sentinel, the Three Brothers, Glacier Point Apron, and Elephant Rock as well as Half Dome, I realize that it is a relatively immediate process. With all that exfoliation going on, climbing the face of Half Dome begins to resemble a game of "flakes and ladders."

Jeff Lowe (b.1949) is clearly one of the pioneers in climbing vertical ice. He has established some of the most creative and difficult climbs in the world including a new solo winter route on the North Face of the Eiger, and many bold lines in the Andes and Himalayas. His 1994 route, "Octopussy," is considered one of the most difficult mixed climbs in the world. He is the author of three books, *The Ice Experience, Climbing with Ron Fawcett, Paul Nunn, and Alan Rouse,* and *Ice World.*

JEFF LOWE:
GRABBING FRIENDSHIP
BY THE ANKLE

Colorado

Michael Kennedy is a resident of Aspen, Colorado, and editor of *Climbing* magazine. Prior to March, 1977, I had met and talked with Mike only once. I was favorably impressed. Many good climbers are very intense, seemingly about to burst at the seams. That sort of intenseness always has been difficult for me to handle, and I have a tendency to shy away. By his reputation, I knew Mike was a good climber, and when we sat down for a cup of coffee together I was halfway prepared for a tense and awkward situation. Our talk, however, was very enjoyable.

Among other things, we talked about independent attempts that we both had made on the East Face of the Moose's Tooth, a huge Alaskan wall that is yet unclimbed. When I asked him the reason for his party's failure, a smile broke through his beard. "At our high point we were hit by an avalanche of ice blocks," he said. "One of our anchors was ripped out, and one of our packs was smashed where it sat on a ledge. That was enough for us." He concluded, "We go out of there fast; man we were freaked!"

Mike was no arrogant, macho climber but a man who admits being scared and can smile at his own fear. As we continued to talk, sip coffee, and size each other up (yes, I'm certain Mike was taking my measure as well), I sensed a fairly strong feeling that the lanky fellow across the table from me would be a good partner in the high mountains. When Mike got up to leave and shake hands, I said, "Let's get together and do a climb sometime." "For sure," Mike agreed. "I'd like that a lot."

When in March, 1977, I found myself in need of another instructor for an International Alpine School ice-climbing course, I thought of Mike. We wouldn't exactly be climbing together, but it would be a good chance to get to know each other and gauge the value of that first impression. By the end of the course, when we were having a rather boisterous end-of-course celebration at the Outlaw Bar in Ouray, I knew I had been right about Mike.

After a long winter of teaching, I had run out of energy and inspiration. Mike had sensed this and doubled his own output: setting up most of the top-ropes on the icefall, demonstrating techniques in an enthusiastic (and competent) way, taking groups of students on two consecutive days up long and difficult climbs, and giving them the experience they had come for. Having done all that, he accepted my thanks for a job well done, saying simply, "That's what I'm being paid for, isn't it?" and then buying me a Heineken.

I asked him over the beer if he would be interested in going to Alaska in June to try a couple of new routes on Mount Hunter and Foraker. My cousin George Lowe and I had been planning these climbs all winter but needed a third partner. "Would I?" he answered. "Is the Pope Catholic?"

Alaska

We met in the airport in Anchorage. George had come from California, Mike and I from Colorado. George and Mike had never met. It was a blind date and we were all very aware of that fact. Nervous. George and Mike were all good humor and politeness: "Ho, Ho," George said when he greeted us at the baggage claim, "glad to see you guys made it. You must be Mike." They shook hands like two businessmen.

I found myself nodding in an inane but hopeful way. Yes, nod, that is Mike, and, nod, yes, that fellow with the young face and hearty greeting is George, the physicist/climber with whom you'll soon be climbing. I was the matchmaker and I prayed that George's serious mien and Mike's casualness would complement each other rather than clash, as can happen so easily on hard climbs.

Two days later we were lying in George's North Face Morning Glory tent at the base of the North Face of Mount Hunter. We had taken the train from Anchorage to Talkeetna and then were flown by pilot Jim Sharp to our present location in the heart of the Alaska Range, near Mount McKinley on the Southeast Fork of the Kahiltna Glacier.

The first objective of the trip could be seen through the arched opening of the tent door. The Northwest Spur of Mount Hunter rises more than 7,000 feet from the southeast Fork to the summit at 14,753 feet. If we were successful on Hunter, we planned to try a new route on the 10,000-foot-high South Face of 17,400-foot Mount Foraker, which is on the other side of the Kahiltna from our basecamp.

But first we had to climb the spur that swept up in front of us. As Mike exclaimed when we first landed on the glacier, "That's a training climb?" Our Alpine-style plans seemed a bit flimsy when compared to the obvious strength of the mountain's defenses. It didn't help to know that three good sized expeditions already had failed on the same route.

But we already had made our preparations: cached spare skis at the base of the West Ridge, which was to be our descent route, and loaded our packs with bivouac gear and food for five days. We planned to climb during the Alaskan night which in June never becomes darker than twilight farther south. That way we hoped to avoid the sluppy snow conditions that were certain to exist during the day. The reggae sounds of Bob Marley and the Wailers helped Mike and me endure the waiting, but George glanced up from his book occasionally with a half-hidden look of disgust on his face that seemed to say, "What are we, rock groupies or climbers?"

At ten-thirty Jimmy Cliff was singing, "The harder they come . . . the harder they fall. . ." George punched the stop button. The sun was off the face; our wait was over. Outside the tent not much was said as we donned our skis and roped up for the short approach to the base of the spur. The silence was almost as heavy as our packs as we began to ski up the nearly flat glacier. We were spaced 150 feet apart on two ropes, and above the noise of the skis as they slid over the crisp surface, conversation was not easy to maintain. None of us really wanted to talk anyway. It was enough just to be starting a big climb, the snow-covered peaks all around us huge and impressive in the subdued light.

Grabbing Friendship by the Ankles

An easy snow-bridge over the bergschrund put us on the climb. At the base of the route we traded skis for crampons. We climbed simultaneously most of the way up the lower spur. Mushy snow covered the ice to start. We made a quick front-point around the end of a rock band, threatened by a drooping serac. Hard-breathing effort took us up steep, unstable snow. The crest of the spur dropped away on both sides and curved up to taper into an ice bulge that barred the way. But the bluish-white ice looked good. A core of ice extruded from a screw as it went in. There was the click of a carabiner. Basecamp looked small already, 1,500 feet below, and the wings of the orange tent seemed like a tiny butterfly lost in a sea of snow and crevasses.

George's crampon points loomed above us as Mike and I belayed him up the steep ice bulge. Mike moved fast up a corridor of snow between ice towers where the crest became broader. We huffed to keep up, taking short rests leaning on our ice axes. The white outline of the slope above us became sharply etched against a sky of opaque blue as the sun rose from its shallow dip below the horizon. The ridge was broken by a flat at the top of the lower section, below a pointed ice face we had dubbed "The Triangle." It was 6:00 a.m. We rested and had a bit of cheese and zucchini bread. Weighty food, perhaps, but more sustaining than "freeze-dried." We had done more than one-third of the climb.

It was nice to sit on the packs and eat and gaze around at the waves of peaks lapping at the sky. I looked over at McKinley, which rises above a row of intervening mountains, and wondered if there were people over there at this very moment staring back, taking a break from the effect of climbing that massive hill. But my reverie soon was brought to a halt. "We've made good time up to here," said George, "but the real climbing is just beginning." My vision followed the sweep of his hand up the 1,500-foot ice-wall and came to rest at the sharp summit. I knew George was right.

The ice face itself looked straightforward enough (though with our heavy packs, we had to belay), but something we couldn't see from where we sat had us all a bit worried. From the apex of "The Triangle" there is a narrow, corniced ridge leading horizontally back from the summit of our spur, connecting it with the main mass of the mountain. From the airplane on the way in it had looked like a ripsaw blade, points coated with marshmallow syrup sticking up vertically. "Let's get started, then," said Mike, who already was standing up and re-shouldering his pack.

Jeff Lowe

On the face, the leader trailed both ropes and anchored them to two ice screws when they ran out. The other two climbed simultaneously, one being belayed by the leader and the other belaying himself with a Gibb's Ascendeur. The climbing alternated between good snow and hard ice. The angle varied from about 45 degrees to perhaps 60 as we headed for the right-hand ridge, which looked as if it would offer easy going for the last few hundred feet to the top of the face. At belay stances we chortled at our good luck with the weather and joked about making the summit in a few hours. Mike led the last pitch to the ridge up a steep and insecure trough.

Our "easy" ridge turned out to be a nightmare of insecurity. George struggled up through mushrooms and cornices made of snow that had the consistency of porridge but not the cohesiveness. It was rotting in the sun, drooping everywhere, threatening to fall into the space around us, perhaps taking us with it as well. George took hours on his lead, attempting to compact the snow so that it would hold his weight. It was like trying to swim up a knife-edge of sand, tilted at 60 degrees. Finally, George yelled down that he had a belay. "But don't fall, I don't think it'll hold." Mike and I shot worried looks at each other as I started to follow.

Several pitches and much time, sweat, and worry later, the three of us were ensconced on a small ledge we had shoveled out of the snow just under the very top of the face. Almost comically our rope was draped around the nearest mushroom. We were not very much cheered by the "security" this provided, but it was all that was available. Mist and light snow moved in. We had climbed for nineteen hours to get to this place. The horizontal ridge that led back from the present location was only 500 feet long, and after that it looked like walking to the summit, but those 500 feet were the worst bit of climbing terrain any of us had ever seen.

We brewed soup on our little ledge and tried to talk ourselves into believing the situation was not quite so blue as it appeared to be. But I had a terrible feeling in my stomach, as if at any moment the whole mountain would fall. "It's impossible," I said, and believed. There was no strong opposition to that viewpoint, but we agreed to rest where we were until the early morning hours had solidified the snow as much as possible; then we would give it a try. After all, we were only 500 feet from success, yet more than 4,000 feet above basecamp. We tried to sleep.

At one o'clock in the morning I started out on the traverse of the ridge. Somehow I had hogged the lead. The suspense of waiting behind seemed worse than whatever difficulties the ridge could offer. I used the shovel in place of my axe because a great deal of snow would have to be removed to get to something that would support body weight. I quickly lost myself in the task, shoveling like a wildman trying to tunnel back to sanity.

The cornices overhung the narrow and incredibly steep ridge on both sides. The trick was to make a trail through them without making them fall. Things went well at first, and after a short while, the rope between Mike and I stretched tight. He began to follow since there was no place to establish a belay. I began to enjoy the tunneling and crawling and balancing, and thoughts of success begin to enter my mind as I approached the halfway point along the ridge. I was happy, too, in a way, as I started to carve on a particularly nasty lump of snow.

With a sickening "WHOOMP," it suddenly felt as though the earth had begun to rush inward on itself. But that implosion was only in my head. The cornice had fallen and me with it. I did not feel too much fear (will Mike and George hold me, or will they go, too?), but I did a lot of flailing about with my feet in a futile attempt to stop tumbling. All in a flash, I felt my left crampon points snag the ice. My ankle made a snapping sound, and I felt tendons rip! Then, just as suddenly, my fall stopped. I was dangling on the rope, sixty feet below the side of the ridge. George was yelling to see if I was all right. "Yeah," I replied, "but I think my ankle's broken."

After a prolonged struggle to regain the ridge, during which the only assistance Mike or George could offer was a tight rope, I crawled back along the path I had so recently chiseled and greeted Mike at the place where he was straddling the ridge. It was the only such place around and he had landed there after being jerked off his feet by the force of the fall! The clouds had descended around us, and it began to snow again. "Well," Mike said, "I guess we get to go down now, huh?"

The descent of the ice face took a long time. First George would rappel down and set up an anchor from an ice screw or rock piton in the bands that crossed the face. Then it would be my turn to hop one-legged down to George. Next, Mike would slide down. The whole process was repeated numerous times, and as the storm got heavier, spindrift began to flow down the face in a continuous sheet. Strangely, our humor was good. We told each other jokes at the stances. George and Mike accused me of creating an excuse to get back to see a lady I had met in Talkeetna.

While we were doing the next to last rappel before reaching the flat area below the face, I stood alone with George at the anchor. "You know," he said, "I'm glad Mike was along on this one. He's solid as hell." Then Mike came down and George slid off on the next rappel. I chuckled to myself to hear Mike say, "Man, it's great to be with a guy like George in a situation like this. Hey, what're you laughing about? You finally flipped out on us, or what?"

We bivouacked again on the flat at the base of the face. George and Mike also made a perfect splint for my ankle from several rolls of adhesive tape and the aluminum staves of my pack. Another day was consumed in getting off the climb, but we finally arrived at our skis, which stuck out of the snow like outstretched arms. Relaxing before the final leg of the journey back to basecamp, I lounged back on an ensolite pad, and the mountain loomed above the injured ankle I was holding up in the air. "That was kind of fun." I said to no one in particular. Maybe it was just the euphoric effect of the Percodan that I finally had allowed myself to take, now that the dangerous part of the descent was over.

Epilogue: The same day we finished the retreat from the Northwest Spur, I was flown directly to Anchorage. Doug Geeting, another pilot from Talkeetna, just happened to land on the Southeast Fork to drop off another party of climbers shortly after we arrived at camp. At Providence Hospital in Anchorage it was discovered that I had suffered a severe sprain and two bone chips.

Mike and George returned to Hunter and completed the route a few days later. After that, they went around to the south side of Foraker and made a ten-day ascent of the "Infinite Spur." These achievements were made even more satisfying to the climbers by the new bonds of friendship that had formed between them. Mike was later to write:

"I felt completely comfortable climbing with George. There were no ego games between us, no competition, and the experiences of the last days had brought us very close."

Andrew Greig (b. 1951) is a professional writer who happens to love mountains. He has been on several major Himalayan expeditions including visits to Everest and K2. He is also a poet and performs original musical compositions, nearly always with mountains as his central theme. His books include *Summit Fever, Kingdoms of Experience and Men on Ice.*

ANDREW GREIG:
A GLENCOE MASSACRE
In which a novice is initiated 20-26 January 1984

As we head north on icy roads in mid-January, Mal enthuses about the conditions. A substantial fall of snow, a slight thaw, now freezing hard. "Glencoe will be crawling with climbers this weekend." I'm less enthusiastic; if anyone will be crawling this weekend, it'll be me. The van heater is broken so I huddle deep in my split-new climbing gear, watching our headlights skew out across deepening snow. We don't speak much, each absorbed in our own thoughts.

I'm keyed up, anxious yet oddly elated. To shut out the cold I mentally run through everything Mal had shown me about the basic mechanics of snow and ice climbing, in the warmth of his principles of belaying, the extraordinary array of ironmongery, the pegs, pins, channels, screws, plates, nuts, crabs, slings. . . An evocative litany but especially confusing when everything seemed to have several alternative names. This was starting truly from scratch.

I try to review it all logically. First, the harness. I smile to myself in the dark. With our harnesses belted on and the full armoury of the modern climber dangling from them, we'd looked like a cross between gladiators and bondage freaks. Then the rope; I tried to picture again the basic figure of eight knot used for securing the rope through the harness loops.

271

Then the basic sequence of events for climbing. The leader climbs up, more or less protected by his second, who's on a hopefully secure stance at the other end of the rope. When the leader reaches a secure position somewhere near the rope's full extent, he in turn protects the second who climbs up after him. Simple and reasonably safe. At least, I hoped so.

We'd rehearsed it on the passage stairs. We stood roped together at the bottom of the stairs. Mal tied a "sling"—a loop of incredibly strong tape—through the bannister and clipped it to my harness with an oval metal snaplink, the karabiner or "krab." This secured my belay stance. Then he took the rope near where it came from his harness, threaded it through a friction device, a descender, and clipped that to my harness. Then with a "see you at the top, youth" he solemnly walked up the stairs while I paid out the rope through the descender. About 20 feet up he stopped and pointed out that if he fell now, he'd fall 40 feet in total before the line between us came tight. So I put in a "runner:" He looped another sling round a bannister rail, then dipped a krab to it, with the rope running freely through the krab. If he fell now, he'd only go down twice the distance he was above the runner till he was brought up short by the tight rope between us being looped through the karabiner.

I thought about it a couple of times till the logic of it sank in. Yes, it made sense. The runner was there to limit the extent of the leader's fall.

It was at this point a woman came bustling up the stairs and gave us a very strange look.

With the merest blush, Mal continued on up, putting in a couple more runners till he got to the top. There he tied himself securely to the rail "On belay!" The cry floated down the spiral staircase. I unclipped the descender, tried to remember the appropriate call. "Take in slack!" I shouted. He took in the rope till it came tight between us. I waited as he put his descender onto the rope. "Climb when you're ready!" With some difficulty I unclipped myself from my belay stance, shouted "Climbing!" and set off up after him.

Some 20 feet up I was going great guns, then was suddenly brought up short with a jerk. I couldn't go any further. Try taking out my runner: Mal called down. Of course, the first runner was preventing me from continuing above it. I unclipped the crab, untied the sling and continued.

At the top, we shook hands most movingly.

And that seemed to be the basic principle and practice of belay climbing. I hoped I'd remembered the calls correctly. I mumbled them over a few times in the freezing van. The rest of the gear—the pitons in various shapes and guises, the screws and nuts—were for use when there was nothing convenient to loop a sling over to set up a belay stance or a runner. We'd gone around wedging them into cracks in Mal's fireplace. It had all been wonderfully ludicrous, but next time it'll be for real. How did I get into this?

After Callander the glimmering countryside grows wilder and more desolate. Long slopes suddenly swoop upwards, the snow deepens as we skirt the wilderness of Rannoch Moor and wind down towards Glencoe. As we near the infamous Clachaig Inn I think back on the last time I was here, sixteen years ago. High on adrenalin, youth and Pale Ale, I'd stood in a corner in full hippie regalia—the gold cloak, quilted tea cosy for a hat, peacock feathers, the strawberry tunic, oh my God—and thrashed out Incredible String Band songs into a small bar dense with steam, smoke and climbers so large and hairy it was hard to tell where beards ended and sweaters began. Climbers must be exceptionally tolerant, and such was the confidence of youth and the mood of the times that I got off with it, even had a few drinks bought me. Then at closing time walked out with a nurse from Glasgow into the black night to tried yet again to lose my virginity, mind intoxicated with Pale Ale, adventure and the great sensed bulk of the mountains. . . .

Now I can't even recognize the interior. The clientele are much the same, only now they look younger and smaller. A motley crew: straggly hair, gaiters, training shoes, bare feet, old jeans, blue fiberpile salopettes, bright red Gore-Tex jackets, moving from table to table talking gossip or snow conditions, arm wrestling, playing pool. A number of girls too, some looking decorative and bored, others decidedly capable.

Mal's clearly well known and respected here. A constant stream of people come up to our table. Climbers' talk. "Tower Ridge. . . still seconding all the time. . . solid for its grade. . . knew he was going to lob, so. . . Whitesnake. . . the crux after the chock stone. . . wiped out in Peru. . . ." It's all new to me, exotic and bewildering, but I sense some interesting interactions behind these casual exchanges. Allegiances and rivalries, the seeking and withholding of information, put-downs and half-acknowledged challenges. How much a casual remark such as "I thought it a soft touch at Grade 5" can imply! It suggests that for the speaker the climb was easy, that he is familiar with real Grade 5s, it inquires after the listener's capability and casts aspersions on his friend who first climbed an rated the route. Just how good are you, anyway? "I found it hard enough last time: Mal might reply mildly. This counter stroke makes it clear that he had climbed it, and more than once, that he doesn't need to pretend a hard climb was easy to bolster his reputation. . . ."

In fact, it's just like the literary world. Competition and cooperation; jostling over places in an invisible league table; ideological, personal and geographical divisions. The Aberdeen crowd here to show the others what real climbing is, the hard men up from the North of England to make their point, the Central Scotland boys protecting their patch. . . Yes, very familiar.

"Who are you?" one youth asks me, uneasy he can't place Mal's new partner. "I'm a guitar player." Pause. "What are you doing up here, then?" "Learning a few new chords." He looks baffled, scowls and retreats. Mal grins and agrees that though climbing itself may be a pure activity, there's nothing pure and disinterested about the social side of it. Everyone seems extraordinarily vague about what they're going for tomorrow.

Tony Bridle and his climbing partner Terry Dailey walk in the door. Tony's one of the lead climbers for Mustagh, the only one I've met other than Malcolm. Handshakes all round, it's good to see a familiar face. I'd seen him last at Mal and Liz's wedding, carried off to do a Dashing White Sergeant by two tall girls and grinning wildly. Even sober as now, he's still bouncy and hyper-enthusiastic. As he chatters away about past and future routes it suddenly strikes me who he reminds me of: Davy Jones of the Monkees. Small, looks as if butter wouldn't melt, innocent brown eyes, hair in a neat fringe, something about Tony makes one want to pat him on the head. He's twenty-three and looks about fifteen. I think he both resents and plays up to it. It's hard to imagine that he's recognized by his peers as having quite exceptional stamina and self-reliance. There must be steel somewhere behind that baby face. Who or what put it there?

"So where are you taking Mal tomorrow?" he asks me, for the benefit of Mal who's locked in conversation about the season's big challenges on "the Ben," i.e. Ben Nevis.

"Oh, I don't know, we'll just poke around," I reply in the prescribed vague manner. "Maybe warm up with Smith's Gully and see what he's up to. Then we'll take a look at something more serious." Now we have a few attentive ears at the next table. Mal twitches slightly but can't get out of his conversation.

Tony grins, replies in his Lancashire accent, "Yeah, he's a bit lazy. The old fella's buggered. Still, he'll second anything you lead."

Andrew Greig

"Thought I'd maybe give him a couple of leads if he's shaping up. . . ."

Mal is saved from further roasting by the arrival of more friends I recognize from the wedding. A big boozy night that was; the climbers all gravitated toward the corner of the room and spent the night talking about the only relevant subject at such occasions—climbing. They're obsessed, but it's an interesting obsession, for the first couple of hours at least.

And so that first night at the Clachaig rolls on. Red faces, swollen knuckles, diminishing pints, growing excitement and anticipation as hopes and plans build for tomorrow. At least they don't train on orange juice and early nights. Their regime seems to be one of alcohol, nicotine, late nights and systematic abuse, both verbal and bodily. Suits me.

I stand outside our chalet door for a few minutes before going to bed. The air is clear and cold, smelling unmistakably of snow. Clouds move across a three-quarter moon and sweep enormous shadows over the glimmering slopes across the glen. Passing voices ring hard in the frost. Orion is rising, the wind whispers over the snow, distant echoing water. I feel uplifted and self-forgetting before the irresistible forces of moon, shadow, mountains, snow. This alone was worth coming here for. I shake my head and go inside. See what tomorrow brings. Hope I'm up to it. I've been training two months for this.

The wind's blew into our faces, but my new gear keeps me surprisingly warm as we plod up through soft, deep snow into Lost Valley. We go over ice-axe braking and the placing of "deadmen" which are in effect snow anchors. Then the fun's over. Time to do some climbing.

My heart thuds wildly as we gear up, I have to force myself to breathe slowly and deep. Concentrate. I buckle on the harness, tie the rope, get the knot right on the second attempt. Then strap the crampons onto my cumbersome rigid-soled double boots.

The cramps are like heavy duty running spikes, with two additional fangs projecting out in front. Then I sort out my two ice axes. Both have sharply inclined picks with teeth notched towards the tip; the head of one ends with a hammer for knocking in and removing pitons, while the head of the other ends in an adze for cutting steps. Apparently this is largely redundant, as the combination of front-pointed crampons and inclined picks make step-cutting unnecessary in most situations.

I feel absurd and overburdened, like a deep-sea diver in a paddling pool, as I follow Mal up the steepening slope. It's not steep enough—he says—to merit belaying. I keep my gaze determinedly at my feet. Slip,

A Glencoe Massacre

flurry, recover. Continue. Untangle these stupid axes. Stop tripping over the crampons. Up and across, don't like traverses, getting pretty high now. Don't look, watch your feet, time for doing, not thinking. How clear the sounds are: scrape of crampons on rock, scrunch of boots in snow, jingling harness, echoing wind, a faint mewing cry. . .

We look up and spot a figure waving awkwardly further up John Gray's Buttress. "Looks like he's got gripped" says Mal. "Kick yourself a ledge and wait here." I feel a moment's pleasant superiority over the incompetent up ahead, then a surge of fellow feeling. Mal tries to persuade him to climb down, but the shake of the head is vehement even from here. I look down. Safe enough really, but just the same. . . Mal climbs further up, secures a belay. In crabbed, awkward movements the man picks his way down. When he finally passes me, he's white-faced and embarrassed. "Snow's tricky in patches," he mutters apologetically. I agree politely.

A shout from Mal. He's waving me up towards a ledge on the left beside a steep drop into a narrow gully, then adds something I can't catch. By the time I reach the ledge, he's disappeared. The rope runs over the edge into the gully, then drops out of sight. I wait. And wait. And wait.

Thirty minutes later there's still no sign of him and the view downhill is beginning to impinge on me, nagging like a toothache. I stood tentatively, feeling foolish. No answer. Adrenalin wears off and muscles stiffen. Now what? Don't think. Wait. Odd feeling alone up here. . . .

He finally appears below me, plodding up the hill looking puffed and not very pleased. "Dropped my glove belaying that wazzock, it slid right to the bottom of the gully." I ask what had happened to the man he'd rescued. "Gripped." He says shortly and indicates our next line. A traverse right across a distinctly steep slope. He sets off. Looks like I'm not going to be belayed. I've had a lot of time to get nervous and don't like the look of it, but follow thinking about avalanche, about falling. . . .

I reach his stance, a narrow ledge beside a boulder, panting hard. Nerves, mostly. "Right, better clip in now, Andy."

I put him on belay through the descender as we rehearsed on his stairway a lifetime ago. He checks my gear, goes over the call sequence and disappears round the corner. One day all of this will seem normal. I peer round to see where he's making for and find myself looking down the throat of an apparently sheer snow chute. I look away, feeling ill. How did we get so high? This fear is like seasickness, invading mind and body. Hands tighten, stomach lurches, legs feel weak, stare fixedly in front. . . .

"Gripped" is the right word for it. One grips and is gripped by an enormous fist of fear. I can't do this. I'll have to cry off the Expedition. What a farce. Then angry at myself, at this instinctive fear and revulsion. A clinking sound drifted faintly back. He must be putting in a runner. Good man. Put in a dozen. Stare at the weave in my gloves, the powder snow caught in the cuff of the wind suit. All sharp and vivid, too clear. "I'll put you in controlled freak-out situations." Mal had said. "You freak out and I'll control them." He knows what he's doing. You trust him, don't you? Yes. So nothing to worry about, just don't make an ass of yourself.

The rope stops paying out. I start untangling myself, take off the descender and clip it to my harness. The slack's taken in, then tugs come down the line. If only we had to face just one moment of truth, not many. Here goes. . . .

"Good enough, youth."

I arrive at Mal's stance and subside, jittering with adrenalin. I've just learned that waiting is worst; climbing itself is too novel, too demanding and intense to leave much room for anxiety, or for memory. Already the last twenty minutes are reduced to a floundering through whiteness, stinging knuckles caught between axe shaft and rock, a flurried impromptu tango when my crampons interlocked, a hurried pull-up, the surge of satisfaction when the pick thuds into frozen turf. All so clumsy and unfamiliar, but something in this lark, perfectly safe really. . . .

Then I look down and that anxiety that is like drowning rushes up to my throat. We're poised out on the edge of space. Horrible. Unnatural. I shrink back into the slope. Mal points out matter-of-factly that the crampons can't grip properly this way. Clinging to the slope actually increases the likelihood of falling. I point out this may well be true and would make a sound Buddhist parable, but every instinct in my body shouts at me not to stand upright.

By now the weather's deteriorating fast; a greenish-grey sky and each gust fiercer than the last. And the pitch above us isn't filled in with snow and ice—Mal points it out, I shudder and try to sound regretful when he decides we've done enough for today. And oddly enough, I suddenly am. He belays my descent along a ridge and down the sheerest slope yet. Perhaps because down is the right direction, I enjoy it and even find the blinding spindrift exhilarating. Then turn outwards and step-plunge down, feeling positively elated. Great to be in the hills, feeling oneself so physically immediate, so simple. And there's something pleasing in the essence of winter climbing; a rope, axes, crampons, things to wedge in cracks, and with these one can go almost anywhere, in reasonable safety.

A Glencoe Massacre

Pointless maybe, but satisfying. And I like the way in which, quite unlike rock climbing, routes appear and disappear, may only exist for a few days every other year, are never the same twice.

In the valley we find an ice slab and mess around on that, reluctant to pack in for the day. Vertical and all of 12 feet high. My first fall of the day leaves me dangling helplessly from one axe wrist loop, unable to go up or down, feet six inches off the ground, cursing a Duff helpless with laughter.

As we plod back, the wind redoubles. The combination of spindrift and fresh snow forms drifts in minutes. A couple of gusts simply knock us over. It's exhilarating. We do not know this is the beginning of the worst blizzard for years in the Highlands and that five climbers will be dead before it's through.

That evening in the Clachaig the sense of siege and drama mounted like the storm outside as one group after another staggered in, red-faced, dazed, plastered from head to foot, head torches making them look like negatives of miners. I floundered through chest-high drifts to our chalet, passed two tents reduced to mangled poles and shred of material. And this on the sheltered floor of the valley. Rumors spread rapidly. All roads out blocked. . . sixteen head torches still on the hill. . . Mountain Rescue team on four calls at once. . . Hamish MacInnes stranded in his Land-Rover. . . someone's taken a fall, broken his collarbone. . . We drank on, increasingly aware of Tony and Terry's absence. They'd left at 5:00 a.m. to go to Ben Nevis. Mal was quite confident in them, but still kept glancing at his watch.

Finally, round 10:30, a small and tall figure pushed wearily through the door. They looked as if they'd been tested in a wind tunnel, a mangle, a car wash, then hit repeatedly over the head for hours with a particularly substantial edition of *Being and Nothingness*. Which turned out to be pretty much the case as, drinks in hand, eyes still unfocused, they recounted their epic day. They'd succeeded in doing Vanishing Gully in appalling conditions ("Very vertical," said Tony, eyes wide at the memory of it, "very"), abseiled off Tower Ridge where their lowered ropes flew straight up in the air like snakes charmed by the banshee howl of the wind, and made it to the CIC hut, mostly on hands and knees. There, unbelievably, they were refused shelter because they were not members of the Scottish Mountaineering Club, so they had to continue. From the hut to the road, normally an hour's walk, had taken them six and a half hours of tumbling, rolling, swimming, crawling, through a world gone berserk. "I once took two and a half hours on that walk," Mal said, "and the conditions were desperate. For Tony to take six and a half hours . . . ." He shook his head. Terry was slumped back, pale now, staring into his pint, completely drained. Tony was starting to recover, and entertained us with the absurdity of nearly being wiped out crossing the gold course ("Thought we might set a new record"), finally being slammed up against the fence ("I thought I was going to come out the other side as mince!"), getting to the car and realizing they'd have to dig it out. Then they'd driven through the blizzard, abandoned it on the road, and battered their way through to the Clachaig on foot.

A definite epic, a tale worth surviving for the telling of it. And sitting in that besieged inn in the wilderness, packed with dripping, excited, exhausted climbers, thinking back on the day and listening to the stories go round I began to see something of what brings them there. Anxiety, adrenalin, physical endeavor, the surge of exultation; a day locked into the mountains, evening in the company of fellow nutters—after this, any other way of spending the weekend would be simply dull.

And one doesn't have to be a top-level climber to feel this. At any level the rewards and apprehensions are the same. This is what makes them risk life and limb, scrape, borrow, hitch, neglect work, lovers, family, the future. The moment you commit yourself to the next pitch all those ghostly chains of everyday worries fall away. Lightness in the midst of fear; all that exists is the next move, the mountain, and your thudding heart.

Come closing time we are invited into the Snug bar among the late drinkers. Something of a ceilidh starts; guitars come out and the songs go round. And looking round I suddenly see how this was the original bar I'd walked into sixteen years before. The door must have been here, the fireplace there. I see again the dartboard, the Pale Ale, my Glasgow nurse, myself singing out my teenage years into the hubbub of men. The place is recognized though overlaid with changes. Me too. For a moment I long to go back, to have that night again, though I know I carry it inside me. Then one of the women's voices, trained and beautiful, lifts in a haunting Gaelic lament, and in the moment's silence at the end we are all briefly bound together by the silken, invisible rope of her song.

Next morning I helped Tony and Terry dig out their car. As we slithered towards Glencoe Village the car radio spoke of 2,000 people trapped

A Glencoe Massacre

in Glenshee, marooned trains, three climbers found dead in the Cairngorms. . . Tony and Terry glance at each other, the slightest shake of the head. Nothing is said. It could have been them but it wasn't.

At the village I waved them goodbye and plodded to the monument to the Massacre of Glencoe. It's a simple pillar of stone on a hillock near the river. The inscription was unreadable, being plastered with spindrift. I thought of the sign in the Clachaig: NO HAWKERS NO CAMPBELLS. Life was precarious enough in those days, no need for mountaineering. Climbing has some of the adrenalin, the release, and the self-discovery of combat; the difference is you're not being asked to kill anyone, and you take no orders but your own. But war and climbing partake of the same odd quirk in our nature—only when our survival is at risk do we feel how precious it is to be alive. Tony and Terry's silence came not from callousness but an acceptance of the risks involved.

Mal spent most of the day in his sleeping bag, looking haggard and listening to Frank Sinatra on his Walkman. Apparently last night's session went on long and late. We ate and slept, marking time. Climbers came, gossiped, picked up their gear and left. Towards evening the snow came down again, thick and swirling.

We went over to the pub for one beer, had several, and found ourselves having a long and surprisingly personal talk about our lives. Our paths have been so different, yet there are parallels. It's hard to imagine now, but Mal worked in insurance in London for five years. "Then one day I looked around me, a long, slow look at all the familiar faces reading the papers or looking out the window, and I saw they were only existing, not living. And if I carried on, I'd be like that in another five years. I thought, screw that for a lark. I handed in my notice to quit that day." He stared down at his ledger with his characteristic frown, part impatience, part perplexity. "That's why I could relate to you from the beginning, because somewhere along the line you've chosen not to live like most people."

I nodded, knowing the unlikely kinship he meant. The turning point in my life had not been as sudden and clear as his. My dissatisfaction with the life I was leading some years ago grew slowly and unnoticed like an overhanging cornice until finally I fell through. I kept on writing because there was nothing else.

And the unhappiness we spread around us on the way makes it all the more important that we do it well.

Andrew Greig

Climbing and writing seem poles apart, but we had both rearranged our lives round a supremely satisfying central activity that seems pointless to many—sometimes to ourselves. We were both now doing what we wanted. That was our basis for mutual respect.

That night he called out in his sleep, "it's too late now." And then, "Better put some more runners in, Andy."

Next morning loose snow still ruled out serious climbing. We spent it working on setting up runners and belay stances, and abseiling. There's something absolutely unnatural in walking backwards off a cliff. I found it also—when you're sure of the rope and the belay—surprisingly enjoyable. Just lean back and walk down, paying out rope through the descender. Pleasingly ingenious.

I spent some time on placing aids. Hammering pitons (blades, leapers, bongs, angles, channels, pegs, the wonderfully named RURPS—Realized Ultimate Reality Pitons) into cracks; wedging nuts (wedges, wires) into fissures. "I lost a couple of friends here last year, "Mal remarked conversationally, fumbling with something on his harness. I didn't know what to say, made some sympathetic sound. "They're worth nearly twenty quid now," he continued. I stared at him. "I know this is an age that sets a price on everything, but this is ridiculous." "And even this one is a bit knackered," he said, and held out a strange object to me with just the faintest hint of a grin.

It looked like a piece of particularly nasty dental equipment, like an adjustable wrench with its jaws turned inside out. They were spring-loaded so one could pull them back, shove them into a crack and then let them expand to grip the walls.

"It's called a 'friend.'" "Not totally reliable, but very useful at times."

We went through the belaying sequence on the floor of a quarry. I was cumbersome and ponderous as I stumbled along pretending there was a 1,000 foot drop on my right, placing runners along the rock on my left. When I shouted "On belay!" my voice sounded absurd and lacking in conviction, like the first time you try to hail a taxi or call "Waiter!" Mal followed on round the corner, walking slowly, treating this charade with elaborate seriousness. He came to the first runner, removed the peg, then abruptly fell back. I instinctively pulled the rope back on the descender and he was held. He came on up again, head down. When he arrived at my stance he looked up, shook his head. "Whew, that was a bit thin, youth!" We laughed. It was a game. The whole activity is an absurd and sometimes delightful game.

A Glencoe Massacre

He led through and we did a couple of pitches on genuine slopes. It's clever and simple, this whole procedure, each climber alternately protecting the other. I was still getting tangled up and several times hit myself on the helmet with an ice axe, but it was beginning to feel more natural. Finding out what crampons can do, working out different moves, reading the slopes ahead. The last pitch was a scramble; the snow deep and powdery, no purchase in it, then loose and shallow over rocks. Spindrift blowing up into my face, balaclava slipping over my eyes. The left axe pulled through and I was off balance, hacking away wildly for purchase, slipping. . . An internal voice spoke very clearly, "Slow down, look for it." I spotted frozen turf, the inclined pick went in and held. Lovely. Pull up, across, come out on the tope and find Mal sitting patient and immobile as a Buddha, wrapped in a cloak of spindrift.

We finished up by building a snow house. It was more of a beehive than a classic igloo, but the shelter it provided was impressive. Absolutely silent and windless inside. "If those missing Army blokes, have made one of these and stayed in it, they'll be all right for days."

Back in the gloaming, in high spirits, for tea and the latest disaster stories. A few casualties, but no fatalities in Glencoe. In the evening I borrowed a guitar and sang a few songs I'd written years before to go with my *Men on Ice*. Mal was very taken with them, insisted I put them on tape, and spent much of the rest of our time in Glencoe wandering about with the earphones on, bawling out the lyrics. When he was over in the pub I wrote some new verses to "Throw me down some more rope," and a middle section. Mal was amazed on his return. "How can you do that?" "How can you solo Grade Five?" I replied. It was good to be reminded there were things I could do competently.

"We'll try a harder route tomorrow," he said as I crawled into my bag. I lay thinking about that as he muttered over a new verse and the chorus, trying to memorize the words:

Halfway up "Whitesnake'"when the blizzard hits,
Can't feel your nose or your toes, everything goes
And nothing grips (except you);
It's a funny desire, wanting to get higher,
Sometimes you wish you'd stayed below,
Sometimes you know that it's right,
Sometimes you know that it's wrong,
And sometimes you just Don't Know
Throw me down some more rope (throw me down)

Andrew Greig

Throw me down some more rope (hey, youth!)
Throw me down some more rope 'cos I'm falling,
Yes I'm falling. . .

We set out in the half-light. No cloud, no wind, blue sky filtering through. The high ridges slowly become three-dimensional as we plod up the road in silence, our sense sharp and clear as the air. A flock of sheep freshly out of a snowdrift are encrusted with icicles; as they move a delicate tinkling like wind chimes sounds across the valley. A buzzard circles into high sunlight, drifting on invisible currents. Three crows beside a frozen stream tear at a dead rabbit. Glencoe goes about its immemorial business.

It was a long day that, on the north face of Aonach Dubh, but only fragments of it remain lodged in the memory, like slivers of ice caught in a wind suit's creases. I was too caught up with what was happening to record, too present to stand back, too scared to take photographs.

The first pitch up a narrowing snow-choked gully made the first day's efforts seem child's play. Relief and exhilaration on arriving at Mal's stance, then half an hour clinging to a stunted rowan tree, fighting off paralysis and panic, hating it. Sitting still is the worst. Time to take in where you are, time to think, time to fear. I look down—too far, too steep, too empty. I glance up—too high, too steep, too endless. Contemplating going on this Expedition is absurd. My body hates this. Don't look, don't think. Keep the rope going. Where's Mal got to? If you think this is bad, imagine the sense of exposure on Mustagh. . . Extraordinary clarity of lichen on this branch, the precise angle of this fork . . . .

It's a relief to be climbing again, traversing onto a buttress of steep rock, soft snow, patchy frozen turf. Gloves off, treating some of it as a rock climb, half-remembered techniques from childhood scrambling. Chunks of knuckle left on rocks, arms with all the resilience of blancmange. Concentrating hard, each movement dreamlike in its intensity. I call for tight rope and get it. Thanks, pal. Over a bulge, there he is . . . .

Another anxious wait on belay, then another pitch. It's beginning to feel more natural. I cease tying myself up in Gordian knots of slings, rope, karbs, and ice axe lines. Even relax enough to snatch a photo as Mal works his way up an angled deft above me. After two hours fear starts to lose its urgency, and though I know this pitch is trick by my standards I push up through soft snow, cross onto rock; find some lovely frozen turf and almost shout with satisfaction as the picks thud home. Hold an elephant, that would. Now pull up. . . Something in this lark after all.

A Glencoe Massacre

Until you pause and catch a glimpse of below.

An hour and two pitches later we come out on top of the ridge. I'm shattered, puffing like an old espresso machine, arm muscles like wet newspaper from working above my head all the time. In addition to the long approach plod, then the physical effort of climbing, I've put out enough nervous energy to light up Glencoe village for a year. But the weather's menacing and the light starting to go, so Mal hurries on and I plod after. We pause on the summit of Aonach Dubh; briefer than a kiss is this final pay-off, that's the joke of it.

Mal points down No.2 Gully. "Follow me as fast as you can but concentrate." I sense a certain urgency in his voice, and follow him down in the half-light. It seems steep, but I haven't the energy to care. Step, plunge, axe, step, plunge. . .it becomes endless, unreal, hypnotic. I begin to stumble, stuff snow in my mouth to stay awake. Somewhere along the line a crampon disappears. No time to look for it, carry on. . . I seem to have been doing this forever, stepping down through the gathering dark. In the distance Mal swings right and up onto a buttress. Eventually I join him. "Well done," he says briefly. Must have been harder than it looked. It's getting very dim now. We start feeling our way down over rock. scree and snow towards the yellow lights in the valley.

Finally his urgency relaxes, the rest is straightforward. We sit for five minutes on Dinnertime Buttress, munching biscuits and looking over at the glimmering slopes across the glen. We say nothing, but it is many months since I felt so at peace. "What was that route called?" "We can decide that in the pub," he replies casually. Understanding comes slowly. "You mean you. . . we. . . ?" I sputter. He nods. "I'd been saving that one up for a while."

A new route for my first route. I'm outraged, flabbergasted, and not a little chuffed. Of course it wasn't hard Grade 2 or 3 he reckons—and all I did was follow on, but the sense of delight and absurdity sustain me on the rest of the trudge back. "Two Shakes" I say finally. "Why?" "Well, there was two tree belays on it, there's two parts to it the gully and the buttress and I'm lying about the amount of shaking I did!"

Finally, we push through the door of the Clachaig into a gust of warmth and light and laughter. Then the simple wonder of sitting down. We've been on the go for eleven hours. I slump back against the wall, totally blank.

"Tired, youth?" Mal asks.

I search for the right epithet.

Andrew Greig

"Massacred," I say briefly, and with some effort raise the first pint of the night to my lips. We left Glencoe two days later. I was relieved yet oddly regretful as the old blue van struggled out of the valley. Five days in this place had been a month of normal time. Grinding and slipping past abandoned cars, cottages up to their eyelids in snow, a snow blower moving across the wilderness of Rannoch Moor, followed by a tiny man in yellow oilskins.

We were silent as we worked our way south toward civilization and its dubious benefits. What had happened to me here, what had I learned? The extent of my fear, yet strengthened for having coped with it. Perhaps one can never overcome fear completely—after all, it is often a sane and appropriate response—what counts is that is doesn't overcome you.

Being a novice climber is like having a weak head for alcohol, people may laugh at you, but you get high more easily. It didn't take much to get my heart thumping, whereas Mal has to push it a long way to get his kicks. Both novice and expert have the same experience, despite the huge gulf in their capabilities. Both know fear, exhilaration, satisfaction, relief. Both have to persist through discomfort and utter fatigue. Both have to recognize their limits, then push a little further. And both experience the great simplification of one's life that is the reward of all risk activities.

But I was thinking most of all about the two Army lads who were found dead today in the Cairngorms, and of the half-buried monument to the Massacre of Glencoe. Our "massacre" by the elements is a self-imposed one, a piece of personal theater. When it is over, all but a few get to their feet again and feel themselves, behind their fatigue, somehow stronger and more alive than before.

For those who do not rise again, there remains the unyielding pillar of stone, the inscription obliterated by drifting snow.

Hamish Brown (b.1934) is a well known Scottish poet, essayist, and fiction writer. He is also a photographer and editor. He has traveled extensively in Japan, Sri Lanka, Malaysia, South America, the Middle East, Africa, and has climbed in Britain, the Alps, and the Himalayas. He is the author of over a dozen books ranging from travel narratives and poetry to fiction including a collection of short stories entitled *The Bothy Brew and Other Stories.*

HAMISH M. BROWN: AGAG'S GROOVE

(Fiction)

Cutting the rope was simply an improbable ploy of the fiction hacks. As if the forensic boys wouldn't be on to that at once.

"Climb when you're ready," he yelled down to his invisible partner on January Jigsaw.

"Climbing" came the billowy response as Betty began to pick her way up the neat holds.

Rannoch Wall would make anyone want to climb. She just wished she'd got Allan to take her years ago. She liked it when Norrie was there too. He was so much more gentle than her husband. But she'd have to be careful—canny—in case Allan thought there was anything going between them. Which there wasn't, "mair's the pity:" she muttered as she lifted a runner off a pink porphyry spike. "Keep your mind on whit you're daein!" She told herself.

Allan and Norrie were partners in a garden ornament business. "Selling garden gnomes" as Betty taunted him on their last screaming match.

"And whit's wrang wi' garden gnomes?" Allan had responded.

"Oh, Naethin. It's jist you become mair an mair like them: Dopey, Sleepy, Grumpy."

287

"Shut up then, Snow-white!" he'd yelled and stomped out to slam the door and set the plates on the dresser quivering.

His anger was the worse because he knew she was hitting too damn close to the mark. They were overdrawn and in trouble and he'd not desire for Betty to discover that or, more importantly, her stuck-up father who was so correct and proper in everything, like ensuring Allan had taken out a good life policy before they married. (Betty of course was already covered, had been since birth.)

"Don't want my little lily left in the lurch, what?" he'd admonished in that smug voice of his.

The last straw had come with the patio Allan and Norrie had agreed to do for the colonel. At the last moment he'd wiggled out from his commitment and they'd been left with the materials come parts of which were already looking tatty of rusting. They'd threatened the colonel with suing him for breach of contract but he pointed out there was not contract, he'd signed nothing and they'd get nothing, except a big bill for the costs. The bugger was probably right too. They gave up on that one. They were pretty well giving up full stop.

The odd Sundays when they could escape claustrophobic Helensburgh and head for the Coe were treasured respites from the pressures of failure. Allan and Norrie had come together through climbing and it had seemed a good idea, three years ago, to set up their own business. "70% of households in Scotland have gardens which are actually looked after," he'd quoted. "Man, there's the market."

Somehow it didn't quite work. People who'd sink twenty five quid for a fancy conifer or aweeping cherry grudged parting with even a tenner for some concrete eye-catcher.

"No taste, folks," Norrie complained.

Allan thought it was probably the opposite. Too many effing people had better taste than to want garden rubbish. Betty's father had creased himself when he'd set eyes on the first Seven Dwarfs set they'd stocked. He did not like his father-in-law; nor his daughter if it came to that.

He'd first suggested she come along on a climbing trip with the gloating hope of scaring the shit out of her but she'd taken to it. Liked it! And she a such a cocksure little bitch she never even noticed how she rubbed Allan's nose in it with her new enthusiasm.

Betty's beloved father had—naturally—raised hell about her climbing. It was far too dangerous. Allan's efforts at explaining that Betty always had a rope on and couldn't fall, not seriously, never got through.

Hamish Brown

"You might fall," he'd remonstrate.

Allan thought, "The way things are goin I'm mair liker tae jump!"

"What's that you're muttering?"

"Nethin. Nethin. It's quite safe. . . ."

But explaining the old man was more at risk every time he stepped into his Rover had not gone down well.

He tried again. "If I'm leading I've got protection on. Besides, Norrie's usually seconding." "Well, he's probably more reliable."

"Thanks."

He kept very quiet about the fact that on a few recent occasions Betty had led routes. Norrie had had a job keeping a straight face while Allan and Betty argued over that.

"Your old man'll kill me!"

"Only if I kill masel:" she countered. "And who's gone to tell? You? Norrie?"

She reckoned she could lead January Jigsaw, or Agag's Groove. Rannoch Wall's exposure was exhilarating rather than scary. It was that verticality that first put the idea of mischief into Allan's head. If she peeled it would be easy to cut through the taught nylon. You could say a sharp edge cut it—except the experts could tell it was a knife cut. There must be some way though. Alas, Allan's preoccupation led to another row on the drive home, which started with Betty's shot across his bows, "Right talkative tonight aren't we?" And only eased off when they ate their chip suppers in the lay-by before home. Actually laying hand on money enough to save their business as well as being rid of Betty seemed a really brilliant idea. But how?

Then, bit by bit, it came to him. Just a straight slip would do. At the top of the climb. There would be no evidence with that. Or would there? Betty's father could well be suspicious and if there was any probing a motive enough would be discovered. Men had murdered for a lot less. Maybe he could do something to the car next time she took it off by herself, her next Keep Fit night? But that's all movie stuff too. He hadn't a clue how to go about it, never mind the time needed. The climbing accident would be best. Maybe encourage her to solo something and con her about the grade. Hope she'd fall. He'd not even be present necessarily. No suspicions then. She was too turned on for that though, she knew just how well she did climb and she'd want to read the description anyway. Oh shit! There had to be a way. If only he could fix it so he wasn't there. Nobody would make any dangerous background checking then.

Agag's Groove

The answer came to him in the owl hours of night. He'd get Norrie to do it. Take her up something. Agag's would go. Promise it was to study the line carefully so she could lead it the following weekend—except there wouldn't be one. When she unroped at the top it would only take a wee shove. People were often careless at the top of a climb. Accidents had happened like that before and never any alarm bells ringing. Great!

Except Norrie's eyebrows vanished into his fringe at the very idea. Sure, he knew they weren't exactly a happy family but that's no reason to actually kill the wife. And by proxy. Use him! "You think I'm effin mad?"

"No just aboot tae gang bankrupt." Allan sneered. "Wi the insurance money we're aff the hook. Betty's nethin tae me."

"Well, I like her."

"Marry her then!"

They argued blue murder every moment they had in private. Norrie simply wasn't the type to do such a thing but neither was he the type to relish the prospect of bankruptcy. A direct threat from the bank had him sick and sweaty with fear. He couldn't even despair at the thought that there was no way out. There was. He looked at the letter in his hands as they sat at the table in the corner of a shed in the yard that served as office and, without lifting the tired eyes, he squeezed out the words Allan longed for: "I'll dae it."

Good lad! Allan yelled, and came round to thump him on the back. He turned away without looking and nearly knocked over the figure of a winged Mercury that they'd been forced to bring inside as a prim lady of known determination had sworn next time when she came to collect her concrete bunnies, she was going to drape a towel round the statue and hide its immodesty. With luck, Allan thought, the old witch would never collect her bunnies. Once they'd got the insurance money they'd be away, at least he would be.

"Onythin just tae be shot of this lot," Norrie sighed.

"Exactly," Allan giggled, to earn a glare, "But I'll be killin twa burds wi the ane stane: the failed business and the failed wife, baith the gither." It was a pity they couldn't do Betty's father as well but then, they'd have no call to see the old man ever again once the proprieties had been attended to.

With the ploy determined Allan even became quite pleasant to his wife which simply drew the response, "It's not like you. You're after summit ah bet."

Allan just stopped himself from crowing, "Hoo much dae you bet?"

He knew and inwardly purred like a cat watching a dinner party and sure of a saucer of cream at the end.

They carried off the ploy quite effectively. The plan given cut was that the three of them would do Agag's together, then the following Sunday Betty could lead Norrie up it, that way placating the old man who objected to husband and wife ropes, even though they had no kids or dependants. But the second weekend would never be.

Allan, as secretly planned, carefully "forgot" his rock boots so dropped the others off at Jacksonville while he rushed on up to the Fort to buy another pair in the newly-opened Nevisport. He'd be back to join them after Agag's. Betty was quite happy with this and Norrie, licking his lips, nodded agreement.

He, poor lad, tried not to think what he was going to do as they wended up to the Buachaille through the heather. In some ways he was lucky being so feckless. He couldn't think deeply. It was as if the worn path through the cloying heather was a track on which he was set like a controlled toy train. It was all so routine and familiar. They hardly even talked as they put on their rock boots and harnesses and checked all the clobber. Norrie led off, surprising himself at his calm, but it was the set gracefulness of long practice. He was so programmed that he just shut out what he must do at the top of the climb.

He sat on the big ledge to bring Betty up. Norrie could feel the red rock warm on his back. His feet hung out over space. There was a solitary blaeberry on the ledge and he popped it into his mouth.

"Climb when you're ready."

"Climbing!"

He watched her picking her way up, hands moving gently, fondling the rock, then gripping while she arched out and up onto the next foothold. She climbed steadily and well. Betty wasn't a bad soul really. It was just Allan riled her so. Ach, life had got everything the wrong way round he felt. And to escape its toils and coils he was going to commit murder. They'd never used the word in going over the details. It was "an accident" always. But the doing of it was his responsibility even if Allan often reminded him they would both be equal benefidaries.

"It wouldna bother me!" Allan boasted.

And Norrie thought, "No, it wouldn't; you're a rich bastard."

The pitches were climbed steadily. The very routine of climbing is one of its comforts. You get lost in it and everyday cares drop away beyond the horizon. Norrie reached the top, pulled in some slack and went straight to the belay. He'd done Agag's three times before and didn't forget moves or such details. It was the finest V. Diff. In Scotland. Classic.

"Climb when you're ready."

"Climbing," came Betty's echo.

Norrie grimly muttered "Falling" to himself and then switched off the nasty future to concentrate on taking in the rope. Betty let her eyes sweep over the Moor, with the threads of roads laid on its sequinned serge and the cocked hat of Schiehallion away in the east, then turned to the kindly rock. Aye, she could lead this no bother. She went up the last pitch and pulled over the top onto Crowberry Ridge.

As so, Norrie stood up, throwing the colorful coils of rope off his legs and began undoing the belay. Betty unclipped the rope from her harness and began untying the figure eight. She turned, as one always does, to look down the sheer 300 foot route just climbed. It was Norrie's moment.

"Betty."

She turned her head to see his outstretched arm.

"Would you like a sweety?"

There were two or three in his palm and she chose a mint. This was all part of their routine too.

"Ta."

They sat in silence (but for a plane high overhead and the occasional rattle of a mint on teeth) and Betty thought happily to the following weekend. Apart from bloody Allan, life was pretty good. Norrie was thinking of Allan too, imagining him coming back from the Fort, the intended hours late, not to find flashing lights and the bustle of police and mountain rescue but an irate wife and a silent partner sitting at the car park. They would be ruined. And so what? He just couldn't do it. He reached out a tentative hand and laid it briefly on Betty's shoulder so she turned to look at him. He gave her a smile that held a hundred secrets in it. Betty smiled back. She put out her tongue with the mint on it like a little girl might have done. They laughed.

Allan, having seen them set off, had gunned the car along the straight to Alltnafeidh and on for the Coe, his voice roaring out a song. They were saved! What a sucker Norrie was, being persuaded like that. Allan just hoped, he could be the person who broke the news to the old man, the shock would be as good as sticking a knife in him. The bastard had even set this up with all his talk a few years back about having adequate life insurance. Well, the insurance would certainly save some lives, and the detestable business.

It did too, though he never knew how—not in the way he'd planned.

He swept round the bend at the Study just as the dithery old couple pulled in to see the falls which took his eyes off the road momentarily. This meant he was slow in reacting to a bulky, long HGV grinding up the glen. All he could do was swerve. The barrier bounced him back and he was exhaling a Whew! of relief when the tail of the lorry smashed in the corner of the windscreen and removed half his head in a single stroke.

Betty's father was more smug than ever when the insurance check came through. And his little lily blossomed. Maybe it was as well however, that a year later, he did not see her solo Agag's Groove while her fiancé, Norrie, looked on. While they were climbing on the Buachaille he was hoeing the rose bed he'd planted round the statue of the winged Mercury which Norrie had sold to him.

Agag's Groove

Terry Gifford (b.1946) is the founder of the International Mountaineering Literature Festival. He is a member of the Climber's Club and recently edited *The Climber's Club Centenary Journal*. He is also a poet with a number of books to his credit, including *Whale Watching with a Boy and a Goat* and *The Rope*, and has edited several volumes of John Muir's works. His latest book is entitled *The Joy of Climbing* which was a finalist for the 2004 Banff Mountain Literature Award. He has climbed extensively in Britain, the United States, and Europe.

TERRY GIFFORD:
BONFIRES IN BORROWDALE

I looked down the first pitch from my stance beside a tree and braced my feet firmly apart to take a fall. The rope ran down in a straight line but disappeared over the top of the steep wall at the bottom. How reassuring the ritual calls are when you're out of sight of each other. Tom's head soon came into sight, and his hands, feeling over the rock, testing holds. "The trouble with these trainers," he said, "is that you have to be careful not to catch them as you lift your feet or the velcro lifts and they might drop off!"

At the start of the next pitch I placed a left foot high in a groove and made a huge pull, wondering if Tom could find the solution to this problem. I needn't have worried. He didn't hesitate to discover an alternative to the left, and in the polished groove of the third pitch, followed by the foot jamming crack of the fourth, before the final wall of the fifth Tom kept coming, talking all the time. On the Belvedere I coiled in the sunshine whilst Tom removed the belay before we moved across to peer over the edge a few feet further to the north. Another team were starting the final pitch of Little Chamonix, the leader spreading fingers and toes across the steep top wall. Tom's eyes lit up. Well, we'd come to that. Tom had just done his first route in the Lakes. When you're seven there is plenty of time to fuel bonfires.

In fact that very night, instead of dreaming routes ahead, time turned backwards as the young climber blacked his face with the rest of his family and swinging a fearfully grinning turnip lantern set out singing the Lyke Wake Dirge to trick or treat "the shepherd's house" below Shepherd's Crag. Later that night, the excitement over and young climbers fast asleep, a rustling at the window brought us peering out into the dark to glimpse a witch in black plastic bags riding a beesom round the corner of the cottage. Tempted closer, after our shock the disguised shepherd of the crag offered us a drop of "real dragon's blood" to calm our nerves. His little lad, Jason, watched these pagan rites from behind a car, as we brought out the turnip's and the pumpkin's flickering faces to see them off again to their home under Tom's high viewpoint of earlier that day.

Tom's route, Jackdaw Ridge, makes a final jagged fling and tumble of rock through the trees before Shepherd's Crag disappears round the corner into the hillside and a marvellous walk up to Watendlath. For connoisseurs of Bentley Beetham's detailed explorations of Borrowdale, and this end of Shepherd's Crag in particular, the Jackdaw Ridge actually starts up Beetham's Ant Highway, which matters little. Tom claimed it like a new route and climbed it again next day together with a 30-year-old who had never climbed before, but knew someone else who would love to do it.

However, the following afternoon Kev and Barby arrived for Tom and I to guide them up Knitting Haws. It's a scrappy scramble, but Tom led up all the bits of boulders and little walls that we could find as, unroped, we strung rock and heather together. By far the finest descent is to turn north and follow a track below a wall to a smoothly grassed spur. We fell through deep bracken towards the lights of Grange as dusk closed in.

A wet day and we were pulling fallen branches out of the fields, dragging them down the road to a growing bonfire opposite the Borrowdale Hotel. And still Little Chamonix was receiving continuous ascents. In an afternoon of clearing weather, Tom and I with three-year-old Ruth, walked into the great bowl of bronze trees that leads to Black Crag. Voices came from Troutdale Pinnacle, a valley route with a big-crag feel that Tom could look forward to climbing at any time of year. I memorized the elegant line of a parallel party on the Super-direct as we slowly explored the orange fell below Greatend Crag. In full autumn color this is a magic corner of the Lakes, not far from the road. Rowans explode in bonfires of berries along the paths.

November the fifth and I wanted to take Tom on a nostalgic climb in Coombe Gill. I must have been 16 or 17 when I did my first climbing here. We were awestruck working class kids from a Scott troop up Newmarket Road in Cambridge. Des Oliver (creator of Troutdale Pinnacle Direct) introduced us to rock climbing on his afternoon offfrom the grocer's shop where he worked in Keswick. I've never forgotten Glaciated Slab since that day twenty years ago when we Fen boys flogged up the bouldered fell towards this whale's back 100ft high. As we youngsters were introduced to the concept of Old Man's Pace up that slope I remember someone stating what became for us the Cambridge definition of steepness: "I wouldn't ride me bike down here!"

The top of Glaciated Slab is the top of the fifth pitch of a Bentley Beetham creation called Intake Ridge, twelve pitches of Mod that wander up the east side of the entrance to Coombe Gill to the top of Bessyboot. Beetham is supposed to have made these linked scrambles for the initiation of kids into climbing. Glaciated Slab is itself perfect for the purpose as Des Oliver obviously knew. He lit something there that was becoming a recurring ritual. Tom silently soloed up the easy scoop at the top end of the slab. I followed at his heels. Next David, who had come up to Borrowdale for Bonfire Night, started out in big boots up the face in the center of slab declaring it clearly V Diff rather than Beetham's grade of Diff. Tom tried hard to solve the problem of the thin crack in the middle but finally traversed across to find an easier way up for his short reach. The chimney also proved good fun, taking us out to the open left edge of the outcrop. Finally, David and I soloed the excellent break just round the comer that finishes at the top of the chimney.

And then to the bonfire, with fireworks provided by the film director Ken Russell. Anyone who has seen just one of his films can imagine his delight in setting off bigger and better displays of pyrotechs. The rockets shot up like flares lighting Little Chamonix. The first Guy, top of the pile of branches and beds, was quickly consumed and so we then brought on our crucified straw man whose candle eyes flamed from the front of the fire. As his body burnt, the turnip head rolled safely out of the fire for a second or third life beyond Halloween, the Celtic year's end.

Bonfire in Borrowdale

The shepherd passed round his taties from a tin hooked out of the heat of the fire to challenge the bonfire toffee already circulating. We stood facing the heat in the comfortable neighborly atmosphere.

"I took our Tom climbing in Coombe Gill today on routes that have all got the old sheep counting names, you know. Trod Yan, Tan, Tethera, Methera. . . Do you know them?"

"No, I've never used them."

"They were named by a guy called Bentley Beetham."

"Now I remember him. I gave him a lift once. He used to stay in a tin hut beside the road beyond Rosthwaite. He was getting on then, maybe in his eighties, and he could hardly walk along the road. He said he'd climbed a route up Bessyboot that you could walk up either side of."

"Intake Ridge! That's where we've been today."

"Aye, and I remember him saying 'They'll never stop me till they nail me down.'"

"Well I hope I'm around when our Tom takes his daughter or son up old Bentley Beetham's routes in Borrowdale!"

As the fire died down at last and we drifted away, the crag bulked black above. It held in the promise of darkness one of Beetham's best discoveries, made a month before I was born. From Halloween to Bonfire Night, Little Chamonix had literally hung over us like the future, to be savored when it comesthe spikey comers, airy stances, the engaging of toes on the slab, the revelation over the knife blade, the unfolding of in cuts on the testing top pitch. Well, Tom will come to that in his own time. Some routes are worth saving to savor in the fired light of leading.

Terry Gifford

TERRY GIFFORD:
BONFIRE ABOVE BENIDORM

"Look Tom, there's the ridge we climbed." Norman was pointing out of the aircraft window, leaning back so that Tom could see. We were flying home after our first New Year holiday on Sun Rock, within reach of Calpe on the Spanish Costa Blanca. For Tom it was his first climbing trip outside Britain and there, clearly visible below, was the best route of the week, Espero Sur Central, a 1,200-foot long Severe which took an isolated ridge reaching down from the summit, left of the south face, of Puig Campana, the mountain behind our twenty-noe storey tower block in Benidorm.

For this long ridge we'd made an Alpine start down the lift of our tower block and out into the mild January night air. As we parked the car it was getting light. A half moon hung over the massif of empty hills around us. We sent Tom off to find the start of the trail towards the dark Puig Campana. The air was perfectly still. A dog barked in the village below.

When Tom returned we loaded him up. Strangely, both Norman and I had developed bad backs before we came away and the hour's walk in did become a little awkward, beating through the bush and climbing over old terrace walls, even before we lost the regular path. But the best of it was the bonfire. As we got closer the rays of the dawn sun broke through the towers of Benidorm to set alight the huge limestone face above us in a bonfire of orange and red cracks and ribs. The black edge on the left marked the perfect arete of our route.

Bonfire in Borrowdale

It is approached by a basin further left, round the back of the ridge. Hidden from the sun this was a chilly place to rope up. But having Tom there, with the promise of a long day's adventure together, generated a warm glow of expectation. Dads (and mums) will know what I mean. Climbing in the middle, Tom was busy tying four knots whilst Norman headed up the first groove towards a tree. Following Norman on the first pitch, Tom got the sack caught as he traversed right from the tree. It was going to be a long day's test of patience, but the first belay brought us back to the sun.

I was supposed to walk 100ft along the broad ledge, but less than half that distance brought me to another tree at its end. In fact, every pitch on this climb was actually shorter than suggested in Chris Cragg's guide. Tom was about to follow when Norman shouted to me that one of Tom's knots had come undone. This is enough to send a shiver down the spine of any climber, but a father has to shoulder a bigger burden, especially on the second of 12 pitches. I suddenly felt queasy with guilt and quietly hoped that Chris had got the grade of Severe right. He hadn't for the supposed "Hard Severe," Via Valencianos at Calpe, the polished crux of which is 5a. We'd not taken Tom on this. It was our first afternoon and we had wanted to get a feel of the grades. But Tom has learned from his father a devious line in cheating only, you understand, if absolutely necessary; when time is short, if the survival (or sanity) of others is at stake.

Two pitches of fluid movement up open grooves brought us on to the arete itself. From an airy belay we watched Norman climb a crack on the left side of the arete leading up to a peg at a bulge. He was raving about the rock, about the situation, about the climbing even, but here he paused, made some of his "watch me!" moves juddering left, then resumed his ravings again. Tom climbed smoothly past the bulge on its right face. Things seemed to be back to normal. When I joined them at their spacious belay ledge Norman broke open a can of tonic water, the first that week that he had actually drunk neat, undiluted by gin.

It is a measure of the pleasure we derived from this route that Norman thought, in retrospect, that he had led the best pitches, and I was equally sure that two of the pitches I led were the best. The next was one of them. I stepped left into the bottom of the hanging chimney which provided steep bridging with plenty of protection. In the still sunshine, high above cowboy country, it was my turn to rave about the flutings of the rock, the beauty of the moves. If only it had lasted for 150ft as the guidebook promised. I'd run out 90ft when I came to the break on the ridge that was the belay.

A scrappy groove led to the crux pitch where the guide offered a choice of lines. The arrows at the start of the leftmost groove (found only after a scramble up a ramp from the ridge) left no doubt about the classic line, with perhaps a move of 4c. The layback start and delicate bridging were somewhat marred by the big block at the top of the line, waiting to tumble on to the belayer below. I forget how many times Norman kept saying "When you follow watch that block. Tom," before he finally reached a belay, out of our hearing. Tom stormed up the layback and again outflanked the crux moves on the right face.

According to Chris Craggs, two pitches now led to the top of the route. One was "easier angled," and the other "the climbing now eases." So I thought I must be off route—although on the ridge it was difficult to quite see how—when I found the next corner blocked by overhangs. Never mind, there were jugs underneath and an exciting swing right for a high step round the arete. A rare peg hinted at the exposure of the steep steps on the crest of the ridge. Tom would love this spectacular "easier angled" stuff.

When his rucksack came into view a grinning face turned upwards. When he arrived at the belay he coolly sat down and tied on. "Look at that Tom" I enthused, needlessly, "feel the sun. What marvelous situations climbing gets you into. This sill last you through the winter, eh? When you're in school on a manky day in February, remember this view?"

He looked out from our perch. "Okay, Dad, okay," he said, "just don't start singing."

But Norman was getting ratty instead of inspired. "I thought it was supposed to get easier" he complained. When his next pitch was up the steep ridge in serious situations leading to a single ancient peg belay he was positively alarmed. We still had to find a way off the mountain, not a crag, and the sun was now getting low. It was January after all. He rushed off into the lead again. running out nearly a rope length. When I joined him and Tom having climbed an overhanging little diagonal crack protected by a peg, I knew he would be fuming. Sure enough. He shot off up slabby rock that thankfully took him quickly to a red dot on the path that traverses the upper part of the mountain.

We stayed roped up, for it was dear when we looked round the corner that the red-dotted path would cross several ribs, down climbing the far side of each of them and in between traverse the loose ground of the upper bowl of the south face. Only after the final steep down climb into the big scree gully could we relax. Crossing towards a patch of the dying sun we sat down, changed into trainers and finished the water.

"You've done well Tom," pronounced Norman, "and you haven't complained once."

As we kept looking back at the mountain a mist drifted across its face, which suddenly cleared and Puig Campana was a bonfire again. Now it glowed only with the last embers of the day, a warm pink bonfire in the sky, rising above us like the final flame of a memory that would warm us all through many a manky day in school that winter.

Paul Pritchard (b. 1967) is one of Britain's new young "hard men." He is an outstanding rock climber who has pioneered many new extreme routes on the Welsh crags. He is also an outstanding writer. His collection of short stories entitled *Deep Play* won the the Boardman Tasker Mountain Literature Award in 1997. He received an unprecedented second Boardman Tasker in 1999 for his most recent work, *Totem Pole* which recounts his near fatal climbing accident.

PAUL PRITCHARD:
A GAME ONE CLIMBER
PLAYED

(Fiction)

I am lying in a long grass, naked I think, foetal. Warm. It's so pleasantly warm. I can hear distant cries. Children playing? I am adrift, going further and further toward slumber. I don't see but I feel I am surrounded by tall hedges. Insects buzz. Darkness begins to creep over me—my eyes are shut but I can feel it. Still warmth and a smiling comfort. Some one takes my hand—she must be knelt by me. I don't open my eyes, nothing need by physically gestured.

Then the hand slips inevitably away and I am left in a cavernous night with all the contentedness of a young child dozing in the afternoon. This is it, the most beautiful part of all my life. Utterly final.

"Paul." A distant voice calls out.

"Paul, wake up." Nearer now.

"WAKE UP."

Leave me alone. Let me sleep. Let me go.

"Come on Paul, WAKE UP." My body is being shaken violently.

In anger now I turn to scold my disturber "why don't you just. . . ."

LIGHT—My eyes open. Someone has just thrown an electrical appliance into my wet dream and 240 volts are put through me. A blur. It's too bright for me to see. I want to ask questions where am I? What the hell is going on? But it's impossible. I am just a single painful thought in a space of white noise. Then somewhere, below me and my thought, a body, I think related to me, attempts to breathe. An implosion of sharp points. The body convulses and is thrown onto its side. Lines, horizontal, vertical, diagonal. Beginning to focus. And colors too. I gain some comprehension of what I am. AND COLOR! A jet of red pisses out of my mouth and then a deafening sigh. Convulsions follow. More red water. Enormous gasps. Daggers are screwed further into my chest. MY CHEST!

"Paul, you're in Wen Zawn and you've just ripped all your gear. You hit these rocks and then you went in the water. This is Glenn."

The words swim around in my head looking for a place to attach themselves. They settle in all the wrong places, though anagramatically they make some sense. . . Glenn Zawn. . . Hit the sea rocks. . . "You've been wedged under water for about ten minutes. I pulled you out feet first". . . Glenn. . . Gogarth. . . "GLENN" I shout but no sound comes. Again I try to inhale the white noise but my throat will not allow it. Something stabs and twists. This is it. You've done it now. You've punctured your lungs for sure. Sleep. . . Sleep. Yeah go on, go to sleep and you'll die you pathetic shit. Is that me or someone else being cruel? I sob uncontrollably. My eyes focus now on Glenn. He's trying to solo up the wall of the Zawn. My whole body feels broken. Is it spread over all these rocks. "Don't leave me Glenn." Still nothing comes out. Like a dolphin I dive in and out of a sea of unconsciouses. I want to continue my sleep, but my slumber is intruded upon.

"Paul wake up—I'm your doctor and I just want to put this tube up your nose. Swallow as I push it in."

The sky, the sea, the walls of Zawn are stark white and ugly. The whole world is ugly. The pieces of my life are shaken through a sieve and the finer particles settle around me. My family, my friends, the woman I love. My body shudders in waves. I'm falling again but I can never tell if it's for the last time.

"Paul, it's raining outside. Lets stay warm under the covers. Let's stay in bed."

Am I this sad for them or for me? What a profound welling up of all the unfinished stories. The potential fairy tale endings or the emotional farewells. From my right temple blood wicks across my wet face. It's still raining. My shoulders feel like they're in pieces. With each tiny gulp of air I inhale more panic, I want oxygen. Another time I slip into blackness.

"Paul, wake up—the stars are out, the weather's clear. We could be at the base of the Torre by eight thirty."

Pain in back, in pelvis, in both ankles.

Glenn has dressed me in his clothes, but still I have gone beyond the shivers. From time to time the rigidity falls from me as though I am soaked in a hot bath. Then, again distant voices laugh and shout. I strain but they don't come nearer. My imaginary saviours drift away. I am held.

"Paul, wake up." Glenn is slapping me about my face. "Don't sleep, it's dangerous." Now he's holding up a piece of frayed wire. "Look, You snapped a bloody wire. And the tide's coming in pretty fast." The bag of bones rattles on the hard, spiky floor. The tide could come in, night could fall, a storm could blow in from the West. I could slip out of my own back door and never return. It's not a problem for the bones. But it is a problem for Glenn. I hear him shouting. He informs me that five hours have passed.

My eyes hinge open. Above, the walls of the Zawn are like the rib cage of some giant animal seen from the inside. The clouds are bent. For a fabulous moment my view becomes the cupola of Madrid's church of San Antonio, a circular sweep of Goya's colorful people against dull grey and green. The saint performs his miracle as the Antonio beckons to us down here. He waves. I feel important, at the center of his miracle. They all wave.

"Paul, they're here. The rescue team."

Rescue? Ah! The cliff top. Adrenalin fuelled ambivalence gives way to momentary excitedness, and more gulping for air. I hear the throbbing pulse of a helicopter and out beyond the neck there is a red boat which says RNLI. A dinghy speeds in and out clamber men without faces. As they lash me to a stretcher one of them asks me "what's wrong? You've done way harder things in this Zawn." I laugh. They are good at their job. I get panicky as I'm nonchalantly passed around inches above a clawing swell, all strapped up. Little gulps. Small gulps.

I am clipped into cables, winched up, swung around, lowered down, winched up again and pulled into a hovering yellow helicopter. The noise worries me. A mask is planted over my nose and mouth, a tap is turned and with a hiss my anxieties dissipate. The men grow faces. I shut my eyes.

The Games One Climber Played

A sloping shelf running with water. I can't swing my feet back onto the rock. I can't hold on any longer. I try to move up but I am strapped down. I slump back and relax. My body and the day begin to fit together.

I had wanted to reaquaint myself with the intricacies of climbing in Wen Zawn before attempting the big new line again up the back wall. It is wild rock down there. Unpredictable, untamable for some. You have to take time to build up a relationship where you and the rock can trust each other. I had been here many times, scared myself and forged partner ships. Conan with Dave Green, The unridable Donkey with Nick Dixon, Rubble (the softest route in the world) with Leigh McGinley. "An easy day" on the direct start to Games Climbers Play, I had said to Glenn. It went near the line of my project and we would have a good view across. We rappeled into the foot of the Zawn and Glenn got a belay about fifteen feet up above the lapping waves. Drizzle steadily fell. The moves became scary and awkward. I had to climb down twice before I could arrange some protection in clay/rock mix. I started to move up, confidently, with all the inflated ego of a seasoned Gogarth climber about to plod up an easy Extreme. A couple more small wires, tips laybacking, then dripping hand cracks through steps of roofs. I was tiring but I knew how far I could go after I had hit the lactic acid wall. The belay was right there. Chalk was turning to mud in the cracks. I hung in there, pumping heavily and my forearms burned. I threw in a couple of extra Friends in case I should fall. "Jeez Glenn, this is strenuous for E4!" In the flared crack, fisting to the cuffs, I was faced with a choice; continue with deadmeat hands for six more feet and step across to the ledge or move right now and grab hold of the same ledge. The decision had to be made in less than a second. I swung right from the crack and grabbed the ledge with my right hand. Water began to make little rivers down to my armpit. My feet cut loose into space so I repositioned them on greasy smears and brought my left hand over. My error became apparant—the ledge was smooth and moist and sloped toward me alarmingly. I tried to mantle. No. Again. No. One more time. Utterly pumped I hung like a rag doll for a few timeless seconds contemplating the inevitable. Without shouting to Glenn I throw myself off the rock to avoid falling badly. I am not too worried as I've got plenty of gear in, but I begin to accelerate.

The horrid notion flashes across my mind that the Cams haven't held and I brace myself for a longer fall. In the confusion I feel myself slow down imperceptibly and almost begin to relax. Then I continue to accelerate again. Instinctively, like other animals, I prepare to land on

Paul Prichard

my feet. Ten pieces of gear explode from the rock. I land atop a sharp ridge sticking up out of the Zawn floor and my right ankle crushes with the impact. In the same blurred moment I rocket head first into a narrow cleft of flushing sea water and stop.

And then I am lying in long grass, naked I think.

Ian Mitchell (b. 1947) is a prize winning author of five mountaineering books including *A View from the Ridge*, co-authored with Dave Brown and winner of the Boardman-Tasker Mountain Literature Award. He has climbed in Norway, Iceland, the United States, and in the Pyrenees and Alps. His other books include *Scotland's Mountains Before the Mountaineers*, *Mountain Days* and *Bothy Nights*, and *The Mountain Weeps*.

IAN MITCHELL:
DEAD MAN'S ICE-AXE

Fiction

Druim Shios and Druim Shuas of Ben Beith; nothing to it. A pleasant winter's outing in the soft snow that had fallen—a little earlier than usual—in late October.

It was a sharp, clear day, blue skies and sun—but with a stiff wind. They breakfasted as they dressed, putting on gaiters, boots and windproofs while the primus hissed and the porridge bubbled glutinously. Then, ready, they sat enjoying a second cup of tea—all the more so since it would be long before anything hot but breath passed between their lips.

He picked up the two ice-axes that he had brought with him. One a glistening metal Stubai with a sheath of blue rubber on the stem, and the other. He looked at it, an old Ashenbrenner, its oiled wooden stem glowing like the embers of a fire. It was his spare, he took it along for anyone who came without an axe in winter. He had initially used it himself, after he had gained it in one of the exchanges of anarchical barter that featured in former days. Gained it for the loss of an old Remington typewriter, which its recipient had used to type his way out of the fish factory and into University. He held one axe in each palm, deliberating. The Ashenbrenner was heavier, though probably less able to break a fall, since it was a quarter of a century old.

He handed the Stubai to his comrade, and donned his rucksack "Here, you take my axe, I'll take the other one."

His companion looked at him a moment before taking it, and tried, smiling, to make light of the issue.

"Are you sure? It's your axe, but if you're happy with that one. . ."

"It's all right," he reassured wryly, "I'm not superstitious."

The chosen weapons were taken, and they stepped outside. Down from the bothy was a huge gap in the mountains, filled with ultramarine sky. The Bealach Ban, a route through to the west. To their right was the sharp Scalpel Ridge, foreshortened to tower over them, and to their left, smothered in snow, was Ben Beith with the ridges of ascent and descent they intended to traverse. Hardly a Grade II, but his friend had never used ax before, and he wanted him to have experience before they tried anything more ambitious. The snow was soft: there had been no frost.

"It'll be a plowter up to the hill through this soft snow," he observed as they started out the path along the rising burn. They walked. Silent. He was not in the mood for talking just yet. Still a bit tired. It had been a rush yesterday to travel north for the funeral, and then back down in the train, to head off again—his friend obligingly driving—to their bothy, their hill. Though he had slept reasonably well on the floor, his muscles were taking a long time to work, to over come his body's resistance. But they would, and then they would chat. For the moment it was enough to scan—as they ascended the pass—the mountains closing in on them, looking much more commanding in the whiteness, the brightness.

He could not see the crematorium, he could see almost nothing. The driver set him down from the bus, fog lights blazing, and assured him that the pole discerned dimly through the mist was the stop he required. If he just followed the pavement he would come to the building. The bus moved off, and he was left standing beside a pole whose legend he could not read.

It had been clear and sunny when he had boarded the train. Only when it had started moving up the East Coast did the mist begin to come in from the sea. And by the time he got off at the station, it was the familiar forgotten raw piercing haar from the past. It left you cold and damp, without there seeming to have been any precipitation. Haar; he muttered the term to himself, and thought for the first time—haar hair. All those years he had lived with it he had never realised. That was what it meant. Deliquescent hair, coming in locks and curls from the sea, to form a wreath.

He could have taken a taxi but he had time to kill. He wondered casually if the buses still plied the same routes as twenty years ago, if he could still find his way about the place. But the numbers had been changed and he had to ask his way of a fortuitously found inspector. Hearing his own question, he noticed the accent returning; the accent he had been born with, the accent the other had died with.

His companion had stopped on the path in front of him, waiting. The blood was beginning to quicken, the muscles to submit to discipline, the breath to come easier.

"Which way?"

"We can start looking for a crossing over the river any time now, and then cut across the moor to Druim Shios. That part will be murder, the moor. The snow will be soft and deep, but once we get on the ridge the wind will have pared it down and the going will be easier. When you cross the river use your axe for balance. I've used it for that more often than for stopping a fall."

"So it's just really for decoration, for show?" was the laughed reply.

"Usually."

The river was not high, and snow had covered the boulders which sat like icing-covered puddings in the water. It proved simplest to wade through, and let gaiters do the job of keeping the icy water out of boots. On the other side, deep snow over sinewy heather roots made for hard going and little talk. But he looked at the still-clear sky. The weather would hold, they would have a good day.

He had walked along the pavement in the mist, just able to see the dank bushes at the roadside. Occasionally he passed an unlit lamp-post. It proved further than he remembered from his last and only visit to the crematorium; twenty, twenty five years ago? He walked on in the void, not seeming to get any further. Each lamp-post was like the last and no cars passed. He had a sudden terror that the path would just go on and on and then stop, nowhere. He pulled his coat closed round his body against the cold, and kept walking.

Then he saw them. As if they were the dead themselves, or the undead, the unburied. Moving silently through the mist, a mist now punctuated by weak spectral lights, was a crowd of insubstantial figures, as if conjured out of a concentration of the mmist itself, as if they were but its allotropes. He moved through the sound-deadening haar, afraid to speak, and approached the crowd, looking for a face he knew. They looked back at him, as though he were not there.

Then he came upon a visage which turned in recognition towards him, spoke in a soft voice, a seeming emanation of the mist;

"Ah, ye heard. Ye got here."

"Aye."

"He'd hae been gled."

No one spoke further. He wondered if they had been talking before he arrived. If his intrusion were the cause of the silence. He felt a panic attack, saw them all there to be buried, to be ushered into the threateningly-hidden building and cremated—not the dead man lying in his coffin, but the dead past that his decease could not resurrect by this reunion.

Pulling off of the moor onto Druim Shios, they used the axes for balance. When it steepened a little, he demonstrated to his partner how to ascend a slope.

"Don't pull yourself up on it. It won't hold. Get your weight over it."

And he showed how to break a fall, holding the axe across the body and falling over the stem, using the curved pick as a brake.

"So what's the adze for?"

"Step cutting, but we won't be doing any of that today. The snow is too soft."

After the lesson they sat to survey the scene and to take some refreshment; an orange, some dried fruit, chocolate. They ate in silence. Then his partner took a few photographs, including one of the axes against the steepening ridge.

"To show my boy what a hero his dad is," he joked. But he noticed that his seated companion did not make a response to the jest, and asked more formally. "Were you all that close to him? I never really heard you talking about him all that much. You didn't seem to keep regular contact with the people from that time in your life."

The man with the Aschenbrenner finished his chocolate before replying, to give himself time to compose an answer.

"I had only seen him maybe four or five times in twenty years. But at that time, in that period, we were close. It was the time when you shared intellectual passions, political passions, life on the mountains. . ."

"And sexual partners?"

He managed a soft smile.

"I told you about that, did I? Well, it was the spirit of the times"—or maybe I should say the illusion of the epoch—"Make Love Not War," "Power to the Imagination and all that." But that is dust and ashes now, just like him. Anyway, let's not get morbid. It's a fine day—one he would have liked, though being a lazy bastard, he might have found an excuse for not going on the hill. Let's enjoy the day."

And they moved off through the changing climb of undulating knolls, steepening aretes, sharp ridges. Varied enough to retain constant interest, and an ideal morphological teaching-aid in the use of the axe. He was feeling better now. Concentrating on the job, the energy-giving air helping the adrenal in-flow. They were walking across the wind-clipped summit plateau to the cairn on the top before he thought again of the man whose axe he was carrying.

The axe's original owner had used it on the hill, but not for long. Though he continued with the mountains, he quickly eschewed anything difficult, like rock climbing or winter expeditions. Mostly he liked the social aspect. The pub banter, the bothy life, the crack—and the women, since there were many camp followers in those days. But when his comrades became serious about this hill-business, he good humouredly dropped into the background. That was why he had divested himself of the axe; he could not take the mountain that seriously.

Nor did he take the politics that seriously either, though he believed in them. He knew that it was there—at that time—that the crowds were, the good times were. And, unashamed rogue as he was, knew that it was there that it was easiest to get laid. And he was more successful in that department than the man he had exchanged the axe with.

"Your problem," he used to say, "is that you think you can't get into bed until you've discussed Marx."

But the dead man had taken his share of the struggle while it lasted; the duplicating of magazines, the handing out of leaflets. And they had never divulged to anyone which of them it was who had dropped the burning tin of paint into the jeep at the U.S. base to show the bastards what napalm was like. But here too there was never the unquestioning commitment, and the dead man withdrew before the others to his private concerns. To the man he had passed the axe to he had said, "You'll never give up, never. I know it."

They reached the summit amidst the snowy tundra, and planted their axes, like pennants, in the cairn. Then sat down to eat again; the fruit-cake and juice this time, and more chocolate. Below them lay the waters of Loch Beith and to the east, the mountains where he had first used the axe, as indeed had its original owner. They sheltered from the wind as best they could behind the cairn, but it was cold. So after a couple of quick photographs, they got ready to leave, to descend. The novitiate asked his mentor.

"Why did he not want you to come and see him at the end?"

The latter lifted the sack and picked up the axe again. He would need it for the descent. They turned backs to the wind and set off down the sloping plateau.

"It wasn't just me, he refused to see anyone. When he got the diagnosis, and the time-scale, he hospitalized himself. He was adamant, immovable; no visitors. I can see him thinking—what good would it do, what could they tell me, how could they help? And also, knowing that, knowing it would distress visitors too, so he took the decision. Again, so typical of him. But we are coming to the descent, so take care."

The Druim Simas is actually steeper than its longer brother. A powdery cornice was hacked away to reveal a steep chimney leading down to a ramp. The leader told his partner to face in, kick in his toes, and use the axe for balance. With a little trepidation his partner obeyed, and they moved on.

"I took a photograph of you coming down. That'll impress your boy," he informed the man with the Stubai, who clapped his back by way of thanks. The ridge now narrowed, but it was never problematic and they descended swiftly. On each side, he noted, the snow was fluffy and a slip would not lead far. Now they arrived at a slabby bluff facing the moor below them. They could see the bothy four miles away and were already thinking of food and rest. The direct way off over snow-clad slabs was ruled out, they would descend the steep snow slope to their left, which led smoothly to the corrie floor. He faced inwards and started to descend, using the axe as an anchor. The snow here was a little harder, out of the sun, than on the ridge.

He smiled to himself as he kicked steps.

Then there had been, that bizarre incident he could never forget. They had been drinking—it was a Friday night—the four of them. They were all merry, and the dead man particularly so, when they left the pub and headed for the bus. They all lived in the same area of the town, an area which was a kind, he thought, of local left bank at that time. They were two couples; the dead man with the new girlfriend he was living with, and himself with the dead man's previous wife, whom the latter was separated from. They were all pals. Sexual jealousy was not permitted in those days. Their group knew many such couplings and uncouplings.

They went upstairs in the bus—for the dead man smoked heavily. And upstairs on the late Friday buses you could get a sing-song sometimes, the drunken prales giving it "Ten Guitars" or "Danny Boy." But that night they had taken over, and got the keelies singing the "Red Flag;" though they lost them with "Bandiera Rosa," he remembered whimsically.

The dead man was like a gangster, in double-breasted suit and Homburg hat which suited his rascality. He was ill, smooring with the cold, against which he had imbibed heavily but unavailingly in the pub. The bus reached their destination, one of their flats where they would drink for a few more hours, and talk. But the dead man would not hear of it.

"Let's tak the bus tae the terminus, and ging for a swim in the bay," he suggested, and indicated that if necessary he would go alone. The rest of the party, more sober, agreed to accompany him and prevent any accident befalling. It was winter, he remembered, though he could not recall the month. But it was cold and misty and the bay was of the North Sea. He smiled again as he remembered the gangster's words, out of sight of the women, as they headed for the silent, darkened bay beyond the last street lights;

"We'll get an orgy once everybody's dais are aff!"

It was not a likely setting for a Bacchanalia.

A black sea crashing in a black night under a black sky, with freezing spume carried by the wind across the shingly beach and black racks by the shore. In the face of the womens'—and his male partner's—refusal to strip, the bandit remained true to his word, and deposited his suit and hat on the each, scuttling crab-like over shingle to the shore and crawled into the sea.

They looked on with a mixture of amusement and trepidation as he splashed around, inviting them to come in, and then watched him disappear under a big wave, whose noisy retreat carried him out to sea, and out of sight.

"Fuck," thought his male companion, "fuck"—and began swiftly and reluctantly to undress, while the women shouted the swimmer's name.

"Fuck," he thought again, as he stepped over the painful shingle and reached the water, looking out to the blank sea, stepping in to his ankles, his waist. And suddenly seeing the body of the dead man being swept towards him on a huge wave. He grabbed an arm and held it as the wave retreated, pulling him to the shore. The swimmer spoke, leering drunkenly.

"What about the women? Are they nae getting their dais aff?" — oblivious to his near mortality and assuming his naked companion had come to join in the orgy.

"You bastard. you bastard," his rescuer had smiled in reply. giving him a hug round the shoulders. The gangster was cured of his cold, and his half-rescuer caught a chill which lasted a week, he remembered as he kicked into the hardening snow. Not a place to slip, he thought as he looked at the rocks on the corrie floor below, consciously making big steps for his companion to follow. They he heard the latter shout; "Stop, I'm going to immortalise you!"

He looked up, saw the camera pointed at him, and halted—though it was not an ideal place. He lifted the axe in salutation as requested. The photographer took his time, trying first with, then without, gloves, to set the camera.

It was then he saw the dead man's name, carved on the axe with candleburn in some boredom of a bothy weekend, and remembered that he had never called him that, but only by his nickname. His attention was taken up; how had he got that name, and who had given it to him? So he was not concentrating, and a little stiff from his immobility, when he moved, stubbing one toe against the other, and headed downwards towards the rocks below.

The pick held him, first time, as he fell on it. He had not come far, possibly fifteen feet, and would not have done himself serious injury, given the length and angle of the slope—a broken limb at worst. He got to the bottom and cautioned his companion to come slowly. When the latter arrived it was to comment, mock-seriously;

"There was no need to go to that length with your ice-axe demonstration."

The leader was looking at the axe, turning it in his hand,

"It held. It's probably never been tested before. Sometimes the wood in these old one's weakens, and on impact the shaft snaps away from the metal. But it held."

Dog-tired now, they headed across the moor, their packs seeming heavier, and speech coming infrequently. He remembered his shock when the minister had used the dead man's real name. A midst the crowd of assembled mourners he had expected to hear, once more, the familiar

Ian Mitchell

nickname; it was as if they were cremating someone else. The minister had given a secular service, and they had ended by singing "Jerusalem" at the dead man's request. He stood by she who had been the dead man's companion at the bay, but was never his wife. He held her hand as they sang, smiling through tears.

One made tea on their return, and searched out a packet of biscuits. Another lit a fire with the kindling and coal they had brought with them, supplemented by some bogwood they had found on the moor. They sat awhile, slowly recovering, and then changed out of damp clothes, hung garments around the bothy to dry.

In the Hotel afterwards, the faces from long ago, when there had been giants on the earth, they had not died out, they had simply shrunk—a little later than the dead man—to human proportions. It was awkward. all knew what they had shared, and shared with the dead man. But it was long ago. To try and bridge the chasm of the years would be like trying to ascend a mountain without an axe in winter, unable to cut steps, to balance, to arrest a fall. The limpid silences and staccato exchanges had to substitute for the sorrow and loss.

"Thought ye micht bide till the morn?"

"Couldnae get aff work mair nor a day."

"The service wis guid, he'd o' liked it."

"He chose the songs himsel."

"Still getting on the hill?"

"Aye, noo and again. Yersel'?"

"Naw."

"Well, that's it then. I've a train tae catch."

"Keep in touch."

"Aye, probably see ye at the next funeral."

The mist had gone when he came out of the Hotel, he could see clearly now. But there was no time to look around the streets. He had a train to catch and could not linger.

They ate their food in the fire glow, and broke open their bottle of whisky, starting to drink as they finished the meal.

"Enjoy your day?" he asked the novitiate.

"Smashing, though I got a bit of a fright when you slipped."

"I wasn't concentrating. My mind was elsewhere."

"Forget it, that's all past. Let it lie."

"Aye."

"And you shouldn't still be using that old axe," his pal suggested,

Dead Man's Ice Axe

as a dram was passed over.

"Maybe. I might look for a new one."

"Burn it. Throw it in the fire."

"No, I couldn't do that. Couldn't do that. You know your Wagner? 'There is a spear that heals as well as wounds?'"

"Aye," joked his pal, "and I know my Bob Dylan too, 'Don't look back'. Drink up!"

They drank in the comfort of the whisky till the bottle was finished.

❋❋❋

The next day they drove off, and it was a long time before they spoke. And when they did, it was not of death or the dead.

Hamish MacInnes (b.1931) is one of Scotland's most influential mountaineers and a leading developer of mountaineering equipment. His invention of the all metal, drooped-pick ice axe (the Pterodactyl) brought ice climbing into the modern age. His MacInnes Box tent helped make possible the ascent of the Southwest Face of Everest. He is also at the forefront of modern mountain rescue theory and technique. He has climbed extensively in the Himalayas, New Zealand, the Alps, and the Caucasus, as well as his native Scotland. He is a film maker and has worked on a number of movies, including "Eiger Sanction," "Monty Pyton films" He is the author of numerous guide books and books on mountain rescue as well as autobiographical works such as *Look Behind the Ranges* and *Land of Mountains and Mist* with Moira Kerr. His latest book is *The Mammoth Book of Mountain Disasters*.

HAMISH MACINNES: MAN O' HOY

By stack and by skerry, by noup and by voe,
By air and by wick, and by helyer and gio,
And by every wild shore which the northern winds know. . .
　　　　　　　　—[Sir Walter Scott, "The Pirate"]

WE WERE ALL SITTING in the small room of the Rackwick schoolhouse, long since without the gay laughter of school children. Their laughter was replaced with the ribald mirth of adults. Mac the Telly, alias Ian McNaught-Davis, had us in fits. He was waxing his most eloquent:

"Here on the remote island of Hoy, providing a phallic fore ground to the wide and somber backcloth of the Atlantic, six climbers pit their feeble resources against this ravished 450 feet sandstone column, the Old Man of Hoy." At least his words went something like that. He was mimicking Chris Brasher's rehearsal of the Outside Broadcast the previous day, when Chris got a bit carried away with superlatives. There was a peat fire burning in the grate and around it were some of the best climbers in Britain, all crammed into that tiny room. We agreed that Mac's impromptu recitation was one of the funniest we had ever heard. Mac with Joe Brown, was attempting a new route up the east face of the stack, whilst Dougal Haston and Peter Crew had the task of making a further new line up the south-east arete, an edge bristling with overhangs on the landward side. Chris Bonington and Tom Patey were scheduled to do the "tourist route," which they had previously climbed when making the first ascent of the pinnacle.

I don't think I had heard of the Old Man of Hoy until Tom Patey mentioned it to me in 1962. Nothing was done about attempting to climb it then and it wasn't until 1966 that Tom, Chris Bonington and Rusty Baillie, a transplanted Rhodesian, climbed this column of sandstone for the first time, taking three days to do so. Tom Patey was then a G.P. in Ullapool, a fishing port on the West Coast of Scotland, a town saturated with tourists in summer and suffering from the overzealous influence of Christianity in all seasons. Tom, even when wishing to climb on weekdays, let alone the Sabbath would drive out of town respectably suited in black, as befitted his station, whilst in the boot of the car reposed his well-worn crag clothes which he would furtively slip into at some remote lay-by. Tom's talents were numerous: he was a fine musician and his old piano accordion was always with him. As a prolific and satirical songwriter his friends and enemies were never spared as he cut everyone down to size with well-chosen words and musical embellishments. His writing, too, was superbly funny and he had the ability to use his own irrational behavior to his advantage. For example, he wrote, "Who else but Hamish MacInnes would phone at this hour of the night with such a preposterous suggestion." Whereas it was he who used to telephone me at all hours of the night, suggesting some apparently hare-brained scheme, though usually they weren't quite so way-out as at first appeared. On another occasion I eavesdropped at one of his lectures and heard him recounting how I had used my longjohns for a sling on a difficult retreat from a climb. "Hamish," he said, amid peals of laughter, "had taken off his longjohns in sub-zero temperatures to use for this abseil sling." In fact they were his well-worn longjohns, not mine, which I had used, much to his discomfort on that occasion.

There had been four other live climbing Outside Broadcasts before the Old Man of Hoy: two in Wales and two in France, including the Aiguille de Midi and the ascent of the Eiffel Tower—a somewhat offbeat program which could hardly be said to have involved the technical problems we were now facing. Tom Patey had prepared a dossier on a possible Old Man of Hoy program, however, without giving a thought to the almost insurmountable engineering obstacles in the way of such a venture, assuming that repeating the climb itself would be by far the most difficult aspect of such a scheme. Nowadays, when planning an Outside Broadcast, we hardly consider the actual climbing of the cliff for transmission; there are so many competent mountaineers available we don't have to, but rather we concentrate on the technicalities of getting a signal out to civilization and also on the sheer cost of such an exercise.

Alan Chivers is a name which should go down in television history as the evangelist of outside broadcasting. Though not a climber himself, Chiv, as he is affectionately known, runs many more risks than his climbers. The whole massive investment and his career are balanced on the knife-edge of weather, notoriously unreliable in mountains or on such northern seaboards, and on a jungle of temperamental electronic equipment. But Chiv was the man who had the boldness and foresight to attempt to televise the Old Man of Hoy climb. When Tom Patey's portfolio arrived on Chiv's desk he was duly impressed, but could his engineers attempt such a thing? He passed the query down the pipeline and patiently awaited an answer. This was an unreserved yes. Chiv never questions the capability of his men. They have to be pretty good to work for him in the first place, and he always has their well-being in mind. As a result both climbers and engineers have faith in him and respect for his cool in times of stress. It is said that no man is irreplaceable, but I feel it would be very hard to replace Chiv's dynamic approach and his nerve in taking on a mountain where failure would stir the wrath of millions of Viewers.

Our earlier Outside Broadcasts were Micky Mouse ventures compared with Hoy, for at this remote outpost of Britain there were no hotels and the stack was a forty-minute walk from the nearest road. The B.B.C. staff would have to stay at Stromness in the Orkneys and the journey entailed a ferry trip to the island of Hoy, then a car journey to the road end at Rackwick, followed by the aforesaid walk, a daunting itinerary when added to the companion problems of getting a small mountain of equipment up the hill and over the bogs to the headland opposite the stack.

Usually all this electronic gadgetry is housed in a large vehicle called a scanner, which is the nerve center of an Outside Broadcast. It is to this unit that the cameras feed their signals and within the Director must select from a battery of television monitors which picture to use at any given time. It requires split-second decisions and he has to be a veritable Argus.

It was obviously impossible to take a complete scanner to the cliff-top at the Old Man of Hoy, so everything had to be derigged, packed, and then hauled by two large tractors with a special sledge to the two marquees at the cliff edge. Part of this operation involved hauling the sledge up a steep hillside, using winches, because the ground was too dangerous for the tractors. My particular job was to deliver the cumbersome electronic cameras to their respective positions on the mainland cliff and also to the rock-strewn shore 400 feet vertically below. As well as this I had to operate a mini-cam on the climb itself during transmission. I had recently perfected a cable way system for mountain rescue work in Glencoe and I put this to good use for the rigging operation. The cable ways involved using a long rope angled steeply to the rocky shore below, then tensioned. The cameras and platforms were lowered down this on pulleys using a separate rope. Several hundred pounds of equipment at a time could be quickly and safely dispatched to their positions in this way with great accuracy and delicacy, but getting the equipment up and down the stack itself involved hard brute-strength hauling. The so-called mini-cam then in use weighed 70-lbs. The whole operation smacked of a military exercise. It was like an offensive against the Old Man rather than a climb; there was no overriding confidence that we could pull it off—the odds seemed to be against us. Somehow or other it reminded me of Alexander's siege of Tyre. A company of Scots Guards acted as caterers to the organization and their equipment as well as the bulky B.B.C. gear had come to Hoy from the Clyde Estuary by landing craft.

Nature suddenly took a hand in the proceedings; she is always close by in the wings when we do an Outside Broadcast and on this occasion she took the form of a violent storm which flattened tents and left a nightmare of soggy equipment for the engineers to swear over for a whole day. There was also a family of great skua, whose home was on the Rackwick path they all took exception to trespassers and consequently dive-bombed us as we commuted each day.

To us Mac's repartee the evening after the dress rehearsal was light relief. All the climbers and Sherpas, a term given to climbers who do the difficult rigging on these programs, had a feeling that the whole thing could be a disaster. Everything had gone wrong at the rehearsal; the cameras on the stack, John Cleare's and mine, were in the wrong place at the right time; the radio talk-back equipment which climbers wear and two of the other electronic cameras had gremlins in them as well. It was more like a Goon Show than a serious rock climb.

Rusty Baillie was assisting John Cleare with the other mini-cam and he had brought his dog Puck with him. Puck was trained for search and rescue, that is for finding people buried in avalanches or lying out on open moorland. Rusty had been one of the instructors at my snow and ice climbing school in Glencoe and had as casual an approach to life as to his clothes, which were often unique. I recall, for instance, a long, capacious anorak, modified from a gabardine raincoat. Instead of buttons he had an arrangement of wooden toggles and hemp rope loops. Assisting me and my mini-cam was Ian Clough, a close friend with whom I had climbed many mountains.

To look after our spiritual needs but on the payroll as a Sherpa was the Reverend Sydney Wilkinson, a minister from Aberdeen. Syd was a strong climber who had lived on Baffin Island where he had made many solo ascents. With the proceeds of his pay he hoped to buy a new washing machine. Syd frowned on the apathy that modern youth presented in an age when climbing and exploration was never so readily available to the working man. One lunchtime he sawed off a section of scaffolding plank about a foot long and placed it between two boxes, then he split it in two with one clean karate chop! I felt there was an implication that we should be doing something more useful with our spare time than singing bawdy songs in the schoolhouse in the evenings. With some misgivings I cut a similar piece of wood and placed it between the boxes. I felt that I would probably be breaking a hand rather than a section of Oregon pine for I had never tried this martial sport in my life. I glanced with trepidation at the edge of my hand, thinking it looked vulnerable compared with his which resembled a blunt blade of an axe. I decided instead to try the wood chopping act using a clenched fist but I didn't deliberate too long otherwise I would have chickened. Wham! I was surprised to see how easily I split the timber without even a trace of pain or injury.

"Have a go, Rusty," I said casually, "it's a piece of piss. I may even dispense with myoid hatchet for cutting kindling when I go back home." Rusty will have a go at anything and he repeated our stunts with ease. Syd, somewhat nonplused at us mere amateurs, rummaged in the pile of planks until he found one that was so knotty that he had trouble sawing it. We all watched in silence, a large group of us now, both climbers and B.B.C. technicians. He placed the wood between the boxes again, but this time with reverence, as if it were a sacred offering. There followed a period of concentration on Syd's part when he seemed to be willing the destruction of the unoffending piece of plank without even touching it. It seemed to me at least that for that second of crucial contact nothing happened. Just a sickening sharp thud but miraculously in slow motion the timber parted just as I felt sure that his hand was going to disintegrate.

The Old Man of Hoy had captured the public's imagination. Cartoons of it appeared in *Punch*, and other national dailies ran features. It took on the expectancy of an international soccer match. In this age of canned and frozen food and pre-recorded programs where everything is respectably predictable, an outside broadcast has that dash of adventure about it. It's like motor racing—people expect something to happen, often the worst. I think I was the first person to dub the Hoy Outside Broadcast as a circus. Really that is what it was where gladiators compete on a vertical and overhanging plane rather than on the level, and where the adversary is a mountain or in this case a rotten stack where a hold can come away like an over-ripe apple at any time or a storm can put paid to the whole enterprise.

Hoy and subsequent Outside Broadcasts did much to make the public aware of the art of climbing and also the pleasures and rewards one gets out of it, other than a fat fee.

Being involved in mountain rescue work in various parts of Scotland, I had contacted the helicopter wing of R.A.F. Leuchars in Fife before traveling to Hoy, to find out if a helicopter could be on call for a rescue operation, should this be necessary. At that time they were not so widely used as they are today. I was told that one would be available in an emergency, subject to weather and refueling facilities on the mainland. This enquiry, plus the wide press coverage of the proposed climb no doubt stirred the imagination of the R.A.F. Buccaneer pilots who were also based at Leuchars and once or twice when we were busy establishing camera positions they buzzed us.

As part of the rigging operation I had spanned a heavy rope between the mainland cliff and a point halfway up the stack for hauling gear across, and for no logical reason took the rope down that night, though in fact it would have been more sensible to have left it up, for we had work to do with it the next day. Just as we arrived at the tents on the cliff-top the following morning there was a roar to the south and we saw a wave-clipping Buccaneer skimming across the sea towards us. The stack is partly sheltered to the south by the arm of a headland, and this had no doubt hampered the style of earlier buzzing Buccaneers. Not this one; he had obviously done his homework for he came in at an angle to the main cliff upon which we stood to avoid the headland, then banked violently so that he was now on a course parallel to the cliff and the sea, reverting the belly of the plane, then with a flick he straightened and before we realized what had happened he had shot through the gap between the cliff top and the Old Man. It was a daring bit of flying which appealed to Chiv who had been a test pilot during the last war. I have often speculated what would have happened if that rope had been left in place. Most likely it would have parted like a strand of cobweb, but on the other hand it could perhaps have created that small disturbance to the flight path which could have been disastrous. Pilots, like climbers, do take risks and after all, the better aspects of life have that spice, that element of risk attached to them.

The great day came at last but we still seemed to be in a state of chaos, though we had managed to get all the cameras in position. Chris Brasher had sharpened up his commentary and Chiv was barking orders from the big marquee as if from the bridge of a destroyer. Large floodlights, appropriately called brutes, had been lowered partway down the cliff face below the marquee for night shots. Ian Clough and I had to cover the "tourist route" and the south-east arete of Haston and Crew while John Cleare's and Rusty's job was to go up over the top of the stack and descend to a point where they could meet up with the emerging Joe Brown and Mac the Telly. Unfortunately, John's camera never worked on the stack so a greater load went on Ian and myself.

Things went surprisingly well for the first day's transmission, considering the chaos of the rehearsal. The weather was kind and purely for the amusement of the watching millions two of the groups were scheduled to bivouac on the mountain. Joe and Mac had a disturbed night in the Mouth, a gaping hole in the vertical face; I say disturbed, for somehow the contents of a whisky bottle which was being guarded by Mac disappeared overnight. Mac blamed the fulmars who the next morning were puking even more aggressively. Dougal and Pete who had been hammering their way up the arete for two days now in a cacophony reminiscent of the Anvil Chorus, were lodged for the night as planned on a small ledge adjacent to the tourist route. Ian and I had the task of climbing to this ledge and then attaching ourselves to ropes as best we could, for Dougal and Peter fully occupied this haven on the otherwise vertical sandstone. It was a late night show, a sort of "before we close down for the night, let us have a last look at the climbers on the Old Man of Hoy." The illumination came from the battery of brutes on the cliff opposite and a sungun, a portable camera lamp which we had laboriously taken up with us. But the long fingers of trade unionism reached out, even to this remote corner of Ultima Thule.

"Who would switch off the generators?" the electricians asked. They were scheduled to knock off at 11.45 and it would be at least 12.15 before Ian and I could get down from the stack. I talked to Chiv over the walkie-talkie, pointing out that the climbers might be snug in their sleeping bags on the only available ledges, but Ian and I were just clipped to climbing ropes and needed the lights to get off the climb. Alan Chivers is a very independent individual; that is one of his charms and he doesn't brook inefficiency of interference even from his most exalted master or a powerful trade union.

"Don't worry, Hamish," he said, "I'll wait for you both to get off and I'll switch off the gennies myself."

Soon afterwards Ian and I were spiraling down the long free abseil to the base of the Old Man to snatch a few hours sleep in the marquee, for it wasn't worth returning to Rackwick that night.

Next morning I yawned as I went outside for a pee; the sky was watery and the yellow streaks of dawn reached out into the Atlantic. I thought of how King Hakon sailed down this coastline on his tragic mission to help the people of Skye and how he later returned, a defeated and dying man. In those days the stack was part of the mainland of the island and indeed it is only in recent times that it lost its spare leg, for old prints depicted it as an arch with a lower leg between the existing stack and the mainland. An interesting stack in the making can be seen close to Cape Wrath lighthouse across the Pentland Firth where a narrow gap has formed round a segment of cliff by a constant nibbling of the sea.

The second transmission from the Old Man was not without incident. Ian and I went up ahead of Tom Patey and Chris Bonington who were now climbing the ordinary route in the day, and beyond the Haston crew bivouac ledge we leapfrogged past them when we were off the air. When covering the crack which leads on to a surprisingly spacious summit, a large chunk of sandstone fell, possibly dislodged by a rope or by its own volition, or it may have been the Old Man, like a fulmar, venting its spleen on us rapists. Anyhow, it headed straight towards me and seemed to fill the viewfinder of the camera. By the grace of God it parted just before it reached me so that a piece fell to either side. These chunks disintegrated further on the ledge upon which I stood and, by a freak of MacPherson's or Sod's Law, missed Ian as well. The subsequent pungent smell of brimstone reminded me of my ultimate destination. I gave a shudder and started to climb the crack to join the others on the summit. The O.B. had been an unprecedented success.

Well, it was all over bar the shouting, or perhaps I should say, drinking; a momentous piss-up was arranged at Stromness. Chris Brasher promised it was to be the biggest booze-up since the last Berserker wake. It was, and followed a sumptuous meal where the unsurpassed seafood of these northern waters featured prominently. I recall quite clearly wrestling with Joe Brown. He always seemed to get to grips with me when he has had his statutory three pints of ale and somehow he fell with me on top of him, his back, which had been a source of trouble for years, received further injury so he had the two following years to reflect on the merits of whooping it up in the Orkneys. Later an enormous Viking bowl of Orkney Gog was produced. It tasted like a mixture of molten lava and nitric acid but Rusty, never to be daunted by taste, quantity or potency, and anyhow by this time his other faculties must have been anaesthetised, swallowed the contents in a long and, for us, breathtaking draught. A roar of approval shook the hotel. That night the citizens of Stromness were tolerant.

I think I was the first to notice that Rusty had disappeared and, being concerned for his well-being, after consuming such a lethal brew, I asked where he had gone. No one knew so we searched the hotel with no success. However, Puck was curled up close to the fire, apparently immune to both the din and the departure of his master and no doubt in a dream paradise of rabbits and buried climbers. As I had helped with Puck's rescue training, I now deployed him.

"Come on, Puck, find your master." His ears pricked up as much as they ever would for he had a pixie look with one ear permanently drooping like a wilting flower. He looked at me as if I was mad but then realized I meant what I said, when he quickly established his master wasn't in the room. Giving a growl, he scampered towards the door. I followed and with nose hovering above the pavement he trotted down the street, followed in turn by the drunken rabble. It must have been a strange procession as we wove our way in revelry behind Puck, a pied piper scene where a somber and worried dog led the drunks in the general direction of the harbor, like a scene out of *A Midsummer Night's Dream*.

Up and down, up and down,
I will lead them up and down,
I am feared in field and town.

The trail ended at a warehouse, with dog looking up and whining at the corrugated side of the building. On the roof above this spot where Puck had stopped was an open skylight. Somebody climbed up and shouted, "Hey, Rusty's sleeping inside on a pile of fishboxes." His clothes apparently were neatly folded beside him and he was wrapped up in his famous gabardine anorak.

Through the good offices of a kindly Orcadian we later found our hotel but not our rooms; we probably didn't have any. A bout twelve of us tried to bundle on to Chris Brasher's bed. Chris as yet wasn't in occupation. I vaguely remember something breaking, followed by an avalanche of laughter. About this time most of us ceased to record events and the rest of the night will forever be shrouded in mystery.

The ferryboat to Hoy next morning was filled with climbers who in turn were filled with resolutions to give up drink. The walk across the moorland to the stack, however, had a sobering effect and that morning we didn't even bother avoiding the skuas who dive-bombed us. Eric Beard, or Beardie, as he was called, had his head cut open by one. This was to be our last day on Hoy as we hoped to complete the derigging. Some of the climbers had already left and Mac was due to pass the stack on the St. Ola on his way south that morning. Beardie, who was better known for his fell-running records than pyrotechnics, suggested, "Let's give Mac a rocket send-off as the ship passes. You've got all those signal rockets, Hamish." Indeed, I had. These had been purchased in case some form of emergency communication was required should the walkie-talkies fail.

"All right," I agreed, "but no reds. We don't want to stir up a full-scale sea rescue for we've got a good relationship with the lifeboat lads."

This was a reference to the Longhope lifeboat which was later to go down with all hands. We were well under way with the dismantling operation when someone shouted, "There's the St. Ola." There was a mad scurry on the cliff top as a dozen flares, which can soar over a thousand feet, were positioned then fired. They exploded in a canopy of green, high above the stack, giving the Old Man a surreal appearance like an Indian totem pole. There was a hoot from the ship and she veered in towards the Old Man, then hove to. Meantime Mac was enjoying the spectacle on board. That was until he saw the skipper obviously answering what he thought was the most grandiose distress signal of all time. Thinking it would perhaps be better to break the news to this mariner that these were parting but somewhat ostentatious tokens of goodwill from his friends, Mac set foot on the bridge to inform the captain. As one of us Mac realizes climbers have an unenviable reputation in some quarters and this was fully substantiated by the opinion of the captain as he hauled the St. Ola round and headed south. It was followed by a rousing cheer from our ranks and amplified by a last rocket, a powerful maroon, whose detonation high in the clear heavens morning roused every seabird from its morning contemplation and they took to the heavens in a flurry of feathers.

Pat Ament (b. 1945) has 30 published books in the mountaineering genre. Ten of his essays have been published in international anthologies. His writing has been translated into Japanese, Italian, and Czechoslovakian. He is a world renowned, pioneer rock climber, and is a karate black belt, chess expert, photographer and pianist, songwriter, and the author of *High Endeavors* a collection published by this publisher in 1990. He lives in Fruita, Colorado, with his wife and three children.

PAT AMENT:
TO BECOME AS A CHILD

Except ye be converted, and become as little
children, ye shall not enter into the kingdom of
heaven. Whosoever therefore shall humble himself
as this little child, the same is greatest in the kingdom
of heaven. — Matthew, 18:3-4

Royal Robbins, king of iron logic, was in control during his days on Yosemite's granite walls. His ideas about rock climbing during the 1960's often are thought to have been the master concepts of the day. And they had an austerity. They were severe and pure. There was something grim about Royal, something condescending, and serious. Now that spearhead spirit has given way to a friendly, more relaxed one—a quality almost childlike. Other meanings for him now are at their dawn of time. There is hardly a vestige of the competitive specter who pioneered the great routes on Half Dome and who was the master spirit of the Salathe and North America Walls of El Capitan.

With 20/20 hindsight, I see Royal as always having had a child's zest and sense of merriment—the hopscotch of those steep, no-hand boulder routes at Stony Point, the magic lantern adventures of Sentinel Rock, the jacks of sorting gear, and that follow-the-leader chicanery of the friction slab of the

Salathe Wall. El Capitan, with its puppets and wires, was for Royal a huge playhouse of rock. The man of that play is a blend, and I think was always, of an elegant seriousness mixed with skip rope revel. Call it jocular grimness, what with his punning and gallows humor, his dark comedy and grins. In bouldering, he applied all the trickery in his soul to gain advantage. After he walked down Half Dome's steep descent route, he wrote in his *Summit Magazine* column, "Even one man went down without touching his hands." Humorous and falsely modest. I remember the conviviality of bouldering. Royal's merciless, bellicose stare had in it also a certain popgun, roller skate feel. The master up there on lead, the great climber of our generation, was, behind the dark glasses, Robbins on a tricycle.

The partners he chose all were laugh-a-minute people, TM Herbert, Tom Frost, Joe Fitschen, yours truly, etc., with their monkey shines, pranks, Vaudeville, sparkle, and their own sour looks. Chuck Pratt, Royal's greatest partner, had the air of a circus performer. He juggled wine bottles, walked slack chains, and performed his unprotected tight wire ascents of ferocious off-widths, often with a cynical grin. And Kor. . . when Layton took on his serious stare it only made us laugh because it was so out of character with the Tarzan, frenetic imp we knew him at the root to be.

On almost every rock he climbed, Layton went up in a violent hurry—almost as though to race to the edge of life, or sanity, and look over, and then race to the next. He risked his life and everyone else's in such humorous and compelling ways that all his friends to this day feel his colorful energy radiate outward from the depths of their souls. You could not help but love that little child who came to live in such a huge and imposing (six-foot-seven) frame. I see his long body stuffed into a bumper car at Lakeside Amusement Park, in Denver, his legs and knobby knees pointed upward out of the car. I see him eating carrots, because he was a vegetarian in a fight with some lung condition. We see him fall through the air because he raced up the rock too fast. There was not time enough for him to discover that he was four moves into rock beyond anyone's ability—including his. I see him place marginal anchors from which he and we had to belay in a hanging position on a terrifying climb. He would race to get off those anchors, as they shifted. That I should allow myself to be placed in such circumstances will, incidentally, say something about me. I think of Layton's climb of the Diamond in winter, that brave, very cold achievement, and dropping acid for a short spell in the late '60s, taking up painting, doing a few psychological full gainers which culminated in his becoming a

Jehovah's Witness. He married, raised a family, divorced, and re-married. Later stories had him sea diving and fishing in the Phillippines. . . . And Layton was one of the sane ones.

I do not exclude myself as having needed much revision along the way.

I am happy to report I have witnessed progress in the lives of quite a few acquaintances, and in my own life. I have seen life and rock climbing smooth people to a fine gloss and turn meanness into intelligence.

I visited a climbing shop recently and met three young, dedicated climbers. Not one of them was familiar with the name Royal Robbins. The names of these young climbers will, in turn, one day blow away against the rocks. As Royal brings himself to the mezzotint, to the woodcut, of life, to the absurdity of his place in it now, some of the mystery and exhilaration of those prime (primal) years as a rock climber still hover about him. He left a bit of himself in those rocks and took away from them something in exchange—some of the serenity of Half Dome, some of the strength of El Capitan. What is he involved with at the moment? A cancer scare with his wife, Liz, early in 1999, was more agonizing than the worst predicament of any climb. The prognosis, fortunately, has proven to be good. Each year he has done his summer trip of several days down Idaho's Salmon River, Middle Fork. I had imagined these kayak adventures to be something along the lines of the movie "Deliverance." Royal shattered my illusions with a description of how other members of the trek boat ahead, so that at the end of each day he arrives at a beach where tables await him with wine, salmon, and steaks.

Those first climbs of El Capitan were done in a spirit of festivity, for climbing above all is play. Climbers are, in essence, children. French philosopher Diderot described children as essentially criminal. According to Diderot, it is our good fortune that the physical powers of children are too limited to permit them to carry out their destructiveness. We would not want a child to be in charge of the nuclear arsenal, for example, although world wars have been the result of people who, as adults, did not progress beyond the selfishness of a child. A vision of the child from scripture suggests that children are innocent and follow their hearts as best they know how. It is this kind of child, a vision of receptiveness and purity, of honesty, and simple play—appropriate models for the climber.

Binet, a French psychologist, introduced at the turn of the century the notion that the mental age of children could be measured. He outlined norms of accomplishment for different ages of childhood. A child a year old is able to place a square block into a square hole and a round block into a round hole. A climber today is expected to do a climb, to place his round head into a square chimney, so to speak. It's interesting that we give the older climber a reprieve. Very little is expected of Royal anymore. If he climbs anything, no matter how minor, he's complimented. People are mystified when he conforms his slightly more rickety body to a glassy alcove. In the face of physical age and decline, the older climber imposes upon himself his own norms. He begins to act free of certain definitions of himself and invents a new idealism.

The climber who has gone over the summit and now is lost on the far side of the great mountain of his prime becomes like a figure in a drawing by Maurits Cornelis Escher. He walks one way, while other figures of life walk in completely contradictory ways. Somehow the figures fit together in the picture. The whole picture feels impossible, yet the figures continue their hypnotic, almost sinister march in and around each other—each without an awareness of the others. Conveyed is a feeling that all the figures are the same one figure seen from many different perspectives at once. Among the mysteries of life is that we are each other. I have seen Royal transform his face into TM's countenance, and TM suddenly will bring to his own face the odd glare of Royal Robbins. Somewhere in myself I know I am Royal, and I think he would admit, begrudgingly, to a likeness deep in himself of me.

If the geezer. . . (already I have run out of ways to say "older climber"). If the. . . "endangered species. . ." was at one time an extraordinary member of his society of climbers, his friends and peers may not want him to show weakness. They may wish that he retire in style, or, in Tom Patey's words, climb gracefully down. Yet to be a beginner again tends to tamper with the illusions a great climber's friends have of his greatness. Thus he must strike a balance, move slowly, and direct his efforts with care to blend old and young. Time will conscientiously take from him a little more strength each year, and the process will happen faster and faster, but he is able to set to work a more relaxed, innocent strength. A more obscure and removed application of ability becomes his play. He no longer struggles to lose weight.

I was amazed when a friend said recently, in an expression of great freedom, that he had lost 125 pounds. I waited anxiously for him to share how he did it. "I divorced her."

Every thought or step for a child is a test to see what works. Life is there for the taking, and a child learns quickly that screaming gets a response. So screaming it is, even though the child is perfectly happy. We scream (at least quietly) on our first climbs, until we realize the rock will not bend by such howls. We realize, contrary to appearances, that we are destined to live, and we need not scream. . . for the moment. As a child, Royal probably did not scream much. He acted mostly in his quiet, inner way, with his characteristic serious glare.

There are examples of how the play, innocence, and good of children may be brought to bear, in favorable ways, upon our adult lives. As the Savior of mankind said, we are to become "as little children." We thus must identify the qualities in children to which the scripture refers. With a threatening tone in my voice, I ask my two-year-old daughter, "Who messed up the entire house!?" She answers, "Baby." She is honest. She has no concept of the malice of which I am capable. Yet for a child to possess such honesty and purity does not presuppose altruism. My child is teachable, pure, and sweet but also possesses the selfishness and self-centeredness of her age. As I learn from her, I try to incorporate one quality and not the other.

To become like a child must be to go back to an early contact with nature, a sense of the glory of a world completely new. . . when we confronted for the first time the beautiful outdoors, when there was enough consciousness to discover and realize the incredible worth of life. . . . Climbing never does get too much better than one's first, young days at it, being on the rock, or near it, the feel of air, the sense of adventure with a friend. . . . I begin another article with the line, "From the moment life called on my spirit to make things interesting, there was rock." There is an unusual, unforgettable magic, when we're young. Things are so beautiful we don't know how to act. We do mostly what's natural. We reach for holds and cling to rock, and our first climbs burn into our souls with a power equal to falling in love the first time.

The older, mature climber must get back to that, where things are new. It is not such an easy task. To start, he allows himself to drift out of shape. Then there is a sense of accomplishment again to climb 5.6 or 5.7. He masters easy moves and keeps it a secret from himself that he was a better climber in some geologic past. He feels the challenge of easier routes and lets their surprise flow through him, as though life has begun anew. It is his calling to make something of this marvelous play-dough called rock. Things are, in fact, probably more fun when we have less experience. It isn't always so happy when we are strong and in possession of a lot of majesty and skill. We get a second ride through love and magic when we shake off a little of the sense of height that our lives through the years gain. The beginnings are high places in and of themselves.

The child puts a premium on play. When it doesn't feel right, it ceases to be play. Fear is, more or less, his guideline for safety. The child's fears are not cultivated, however, and he reacts more out of instinct than from a rational understanding of danger. Later, we know exactly what we are afraid of and back away from places that don't send the right surge of feeling through our veins. We play with the way things feel. Fear has its allure, as we begin to face ourselves in it. We defy our instincts somewhat and grow knowledge.

By definition, the very young child is not too sensitive to the needs of others. He finds delight in doing things for others, nevertheless, and he is able to communicate his/her good spirit to others. Yet dependence on others to supply virtually everything requires a young person's full concentration on his needs.

One of the first things a child learns he can do, by and for himself, is climb.

The child is loud sometimes. Most self-respecting climbers prefer to be in the quiet of a tranquil setting. At the same time, we do not wish to go quiet into that good night. We make our little noise, almost by necessity—to remind ourselves we're engaged in life in an actual and living way. I recall a climb with Royal when he didn't say a word during the length of the climb. Yet he spoke in his manner, rather bluntly, with his silence. We speak, and sometimes we sense the joke of our noise. We are quiet, and words transmit in spite of our silence. Our thoughts travel soul to soul, as companions. As adults, our conversation is subtle and practiced. We hope to be pure, innocent, and happy, yet we know things. An adult is one who has had his or her disillusionments and, to become as a child, must continue to believe in sun, sky, rock, and play.

When I think of Royal, I think of his youth. As a teen, he already had a sense of art and classical music that went normally with a more mature person of about twenty-five or thirty. He had a good sense of organization and protocol. I was beyond my playmates in terms of spontaneity and creativity but behind in the formalities, rules, and conventions of social interaction. Now as I try to become more a child, in the good, spiritual way, and as I look for the joy and newness of life, it seems I too always have had a flair for a certain comedy. Many of my actions and activities can be identified, with a certain pride, I might add, as those of a child.

Pat Ament

During the '60s in Yosemite, pioneer climbers and their companions seemed to be in a fight as to who would be the youngest of them. With cannonades and banners in their souls, they carried themselves and their beautiful eyes. They looked upward into the granite, into its blacks, grays, and boundless whites.

Dave Rearick was the silent one, the man who came to Colorado from California. To the chagrin of Colorado climbers denied permission to attempt the sinister Diamond wall on Longs Peak, Rearick was given permission—along with his partner Bob Kamps. If there was a right hero for me, it was Rearick. His personality was suited for a monastery more than climbing, but he could play along with the most immature of us in the simple way of a child. I may have inspired some of the play in him by the notion (so visible in me) that suddenly I had made myself his friend. His restraint and detachment accounted for much of the humor. He had none of the shrieking, childlike craziness and laughter of Kor, yet he smiled. You had to put a little effort into seeing to it he did. Dave took on the costume of the climber and acted out the part but was in fact a climber and, in his day, one of the best. He methodically proceeded through the steps of a climb, as though to act out some formula in calculus.

That Dave should be a math professor was an older, less desirable part of him. Yet he was open to what I said, though I twice had flunked general math in high school. He tolerated, in a humble, childlike way, much silliness and absence of logic, etc., that resulted from my attempts at conversation. You have to remember the sun was shining. There was a lot of green. There were lots of pines, which would make a person forgive almost anything. The sky's blue was as rich as the deepest, brightest lake in summer, and in Eldorado the wind rushed at you at amusing, unexpected times.

As climbers in the early 1960's, we were free to use those Eldorado and Yosemite rocks in the way we wished. Caught up in sandstone and wind, frightened half the time, ecstatic other times, panicky and giggly, the pleasure of our thoughts included friends. I wanted to have absolute friendships. I do not know how many of that kind, if a single one, I achieved. Royal befriended me and was the best possible teacher and companion. We had a friendship born in part through the tests of climbs and through the oddities we noticed about each other that made us chuckle and muse. There was a sense from the beginning that our friendship was eternal. We found in one another all the light of Eldorado or Yosemite or Longs Peak to make us our richest selves. On rock, we were our most luminescent. It already was bright enough without us, but we went up there and took with us our spirits.

My various Boulder partners and I became joyfully lost in the steep, vertical, shrine-like coves of Eldorado and were happy. We were, I suppose, human beings in trouble. We did not exactly know where life was to go or where it was supposed to take us. We did not know what to think, with regard to our lives. Life was simply incredible. We settled for each other's jingle-jangle company and shared each other's fortunes. We were not able to share so well our fortunes with the world—for they took our joy to be a statement of happiness, something not permitted in some circles. They did not like the suggestion of alienation. It was a menace to their sense of conformity, a bad contrast to their absorption into regular, more approved behaviors. It's for the very reason that climbers do not fit well into the comprehensive community of the world that they strike upward, alone, into the solitude of rocks.

In time, a number of my friends and I would, more or less, abandon one another, yet the few years we had together remain in memory (I'm sure I'm not the only one who remembers). I cherish those years and those people. We were in love with the ease of the climbing, the ready existence of finger and hand holds. From a distance, the rock always appeared holdless. You could show off for your family who on rare occasion came to watch and, from the road below, wondered at what magic held you there. It was a joy to see the right holds appear in the right places on climbs, and it was a fertile aspect of the experience to see and identify those holds and how they worked together. To use those holds as we flowed past them was similar to how the years of youth passed. Quickly.

We were amazed at how abundantly able to make first ascents we were, how many climbs were given us. In some cases, they were discovered simply by our starting upward in a certain direction. We let the rock show us the way. When the line was drawn up the rock, by our ascent, we saw the creativity. Such a creativity had been there, on and in the rock, alone, and it had waited for us to come and give it human implementation and make its existence, and ours, official.

Life has so much to offer, and I was perplexed, disturbed, and worried about how I was going to have it all, take it all in, take everything apart, and put it back together, in the few years I would be permitted to live. Eldorado, one very impressive environment of the world, and the forests around the Flatirons, the airy summits, natural rock shelters, caves, mornings, afternoons, storms, and starlights were a complex terrain and showed me their deep mysteries as I began to learn of my own. Any ledge, any foothold there, was a place to be a child, when in fact I was becoming an adolescent. A child is very dependent upon others, whereas a crucial turn of experience for an adolescent is to realize his or her independence.

All those times, as a child, when I stood beside my mother who I loved with all my heart, I was unable to grasp, nor perhaps could she, how quickly life would be climbed, how fast the earth was to rotate and bring us toward a descent. I felt safe in her company, under her care and guidance, and she loved that I climbed. She understood what it meant to me. The world was strange enough, and she did not press me to explain what I felt—which would be stranger. It was enough for her to feel in me the secrets I'd been finding up there in dihedrals and on airy aretes and corners in the high exposure of Eldorado.

What my life should be about. . . was answered promptly, as a climber. I would do all sorts of other things in life too, such as write, but climbing was a catalyst. It would open to my soul the world and let it teach me about myself so I could apply whatever principles I might glean, the principle—for example—of going and doing and being alone among friends. I suppose I do not need to point out the contradiction of those words, "alone among friends." A climber, by definition, has acquaintances who, in a sense, teach him. . . when they are not subjugating him to their wills. They have their instructive perceptions, their lives, their own aloneness, and their mortal probation. . . which are worth the effort to observe, if you are their partner. Each of us knows life at least a little through the eyes of others. It was possible for me to move somewhat along the footsteps of my friends. They did the same for me at times, allow me to teach and help them by what I was and am. They would not, however, wish to admit now that the most difficult thing each of us could know, because we were so young, was the extremely delicate and sacred nature of our relationships.

I did not have to grow into the world very far before I sensed and saw the spiritual carelessness and sometimes viciousness of the climbing world. There were poisoned spirits in the Boulder community and also in the general world of climbers. There was the jealousy of one, and there was the smallness of another. C. S. Lewis said. "We must picture hell as a state where everyone is perpetually concerned about his own dignity and advancement, where everyone has a grievance, and where everyone lives the deadly serious passions of envy, self-importance, and resentment." Such a statement attaches itself to the way things began to exist in and around climbers, as I began to make that transition out of childhood into adolescence.

All my life, I have been plagued by the stares of those in an ongoing campaign to note that I am not of their society. Yet they would never let me join their society in fact, for deep down they know my spirit, with all its conflicts and faults. They would never allow themselves to be compromised in the way it would feel to them were I to be of them. In the end, the members of such a society will not know each other well enough to know who is currently of them or who is alive or dead. They don't mourn the loss of one from their midst. Climbers of this sort are more like jackals than a community of friends. They have families and group feeds. They bite at each other, are competitive and ruthless. They are cunning and able, yet are fundamentally the scourge of the higher, more sane, and beautiful world of beings.

By the time I had dug all the javelins out of my back and been judged and lied about and defamed in every possible way short of altogether destroyed—which appeared to be the goal of a number of whom I never had met—I began to replace sincerity and imagination with reality. It did not take too long, as a young climber, to lose my childhood. I was the enemy almost immediately, for no other reason than my relatively noticeable abundance of experience. I never intended to cast any questionable light on them. They could have only been moved by some deep insufficiency of their own.

It wasn't climbing that caused such spiritual conditions. Most people are removed from their evil selves during the course of a climb. It's after and before that the devil owns them. If climbing is some type of spiritual tool placed on the earth for our benefit and through which we might grow and perfect ourselves as children of God, then there are ready candidates by the thousands whose general state of character fits the description of being very much in need of improvement. The carnival of the climber procession is a bit like the old movie *King Of Hearts*, where the people go away and leave the insane to take over the streets.

Self-understanding comes with a more generous understanding of others. I get to the truth when I think about the canyon's voices that have found me and found in my heart what was good there. Mutually-sustaining friendships have survived. I speak of Royal, for example, and I speak of people who once fell under each other's spell, under the spell of climbing, who saw or sensed in one another the genius, the beauty, the worth, and who had a sense of imagination and childlike play. There are individuals who completely rose above the muck and mire. The names John Gill and Chuck Pratt come to mind, two individuals who stayed relatively removed from the climbing community and were individuals blessed with child-like gifts.

It's wonderful to discover people who now have more kindness in their eyes, who are more child—the kind of child we desire. The sponsored-climber, piercing and tattooing, goateed, Madonna, Marilyn Manson, levitating in ecstasy, bolt-happy. . . manifestation of climbing appears to have gone right past play into banality. I make my playground solitude in a last few private environments I create around and in myself with the help of memory and imagination.

While we long for something that once was and never can be again, while we wish for a true feeling or slight redeeming reverence, or purity, in today's climbers, we note also their greatness. A few are possessed with the grace and qualities of good people, and so many gifts, so much ability, and simple, child-like humility to stand as an ensign to all that climbing wishes it was or could be.

I am content now to act out new joys with my wife and kids. We were in a tent in a remote campsite of Yosemite a few years ago. My wife and I felt close, as we settled into our bags. It was an awkward situation to be romantic, what with the kids in the tent. Fortunately they fell asleep and slept well. I realized here, in this tent, an important element of truth. We were at play. Life had presented us with a sacred opportunity, to be together, to be in Yosemite, and in life, and to see what we could make of the materials at hand. It felt like a beginning, an innocence, as happy as when I first rock climbed. Robin moved closer. Then a kiss, and the fear of bears began to diminish.

There is nothing better than the love your child generates in you. At the age of two, my daughter Maren listened attentively as I said, "One day you and I will go up on the rock and climb. We will spend the night on the rock and eat dinner. We will look at the stars, and then we will sleep, and the sun will come up. Then we will continue to climb. . . ." She said nothing. Two months later, to my astonishment, Maren, eager to fulfill the little prophecy of the universe she is, stated.

"Daddy, I want to go up on the rock and climb and spend the night and look at the stars and eat dinner and sleep on the rock, and the sun will come up." She had internalized those images.

To Become as a Child

A few days later, Maren said she wanted to climb. It was snowing outside, so I asked, "Can you see the rock? It's right here?" We were in our living room. I pretended to reach for holds and pull myself up. She did the same and acted out the part with her hands and face. She put on the demeanor of struggle and made a small grunt of strain. To my surprise, she walked over to a lamp on a table and turned off the light. "The sun is going down," she said. The couch was a ledge, and we sat together and readied ourselves for sleep. "Do you see the beautiful stars?" I asked. "Yes," she said, looking up at the ceiling. She then hurried over to the light and turned it on. "Sun's coming up," she said with a happy, beaming countenance. She reached for the holds again, strained her face, and we repeated the process two or three times. What my daughter and I shared this occasion was everything climbing had meant to me. I was with a friend. We were able to have an adventure. We were in a beautiful environment. There was physical effort, and a sense of play. I would remember this experience as one of the best I'd ever had.

Jeff McCarthy (b. 1965) is an English professor who has lived, studied, and climbed extensively in New England, Scotland and the western United States. He has organized expeditions to Alaska, North Africa, East Africa and Asia. His mountain writing appears in *Climbing*, *The Mountain Gazette*, *Alpinist* and the *American Alpine Journal*. His academic work focuses on the convergence of environmental philosophy and mountaineering experience. He received a Fulbright Fellowship to work and study at Whyte Museum in Banff.

JEFFREY MCCARTHY:
ALPINE TIME

A frican snow is melting down my back and this altitude makes my head throb. The natives are restless in my skull; their drum beats a message I recognize—"ep. . . ic, ep. . . ic." Not again. My knee hurts stepping up in this sling, so I wonder "why am I aiding at all? This part is supposed to be easy, but it's overhanging?" The funny thing is, I'm glad to be here. Well, maybe not right here, but I'm glad to be up here. Did I mention the lightning?

The thing about climbing in the mountains—whether you're in the Rockies or East Africa—is that you develop this internal clock, counting down, down, down, to the moment you have to turn back, to turn around, to retreat. You have to hear that warning if you want to live very long, but you have to ignore it every once in a while if you really want to summit. Not that I'm too proud to turn around—I bail like a leaky rowboat—it's just that sometimes I don't.

So, here's a story for you. Last year, Bob Palais and I had some fun on Mount Kenya where we likely should have bailed but are glad we didn't. At over 17,000 feet, Mount Kenya is the second highest peak in Africa. It's a bigger prize than Kilimanjaro in the alpinist's mind because it is steep and intricate with no easy way up or down. Maybe the most notable feature of Mount Kenya is that the thing has two summits: Nelion is 17,021 feet and Batian is a story higher at 17,058. The problem is you have to drop into the spooky "Gate of the Mists" to get from Nelion to Batian, and then climb four hundred feet back up. Sounds like just a couple of pitches, doesn't it?

Our plan was to get porters in the less visited east-side town of Chogoria, climb the peak, and then descend to the west against the flow of trekking parties coming from Naro-Moru. Four days in, two days for climbing, one day out. Back home in Salt Lake City we'd eyed various routes in the guide book looking for a challenge. Once on the hill we hurried to throw ourselves at the easiest route we could find. The Normal Route was pioneered by Eric Shipton and Wyn Harris in 1929, and we could claim a burning interest in historical climbs and avoid the longer, harder routes on the Diamond Buttress. Best of all, the Normal Route would let us visit both summits and get back down in one day. Around fifteen pitches of climbing gets you up Nelion, then there's that rap into the Gate of the Mists, an icy traverse to Batian, some route finding to the summit, then follow your steps back to Nelion, and descend in triumph and warm sunset light.

So that was the plan. The books didn't support the one day blitz, but just because they recommend two days to hit two summits didn't make me want to carry bivy gear. Our head porter wasn't altogether cheering either: "It's too far, you will not make it," he insisted.

There's the background. The foreground is the way this route kept signaling us to turn back. On Mount Kenya we started filtering unwelcome gastrointestinal news on the approach—we were as sick as jackals who'd sampled bad zebra, and about as friendly. In fact, I had my first sight of the Southern Cross during an extended barfing foray. At the time I tried to feel adventurous—stiff upper lip and all that—but mostly felt dehydrated and cold. I'd come to the opposite side of the globe, bought food, suffered a surreal taxi shuttle from Nairobi, paid porters, organized gear and dragged myself uphill for days only to feel dizzy, nauseous and weak. The peak was right there, and looked great—an alpine dream of stern buttresses and shining snow. It would have been frustrating to a smarter team. But we didn't let the facts stop us.

Four days took us to the Austrian Hut—a wood and tin structure at 15,800 feet, held together by the residue of old meals and a thousand kerosene stoves. Here we rested for a day and wrestled with the decision: climb tomorrow or wait to feel better? Nelion's summit stared down at us all day through a shroud of mist. At some point I decided to stop looking at it. A walk in the afternoon cleared my head, and then—recklessly—Bob admitted to feeling strong. You see, climbing is an awful lot about sharing—sharing the plan, sharing the risk, sharing the suffering—and if he was ready to try and climb, I figured I should be too.

A decision in the mountains has momentum to be welcomed and feared. With Bob's announcement the various components of our trip went into motion—organizing gear, packing the tent so the porters could bring it and other non-climbing stuff down valley, ferrying a load across the glacier to scout the approach and make the morning lighter, scoping the face one last time in the dull glow of an early sunset, and then settling in for a short night in the hut. We dosed ourselves with drugs and denial, and prepared as if our infirmities would evaporate in the clean light of summit day.

That night the Austrian Hut was blessedly free from trekking parties but filthy, dank and smelly with wastes too scary to name. I chose the clearest bunk space I could find—a platform about five feet off the floor with a "stepladder" of balanced stones. Our high-altitude diet of rice and tea made dinner efficient, and we settled into our respective bunks to listen to the wind and think those thoughts that anticipate a long climb.

At three I was up and inching out of my bag to check the weather. I teetered down the stones and shuffled outside. Cold and clear. The stars were bright and the wind was down. More promising still, my internal weather seemed settled—no dizziness, no nausea—all in all a favorable report. I came back into the hut feeling hopeful and healthy about the day, and looked forward to one last hour of sleep. I was full of confidence when I stepped on the rock pile and turned to give myself the outward-facing boost up onto the platform—but then the top stone rolled. Disaster! The energy from my boost pitched me forward—legs across the stones—and into a resounding face plant. Stars in the hut. No more smiling.

My right leg was throbbing and bleeding, my brain was ringing from the Petzl pattern I'd just branded into my forehead. Hurt, embarrassed, groaning, I pogoed back up to my bag—carefully —and lay there trying to decide if this was really as rotten an omen as it seemed. Maybe I was just getting all the bad luck out at once? Could I climb? I pretended to be asleep while one of the porters came out to see what in God's name was causing all the racket. I struggled to rationalize my tumble into a good sign: but to get within hours of a big climb and brain yourself on the nearest pile of stones. . . that seemed inauspicious from any perspective.

At least no one had found me there—Icarus in polypro—I'd make it my secret forever. I thought all this and more while the morning throbbed forward. When the alarm went at four the bleeding had stopped, the knee was only a little swollen, and as for the concussion, well, I'd been raising my threshold for nausea and dizziness already. The climb was still on. Later, Bob asked, "Are you limping?" and I pretended not to hear.

Scree in the dark, a glacier by headlamp and then long shadows as the sun met us on Nelion's big east face. We soloed the first few pitches and then geared up for Mackinder's Chimney and the steepening rock above. The climbing was good—steep and airy on book sized holds. When the full sun hit us there was only rock and ropes and the joy of moving high over foreign plains. Later, there was a dose of simul-climbing, a couple of route finding decelerations, and one short section of steep pulling that had my head throbbing in imaginative ways. We were getting closer. A steady breeze tugged at my conscience and clouds built to the east while we negotiated the final pitches to the lower summit. At 11:30 I sat beside the improbable Howell Hut—an aluminum bivy shelter of lunar module appearance hard by the summit. It's nice to be on top. The highest point was flat and comfortable, and I watched the clouds congregate and bicker in the middle distance. The rope piled beside me as loose as the scree we'd crossed in the dark, and I heard the jingle of carabiners before I saw Bob.

Bob poked at the Howell Hut curiously and we shared the hope we'd not be spending the night in that small space. The two of us had agreed that if we could reach Nelion by noon we'd press on for the real prize— Batian. And there it was, a gloomy mirror of our gray summit, but, painfully, forty feet higher. And here we were, a long way from Batian and a long way from the ground. The only thing we seemed close to was noon. It was decision time.

The higher summit was close, like some neighbor's house, but it looked haunted, and darkness slammed like a door every night at seven here on the equator. Would we be pushing our luck to try and descend Nelion's intricate face (on a line different from our wandering ascent route) starting as late as four? We jittered there in the breeze, trying to decide. The clouds were moving in, the rappel seemed really complicated, my knee hurt and wouldn't a cup of tea be nice? The wind slapped a piece of webbing into a tattered pennant beside me. On the other hand, it wasn't noon yet. Batian actually is the summit, and my falling out of bed debacle had me needing some glory.

Jeff McCarthy

How do these decisions work? I'm not sure any climber could map it as a logical process. Whether you're in the Tetons or the Karakoram, it seems like the biggest decisions you can make happen in a subterranean mingling of desire, fact, hope and chance. You choose the facts you want and cling to them. We moved across broken ground toward the icy col separating the peaks.

The storm accosted us once we rapped into the Gate. Do mountains sometimes disapprove? This one seemed to resent our presence beyond Nelion, and the Gate of the Mists was a blowing mess of snow and fog. The summit was right there, but you sure couldn't see it. In fact, you couldn't see much of anything at all, and I found the stinging wind demoralizing when I looked into it too much. But hey, we'd fixed a line for retreat and it was only noon, what could go wrong?

As happens, a lot could go wrong. Snow and then verglas accumulated on anything horizontal, which made the climbing tricky, and now there was lightning in the mist—harsh and abusive as an unwelcome guest. We got across the Gate of the Mists, but now we couldn't see ten feet and we'd need to traverse onto Batian's south face with no reference points, like tourists in some snowcone.

"You can turn around," a voice in my head reminded me. One quick rappel and a horizontal pitch back to the fixed line would do it. But, if we headed across that dark south face we'd be pretty well committed. The clouds around us lit and then drummed with the falling-down-stairs clamor of close thunder. Not my favorite sound track. We were at another point that tested us to make a judgment. Part of the decision making process was a silent self-examination of fatigue, desire and ability. The rest of it was along the lines of "if we're cold, wet and scared here, let's be cold, wet and scared on the real summit." Not exactly Freedom of the Hills, but we had to move and we decided to move for the tippy-top.

And we were away again—avoiding the voices that said "stop," and listening carefully to everything that said "go"—delivered to the uneasy pleasure of commitment. The pitches unfolded into the mist, and after a couple of dead ends, an unpleasant pendulum, and a legion of squeaky blocks, I was fully engaged with steep rock in the wrong gully at 17,000 feet. Nice work, I know. This was a region of great stones tilted and stacked into chimneys and corners. Above was a brooding overhang weeping sooty tears, and the snow swirled in drunken gusts. Trust me to die of hypothermia on the frigging Equator. I focused on the climbing that was supposed to be a scramble but instead was kicking my ass. I was panting and my head hurt. Off came the gloves. The crampons were already hanging from my harness (a tingling reminder not to fall). The first move was a mantle onto a block and then I teetered right along a steep, snow frosted traverse to a headwall and an old, old fixed rope swinging like a hanged man. I couldn't resist tugging it and I wasn't even surprised to get pummeled by rocks in reply. Dumb move. Keep climbing.

On the headwall's right side I got myself into a crack system I figured I'd free and a few feet higher decided I'd aid. Thirty feet up this crack I weighted a sling and then the Camalot shifted. This is not a good feeling. The umbrellaed cams became my whole world and that frowning sky and those toothy ridges spun down into them—hold, hold, holding. My heart did its tap dance on my stomach and settled. Then it was a good nut and up into a shattered corner and finally I faced ten feet of traversing a tricky slick ledge with a rotten seam for my hands. The steep aid had given me a headache and some rope drag too. Now this loose, skating traverse was going to kill me. All that stuff about the freedom and glory of commitment sounds good from a safe distance, but there, on the brink, part of my brain wondered why I hadn't stayed in Utah—I'd be at Alta, not sketching on this crap rock, but rounding up some folks to hit the bar. Instead. . . the welcome anticlimax of survival—rope drag, deep breathing, snow falling on holds, more lightning, and shuffling steps until, finally, a flake to sling. "Off belay!" My focus expanded, the summit was close and the mountain was beautiful under a low sky and fading thunder.

On the summit the watch beeped four. Four! This was not a time for extended congratulations—we were behind schedule, dehydrated and a long way from home. It's funny for me that my proudest summits are places I spent less than a minute. The glow is really for later, and though I felt satisfaction there atop Nelion, mostly I heard the clock ticking on the sunlight and on my endurance. The descent from Batian to the notch above the Gate brought a welcome kiss of sunshine through the clouds. That was one hopeful sign anyway. We had the reward of tattered views and then a Brocken Spectre—a shadow of ourselves cast in bronze clouds—to reflect our rappel efforts in an eerie mist rainbow.

The glow of sun and accomplishment was the fruit of our decisions, but that glow would fade fast if we got stuck up here. Four raps down the east ridge, crampons on for the icy Gate, crampons off for the hard pull back up the fixed line, organizing gear with a muddled head, soling back up to Nelion on the busted rock that had seemed hard before we'd wrestled Batian. Six pm and there we were by the Howell Hut, again, the

Jeff McCarthy

sun dipping to the horizon and a choice to make, again. Was this happy shelter a clue that we'd better stay? Onwards into the gathering shadows, or bivy here and handle the intricate raps and traverses in the clean light of morning? Stay or go?

The problem with the clean light of morning theory, of course, is the cold dark between now and then. These equatorial days have a pleasant symmetry to the. . . until you're up a mountain and want more light. Every second of deliberation thickened the puddles of dark around us. A night in the meter-high shelter wouldn't kill us, but it would be chilly and morose with headache and dehydration. On the other hand, if we got halfway down the face and lost the rap route, or hung up the rope (which verged on likely given the blocky ledges below us) this summit shelter would be just a cozy memory for two guys shivering in their harnesses. So, there it was again; the hut called a siren song—"stay, stay," while we wondered if we should commit ourselves to an uncertain progress.

I think it was momentum that pushed us onwards. We'd already been moving for thirteen hours, why stop now? Bob knocked good luck on the aluminum wall and we were off along loose ledges to the first rappel. Sunsets are nice—at the beach—but not so nice suspended between the stars and the scree on thin lines of nylon and hope. The palette of colors, the play of light on the landscape, all this was a palpable backbeat to the song in my head, down down down—stacking ropes, scouting for anchors, cursing prayers over jammed lines, downclimbing, slinging blocks, spinning in a surprise free rappel, and then, inevitably, digging out the headlamps and seeing only stars where blue day had been.

By dint of some luck, some perseverance and some guesswork we hit the ground just after 8:30. I was tired. Eight raps and a fair diet of downclimbing in under three hours—I'll take it. We still had a three hour limp over rough ground to our new camp, but I didn't know that then. So, once the ropes pulled and the gear was packed, we had reached the end of our decision tree and needed only stumble downhill in the slow motion of alpine time. And stumble we did, one foot in front of the other, into our headlamps' frail light as yellow as any traffic signal that says caution to heedless, happy souls like ourselves.

Peering Over the Edge:
The Philosophy of
Mountaineering

Geoffrey Winthrop Young (1876—1958) is considered by many to be Britain's most influential pre-World War I mountaineer, having made many important climbs in the Alps. He began his climbing career while at Cambridge University by climbing various university buildings. He produced a guide book entitled *The Roof Climber's Guide to Trinity.* He also organized holiday climbing meets in the Snowdonia region of North Wales and served as a mentor to many of England's best climbers, including George Leigh Mallory of Everest fame. Young lost a leg in action during World War I but designed his own prosthesis that allowed him to continue to spend time in the mountains. Among his published works are *Mountain Craft* and *On High Hills.* He was president of the Alpine Club from 1941 to 1944.

GEOFFREY WINTHROP YOUNG: THE INFLUENCE OF MOUNTAINS UPON THE DEVELOPMENT OF HUMAN INTELLIGENCE*

To William Paton Ker mountains represented the background of sane living; an attainable background, of beauty, health and adventure, in front of which the drama of human life was continuously enacted. It was the fate of human beings, their behavior and their modes of expression, which were the chief interest of his deep and acute mind, and of his sensitive and sympathetic nature.

Languages, literature and his own learning were to him manifestations. They interpreted the progressive variations of human genius, as human society during the earliest stages of its evolution developed form and fashion in compliance with the climatic and geographical conditions environing its original distribution. The background of the mountains to this drama fascinated him, because of the long mystery they introduced, in remote height so long unattainable and in depths so long defended by barriers of superstitious fear. It was as consciousness of a survival within himself of this primitive and mysterious awe, combining with the modern awakened appreciation for mountain beauty, which drew him actively to the hills. It was this which softened the usual severity of his pronouncements—or his silences—when made in the sphere of learning and scholarship, to a happy lyricism in several languages when mountains were his theme.

In other company than that of the hills, Ker's silences were his natural expressions of emotion; and I feel an intruder, and perhaps noisy, in breaking in upon them before an assembly and in attempting to summarize his feeling for mountains, and their influence, in my own words.

It was my fortune to meet him most often in the company of another great Northerner, Norman Collie, Professor of Chemistry in the University of London, who was probably the first discoverer of the Cioch. A fine artist, a great connoisseur, and a faultless mountaineer in many ranges, he returned to Skye in great age and in solitude, to end life among the hills he thought the most beautiful. Norman Collie, in society he liked, was a consummate monologist, pouring out emphatic and often sardonic commentary and speculation on every branch of knowledge or art. Ker maintained his share in the conversation by a stillness as varied, as emphatic and as convincing words seemed inadequate for his seething inward interest in any good subject. With gleaming eye, flushing cheek and an invisible lower lip the fine shades of his agreement vibrated perceptibly through the pauses, or his criticism even scorn could be felt in devastating absences sound.

But to beauty he responded even audibly. To his favoured pupils, and all in whom he discovered grace mind, he could flow in a dozen languages, and to mountains, the deep love his life, he answered even with poetry. No passing was ever more happily timed than his. Upon the slopes the Pizzo Bianco he had just looked round, and said, "I always thought this to be the most beautiful place in the world, and now I know it." And he died in that moment perfected vision.

Mountain literature, by which we usually mean the short century mountaineering writing, could itself, afford no field of study commensurate with his scholarly interest in languages and literatures as interpreters of human history. It has been a short story, and not a very profound one, since in the last century men were awakened to consciousness of the beauty mountains of and began to climb them, and then to write about their climbs. To make an adequate literature of this, we have customarily to move backward in thought and fill out the thin borders of material with sporadic quotations from Shelley or Coleridge, or from Ruskin's more or less distant views of, or view concerning, mountain scenery, or we borrow references from the beginnings of the romantic age and a few extracts from earlier literatures, often taken from their context and forcibly interpreted in our modern mountaineering sense.

The feeling for mountains, ever since we have been made aware of it, and have yielded to it, is an absorbing passion. It can seize upon a youthful mind like an obsession. Like a religion, it can drive us to support our faith with evidences "compelled to come in." I recall now with some wonder how in youth I used to ransack whole libraries, author after author through past centuries, dramatists, poets, essayists, even theologians, for the single word "mountains" to flash up like fire from the page, illuminating it with the glow that fills the room in the presence of first love. As others have done, I was putting my own interpretation upon the references, forcing words, which some writer had used to build up the scene for a character or event, to belong to the abstract mountain passion, to the realization which had only arrived with our mid-nineteenth century recognition mountains and mountaineering.

Were we then the first genuinely to feel it, as well as to realize it? Or was the emotion that possessed our minds with a recognition at once familiar and yet strange, fascinating but touched with awe, something deeper, more primitive, rooted in racial memory? The very recency of our awareness of the mountain spell makes evidences the more difficult to define. The more difficult also because of nineteenth century convention. We date the beginnings awareness of from the first Alpine adventures, only a century ago: from Alfred Wills's *High Alps*, followed by Whymper's *Scrambles*, a work moving journalism which influenced a whole generation of younger minds. A literary respectability was given to the movement by Leslie Stephen's *Playground of Europe*, which introduced artistry and humor into the straightforward narratives of the pioneers. All these first records were handicapped as evidenced by the conventions of the period, which shunned emotional expression, and assumed that adventure must be unworthy of a grown man's interest unless it was undertaken for a serious scientific object. John Tyndall's enterprising spirit, for example, was obviously shackled by this prejudice, and the few adventurous Swiss who first explored their own glaciers all bore the cloak of professorial titles.

The romantic reaction after the formalism of the eighteenth century, and the influence of John Ruskin following upon the revolutionary era of Rousseau, did gradually enable the later nineteenth century to escape from this convention. The "forest and the platform wild" were admitted here and there through the rigid hedges of aesthetic interest. Much in the same way as our historians were released from their generational point of view during the same illumination period, and grew capable of purely objective judgment, our adventurers achieved a like power of detached appreciation of mountain greatness, and a growing liberty to express it.

This recognition, or awareness, of an innate mountain feeling almost amounted to a secondary "breakthrough" in our evolutionary progress. Its revelation has led to the deliberate pursuit of mountain exploration over all the globe, and to a hurried flood of record. In this we might have found the answer to our question as to the origin of our feeling. But here an invariable human change, one belonging to the history of all our arts, again impedes us: the steady shift of emphasis from inspiration to skill, from impression or inspiration to personal performance. Record, in the beginning concerned only with the discovery of novel beauty, with the mountains themselves and the human response to them, has tended always more, and more rapidly, to concentrate upon the human achievement. We must look elsewhere than in conscious recording. Of greater interest to us than any mountaineering stories of our modern response, emotional or judgmatic, to natural scenery must be a consideration of the remoter ages during which that judgment was being formed and that aesthetic sense developed, and of the conditions, climatic or scenic, which inspired and guided those beginnings.

Men who were born among mountains, from the earliest ages onward, have left little trace of any awareness of mountains as entities, and none of seeking to climb them for pleasure. Their environment has never made them mountaineers, in the meaning we now attach to the word. As mountainy men, to use an earlier Irish term for hill-dwellers, they have not seen any mountain detachedly. In a familiar environment of height they have seen no beauty or attraction to suggest an ascent for its own sake.

To the native hill man the visible skylines of summit and ridge have always been as much part of his being as the furnishing of his homestead.

G. Winthrop Young

He cannot see the neighboring slopes except in their homelike detail; the rock or the tree upon the hillside is where he has played, the stream has no continuity for him—it has always existed only as this pool to be explored or fished, or that rapid to be tapped for power. The view is all detail, and all a part of his life, of his unconscious self. In his physical essence he is himself the outcome of his hills. His body and brain are chemically built up of the products of these nearby slopes and of the waters that fall from them. Our kinship with a native soil is closer physically than we recognize. The divorce from it can do more injury to the individual, and to the stock, than our present knowledge or methods of human conditioning can provide against. In the uprooting of the first war I saw old men and women dying in Flanders like seaweed torn from rock; and the long-term effects upon races have since become apparent in national depreciation.

We need feel no surprise, therefore, if no traces are left in mountainous countries, such as Scotland, Switzerland or Norway, of any abstract appreciation of local mountains. It is a fact that, the wider the distribution of hills over any area, the less can we expect to find a mountain consciousness. In its enveloping walls the local mind sees no more than the springs that make the lower fields fruitbearing and the sunwarmed or shaded pasture slopes upon which to grow vine and olive or the sparse crops, or to graze the flocks at different seasonal levels. By every law of nature and of custom, this could be the only point of view of any small community rooted in its own soil, with its growth conditioned by its uneven environment.

During the long evolution of man there have been, of course, forerunners partially anticipating an aesthetic awareness; artists among the cave men, who decorated the rocks with an abstract vision of animal life. There have been also northerners who became poets as they wandered alone year after year on fell and moorland; Scottish crofters and Kerry cottagers whose solitude among mountains made of them Greek and Latin scholars, religious visionaries, or romantic ballad-mongers and storytellers. But it was not specifically their mountains that made them so; nor did they become lovers of mountains in our sense. It was the long communion in solitude with their home world, with natural surroundings so familiar as to frame but never to interrupt thought, which produced them. All solitary living with nature can effect this, even to the production of a supreme ploughman poet upon open plains. In the evolution of human intelligence these more sensitised or dynamic beings have. been the nec-

The Effects of Mountains upon the Development of Human Intelligence

essary precursors, assuring progress in culture. In certain instances the sympathy with nature has been so intense that they have experienced a sense of mystical fusion with the natural world about them.

Where that natural environment has included mountains, these have no doubt had their part in producing the mystical absorption. But, so far back as record can be consulted, the presence of mountains has been in no case essential, never a principal cause. Mystics have occurred even more frequently on the quiet amplitude of the plains, or inhabiting inhospitable desert spaces. If then in this growing response to nature, in these individual cases of articulate sympathy or mystic acknowledgment, we are unable to assign any separate or particular effect to the mountains in an environment, can we trace any more general and fundamental influence contributing to the growth of human intelligence, which was exercised by the mountains alone? I believe that this formative function has been exercised, that it has produced particular qualities of character and of racial genius, acting subconsciously under certain conditions of distance, scale and distribution, and that the break-through of our awareness of this original element in ourselves has been responsible for our modern mountain passion.

Until the human race had mastered all its competitors upon the globe—the animal species, hostile until exterminated or subjugated, the vegetable kingdom, overrunning and overwhelming until tamed to human service—details of scenery can only have interested primitive men in so far as they resisted or helped to maintain human existence. The rugged walls of interrupting mountains, the slow clearing of the forests, and the gradual conquest of the plains for pasture and production, represented the last lines of this natural resistance, the last lairs of the unknown in darker ages, when the unknown was always inimical, and often fatal.

A spirit, evil or benevolent, had its abode in every natural object. But, as their cults developed, spirits had to have some place of origin and common meeting place; and the sky overhead with its brilliant planets and stars supplied a lofty and remote, but ever present and presiding, residence for the super-natural. The mountains, boldly contradicting the level habit of earth, and rushing up into visible contact with the colored mystery of the heavens, became the bridge by which thought and imagination, as they evolved, traveled between the two worlds. Concrete the link had to be, for early mind; Jacob could only dream of angels ascending and descending upon some such actual stairway. Height itself, the magic bridgeway, necessarily became invested with superstitious fears, peopled

by shadows of halfway presences between man and spirit: gnomes or demons in the cold rock recesses, or more amiable inhabitants for the useful springs and water-falls. About each prominent hill, during the ages,
a whole hierarchy came into being, occupying ascending circles of the
unapproachable, as we see reflected far later in Dante's *Divine Comedy*.
As religion took shape out of a vague omnipresence of elemental forces,
with the progress of thought, more attractive gods and goddesses were
placed upon the greater heights, that looked to be above earthly clouds;
upon sacred Prescelly mountain, upon Olympus, upon Ida, upon Sinai.

In effect, the visible mountain ladder, cloud compelling and control-
ling rain and sun, added a third dimension, that of height, to the length
and breadth of surface supporting man in the dawn of his intelligence.
It gave a new measure to his concrete vision of earth. By so doing, by as-
serting the existence of a higher world and of a higher order inhabiting
it, mountains became the first forces to lift the eyes and thoughts of our
branch of animal life above the levels of difficult existence to the perception of a region of spirit, located, as children would locate it, in the sky
above.

It is a bold claim to make for mountains, that they contributed a third
dimension, of height and depth, to man's intelligence; and, by means of it,
adumbrated even a fourth dimension, that of spirit, not permeating it but
placed above it. And yet, when mind first grew capable of comparison,
when man's mastery began to move upon the earth, and he was released
from labour only and from a surrounding darkness of fear, a mountain
peak first sighted upon the skyline must indeed have seemed to belong to
some sphere "visited all night by troops of stars." Just as the first flash
of sunrise upon a snow summit, for the first time realised, must have revealed the golden throne of a god.

In primitive mind the first shadows of the supernatural had to take
concrete shapes. These, we observe, varied in character in different parts
of the world in accordance with the influences of climate and of position.
The chill and cloud of the north, the proximity of sea mists, peopled
height and space with darker hierarchies. On the other hand, the southern
and sunny salience of Olympus or Parnassus had to be occupied by beings with more definite outlines and even, in our view, moderately divine
attributes. In many ranges the occupation still persists. Mysian Mount
Ida, when I climbed it, was for the Turkish soldiers with me too thronged
with fiery devils for the summit to be safe to approach. On Mount Athos
the summit was enduringly defended, on behalf of the angels, by a ruined

chapel and a hermit. But, immediately below, there was a zone or circle held by demons, only a degree less perilous than the belt of forest below that again, inhabited by the lawless charcoal burners. Some of us may still remember how the Swiss Alps, for all the crosses of pilgrimages and sanctifying chapels, were still uncomfortably infested with malignant Geister, with a well known hostility to the local peasantry.

It was not only variations in climate and atmosphere, breeding differences between the spirits dark and light inhabiting high mountains, which helped to fashion beliefs. The scale and the characteristic of the mountain scenery itself have influenced human development as strongly. Physically, of course, a mountain environment has had a constant significance for humanity, according to the fertility, or lack of it, which it provided, or the severity of the barriers which it put in man's way. But the scale upon which the mountains were built, the measure of their height and depth, have had an even greater influence upon the progress of thought and imagination.

This is an aspect of the relationship of man to his environment which has received less attention. The influence upon the origins of mind exercised by scale, arrangement, and compatibility or the reverse may be as determinative as the connection between body and soul. For instance, in vast ranges—the Himalaya, the Caucasus—the scale has been humanly overwhelming. Man and his fields of labor, his villages and temples, have stayed negligible in the scene. In relation to the encircling peaks and gorges no inhabitant could ever have felt anything but an oppressive insignificance. The visible scale of all in sight has disregarded him. Nothing that he himself might create has had any relevance, in size or form. In the result, the dwellers on such slopes have had no inspiration from height, no influence upon their culture. Their environment has remained ungraspable, and therefore inimical or at best neutral in effect. Even in the greater Alps, the modelling has been on a scale too great for an interoperative relationship with primitive man to establish itself, or for any direct mountain inspiration to have produced an imaginative racial development. I have myself, when traversing the great undulating glaciers of high Alps, felt that they did not belong to our ordinary inhabited world. The populated valleys, seen only as dark grooves scarring the icescape, looked to me openings down into an underworld on a lower level of living. Or conversely, when I was looking up from the valley at some remote white summit, the all but invisible human dots discovered by the glass bore no relation at all to the mountain magnitude and splendour; an invisible shifting of snow upon that vast panorama, and the dot would have vanished and left no change.

The inhuman disregard expressed by their great size dissociated the Alps, mentally, from early local life below them, and dislocated any possibility of intimate influence. Primitive man, struggling for existence and subsistence among high ranges, only learned to reckon with human needs, the advantage or disadvantage of the conditions to his own hardy continuance or that of his family and tribe. Height only signified to him because of the other human beings existing upon it; because of the friends or the enemies dwelling upon his own side of some great divide, or beyond it. The pass, communicating across the range with an ally or friendly tribe, or offering access to some enemy beyond it, was the only feature he observed, or recorded, of hills. Those passages from tribal chants, to which our later conscious love of hills gives a happy symbolical meaning, are familiar examples: "How beautiful upon the mountains are the feet of him who brings good tidings;" and, "I will look unto the hills from whence cometh help." In them, it is the human aid coming from beyond the pass, or the sight of the feet of the messenger already descending upon its visible nearer slope, to which appeal and welcome alike apply. The summits were left in that primitive silence of tabu wherein the name of the spirit and of its abiding-place remain unspoken, and its territory is a region of terror, for distant propitiatory sacrifice.

In the proximity of great ranges we should not, then, expect evidences of relationship between mountains and the beginnings of creative art or thought. Among lesser hills, again, where (as in parts of our northern hemisphere) climate and its opacity are for every magnifying height, distances, and the sense of mystery in obscurity, so as to produce the impressions of Himalaya upon sight and imagination, there to the eye for color and proportion, and the communicated sympathy that produces appropriateness, have not been implanted among the native peoples. We are even now constantly struck by the incongruity of past erections or present creation, the infliction upon some noble native hill of a crude chapel, a squalid farm or utilitarian monstrosity. Even the coming, in our present century, of conscious observation and of scenic appreciation has not served to correct a misrelationship as old as time. Traces of what may have been an original inspiration, and a closer affinity, survive here or there upon our downlands, in the rounded aboriginal dwellings and barrows, or the rock-rugged stone monoliths, dolmens and henges, sympathetic with their setting. But, following the inevitable procession from art to execution, any harmonic inspiration was soon lost in the exulting progress of utility and ingenuity.

The clearer atmosphere of the south, illuminating often a mountain environment of vivid outline and comprehensible size, has produced, we note, a closer relationship between certain Mediterranean races and their scenery. The eye has discovered and the imagination has been kindled to a sense of color, of proportion; and there has been a resultant response in appropriate creation. The luminous height of the walls of Apennine, or Carrera, the sun or snow-touched barrier of the Dolomites along the skyline, have been seen on a scale, and with a clarity, that invited human comparison and contribution. By the time Italian architecture has become conscious, the medieval town pinnacled on green hillocks, the white castello in the orchard on the ridge-crest, the campanile above the morning and evening mists of the plain, and the rambling hillside villas with red tiled turrets, are built in the spirit, and with the measure, of lower Alpine modelling. Even the very recent introduction of the dark columnar cypress, tapering in clusters above the buildings and prolonging them upon mountain or sky, has yet further helped to accentuate the sympathy. The visible and comprehensible balance between mountain and plain and lake in an Italian prospect can be attributed the steady progression in artistic vision through the centuries, no less than the moment of fresh revelation under Greek influence, the second break-through of Italian inspiration in the Renaissance.

Under Greek influence, what was it, in the case of the racial genius developing in Italy, which interrupted the effects of lighting and of scale, which drowned the inspiration by dilution, so that it would have died but for the recourse to Grecian sources?

There was, for all its beauty, a structural disproportion in some great part of the Italian scene, which dissipated much of the concentration of environmental effect. Behind the admirable balance of lower hill and lake, of high-set castle and green valley, the view is often lost, and the mind depressed accordantly, in vistas of a monotonous infinity of plain. Over few areas is the proportionate distribution of the mountains complete, or not depreciated by flaws and excessive breaks. Under these conditions, the original artistic vision was imperfect; and it suffered the sooner from the inevitable human progress from inspiration to technique. Ruskin, who possessed probably the first prophetic insight into the meaning of mountains for mankind, has appreciated also this aspect of the relationship, in one of the great prose passages of our language. I quote only a few lines of his juxtaposition:

Higher and higher around the approaching darkness of the plain rise the central chains. . . a wilderness of jagged peaks cast in passionate and fierce perfusion along the circumference of heaven. . . precipice behind precipice and gulf beyond gulf. . . Out from between the cloudy pillars as they pass emerge for ever the great battlements of the memorable and perpetual hills. . . And, under all these, lying in her soft languor, this tender Italy, lapped in dews of sleep, or more than sleep. . . .

The sheer, and undistributed, vastness of the Alpine chain along the remote skyline has been responsible for this restricted, and intermittent, effect of the mountains upon the growth and energy of the sensitive Italian mind. The initial breakthrough was never more than partial.

Greece, however, the Peloponnese and Attica, is the one wholly mountainous land of racial antiquity and of a long recorded culture. Mountainous, it is also the land with the most pellucid atmosphere, the clearest lighting. It was the definiteness of Grecian sunlight, and its positive shadow, which gave to the Greek eye, and so to the mental realization, the first detached vision of natural beauty, the first perception of the relationship of form to color, of a human being to his environment. It impelled the Greek to express this discovery in the first faultless artistic forms.

In that atmosphere, as we can still see now, all colors have an intensity, an incandescence, that can blend the sharpest contrasts. The eye welcomes the vivid green, the warring scarlets and violets and jet blacks, even the blues and pinks and mauves. All the startling conflicts in progress over the landscape, between the varying tints of rock and soil, of silver-grey woods and orchards and the flower-hung cottages, are reconciled. The peasant costumes, garish in isolation, are a delight as we see them dotted or moving in starry dispersion over the fall of field and sun-burned hillside.

The same lucent and exciting atmosphere which first revealed the differing charms of colors discovered also first to the Greeks the modulations of light and shadow on the surface curves and moulding of column and arch, and on the human form; inspiring a primitive artistry to achieve in less than two miraculous centuries the perfection of sculpture and of architecture.

But the revealing light upon that mountainous, sympathetic, and therefore formative environment did more than create the artistic vision; it, first, taught the human mind to reason. In Greece occurred a simultaneous miracle, or, as we may term it, breakthrough, in the evolution of mankind. This small people not only first acquired detached artistic vision; it achieved coincidentally the sudden break-through of the intelligence into abstract thought and logical reasoning. For this, the cause, the influence exerted through numberless ages upon the succeeding human generations, is to be found, as we ourselves can still see it, in the unique balance, the perfect proportioning, of the landscape—which encircles us, no matter which way we turn, with an absolute harmony of relationship between hills and plain and sea and sky.

We can observe how far situation and climate have modified the development of many different races over the uneven surface of many arts of the earth, differentiating their qualities of imagination and of capacity for reasoning. The conclusion is almost forced upon us that, if ever the moment of self-awareness, of that self-consciousness which distinguishes man from his animal ancestry, were fated to arrive, as a break-through in evolution, it had to be as the result of the long pressures of an environment ordered, balanced, and illuminated to impinge with enduring clarity upon the eye and mind of some branch of the human species.

This moment, as we know, arrived in Greece; and supremely in the limited area of the Attic plain, between hills and sea. Approach Athens from the sea, and, disregarding for a time the lighting and the color, the impression of balance, of proportion, is overwhelming, in the relation of the hills to the curving lines of the bay, to the height and distribution of the islands, to the arena of plain in its enveloping mountains. The scale, and the balance, of the triangle of mountains on the circumference, Parnes, Pendeli and Hymettus, frames and emphasises the central heart of surprising pinnacles, Lycabettus and Acropolis. Look outward again, from the heights above Athens, over the gulfs: there is the same balanced harmony of scale and form. The spaces of visible sea, the silver-blue straits, are never wide enough to diminish the height of the azure island separating them. The sea inlets, mirrors of rainbow sunset at evening, alternate with the land, matching in scale with the mountain heights about them and beyond them. The all-pervading mountains themselves flowing to the horizon like waves on crossing tides, with here and there wave-breaks cresting into snowy summits, never dominate unduly the in breaks of coast-line or of intervening sea. They are in the same accordant measure with all visible spaces of the sky. There is no over-wide view across ocean, such as in the end becomes monotonous; no overbearing proximity of height, always in the end oppressive to the eye and mind.

In all this visual balance, and in the influence it has exercised, the mountains play, and have played, the principal part. It is the heights which have given the measure. They are set like upright rulers, to mark the scale, against the perspectives of plain and sea and sky. In their constant contemplation, illuminated by a lighting definite and brilliant, upon color and shadow positive and luminous, primitive mind had no alternative but to acquire, as part of its growth, laws of measure, of order, of proportion, in thought no less than in vision. From the acquired ability to compare, to discriminate, reasoning could emerge. Detachment in thought, reasoning, speculation, with measure and proportion, dawning upon the human mind in the genius of the first Greek philosophers and in the sculpture and building of the first Greek artists, began or hastened the beginnings of civilization and culture in every western race.

It is a mistake, when we have understood the nature of this process, to look for any particular recognition of mountains in Greek literature. Their function as the agents in human development, as one element in a formative environment, precluded any detached evaluation. We must be content to judge of their impression by their effects. Height, the bridge into the unknown, provided in Greece, as elsewhere, a third dimension guiding imagination into a higher spirit world. Upon headland and cliff we can see the resulting tributes of men, as soon as men became capable of responsive expression. Here they are no longer the products of disproportion, or of the great and dissociated height, such as we see in the crude monuments elsewhere offered to strange or antagonistic forces. In Greece the statue or temple belongs in scale and appropriateness to the natural scene. The creations of men, intrinsically beautiful, are never out of keeping with the beauty of their open-air setting. The fluted white columns of the great temple of Poseidon, on Cape Sunium, are at one with the rugged cliffs, with the small wild flowers jewelling the turf, with the wide break of surf below, and the sunlit arching of the sky. The temple of Bassae, remote from all but the passing of the seasons and of time, on a lonely hill in Arcadis, belongs inseparably to its mountain isolation.

The impulse which shaped these forms, and inspired the statuary of the two great centuries after the primary revelation, we feel to have been the product of direct inspiration from nature, and from the divinity revealed in nature to men. The creations are alive with the nobility, with the aura of reverence, with the sense of living movement in rest, which belong—which we can still feel—in the sacred places of the earth, and to the sources of beauty in nature.

Nowhere, I believe, can we become aware of this more movingly than at Delphi. Withdrawn and severe, these eagle-haunted crags upon a mountain shoulder, overlooking valley and sea and the long recession of mountain ranges, preserve an atmosphere of sanctity, of awe, inherent in the scene itself. The feeling of suspense, of a brooding presence, concentrated in a heart of nature, which for a thousand years remained the heart of religion. It is as though, through the silence, we felt the heartbeat throbbing in color and in form, in height and in distance, and in the spirit informing their power. To most of us it comes as a surprise to discover that the impression of sanctity or divinity, which we expected to receive from the cascade of splendid statuary, the ruined temples and shrines descending upon the shattered terraces and ledges of masonry, does not emanate from them, but belongs to the penetrating emotion of the great mountain scene itself. The numen of Delphi dwells in the balance, the proportion, of the views surrounding us, in the tension, of which we are sensible, between mountain and precipice, sky and sea. The superb monuments, crowded and subsidiary, are no more than the tributes to the spirit of the mountain sanctuary offered by those who, through the ages, have experienced for it, and here, the same feeling as we do now.

No one, since in the last century mountains have grown into our consciousness, has better summarized the nature of this deep mountain influence, or the inspiration of such places, than the great philosopher, statesman and soldier, Jan Smuts. "So it has come about that all moral and spiritual values are expressed in terms of altitude. . . . The mountain is not merely something externally sublime. It has a great historic and spiritual meaning for us: it stands for us as the ladder of life. More, it is the ladder of the soul, and in a curious way the source of religion. . . ."

The awakening of reason and of spiritual imagination, in that short and miraculous period in Greece, brought to life our western civilisation. The measure slowly impressed by hills upon primitive mind still rules the reasoning of men, however far they may travel from that first impetus into speculative regions, or into interstellar space.

We know it now to have been inevitable that even in Greece the inspiration should fade, as artists and writers perfected the techniques of their craft, and their more exact appreciation of beauty substituted observation and reproduction for the first sublimity of artistic vision or poetic thought. It is part of the human tragedy, of our destiny as beings in isolation and in egoism, that the more we become aware, and the further we progress in perfecting our skills and executing our ideas, the less we can continue to derive original inspiration.

We can see a small but striking instance of this in our short history of mountain climbing: not frivolous, because not inapt in a mountain context. The mountain influence, working in early ages subconsciously, then through conscious and artistic appreciation, and abruptly in this last century awakening to a passion for contact and achievement, is now progressing by our human law always more towards technique and perfected method in climbing, and it can recapture always less of the first magical awareness of the inner mountain feeling.

Is then the influence of mountains upon us diminishing, its work accomplished in those first ages? May we expect it to lose all hold when once the novelty of climbing as a skill is exhausted, when every range has been explored, and when mountaineers have made themselves so secure with protective and suspensory devices that the effort alone is merely monotonous? We may now accept, I believe, that the feeling for mountains, that sense of intimacy and almost of kinship with them which obsesses us in youth and may even endure into age, does not belong to the category of our seasonal or sporting enthusiasms, which alter with our growth. It is a disposition which we carry within us, already part of our heredity when man became homo sapiens; and it remains a potential response to music. Among a percentage of men in every later generation it has been emerging more and more into consciousness; and it does so among an always greater number, now that the mountain feeling has been recognised and defined. We know how in dreams the terrors of primitive mind, and a capacity for fear unknown to our waking hours, can return upon us; fears felt in some human past lived under the shadow of savage environment, of forest, of darkness and of pursuing death. In the same way, in what we may even call the day-dreaming of sensitized younger minds, the inherited memory of the original mountain influence is alive, drawing men to mountains as to a home.

Others must often feel as I did, and as Ker did, when in youth, and before familiarity and acquired skills had dulled the first keen and magical wonder, we raced for the hills, there to hurry until the last man made wall or the last trace of human occupation had sunk below sight; when, with only the hills about us, we know ourselves again among friends,

The Effects of Mountains upon the Development of Human Intelligence surrounded by forms, by measures, by an influence, to which we feel that we belong, an influence more a part of ourselves than even our own consciousness of it.

However mechanized, or automatized, the conditions of human life may become, the same number of human beings will, I believe, continue to carry this inherited memory, reinforced for action by the new awareness of mountains and of mountaineering which has come with this last century. There will be men and women who find among hills forgetfulness of fear and of their anxieties, in the restoration of their sense of proportion, the recovery of reasonable measure, which was the mountains' original gift to men; or who, like Smuts like so many, will see again upon the mountains spirits of religion—true symbols, founded upon the same inspiring mountain principles of measure, proportion, order, and of an uprightness which points a way beyond clouds and, at least, towards the stars.

---

*Delivered as the seventeenth W. P. Ker memorial lecture in the University of Glasgow, 2nd May, 1956 and was published in 1957.
William Paton Ker. A leading British literary scholar who held the Quain Chair of English language and literature in University College, London. He was an alumnus of Glasgow University as well as a member of the Alpine Club. Ker died climbing in Italy in 1923 mountains to this drama fascinated him, because of the mystery they introduced, in remote height so long unattainable and in depths so long defended by barriers of superstitious fear. It was his consciousness of a survival within himself of this primitive and mysterious awe, combining with the modern awakened appreciation for mountain beauty, which drew him actively to the hills. It was this which softened the usual severity of his pronouncements—or his silences—when made in the sphere of learning and scholarship, to a happy lyricism in several languages when mountains were his theme.

G. Winthrop Young

Phil Bartlett (b. 1955) is a university researcher in physics and a freelance journalist. He has taken part in expeditions to Greenland, Pakistan, India, South America, and Arctic Canada and has climbed extensively in Britain and Europe. He is the author of *The Undiscovered Country.*

PHIL BARTLETT:
RETURN TO THE PRIMITIVE

Mountaineering prompts an ineradicable streak of nostalgia, a dislike of progress and change which runs deep and affects the front-runner as well as the average performer. So what do they fear, these people who prefer the past and see in contemporary climbing the destruction of everything worthwhile?

Fears for the future have existed since mountaineering began, but that does not mean they should not be taken seriously. The reactionary trait is a fundamental one, and it means something. Sometimes it is mere jealousy, envy of the successful or blindness and stagnation of the individual; but beyond these lies the realization that mountaineering is not only about new horizons, least of all new horizons of extreme peril, but includes another element, related to a sense of "belonging" in the world, which can easily be swamped by egocentricity, and the loss of which would ruin everything. And mountaineers believe they have discovered something about this "oneness," or sense of identification, which is worth stating explicitly: you cannot feel it in the civilized world, only in the primitive. The town will not do, only the country.

Eric Shipton was well aware that is was really this rather than climbing which attracted him to the unspoiled places of the world. "There is nothing unusual in the feeling for wild country which has been the chief and most constant influence shaping the course of my life," he wrote. Those dreams in early childhood of chasing the moon over the wooded spurs of the Nilgiri Hills were symptomatic; the emotions they engendered have been repeated again and again through the years in a sense of fusion with the surrounding wilderness.

Shipton was primarily a mountain traveler and explorer rather than a technical climber, yet he never seems to have felt sad about this, or jealous of the technical achievements of some of his friends. On the contrary, he was shrewd enough to realize that hard climbing misses something. Everest in particular came to represent an undesirable narrowness of outlook. He far preferred wandering around the lower slopes, peering into odd comers of unexplored glaciers, feeling free; climbing peaks, as high and as hard as you can, has a way of elbowing all that out. So pity the man who is so talented he never escapes from it!

Shipton's "sense of fusion" is nothing less than the mystic vision, and is the deepest reward of the mountain-walker. In practical terms the question which follows is of course this: how wild does it have to be? Shipton devoted his life to exploring lands which were true wildernesses by anyone's reckoning: Africa, Patagonia, the Himalayas. But Sunday fell-walking in the Lake District can provide a feeling of fusion too, and though this country rather than town it certainly isn't wilderness. In fact much of what is most central to the Lake District's charm—old stone buildings and walls, roads which weave round the lie of the land rather than through it, copses and fields which lap the valley sides—all of this we have made.

The essential element, the common factor which connects the Himalayas with the Lake District, is a sense of nature's mastery. In the Lake District human activity is very evident but that does not prevent our delight, because we still feel that it is the rhythms of the natural world which are in control rather than ourselves. The stone-enclosed fields are delightful precisely because they show humanity coming to terms with the hills rather than being crudely used for our short-term fancy. Quarrying on the other hand can seem like rape, for here it is made clear that the hills no longer rule and the comfort of the Great Outdoors that we seek. the feeling that nature decides and we accept, has been thrown out. To be comforting the natural world does not have to be static but it does have to change in its own time and not in ours. In a recent book about rock-climbing David Craig had pointed out that one can delight in change, but only if it is evolutionary rather than revolutionary;

"...since 1983 a ten-foot pendant fang has dropped off a fine steep route called Sostenuto and made its start much harder. But frost and spate and drought are to be expected. When you climb in such a place, you are working with the grain of nature, immersed in its atmosphere, and your very heartbeat feels eased into more inevitable, less forced rhythms."

A fang of rock dropping off a climb is a sign that nature has its own time scale, its own moment for doing things, and we feel, at least in our contemplative moments, that to accept these, to rejoice in them even, is wisdom. Changes that we make ourselves are very different. They remind us that the human race can step outside evolutionary time and impose itself. This is not welcome to either Shipton (the explorer) or to Craig (the rock-climber), and the gloomy predictions of the nostalgic and reactionary begin to look justified.

When we go to the hills we do not attain joy by imposing ourselves, because that implied responsibility. On the contrary, we want to forget our responsibilities for a while and submerge ourselves in something greater:

". . .when I sit on a six-inch ledge with my feet dangling above a two hundred-foot drop, the hart's-tongue fern and dwarf hawthorn a few inches from my eyes, the air smelling of moss, wood-pigeons clattering out of the tree-tops down below, then at least for a time I have grafted myself back into nature, and the sense of rightness achieved, or regained, is unmistakable."

The mountaineer's sensibility to have nature has its deepest roots in timeless traditions of nature mysticism, but in terms of cultural fashion it springs from eighteenth century romanticism. Romanticism was a broad reaction against the unqualified belief in the powers of rational mind and reason which seemed to be increasingly gripping civilized man. So, if civilization was bad, what was good? Primitivism, obviously, particularly a primitivism which included whose characteristics such as spontaneity, naturalness and faith in the emotions which seemed to be increasingly lacking in contemporary civilization.

Primitivism may be all in the mind or one can attempt to live it, and the eighteenth century saw merit in both. But it is back-to-nature as something to do—the primitive lifestyle as opposed to trying to think oneself into the primitive mentality—which is the mast to which mountaineering stakes its colors. The mountaineer is someone who believes that the benefits of spontaneity, naturalness or whatever else might accrue from primitivism are to be got by going there rather than by imagining it.

This attitude is a part of the uneasy relationship between active mountaineering and imagination which Boardman, and before him, Ruskin, was so well aware of. It is certainly enough to set mountaineering apart from "high" Romanticism, that is, romanticism as a purely aesthetic or artistic movement. For the high Romantic the crux of the thing is not a geographical place like a Pacific paradise or a rural idyll, but a mode of thinking and feeling brought about by imagination. This the sphere of meditation in all its myriad forms. It uses the imagination purely; man becomes sufficient unto himself. But the mountaineer's creed is different. It aims to encourage new modes of thought and feeling, but only by using outside stimulus. We return to the hills to be reminded of what we have forgotten; also to feel again those things which we find too subtle to be remembered and which have to be experienced.

It is easy to exaggerate the primitivist urge. Our ancestors spent most of their energies trying to escape its realities, and we would be doing the same if we did not lead a generally civilized and comfortable existence. But to say that civilization has actually created the attraction would be going too far, and one of the things that justifies this belief is our modern realization that primitivism involves not only the experiencing of a more primitive life-style but also of more primitive ways of thought for which some of our most important thinkers would claim a permanent and fundamental importance. Carl Jung for example believed that ". . . every civilized human being, however high his conscious development, is still an archaic man at the deeper levels of his psyche." He believed that the archaic man within each of us still demands expression, unchanged by culture of education.

Not that everyone agrees with him. Freud regarded many of Jung' s archaic needs as neuroses, malformations of the individual with no essential basis at all. And clearly there are many people in the world today who feel no need whatsoever to return to the primitive. By no means everyone longs to escape to the wilderness and commune with nature for the good of their soul. All one can say for certain is that many, very many, people do, and that their longing seems to be more serious and more deeply felt than any mere "escape."

One of the attractions of a return to the primitive is a sense of simplification and thus of freedom—freedom from the endless complications and decisions of modern life. It is not just that primitive people do the one thing, the only thing, but that they think the one thing, the only thing.

According to Jung such people do not consciously think; the thoughts come to them intuitively, and this because their whole mental life is rooted in the way things are. Life presents them with a fait accompli; they must live and work within the situation as it is, and there is not time for western angst, for wishing that things were different. They are what they are and they are immediate. Primitive people must do this and they must do that, or they will starve. The environment is that real.

But if this is a cruel reality it is also a mentally simplified one. Moral anguish becomes irrelevant, and the primitive mentality is thus essentially amoral. The universe is not good and it is not bad, and wondering about such things is little more than a diversion for those who have lost contact with the primary facts of life. The universe just is. What is important is that we should simply submit, such a submission implying that "the world" is more powerful than we can ever hope to be. We can worship it by all means, and we can perform rituals, but we do so as supplicants; we can remind ourselves of our dependency, but we cannot change it. That, indeed, is one of the prime sources of our religious feeling.

The crucial point is to get back into contact with the things that really matter. There are only a handful of them, yet oddly enough they are what we seem to lose sight of most easily. Simply surviving is the root, and, after that, trying to eliminate pain and danger. These are not matters we normally give much attention to, but returning to them refreshes one's appetite for life enormously. Most serious mountaineering takes place against a background of danger and discomfort, but only so as to provide something against which one can then play the game of trying to get as comfortable and as safe as possible. There has to be something to kick against. Life in the mountains gives you the opportunity to make use of all sorts of subtle tricks for looking after yourself. Boardman called it "serious play:" this is what he was doing building a snow-hole with Scott on Kanchenjunga, digging out a platform for the tent on Gauri Sankar. Serious play is a good phrase, because in bringing out the apparent contradictions of return to the primitive it also brings out its depth. In "normal" life, perhaps because we are so tied up in our own little world, we are convinced we can "do"; if only we could decide what to do. Life demands that we make decisions and we are convinced these decisions matter. Yet simultaneously we are forced to despair, because nothing makes any difference; cause and effect are too tenuously connected. We cannot change anything. The world is too complex, and everyone is pulling in opposite directions.

Mountaineering can be an antidote to all that because the game is being played against real problems for once, not against the man-made, utterly trivial problems which seem to constitute so much of life. You may die if you decide wrongly. Yet at the same time it is a seriousness which is free, even carefree. When one makes decisions in the mountains they are important enough to make one feel truly alive yet they don't produce the sort of anguish which inevitably accompanies a belief in one's own omnipotence. In mountains it is always worth trying to mould events, to exert will, yet in the end something greater hangs over everything. The result is that beyond a certain point one surrenders responsibility for events and becomes fatalistic. "What more can I do?" takes over. One has self determination, yet under the widening perspective which the world's wild places encourage, fate has the last word and nothing matters.

When the French climbed Annapurna I in 1950—the first success on an 8000m peak—two of the summit team, Maurice Herzog and Louis Lachenal, contracted terrible frostbit. On the summit the exhilaration and the beauty swept all else away:

Our hearts overflowed with an unspeakable happiness.
If only the others could know. . . If only everyone could know!

On the descent Herzog is "still blissfully floating on a sea of joy." But later, when the extent of his frostbite has become apparent and he thinks he is going to die, elation has been replaced by a vast resignation.

There is a supernatural power in those close to death. Strange intuitions identify one with the whole world. . . All would end well. I should remain there, forever, beneath a few stones and a cross.

Our ancestors faced fundamental problems such as how to survive and how to get enough to eat which we rarely experience today and for all their drawbacks, offered a kind of simplicity we still crave. In mountaineering we create such a simplified reality, by making a distinction between tactics and strategy. We commit ourselves to strategy—to climb this mountain, to cross that piece of country—and having done so we are left with the freedom to choose our tactics. Strategic decisions may have moral complications, but tactics are nothing to do with morality; they are to do with practicality. So by defining the strategy and only allowing ourselves to think about tactics we simplify the mental life and avoid the questions with no answers.

Phil Bartlett

Chris Bonington has expressed this well; the satisfaction, relief even, of a simple primitive aim which leaves the dilemmas and the questioning far behind. Nowhere in his writing has Bonington seriously attempted the strategic question, Why climb at all? And he is probably wise in this; he is no philosopher. But he is good on the freedom of tactics. Involved in a first winter ascent on the North Face of the Eiger, he and Mick Burke landed on the summit by helicopter in order to meet the climbing team who were approaching the top in the teeth of a storm. Whisked from the comfort and security of their hotel to the savagery of the mountain, they dug a snow hole in darkness:

Eventually I found a snow bank, brought Mick across to me, grabbed the shovel and started digging. At least I was able to keep warm as I worked away in the shelter of the snow, while all Mick could do was to sit, huddled outside, waiting for me to dig out enough snow for him to creep in behind me. There was an odd sort of enjoyment about the entire venture. Perhaps it was because we were on our own, with a simple, independent aim. And although now in the midst of a most savage storm, we still felt in complete control of our destinies.

What mountain shall we climb today? That's difficult. But once the decision is made the rest is tactics, and one can be happy struggling with tactics. Every mountaineer loves planning the route, the places to bivouac, the logistics of what to take. One feels freed tom the abstract and unsolvable and returned to the real and important. The aim is so beautifully clear. You can even see it.

The great joy this gives runs right through Bonington's writings. He is as egocentric as anyone and hates failure, but even failure is bearable if it leaves opportunities for a primitive struggle with a clear objective. "As a youngster I was very keen on model soldiers and that has grown into an enthusiasm for war gaming," he wrote recently. Something of this enthusiasm contributes to his love of climbing. On the North-East Ridge of Everest in 1982 he was forced to admit that he was not as strong as his companions Boardman and Tasker, both twenty years younger, that he had no real chance of climbing the route, and that the only sensible solution was for him to accept a support role. And the most useful support he could give was to set up a camp on the North Col of Everest to act as the key to Boardman and Tasker's descent and a possible escape route. It wasn't a question of giving moral support from base camp but of doing something physical which made a direct contribution. And with that, the pleasure he derives from his mountaineering life returned:

I was not depressed by my own failure and was even relieved that I had made the decision to withdraw from the summit bid. . . I felt a vast relief of tension and actually looked forward with anticipation to our trip to the North Col. This was something which seemed a useful contribution to the expedition, was within my capabilities, and a goal in itself.

There was still a useful challenge to go for, with all the criteria —immediacy, danger, decisions—of "serious play."

However, it is the mountain explorers who really exemplify the longing for a kind of re-found primitivism in mountaineering, and who tell most clearly of the joy it can give.

The doyen of early twentieth century British explorers is Dr. Tom Longstaff. "Once can still see in the mind's eye the slight figure, jutting beard, keen eye, strong graceful hands and ever youthful spirit," remembers Peter Lloyd. When Longstaff confessed his ambitions to be an explorer to his father, he advised him to take a medical degree, "every man, he said, ought to have profession to fall back on." Longstaff did so, but never lost his interest in adventure and exploration, and as well as being a mountain explorer, climber and surveyor was a noted seaman, making hazardous journeys in Spitzbergen and Greenland.

However much he enjoyed climbing, the pull of unknown territory was always irresistible to Longstaff. When he first went to the Himalaya in 1905 it was with the intention of attempting Trisul, one the highest peaks in India. Then suddenly, and quite unexpectedly, he was presented with the rare opportunity of traveling to Tibet. "What a chance! My plans for a mountaineering expedition would change into the prospect of a walk of some thousand miles across and round the Himalaya." He couldn't resist it, though he did find the time to make a spirited attempt on Gurla Mandata, an important summit on the Tibet-Indian border, on the way. His team set a speed record by descending 3,000 feet in "a minute or two" in an avalanche. They all survived.

In the early decades of the twentieth century the mountains of the Indian Himalaya were particularly attractive territory for British explorers. They fell within the British administered territories of Kumaon and Garhwal; they are much closer to Delhi than the Karakoram; and Kumaon and Garwhal are amongst the most beautiful regions on earth. Longstaff returned here in 1907 and succeeded on Trisul, which at almost 23,500 ft became the highest peak yet climbed. True to form, the ascent was made at great speed, Longstaff, a Ghurka soldier and two alpine guides he had brought from Italy reaching the top in June using what Longstaff called his "rush tactics," they climbed the last 6,000 ft of the mountain in one ten hour push and the descended 7,000 ft to their camp in the next three. It was an impressive performance, which owed much to the fact that the whole party had been at over 15,000 ft for most of the previous month and were therefore very well acclimatized. Shades of Messner's recent performances.

Like all great mountaineers, Longstaff had an eye for the future. He had seen and noted Changabang, the mountain which three quarters of a century later was to be at the forefront of technical Himalayan climbing when Boardman and Tasker climbed its West Face. In fact he was to print a photograph of the West Face in his autobiography. He must have sensed that a mountain of such appalling beauty—its most obvious comparison is with Cerro Torre in southern Patagonia—was destined to playa significant role one day; "a sheet of palest granite draped with vast icicles, one a thousand feet long. In some ways this was the most amazing mountain I have ever seen."

Longstaff's mantle was in due course taken over by Eric Shipton and Bill Tilman, the two men who between them were to dominate Himalayan exploration in the 1930s. Like all explorers, Shipton and Tilman craved the freedom of the exploring life. Longstaff was apt to say that Everest in particular was a millstone round mountaineers' necks, and that the sooner it was out of the way the better. Shipton and Tilman felt much the same. All that grandiose rhetoric put forward so interminably by Sir Francis Younghusband and others—the glorification of man, his preparation for loftier living and so on—once the mountain was. climbed it could all be put aside and one could be last concentrate on simply enjoying oneself.

Of the two, Shipton is the more immediately attractive character. He was the son of a Ceylon tea planter, but neither made nor inherited much money and was short of funds throughout his life. He eked out a living as a lecturer and writer and during the Second World War served as British Consul in Kashgar. The post-war period was a difficult one for Shipton. Although he led the Everest reconnaissance which climbed the Khumbu ice-fall in 1951 and the hugely successful (in terms of mountain exploration) Cho Oyu expedition of 1952, he was ousted from the leadership of the '53 Everest expedition, divorced in the mid '50s, and to regain his spiritual equilibrium spent several years as a forestry laborer in Shropshire before enjoying a second concentrated period of exploration in South America in the 1960s. Shipton made some difficult climbs, most notably perhaps the West Ridge of Mt. Kenya with Tilman, but it is as the archetypal romantic explorer, searching for something inward of which the mountain is only a symbol, that he is rightly remembered.

Tilman, born two years before the turn of the century, was ten years older and fought in both world wars. In the 20s and early 30s he planted coffee in Kenya, where he first met Shipton. When he returned to England he resolved to devote the remainder of his life to exploration and adventure, though shortly afterwards he fell from a climb in the Lake District and seriously damaged his back; he was told he would never climb again. Tilman inherited family money, never married and was a self-sufficient individualist, as demonstrated by a comment recorded by Jim Perrin: "I've had my peccadilloes, but the trouble with women is, they get in the damned way." Like Longstaff, he was attracted not only to mountains but to all wild places, and in the second half of his life became as distinguished in the field of adventurous ocean sailing as he already was in mountaineering. He could be brusque and reserved and as a sailor was notorious for driving his crews hard. (A famous advertisement in *The Times* read: "Hands wanted for long voyage in small boat; no pay, no prospects, not much pleasure.") At the age of 79 he disappeared sailing whilst on an expedition in the South Atlantic.

In 1934 Shipton and Tilman applied their energies to Nanda Devi, the highest peak in the Indian Himalaya. Standing at the centre of a great ring of mountains which block off almost all lines of approach, Nanda Devi is strikingly beautiful and has the extra allure of inaccessibility. Longstaff himself had tried to reach it, and he was by no means the first. They did not succeed in climbing it—Tilman did so with Noel Odell as part of a British/American expedition two years later—but they did reach its base, and the '34 venture has come to enjoy a very special place in mountaineering history, standing as a glorious example of the small, informal, expedition philosophy for which Shipton and Tilman retained a deep preference all their lives, echoed in Tilman's much quoted view that if an expedition cannot be organized on the back of an envelope in half an hour it isn't worth organizing at all. It is a view which can never fail to appeal to our sympathies, and when Tilman made a rare appearance at a British mountaineering conference in the late 1975 (not the sort of event he had a natural sympathy with), he stole the show.

So what is the explorer's special reward? Little-visited areas have a timelessness, a sense of being part of another era, which the Tilmans and Shiptons of this world crave. I was reminded of this on a recent visit to the Kurdopin Glacier in the West Karakoram. The Kurdopin was first visited by two Dutch explorers, Philip Visser and Jenny Visser-Hooft, who made several Himalayan journeys in the 1920s and '30s, bringing guides from Europe. On the Kurdopin they were eventually stopped by a considerable icefall and forced to retreat. Descending the side of this ice-fall half a century later I was delighted to come across two superbly made stone cairns. Who had built them? No hunters would come so high. I like to think the Vissers' party left them to mark their high point. Sitting by them, the first human sign for many days and so unexpected, put time and timelessness into a new perspective.

Later, below the ice-fell, we escaped thankfully from the tottering blocks of ice and descended the glacier's brown moraines in the late evening sun. We needed water, and ahead could see a likely spot; below a mountain ravine a scree fan, dotted with gorse and grass, spread out and blocked the path. And then movement: before we could make out their shapes a dozen large animals fled the horizon. They were Himalayan goats, Ibex, *markhor*— something of the sort. How I longed to see them close! One day, when I'm too old for climbing, this is what I'll do; come here, to the high scorched pastures below the snow line and sit in a mountain eyrie with the silence and the longest lens a man can buy, waiting, waiting, until the rare inhabitants of these places, those most private and magical lives, reveal themselves. Diemberger's crystals? These also are they, elusive and rare, fleeting moments which cannot be told.

Whether any of this is an accurate reflection of real primitive peoples is questionable of course. Having recognized that contemporary civilization is missing something, it is all too easy to idealize primitivism and create a false image of the noble savage, a silly romanticism in which nature is the only good. But a more immediate way of living is certainly possible and, rightly or wrongly, primitive peoples and their lifestyle stand as our symbol of it. When the Italian mountaineer Fosco Moraini visited the villages of the Kalash Kafirs of Afghanistan in the 1950s he felt he was witnessing a scene "eloquent of fundamental realities." There seemed to be a wisdom embodied in the life of the Kalash which a more sophisticated urban society had lost. It is to be regained only by intentional culture shocks which force us to question our assumptions, and life in the mountains, essentially the life of the vagabond, is one way of doing that. More generally, travel—not package tour travel but "real" travel—can return one to a sense of fundamental things.

During a round-the-world motor-cycle trip the middle-aged Ted Simon found himself in Thailand, overwhelmed by the change that has taken place in our perceptions of life and death. . . it began to seem quite extraordinary to me that in the western world a person could, and probably would, go through life without ever witnessing death, let alone viewing a naked corpse. . . I could not bring myself to believe that this was "healthy." Mountaineers are led to the same conclusion. Every climber is likely sooner or later either to see someone killed or get so close to it themselves that it makes them think. Anyone who is seriously involved in climbing in the greater ranges has a list of dead friends. And walkers too are apt to find that the primitivist nature of what they do invites thoughts about "fundamental realities." Food, warmth, shelter; where does it come from? Climate; how does it affect us? Suddenly we realize that in modern life we are indeed "dangerously detached from the basic facts of existence," taking things for granted and never seeing them at first hand, only on TV screens.

So it is hardly surprising if some of those who have experienced the primitive life at first hand come to scorn modern comforts altogether, and despise the squeamish refusal of the rest of us to look the harshness of life in the face. There is a marvelous passage at the end of *A Short Walk in the Hindu Kush* when Eric Newby and his companion Hugh Carless come face to face with the almost fabled explorer Wilfrid Thesiger. Not quite Burton meeting Livingstone, because this is not a meeting of equals. Newby and Carless are essentially modern men, innocent but adventurous, returning to the primitive on a temporary basis only, just as most of us do. That is why *A Short Walk. . .* falls within the scope of this book. Thesiger on the other hand is not returning to the primitive; in Newby's pen-portrait he is a primitive, though also the classic imperial Englishman. Over supper he tells them about his medical experiences:

"Do you do it? Cutting off fingers?"

"Hundreds of them," he said dreamily, for it was very late. "Lord, yes. Why, the other day I took out an eye. I enjoyed that. . ."

The shock of the primitive, its different assumptions and its different modes of thought, makes one more critical of western ways, and there is so much to be said for the view that if you don't come back thoughtful and uneasy from a climb in South America or a trek in Nepal the whole thing has been pointless. The money you spend, the western materialism you flaunt—it mountain tourism goes no deeper than that then it is a sad affair. Return to the primitive should make you a radical.

Death for example; perhaps our fear of it is not healthy after all, but a tool of repression? The fear of death can become a fear of life, so that instead of living we surround ourselves with endless safety regulations and the rewards of that, though they have to be paid for, are very real.

One way to talk about death is to do it humorously. The late Tom Patey was a master of black humor, and so was Don Whillans. Patey attempted the Eiger with Whillans, and wrote a classic portrait of the man;

"Somebody left a boot here." I shouted to Don.

He pricked up his ears. "Look to see if there's a foot in it," he said.

Mountaineering is dangerous, though the dangers are generally less than public perception makes them. What is more widespread, and probably more insidious than literal tragedy, is the keener sense of death that it offers. And this, though exhilarating, has a danger of its own: it is liable to make a lot of modern life seem downright irrelevant. The triviality of everyday life, that key existentialist sentiment, is something mountaineering can make one feel deeply. On the return from any major mountaineering experience one's feelings are inevitably two-fold: on the credit side an exhilarating sense of living on a higher plane than normal, above trivialities; on the debit side the problem of learning to take those trivialities seriously once again. For however pointless earning a living, say, might seem when one is struggling for life in a blizzard, the person who cannot take everydayness seriously is in danger of going mad.

Re-adapting takes time, and is never easy. "Even though Terry is the most understanding husband I could have, every time I go away we have problems with our relationship," wrote Julie Tullis. "I am immediately plunged back into the routine of a housewife. The initial difficulty is that I do need time alone to come back from one world to the other, which appears very anti-social when I have been away for so long. . . ."

These problems are only too common. Returning to everyday life, it is difficult to take anybody, or anything they are doing, seriously. A return to the primitive encourages a mental retrenchment in which forgotten elements of life regain their rightful status and the trivial things are seen for what they really are—trivial.

The root of it is a completely new sense of the physical life. Mountaineering is a sharp reminder that one is only flesh and blood, that in normal life we tend to forget the vulnerability of our bodies, forget that at its core life is about physical survival and that nothing else matters. Even when physical actions are serious, as in driving for example, we are generally unaware of it. But in the mountains or on a rock climb we rely on physical prowess and are acutely aware of it. It is one more feature of the game which helps to "graft us back into nature and a sense of reality regained." Who are these people who say mountaineering is not real life but an escape? Up in the hills they seem like blind fools, and one is more inclined to question what is so "real" about "ordinary" life.

Yet in one sense return to the primitive is undeniably an escape. It is an escape from the individual ego.

The human ego is a burden as well as a pleasure; everyone is trying to get on, everyone is trying to be a success. The attraction of the primitive life is that it takes one away from these pressures which make it impossible to feel psychologically free. Most anthropologists agree that primitive peoples have a quite different sense of individuality from ourselves, being less obsessed with leaving their mark on the world, less afraid of death—and, as a result, more free.

But this does not mean that the primitive has no sense of self. Discussing Melville's *Moby Dick* the critic Michael Bell has pointed out that the peculiar advantages of the primitive mentality are summed up in the whaling ship's harpooner, Queequeg. whose "unquestioning cosmic acceptance seems to give him an extraordinarily impersonal sense of his own existence." He is truly an individual, yet believes deeply in some greater scheme of things which, because it is beyond his control, removes the more stressful aspects of ego-centricity. He is both more and less ego-centric than ourselves.

And really there is not contradiction here, for it is only becoming fatalistic that one can break free from fear and actually concentrate on being oneself. Is there anything less inspiring, less individual, than modern man, obsessed by his own individuality? Is the answer to life really the avoidance of physical risk and continuing to live as long as medical science makes possible? The result is so often a poor sense of self spread ever more thinly. Yet the primitive radiates a sense of self which we envy.

The eastern concept of dharma, life's duty or purpose, throws some light on this. Dharma is a state of mind now largely alien to the West, and thus increasingly alien everywhere else too, but it still produces in some peoples a sense of identity and meaning out of all proportion to their material wealth. The shepherds of the Gaddi, migratory sheep and goat herders of the Kulu region of the Indian Himalaya, are able to explain an aspect of dharma which to us seems quite radical; that one's actions should not be determined by what seems logical or most efficient, but by what is traditional. Only in this way can one gain a sense of real purpose. The Gaddi travel constantly, with all the inconveniences and difficulties that implies, and to the western observer it is not clear that such constant upping of roots is really necessary. But that is to miss the point. Necessary or not.

We are a shepherding people. We are in the habit of going with the flocks: it is because of the dharma that Lord Shiva gave us. It happened like this. The gods were making their way through the Himalayas. They came to a particularly high, snow-covered pass. They struggled to get over it but failed. In despair they sat down, tired and bad tempered. Lord Shiva was the angriest. . . In a fury he took a pinch of dirt from his body and hurled it to the ground—out of his dirt sheep and goats were created. The flock walked across the snow and as they went they made a path. Then, following that path, the gods were able to cross the pass. In thanks Shivji (the familiar name for Lord Shiva) gave the Gaddis the privilege of looking after the flocks. But these days it is very difficult, so young men. . . are going into the army, government service, and shop keeping. That's good, but it's not our dharma.

However fanciful they may seem to rational minds, such myths have a great power to order and make sense of life. Primitive peoples know quite well that they can be shot down in flames by rational argument, so if they are wise they take steps to prevent such argument taking place. That is why they will not tell their stories willingly.

Jung recognized this clearly. At one point in his life Jung spent some time with the Pueblo Indians of North America. He discovered that their religion was a form of sun worship. But it was a worship which the Pueblos believed influenced and was even essential to the sun itself; they believed that without their rituals the sun would quite simply be unable to cross the sky. "I then realized," says Jung, "on what the dignity," the tranquil composure of the individual Indian, was founded. It springs from his being a son of the sun; his life is cosmologically meaningful, for he helps the father and preserver of all life in his daily rise and descent. . . That man feels capable of formulating valid replies to the overpowering influence of God, and that he can render back something which is essential even to God, induces pride, for it raises the human individual to the dignity of a metaphysical factor.

Well, we have lost that. We have been giving up the notion of cosmic significance since Copernicus gave us a rude awakening. And perhaps that contributes to our current obsession with our own individuality—what else is left?

But mountains offer us an alternative, because they present us with such a grand arena that we are almost bound to reflect on our personal insignificance. They have a sense of permanence and stillness which can be profoundly affecting. Once again, the result is to remind us of the narrowness of our everyday thoughts and concerns. "It is this feeling of steadfastness of timelessness, imbuing every rock, that is such a comfort and so staunch a support in these days of outward change, of flux and uncertainty."

This is the quality which underlies the fascination antique lands like Tibet or Bhutan still have for the western mind. A fine but depressing book about Tibet, *Land of the Snow Lion*, has recently been published by the mountaineer Elaine Brook. Like thousands before her, Brook goes in search of the mystic vision and its benefits, but whether it is the fault of the Chinese or the tourists they have let into the country, Tibet has changed, and the image that stays with one now is not of timeless wisdom but of surly Chinese bus drivers constantly looking at their watches. The country which for so long stood outside time has at last succumbed like everywhere else. In the Potala Palace in Lhasa a sad young monk, finding that Brook speaks Tibetan, gives her a book of Buddhist prayers. "Take it," he says with tears in his eyes. "It is finished here."

Aldous Huxley also has some interesting things to say on how to find a new outlook. Indeed, Huxley has a more than passing interest for any study of mountaineering consciousness. He was deeply interested in how to raise man's awareness of life, and this is perhaps the central concern of mountaineering. In his utopian novel *Island* Huxley used rock-climbing as a tool for raising the awareness of the young. He wrote extensively on the visionary experience, and in Heaven and Hell talked of taking consciousness to those "antipodes" of the mind of which we are normally unaware by invoking the power of static, as opposed to dynamic, objects.

The sculptured figures of Egyptian Gods and god-kings, the Madonnas and Pantocrators of the Byzantine mosaics, the Bodhisattvas and Lohans of China, the seated Buddhas of Kymer, the steles and statues of

Copan, the wooden idols of tropical Africa—these have one characteristic in common: a profound stillness. And it is precisely this which gives them their experience, far away, towards the visionary antipodes of the human psyche.

Mountains have that stillness. They encourage visionary thought and attract anyone looking for a sense of unchanging values:

To whom the mountain stillness is a song
More sweet and strong
Than all by human art and rapture poured From voice or chord
An ecstasy that thrills and fires the blood,
Half understood. . . .

But such states of mind are very fragile, and easily destroyed by the incursions of man. In discussing landscape painting, Huxley holds that though the inclusion of the human dimension may make a scene classically beautiful, it will certainly prevent its being visionary. To Huxley, visionary landscape can never mean "the middle distance;" it can only mean the distant view or the close-up. The reason is that only these exorcize human involvement, leaving an emptiness and silence in which the mind can breathe and be transported towards its antipodes. The panoramic view can be visionary; so can the close-up, one's face pressed against a cliff, and Mummery realized this clearly a hundred years ago. But if the panorama includes a thousand fell-walkers, or the cliff cannot be seen for climbers clambering over the rocks like so many chameleons (to rephrase Patey), those visionary qualities will be lost.

In mountains, less often on a roadside crag, the sheer power of the forces of nature are displayed to shame us into a little humility. Nowhere, not even on the sea, are their scale and uncaring nature seen to better effect. In the avalanche and the rock scar and the grinding of huge boulders along glacial torrents we gain a sense of change, but change which proceeds on its own time scale, inexorably, and oblivious to man and all his works. The mountain village, perched beneath a crag or in the alluvial fan where two rivers meet, seems to be there as a temporary favor. Surviving on a long lease, it will be uprooted in the end.

And in a mountain storm we know we are powerless. We are presented with forces beyond any sense of human powers and the result is both an exhilaration and a tremendous relief. It is a relief to realize there are forces greater than ourselves, and every mountaineer has taken pleasure in the battering rain, the wind howling, and the snow piling ever deeper against the door. If one feels safe one even takes pleasure in being out in such weather, in feeling its force and observing its magnificence. Most of us feel better for rubbing faces with nature in the raw, partly because it is all good exercise, more fundamentally because it takes us out of ourselves. Compare this with "normal" life, in which nothing demonstrates our separation from nature more graphically than our inability to accept its tantrums. We think weather patterns are there just for our benefit, and are absurdly affronted when trains grind to a halt and cars get stuck in snowdrifts.

Many of these ideas can be summed up in the concept of "natural piety." Natural piety is the core characteristic of the primitive mentality, and quite rightly has a religious connotation, for nature is indeed sacred. It is infinitely more powerful than we are, and beyond our comprehension. In some sense it is to be worshiped, propitiated, looked up to. And one is bound to wonder whether the religious life of mountain peoples is ever really the result of dogma, and not always an intuitive reaction to the natural world. Mountain peoples are in general remarkably stoical, and this characteristic is reflected in their religions. God will provide, Allah is all-powerful; such sentiments are ideally suited to people living in mountains. The concept of deity who is all-powerful and who always knows what is for the best reflects perfectly the attitude they have to adopt, whether they like it or not.

But whilst for primitive peoples natural piety is both real and convincing, for us it can be only a feeling. Primitives are animists and see nature personified in Gods who have a more or less human character and need to be kept sweet. The trouble for us is that we cannot accept such ideas unless we keep them vague; they are altogether too fantastic. We have to avoid an overtly religious interpretation, and the result is that there are many people today who welcome the feeling of natural piety and are attracted to mountains because of it, but who nevertheless regard themselves as atheists.

Natural piety is a kind of cosmic ecology. Ecology is the science which stresses the interdependence of all living things and teaches that if you tamper with nature the effects will ripple through the system and be more far-reaching than you expect. Ecology as we know it is hardheaded science, but its principles and emotional content can clearly be extended so that it includes not only living things but all objects in the world, so that the interdependence is not only physical but spiritual. Byron expresses it when he writes:

I live not in myself, but I become

Phil Bartlett

portion of that around me; and to me.
high mountains are a feeling. but the hum
of human cities torture; I can see
nothing to loathe in nature, save to be
a link reluctant in a fleshly chain,
class'd among creatures, when the soul can flee
and with the sky, the peak, the heaving plain
of ocean, or the stars, mingle, and not in vain.

We all of us have had our "moments," and surely many of them have been just this: a sudden realization of being a part of a whole. At such times the present moment is heightened yet we feel simultaneously bound up with the past. Ritual helps that, so ritual is central to anything felt to have a spiritual component, including mountaineering. The finding of a camp, more likely than not in a place where others have camped before you, all the elements of domesticity and the making of a meal which at home seem such a chore, ensuring one is as comfortable as possible, then lying out in a sleeping bag and watching the stars and a vast silence—that familiar routine can take on a deep joy.

But as with visionary landscape, to be successful it requires the avoidance of other people and the facilities man-in-the-mass invariably demands. There is nothing spiritually uplifting about approaching a modern alpine hut for example, though such places have other advantages. There is, on the other hand, something uplifting, something ritual, about an old camping ground deep in Himalayan country, about making oneself at home in old sheep pens and collecting water from a stream where men have done the same for centuries.

Is this sentimental? Surely not; the sense of "rightness regained" is genuine and deeply felt. It would be sentimental to expect primitive peoples to keep living like that just to please us, but there is nothing sentimental about returning to do it ourselves on a temporary basis. To admit to having lost something is not to deny our other advantages, and what we have lost is". . . an absolute authenticity of environment, a sense of the past in the present, a complete identification between people and place. . . . It is the mode of living central to all the classic mountain explorers, who tell us that wild country is an inspiration in a way that nothing else is because it encourages a sense of harmony between the environment and the individual, the feeling that one is but a part of something greater. It is this which brings those moments of sheer delight, and it is unspoilt country rather than technical climbing which is the key to it. "I now felt myself to be on terms of intimacy with this wild region which, to my mind, is the highest reward of any mountaineering venture," the lasting reward of such activities, whatever the pure excitement at the time.

It is also the reward of mountain walking. Natural piety is the philosophical idea which comes over most strongly in modern writings by walkers and backpackers, where it is made perfectly clear that natural piety is more complex than a simple appreciation of nice views, and that its roots go deeper than aesthetics. Two hundred years ago Wordsworth was saying much the same thing.

One of the things we have to do when we walk or climb is be rhythmic. The rhythms cannot be chosen by us but must be attuned to the environment and one feels, however irrationally, that there is a connection between rhythmic grace and the primitive mentality. The beauty in movement of primitive peoples, whether it be the dance of tribesmen in Africa or a Hindu woman walking, walking, across the dust of India, stands in stark contrast to the bustle of any modern city. We are put to shame by our gracelessness.

The world's children, young or old, run up hills with excitement and flop down exhausted after a couple of hundred yards, but those with experience of the hills let the terrain dictate the pace and in so doing demonstrate an involuntary respect for the land. One does it to avoid wasting energy, but it them emerges that there are other, unexpected, rewards. Efficient movement over the land, neither too fast nor too slow, promotes a sense of peace and makes one feel closer to the natural world. This is quite unconscious, but it does develop an unmistakable sense of "rightness." And I suspect that many of the nostalgic feelings for the past which are there in every generation of mountain writing are in fact sincere attempts to explain this deep feeling, attempts which have simply gone wrong. All that comes over is a sense of bitterness and dislike of progress, when what was intended was a plea for the importance of rhythm. That such attempts do go wrong is not surprising. Rhythm must attune itself to the land and by its very nature it avoids the most extreme situations. On its own, therefore, it rarely accomplishes anything new, and is in constant danger of deteriorating into the boring and the mediocre. The backwoodsmen's appeals to "the old days" are almost inevitable uninspiring; we are more inclined to remember desperate struggles on climbs at the absolute limits of our ability, occasions when there may not have been much rhythm evident but at least we achieved something.

Phil Bartlett

The difference is reflected in our aesthetic reactions. Someone struggling and about to fall off is very exciting to watch—exciting rather than aesthetically pleasurable. We are given a sense of fighting nature, of conquering it. Movement over the land which is neither too fast not too slow on the other hand, or graceful and controlled movement up a difficult rock face—these things are a pleasure to watch, but they are not exciting.

There is a peculiar feeling of well-being to be gained from rhythmic, economical movements. It is a sensation open to anyone who enjoys watching their feet moving neatly, and many mountaineers have felt they would continue to climb "even if there was no view and no technical difficulty, nothing except the simple movement upwards." It is a satisfaction which can be found in all forms of mountaineering, though solo rock-climbing, in which the climber carries with him nothing but his own body, it perhaps the closest of all to a pure celebration of human physique and the exhilaration of muscle and co-ordination used to the full. At no time has this been truer than today when the aesthetic element in rock climbing is reflected in color co-ordinated clothing and full-blown narcissism.

Not that the "rules" of aesthetic style need to be constant. Not so long ago the received wisdon in rock-climbing was that one's weight should be on the feet not the arms, with three points of contact with the rock at all times. That was the static or "old school" style of climbing. perhaps best summed up in the principle that one should be capable of climbing down anything one has climbed up. I was first taken climbing at the age of eight or nine by one of the few full-time professionals of the old school, Jim Cameron. Jim lived in the Lake District and carried on working with his regular clients until well into his 70s. I had a few days climbing with him every summer for a number of years, and every year the question on my mind was the same: would we at last forsake the boring old routes on Shepherd's Crag we had done a hundred times, and at last go somewhere exciting? We never did; and perhaps it was a good thing. Jim's equipment was rudimentary and he still used shoulder belays. Neither his equipment nor his philosophy encouraged one to discover one's limits.

My unsatisfied longing to see into new worlds led to great frustration. But there were compensations. Jim knew all the routes he used like the back of his hand and what I remember about climbing, apart from his obvious love of it, is rhythm. Everything was in control, everything was pleasing to see. He never grabbed but moved smoothly, his nailed boots balanced on minute holds he had used a thousand times.

Progress has put the static style in the museum. Strong arms are indispensable to today's hard climbs; no-one would expect you to climb down, and even to climb up an element of premeditated "un-control" may necessary. But none of this has altered the importance of rhythm, and today's experts are every bit as aesthetically pleasing as their predecessors.

But rhythm is more than an aesthetic titillation, or simply the best way to improve your climbing standard, and what makes it so is its mental effects. Mountaineers have found that physical harmony (of rhythmic movement) has a knock-on effect in promoting a mental harmony (of natural piety). There is no need to "do" anything, least of all thing anything; just be rhythmic, and a new perspective develops of its own accord. It is in many ways a more comforting perspective than we are used to, and it explains why increasing numbers of people are forsaking the Sunday papers and going out for a walk in the hills instead.

These ideas crop up continually in Winthrop Young's writings. For Young, climbing is "the supreme opportunity for perfect motion," and the knock-on mental effect is never in doubt.

"A striking figure with the appearance and culture sophistication of the highly cultivated late Victorian intellectual," Geoffrey Winthrop Young was both the shaping personality of rock-climbing in North Wales at the beginning of the century and a superb Alpinist. A polymathic figure, he avoided falling into the trap which now lessens the standing of so many other once-prestigious climbers: blind conservatism. He accepted change, and he sympathized with youth's ambitions. Perhaps it was the unusual breadth of his experience which enabled him to do this. He was proposed for membership of the Alpine Club by Sir Alfred Wills himself, yet he knew Joe Brown, the most important figure in post-war British rock-climbing.

In the years leading up to 1914 Young was pushing forward the technical standards of Alpine climbing much as Mummery had done a couple of decades earlier. The ascent of the South Face of the Taschhorn in Switzerland by Young, V.J.E. Ryan and the guides Franz and Joseph Lochmatter and Joseph Knubel (Franz Lochmatter was later to accompany the Vissers to the Karakoram), was an astonishing performance; the hardest alpine rock-climb of its time and still one of the most serious of its kind.

The way Young scrambled and heaved, using every trick he could think of to get up the thing, including his teeth, while Lochmatters pulled on the rope for all they were worth and all five of them wondered whether they would ever escape. "Our chances are about one in five," announced Young, after some consideration—all this has helped to produce a classic adventure story out of what was certainly the era's major feat.

On the outbreak of war Young served at Ypres as a non-combatant and then in northern Italy. In 1917 he was seriously wounded and subsequently lost his left leg, a particularly cruel fate for someone whose delight in life was based so deeply on masterly physical movement. It altered the mountaineering game fundamentally for him, but perhaps because of that produced his most important writing.

Young was to return to the Alps after the war with the same outlook and the same ambitions he had always had: to celebrate his physical prowess and so gain a feeling of exhilaration, a "delight of rhythm that may reach almost to ecstasy . . . ." For the first few years he refused to believe he could not recapture it, even though the result was full of frustration, by contrast with what had gone before, a nightmare. But finally he was forced to admit that the old prowess was no longer there, and that the comparison of the present with the pre-war years was too painful:

"This was not the least like the sort of luxurious, rapturous transfiguration, with the rhythm of movement still tingling in the muscles and the song of life humming through the silence in one's ears, which had surrounded such high moments in the past."

What was wrong? The trouble was that he was no longer "in tune" with the mountains. There is in them a rhythm and a wholeness, and to be truly satisfying one's mountaineering, whether easy or difficult, walking or climbing, has to produce a rhythm of its own which reflects that. Looked at in this light the root of the problem is obvious: difficult climbing with one leg was an utterly unnatural and unrhythmic thing to do, so far from bringing one into a closer mental contact with the natural world it merely underlined one's separateness. It was mountaineering undertaken purely as a challenge, to prove one could do it, and this could never again deliver the real delight of the game. The key to happiness now was above all things to feel that one was "obeying laws of movement and of living inspiration which have correspondence with the same principles on a deeper plane of existence." In fact Young was to claim that had been the real root of it even when he was at the forefront of difficult

climbing. A new route, achievement; these had been secondary even then
to a sense of harmony. And harmony would always imply matching one's
ambitions to one's abilities:

> It was made clear to me that neither in the mountain nor in myself
> had the virtue of my mountaineering lain; but only in the relation-
> ship which could be created, and constantly renewed between us;
> and that this, on my side, depended upon the technique of climb-
> ing. . . I had lost the secure technique which greater Alpine moun-
> taineering demanded, and I had become dependent upon sheer
> effort, and the technique of others. Further, owing to the excessive
> call I had to make upon physique alone, I could no longer bring
> the wholeness of myself, observation, thought, apperception, into
> natural contact with the completeness and complications of great
> mountains. The right balanced relationship therefore never came
> into being between us at all; and the confident joy that belonged
> only to the right relationship could never follow.

There could be only one conclusion: he must learn to be content with
less demanding mountaineering. But once he saw that, and accepted that
is was not what one achieved that mattered but the matching of ambition and ability, he had solved the problem. No amount of determination could make up for the mismatch and make hard climbing pleasurable again, but by to fell-walking, which is what he did for the rest of
his life, he re-established harmony and his pleasure was as great as ever.
"We discover that there are degrees of mountaineering difficulty which
can be associated productively with every stage of our altering energy:
That the gentler approach of later years can be every bit as fine as the one
glorious hour of youth is wisdom." But without the sort of crisis Young
experienced, it is a wisdom which is easy to ignore.

Mountains teach us to accept natural rhythms rather than fight
against them. Such rhythms are amongst the "fundamental realities" of
which Maraini spoke; they are elements of natural law. In wild country
we are aware of the season: mountain rivers in spate in the spring as glaciers melt; the race against time to grow crops in high mountain valleys
before the onset of winter; above all the harsh contrast between summer
sun and winter's cold. And it seems to be only in wild country and among
primitive peoples that we can accept the cycle of birth and death. Primitive life encourages an attitude to the individual's death more stoical and

accepting than our own, because the natural world has impressed on the primitive something from which modern man is divorced; the primacy of the rhythmic process, not only inevitable but "right."

There is more to mountaineering than this of course, because mountaineering is also expansionism, and expansionism by its very nature is trying to transcend our individual mortality, to transcend our personal unimportance. When someone dies in the mountains one would have to be very cold-hearted to feel it was "right." Inevitably, one wonders about potential that will never be realized, achievements and pleasures that can never now come to fruition. Yet there is a sense in which one accepts more readily because of the environment, because of return to the primitive. Most mountaineers, I think, would rather see a close friend, or even themselves, killed in the mountains than in a car crash, even though the result is exactly the same.

The nomadic life-style has a part to play in this too. One thinks of Conway, walking through the Alps from end to end and arguing passionately that the true pleasure of mountaineering is to be an eccentrics. (Not an "eccentric" but an ex-centrist, someone who doesn't stay in one center but travels around.) Crag-climbers are not nomads, but explorers are, and so are backpackers and Himalayan trekkers.

Are human beings nomadic animals? It is possible to see the nomadic urge not only as proof of our wish to expand, but equally as a way in which we can forget for a while our individual mortality and the hopelessness of trying to escape from it. In any event, temporary nomadism is endlessly attractive. Longstaff explained why:

Since happiness is most often met by those who have learned to live in every moment of the present, none has such prodigal opportunities of attaining that art as the traveler. Every day as he moves or halts there is something new to enjoy. At every evening's camp is the charm of taking possession of some new home. Attainment of a set objective is but a secondary matter; the traveler should not anticipate the journey's end. So long as he loses consciousness of self and is aware in all his sense of the present scene, almost any part of the world is as good as another. Mountain or desert, it is all one. We shall have realized ourselves as being a tiny portion of the universe; not lords of it.

This sums up certain aspects of the mountaineer's return to the primitive and reminds us that whilst it is very different to the expansion into new worlds with which I began this book, it is not simply the reverse of it. If one of the rewards of expansionism is a heightened sense of existing. of being alive, of being important, the same is true of return to the primitive. Once again, the effect of raw nature, more powerful and magnificent thatn humanity in every way, is not to deny us a feeling of significance but to confirm it.

The difference between the two is not so much to do with whether humanity is important but whether the individual is important. Expansion gives us a sense of self as individuals; it is ego-confirming. The power of a return to the primitive is also to give a sense of self, but without a belief in individual importance. Life in general. yes; me in particular, no. The search for a personal uniqueness is always a struggle, and when we speak of going to the hills to find peace, to escape the rat-race, to work off frustrations and get away, what we are trying to get away from is the pressure to be recognized—in short, to be significant as isolated individuals. The mountains comfort us, because under their influence we realize that it doesn't matter. "Life," in some generalized sense, will carry on. The individual life will not. And in natural piety one's sense of place in the universe is not in spite of the fact but is founded on it.

Phil Bartlett

Galen Rowell (1940—2002), American mountaineer, author, and photographer, participated in over a thousand climbs throughout the world, including Yosemite, Alaska, and ten Himalayan expeditions. He, along with Dennis Hennek and Doug Robinson, made the first "clean" ascent of Half Dome in 1973. He is author of numerous books including *The Vertical World of Yosemite*, *In the Throne Room of the Gods, and Mountains of the Middle Kingdom*. Galen died along with his wife Barbara in a plane crash near his home in Bishop, California.

GALEN ROWELL:
STORMING A MYTH

Just after Thanksgiving in 1958, a party of three climbers reached the base of the summit overhangs on Yosemite's El Capitan. Only a hundred feet above them a celebration was beginning. El Capitan was about to be climbed by its 3,000 foot south face for the first time. An assorted group of friends, lovers, media people, and ambulance chasers had hiked up the trail on the back side of El Capitan to greet their heroes. A feast of food and wine lay waiting, but long hours passed without the arrival of the honored guests. Someone grew impatient and threw a rope down over the edge. "Here, Warren, just prusik up this rope and we'll get on with the party."

Warren Harding was drilling. He ignored the rope. He wasn't about to take the easy way out after spending eleven straight days climbing under his own power. The summit overhangs were massive and nearly flawless. He saw no continuous cracks in which to place pitons, so he was drilling by hand with star drill and hammer straight toward the voices overhead. Under ideal conditions he could drill an inch-deep hole in fifteen minutes. Hanging in slings from the overhang, it was now taking forty minutes per hole. On a tiny ledge below were his companions, Wayne Merry and George Whitmore, belaying his safety rope and waiting patiently for the ordeal to end.

Darkness fell and Warren continued to drill. When a hole was completed he would insert an expansion bolt, attach a sling to it, move five more feet, and renew drilling above. The night was marked by the passage of bolts. Five bolts. . . ten. . . fifteen. . . twenty . . . . Dawn came and the super-marathon of drilling was not yet over. At 8 a.m., seventeen hours after he began, Warren Harding crawled onto the summit from a sling attached to his twenty-eighth bolt. "It was not at all clear to me," he later said, "who was the conqueror and who was the conquered: I do recall that El Cap seemed to be in much better condition that I was."

In the twenty years since that historic climb, many climbers have criticized the final bolt ladder on El Capitan's Nose. They say it makes the climb easy. Novices can clip their way up Harding's bolts instead of working with the rock to follow natural weaknesses off to the side; that is, novices who have climbed thirty-three pitches of vertical rock to get into position to clip up the bolts. And they also say that, if they were presented with the obstacle of the summit overhangs, they would find a way up without using bolts; and they would, because big wall climbing has gone a long way since 1958.

I began climbing at just about the time the El Capitan ascent was made. Given twenty years of experience, I know I could bypass the bolt ladder now. But I remember a time when I couldn't; a time when that very "easy" bolt ladder was the most difficult obstacle I ever encountered. Climbing it in 1966 on the fifth ascent of the Nose provided the most dangerous moments I have experienced on any route on any continent.

Climbing big walls was serious business in 1966. On the way to the base of the climb I didn't look up. I was too scared. Several times before, I'd walked in the predawn darkness with big-name climbers who looked up for a few moments too long. They lost their nerve, and made up an excuse to retreat. A telltale cloud, a runny nose, a worn haul bag, a missing piton, things that wouldn't give a moment's hesitation to the wall climbers of the seventies who have broken so far through the fear threshold—they aren't even aware—it once existed. In 1966 we had no helicopters buzzing in the back of our consciousness; if we were in trouble, we were on our own.

Something more subtle entered into our fear of big walls. We tended to intellectualize and philosophize climbing. We never called it a sport, it was an art, or better yet, a "Way of Life." We walked around assuming we were involved in something special. Debates about rating systems were far more serious to us than events in Vietnam. One climber backed off a half day climb six times. When he finally made it, he wrote home, "I have mastered the realm of the Yosemite Grade IV."

"These guys can't even write third-grade English," Jim McCarthy recently told me, "yet they can climb things we never imagined were possible." McCarthy was the outstanding East Coast rock climber of the sixties and every bit as much an intellectual snob as we Yosemitephiles. He was referring to the top rock climbers of today, who aren't afraid to call climbing a sport, to train for it like football, or to use sheer guts and will rather than reasoning and logic to overcome what we pigeonholed by language as "impossible," whether we intended to or not.

Talking with McCarthy, it suddenly dawned on me why we had been so scared in the sixties: we believed the written word. When we read Royal Robbins's account of two long leader falls above horrible protection on the Arches Direct, we vowed never to climb that route, or any that remotely resembled it.

I now realize that the prime movers of yesterday were really the anti-intellectuals. It is no coincidence that, amidst a great reservoir of technically skilled Yosemite climbers, a hard-hat construction worker named Warren Harding made the first ascent of the face of El Capitan. Nor was it coincidence that my presence on El Capitan in 1966 was due to the push of a Colorado bricklayer, Layton Kor.

In the winter of 1965, the immense Kor made his annual pilgrimage to Yosemite with a scrawny six-four teenager named Tom Fender. Like his mentor, Tom laid bricks, drank beer, and climbed with incredible energy. One evening Tom and I were talking about the dreaded west face of Leaning Tower, a climb involving a severely overhanging 1,100-foot cliff that had been repeated only a couple of times by preeminent valley climbers. The first ascent party had ominously written that, since a normal retreat was impossible, future climbers should carefully consider the problems before committing themselves. Layton listened intently for a few minutes, stared at us, and said, "Bullshit. You guys can climb the Tower right now, no sweat, and when you get done with that you'll be ready for El Cap."

Tom and I made the first "podunk" ascent of the Tower a few days later. We found it strenuous, but well within our limits. Once we proved that normal non-supermen could climb the Tower, there was a line-up for the rest of the season. Even with our success on the Tower behind us, we were intimidated by the idea of mere mortals venturing onto the hallowed ground of El Capitan. Early in 1966 we started out with a three-man party. A hundred feet above the ground, our third man's nerves turned to jelly and we lowered him, babbling, to the ground. A week later we came back in the early morning and snuck onto the face before the harsh light of day could strike fear into our hearts. To our surprise the climbing went well, and after two days we were nearly halfway up the wall.

We were climbing in perfect March weather. There had been no precipitation for forty-five days. Yosemite wall-climbing weather was legendary. One of the head gurus, Yvon Chouinard, had written, "Bad weather in California means hot weather. . . the threat of stormy weather is not serious." Naturally we didn't take it seriously when rain began to fall as I nailed my way past the infamous Great Roof in the afternoon the rain changed to snow. We were enshrouded in a quiet mist of flakes. We thought about descending, but considered the seven pendulum traverses that we had made as probably irreversible, especially in bad weather.

Throughout the afternoon, our world changed. It tilted on edge when the vertical fall of the snow became increasingly horizontal in a growing wind. The coming of darkness was disguised, and quite suddenly we couldn't see to climb. We drove pitons into cracks and strung out hammocks for the long wait. I didn't sleep a wink; my hammock filled with snow that melted from my body heat and soaked me to the skin.

At first brush of light we were off and climbing. Snow pelted our faces and numbed our hands. The climbing itself was easy, so easy that I marveled at how simple big wall climbing really was. We were in a single crack system aiming for the summit. We moved, not like acrobats or athletes, but with the jerky, repetitive motions of common laborers. I would bang in a piton, hang a sling from it, step up a few feet, and bang in another. When I reached the end of the rope, I would tie it to several anchors and sit in a nylon seat waiting for Tom to jumar his way up. Then Tom would play sky carpenter for the next hundred and fifty feet while I tried to renew feeling in my hands. Throughout the day we alternated leads, each time eager for the switch, the leader always wanting to thaw cold fingers, the belayer always seeking movement to warm his chilled body core. Both of us reverted to minutes of involuntary shivering after stopping each lead. Had we been winter climbing in the Sierra or Canada, we would have come equipped with tentage, waterproof outer garments, and a stove to make warm drinks. But we had nothing except the sloshing clothing on our bodies and the wet down sleeping bags offering less loft than cardboard.

Galen Rowell

A hundred feet from the summit our crack system ended. We stopped and contemplated the summit overhangs from the same point that Warren Harding had eight years before. I breathed a sigh of relief. We had been moving for thirteen hours with the power of desperation. Now all that separated us from the top was an easy bolt ladder, a matter of clipping into existing anchor points.

Somewhere behind the clouds, the sun sank below the horizon and the temperature dropped rapidly. Our ropes, soaked from water running down the face, began to change from the consistency of spaghetti to that of steel cable. I started up the bolts attaching two carabineers to every other bolt for the safety rope, hoping to cut down some of the rope drag I would encounter when clipping into each point. Nevertheless, the rope drag became increasingly strong, the rope was freezing into position as it ran through each anchor, and it took all my strength to pull through a new hank so that I could move on. Finally, it wouldn't budge. Time was running out and darkness was near. Tom, shivering wildly, was urging me to move faster.

We had two ropes. One was now frozen into the anchors, while the other ran freely from my waist to a haul bag that hung from a piton next to Tom. In desperation I told Tom to tie all the extra equipment to the haul bag and to cut it loose. I then pulled the bag up hand-over-hand and hung it from my waist. Breaking every rule of climbing, I untied from the belay rope, tied one end of the haul rope to it and the other to my waist. Now I had a static belay with one hundred and fifty feet of slack. But I could move. Even with the ungainly weight of the bag tugging at my midriff, I was able to go much faster than before. Minutes later I stood on the last expansion bolt in the highest loop of my sling and my hands touched the top of El Capitain.

I had a rude awakening. Instead of being home free, I was hanging from the lip of an overhang with my hands in two feet of fresh snow that covered steeply inclined slabs. In summer I could have stepped onto the slabs and walked off; to try that now would have been fatal.

I was at the top of El Capitan, a life's goal, yet no friends greeted me, and no one was celebrating. I was in more danger than ever before in my life. A slip would mean a fall of over two hundred feet, very probably a broken rope, and another three-thousand-foot fall to the ground. The one bolt I was on was certainly not a place to belay, and I couldn't see any place above me to anchor. Digging through the snow, I discovered a shallow crack in which I placed just the tip of a small piton. Tying it off,

I attached a sling and moved up another two feet, feeling even less secure. Digging away more snow, I found that the crack continued, and for the next hour I nailed my way up a thirty-degree slab. Finally I was able to stand up. I walked toward a tree, but was caught short by the rope. Even by untying my slings, runners, and belt, I couldn't have gotten enough cord to tie to the tree. Then I saw the sapling.

A tiny Jeffrey pine stuck out of a crack within reach. It was three feet high and an inch in diameter above its lumpy, gnarled base. I could bend it to the ground quite easily with one hand.

A minute later I yelled, "Okay, Tom, you can come up now." For a long while I listened only to the whistle of the wind. The rope ran tautly downward through a groove in the snow. Untied from it, I was lying on a narrow ledge clutching the sapling just above its base so it wouldn't bend.

I heard Tom begin to moan and groan. "I can't do it. My jumars are slipping," he yelled. Then again all I heard was the wind.

I'm not sure how long I lay on the ledge holding the tiny tree with hands that could no longer feel. It may only have been minutes, but it seemed like hours. The teeth inside Tom's jumars were clogged with ice, and the gadgets would not work even after he laboriously tried to clean them. I was convinced that he would never make it. Even a short fall would probably jerk out the sapling and send him flying down the wall. I couldn't wait out the night where I was, and Tom's situation was far more desperate. I had the bivouac gear, food, and water, His only hope was up.

For five days my world had been three thousand feet of granite. At the end of each lead I had calculated how far I had to go. Here I was at the end of that world, yet in the middle of a fight for both our lives. The storm had worsened and visibility was only a few feet. The wind twisting over the summit created a ground blizzard. I wondered what I would do even if I abandoned Tom. Could I survive a night here? Could I walk seven miles through deep snow in the dark to civilization?

Suddenly the sapling began to bend. I held it more tightly and watched the rope quiver. A shadow appeared on the horizon. Tom was at the very lip of the overhang with his full weight on the rope. He had clipped up the bolt ladder without a safety rope, and now, at the end of the bolts, he had grabbed the rope with his remaining strength to pull his way up the final slab. I concentrated on holding the sapling until Tom's eyes met mine. He looked back and forth from me to the pitiful anchor point, but he didn't say a word.

We talked only about the future—what we would take with us and where we would head. El Capitan does not have a classic small summit. The top is a peninsula of granite jutting out a full quarter mile from the rim of Yosemite Valley. We left all our gear except clothing and packs, then walked in a straight line away from the cliff. Each step was a struggle against the elements. We were in the same realm as a powder skier, but without skis, in darkness, totally fatigued, and moving uphill. The elements were all one to us. The clouds, the air, and the ground were all composed of varying amounts of snow. We pushed forward until the mist strangely darkened and the wind hit us more from below than from the side.

Tom was leading the way. Suddenly he turned and grabbed me, shouting, "Jesus Christ! We're walking off the edge of the West Buttress!" Adrenalin shot through me as it never had during the climb. A roped fall is something a climber can deal with in his head, but not an unexpected plunge into darkness.

We once again aimed for the rim of the valley and pushed through the snow. Minutes later the darkness and change in wind came anew. We were now near the edge of the north American Wall. We tried again and again, sometimes finding our own tracks, but we were unable to keep a straight path in the darkness and the storm.

I collapsed in the snow, too tired to walk any farther. We gave up and tried to survive the night, lying inside haul sacks, bundled into sleeping bags that had turned into thin sheets of nylon occasioned by lumps of wet down. I'd never been so cold.

With morning came a brief window in the clouds. It began to snow again, but we were able to chart our course to the valley rim. From there we found it relatively easy to parallel the edge, although it was quite impossible to locate the summer trail. We wallowed through endless fields of manzanita, a masochist's delight were it not for the fact that we could no longer feel our skin being torn by the hard sharp brush. I thought about how smugly I had sat in living rooms of non-climbers telling them that climbing was some kind of ultimate chess game played with mind and body. Pro football was more erudite than our descent from El Capitan.

I also had my first inkling of something that is now common knowledge to all experienced rock climbers—big-wall climbing is a dead-end gambit. Climbing the longest and steepest walls is not the essential fulfillment of the sport. I had just completed the goal of many climbers, yet the climbing itself was remarkably unchallenging. After a day on the wall, the routine became almost easy. Any reasonably fit person could learn enough to do El Cap after a few months of practice. Our greatest difficulties lay beyond the start of the bolt ladder that was supposed to have made the finish too easy. The very idea of wall climbing imparts a purpose to the activity that isn't really there: to get to the top by overcoming specific obstacles of steepness and distance.

Setting up situations where climbing offers rational rewards is simply an intellectual pose. Now, twelve years since my El Cap adventure, it is obvious that elevation, steepness, and distance have been conquered on most of the world's major mountains, from Yosemite to the Himalayas. What is left is style: the disciplining of a natural human act into a satisfying precise ability. The expression of that ability is not necessarily rational. The purpose of climbing is no more than the conquest of summits than the purpose of a mountain stream is the eventual production of electricity, although calculating minds might belabor both points.

At the end of my El Cap climb I staggered into a waiting line of high-heeled women and sport-coated men at the registration desk of Yosemite Lodge. Leaves, blood, and rags covered my body. Muddy water ran onto the clean floor. I checked in to a room with one hand while I held my pants up with the other, I didn't know it yet, but I'd lost twenty-five pounds.

Tom spent the next few days sacked out on the seat of his aging truck. Then he headed for Colorado, worked construction, and began to raise a family, he stopped climbing walls.

My vacation was over. I returned to my automotive business in the city. I might never have climbed a big wall again, except for an invitation from Layton Kor the following spring to do another route on El Capitan. On that climb he shared with me his many doubts about what he was doing, year after year, climbing one wall after another. Our climb together was his last major effort. He surprised everyone with a sudden conversion to the Jehovah's Witnesses. I soon changed careers and became a full-time journalist, but I never wrote about either of my early El Capitan ascents. They were too far outside the confines of what climbing was supposed to be about. The first provided suffering; the second, relaxed joy. In neither case was the overall feeling related to the technical nature of the ascent.

Galen Rowell

Now I know that climbing is merely a vehicle, a tool, and the climber a tool user. As a tool, climbing can be used to overcome 5.12 cracks, the difficulties of a Grade VI wall, or an 8,000-meter peak. But held only to this narrow definition, it can eventually bring boredom and despair.

The climbing tool has a spiritual component as well. At the heart of the climbing experience is a constant state of optimistic expectation, and when that state is absent, there is no reason to continue climbing. "I have found it!" can apply not only to those who feel they have found God, but to those, like me who continue to find Shangri-las where we experience fresh, childlike joy in everything that surrounds us, including memories that are the most long-lasting and intense of our lives. It was in this spirit that I first ventured onto Yosemite's walls.

Doug Scott (b.1941) is clearly one of the leading mountaineers of the twentieth century. He is completely at home on big walls, hard-water ice, or giant mountain faces requiring mixed skills. He teamed with Dougal Haston on Bonington's 1975 Southwest Face of Everest expedition. He is the first Englishman to stand on top of the world. He has reached the summit of dozens of peaks the world over, and with the exception of Everest, nearly all his climbs have been lightweight and oxygen-less. To many he is the consummate mountaineer. He was awarded a CBE (Commander of the British Empire) for his contributions to mountaineering and exploration and is a past president of the Alpine Club. His books include *Big Wall Climbing, Himalayan Climber,* and *The Shishapangma Expedition with Alex MacIntyre.*

DOUG SCOTT:
ON THE PROFUNDITY TRAIL

The rock-shod ice swept away the forest and soils and gouged out the bed-rock for hundreds of feet. Ten thousand years ago the ice retreated and the ancient Merced River valley emerged, dramatically straightened out and over-deepened. The river no longer flowed gently through forested hills, but instead wandered down the flat floor of a vast canyon Yosemite Valley.

The longest, and in some ways the most demanding route out of this valley is by way of the Salathe Wall of El Capitan. Climbers taking this route must ascent 3,000 feet of vertical granite to reach the undulating, forested hill country above. Through so doing, they will come to know better than most the true significance of John Muir's paradoxical name for this part of the "Sierra Nevada the gentle wilderness." And, as they too ponder a dramatically increased sensitivity in all their faculties, they will discover why it is that big-wall rock climbers are so sold on self-analysis.

This is not the easiest way of reaching new heights of self-awareness, but, as I shall try to show, the rewards are correspondingly greater. Our ascent of Salathe Wall was a case in point, although it did not have a very auspicious start.

Most of the acid heads, wrapped up in old blankets, were lying huddled in a heap around a burnt-out fire. A few more were reflecting by the Merced; smoking weed as the mist rose out of the river into the cold morning air.

Peter Habeler arrived, threading his way down the camp road between the jutting caravans and cars of the tourists who were now swelling the camp to capacity.

Peter was also on his first visit to Yosemite, and it was a fortuitous set of circumstances that brought us together. We had both served a rather hectic apprenticeship in the Valley. Peter had got involved, briefly, with Yvon Chouinard, while I had tried to follow Royal Robbins with limited success. On the lower crags, we had both led free climbs comparable in difficulty with the hard pitches of Salathe; and we had made competent ascents of the Leaning Tower, which involved 900 feet of pegging. In theory we could manage Salathe, providing we kept our heads at altitude.

"Come Doug, it is time to go," hissed Peter, trying not to wake the tourists or our climbing friends still asleep in their tents between the caravans and trees. It wasn't the first time he was to ask me to hurry!

I scrambled round, bundling gear into my day sack (I should have packed it the night before), and we left this corner of Camp 7, heading towards El Capitan, for we were going on the profundity trail via Salathe Wall. Not for us popping a pill or drinking spiked apple cider to get eight hours of un-imagined sensory splendor, but a hard, upward, four or five day slog.

We had none of the usual doubts that assail the mind when one is approaching a big climb. It wasn't that we had acclimatized ourselves to them it was simply that we had committed ourselves the day before by putting our 100 pound haul sack some 300 feet up the wall. This is one of the customs the Valley climbers have developed to cut back the odds to more manageable proportions; we were glad to adopt it.

No photograph I have seen really shows the characteristics of the solid, squat bulk of rock that is El Cap. It is monolithic from a distance, but on closer inspection the surface rock is far from uniform. On the contrary, it is highly featured: the granite has been sculptured into elegant buttresses and deep bays, which merge into the spreading slabs and walls that drop down to the forested screes and glacial drift below. When the light shines obliquely, casting shadows across the face, a closer scrutiny reveals long, vertical cracks, precariously perched flakes and splinters of rock, jutting overhangs, and wide expanses of unbroken rock rippled by glacier ice.

Our route included many of these features. It was not at first direct, but it was obviously a natural line and gave a variety of climbing at a continuously high standards.

We reached our "third man," as we called the sack, and took out another little helper in the shape of a topo map of the route. This ensures that climbers don't get lost and are not troubled by the unknown, for every pitch is graded and every feature marked, as is each pendulum and abseil, and the number of pegs needed. But to us, as we looked up from the third pitch, the topo was not at all encouraging; it showed only too clearly that we had thirty-four pitches to go and that reaching the top was a very remote possibility.

To overcome these problems we broke them down into four daily objectives, which loomed so large in our minds that they became like summits in themselves. For the first day we aimed to make Heart Ledge, and forgot about everything beyond.

The first day's work was not the best exercise in European collaboration. We were both humiliated into using sky hooks whilst leading the two 5.9 slab pitches. Neither of us had the slightest idea how the pioneers had stayed in place to put in the bolts which we so thankfully grabbed.

Peter made up for this by leading the huge shield of rock known as the "Half Dollar" in fine style. He couldn't pull the haul sack up and I cursed him as I climbed the narrow chimney pushing the sack in front of me. This procedure was repeated on another 5.9 jam crack above. Peter was in a rage at the restriction the sack was imposing on our progress. We hadn't hauled anything like that weight before and had not yet come to terms with it.

I slung the sack over my shoulder and walked along Mammoth Terrace to the abseil bushes, looking for all the world like a drunken sailor. We both descended to Heart Ledge and our first bivouac site.

It should have been a happy occasion, but I could only think bad thoughts about my partner, while he, no doubt, was wondering what he was doing up there with me! It was like this: he wouldn't stop moaning about the haul sack, about my hitting the pegs too hard, and then about my moving too slowly up the free climbing. All of which was true enough.

On the Profundity Trail

But I couldn't help laughing, he was such a smart little bugger, always pestering his blond hair down with the palms of his hands. Unknown to him, however, he was rubbing aluminum dye all over his face. In the end, he looked as though he'd spent the day down a coal mine. Then he was very fastidious. He would take boiled eggs out of a plastic container and slices of bread and butter from his snap tin. And then I found he had put salt into the flour gallons of water to stop us getting cramps. I nearly threw a fit at home when they put fluoride into the local reservoir and now we had to quench our thirst with salt water! No, we were not very happy—and if he'd been anyone other than a bloody Kraut, I'd have gone down. And if I had been anyone else but a patronizing Englishman I'm sure he would have gone down too. Nothing was said, mind, but that was half the trouble; we couldn't communicate emotionally.

The only generous and charitable thoughts that came to mind were for the first ascensionists—Tom Frost, Chuck Pratt and Royal Robbins. They first climbed up to Lung Ledge, just above Heart Ledge, and the descended, leaving ropes fixed. Returning a few days later, they removed their "life-line" and went for the top, over 2,000 feet higher, taking six days to negotiate the unknown and uncharted rock. It was a fantastic achievement, as we slowly realized over the next few days; it was also a considerable breakthrough in big wall climbing, paving the way for single-push first ascents.

Next morning, Peter was up and about bright and early. I cursed him (under my breath) for breaking into my fantasy world.

"To rest is not to conquer," I mumbled, sarcastically, and had some cheese and water before leading off from the ledge. I took ages on the first few feet, until Peter used some basic psychology to get me moving by offering to do it himself! That was all I needed to reach a pendulum and a surprise bolt at the end of it.

"Get a shot with my cameras," I shouted to Peter.

"Doug, we have not the time," he replied, quite truthfully.

"Get those bloody cameras working," I yelled, and, as an after-thought: "to rest is not to rust."

Well, that did at least clear the air, and we carried on in better style and better humor.

Actually, I think the reason for the improvement was that we now felt more or less committed to the climb. Up to Heart Ledge we had not had that feeling, but now, nagging doubts about continuing were removed. There was only one way out-up and over the top.

Doug Scott

We were both putting pegs in and ripping them out with an increased economy of effort. After Hollow Flakes the climb steepend, and sack hauling was less of a drag. Wide jam cracks and sinuous aid cracks followed one another. In between the stances were remarkably spacious. Peter led the Ear, a flared horror chimney which opens out at the bottom to disgorge the failure into space. Peter was no failure and his wiry figure went up and into it with ease, just as the sun left the face. Although it was early April and the sun had not been anything like as hot as it can be in July and August, being in the shade was as good as a cold drink.

There followed a 150 foot pitch where was A1 and 5.9, and I led it in half-an-hour-the only good thing I'd done all day. This burst of energy was prompted by the long shadows and the thought of not reaching El Cap Spire—our next "summit"—before dark.

Peter led the chimney behind the Spire in the dark, with the pegs jangling and the bongs booming behind the big black tower. An hour later I joined him, climbing up behind the sack and taking the few pegs out by the light of glowing granite chips that momentarily flared into life under my badly aimed hammer.

The bivouac on the flat topped "Spire" was magnificent. It had been eroded into minor undulations and we each found a hollow in which to sleep. But first we ate and drank in true communion, chatting about the route and our reactions to it—quite a change from the previous bivouac. Before, my irrational fears of the route had caused me to build up a shell of self-pity and, as a sort of defense mechanism, to castigate my companion. That also was irrational, for he was a first class climber and companion. A wave of contentment swept through my tired mind as I lay flat out, looking up at the clouds scudding across the night sky, and felt the blood oozing around my worn-out fingers.

That day we had climbed ten pitches of hard jamming and long, tedious pegging. Every peg had to be placed, and the sack hauled; then the second, using jumars, prussiked up behind, removing all the pegs and slings and racking them ready for the next pitch. Wear and tear on the hands could not be avoided, but we both climbed as carefully as time would allow, so as not to cut the flesh. A sharp burr of chrome-moly could easily open the fingers, making climbing an agony. As it was, granite crystal in the cracks chaffed the backs of our hands badly. But it was de-pegging that caused the most damage, because we soon found that it was quicker to take the pegs out under tension. That is, whenever it was convenient, the prussik rope was left attached to the peg which was being extracted. On overhanging walls and diagonal traverses, the sudden release of tension as the peg came out made for some exhilarating swings, but we had to look sharp so as not to catch our knuckles as we went.

Next morning we stepped across from the Spire, pegged up the wall above, and continued to peg for most of the day, from dawn to dusk.

Despite the intense concentration I gave each pitch, whilst placing pegs or removing them, I can barely remember features and details. Yet I do recall seemingly trivial thoughts and actions that occupied my mind and time at the belays.

On Broad Ledge, a frog leapt on to the scene. My surprise changed to wonder as I contemplated that little frog and its place on the vast monolith of El Cap. How many more were there, I wondered. Perhaps enough to fill a ten foot square box. Then he hopped away into the rock, so perfectly camouflaged that I couldn't spot him again. I felt really good up there because of that frog; he seemed to show that we were all in it together, not just the El Cap scene, but the whole business of being alive.

I looked around with a new intensity and watched a drop of water trickle down the dusty granite, a clear crystal that flashed a brilliant light and was gone, to be burnt up by the sun that had momentarily given it life. I traced its wet patch upwards to a crevice and considered its route down through the rock from the melting snow hundreds of feet above.

I felt completely relaxed, and my mind ranged over the problems that had been troubling me and saw them with a new clarity. I had found in Eric Shipton's book *Upon that Mountain* a very inspiring way of looking at mountaineering. One phrase stood out, he wrote that it was not the approach that mattered, but the climber's attitude of mind whilst actually climbing. And indeed it no longer seemed important that anything should come from this climb other than the sheer pleasure and satisfaction of having done it. I had been plagued with doubts about my approach to big wall climbing because I felt that I was doing it partly for the wrong reasons, such as making money and achieving fame whilst lecturing and writing about it afterwards. Well, they no longer had any bearing on the matter. It was not that I felt humbled by the vast sweep of rock, but that I had got so much out of the route already. I was thinking and feeling and experiencing all the elements of joy and peace to such a degree that tears welled up into my eyes.

"Doug! Let go the sack," yelled Peter. "I am ready for hauling." Tears of joy were soon replaced by tears of sweat as I hammered up another hundred feet, taking out Peter's pegs. In fact, they didn't need much hammering, as they were mostly tied off, with only the tips biting into the rock.

One pitch I do remember. Dirty and awkward, it was marked A3. It was also wet and deceptively 150 feet long. After using a variety of smaller blades and angles in awkward, blind cracks, I found a two to four inch fissure which went out under a block for 15 feet and then up another 25 feet to a ledge. It was here that I learnt to stack three angles across each other and put my full weight on them. We seemed to be short on bongs and I had to hand-jam the overhanging crack for 15 feet before I could use regular angles. I arrived on the stance soaked from the dripping lichen of the lower part and stripped off to dry my clothes in the sun, now hanging low above the Leaning Tower.

Peter came up fast after another pendulum—this time from under the jutting block-forced on him after he had taken out the last peg under tension. We moved together on the next pitch and then, after some navigational problems. Peter led round some black flakes after a downward tension traverse and climbed up to our third bivouac, "Sous le Toit Ledge." Sack hauling here was made awkward because of jutting flakes, and the sack had to be pushed from behind. I arrived at the bivouac ledge tired after these exertions and was a bit disappointed to find that we could not lie out flat. I had become soft after the other two bivouacs where ten men could have found space to stretch out.

Peter fixed the ropes up another hundred feet, to just short of the 20 foot overhang which undercut the leaning head wall above. When he came back down we made a sort of hammock from the sack hauling rope and settled down for the night. Half-on and half-off the ledge, we watched the tourists going home, streaming down the valley back to civilization. Really, they had hardly left it, for they had brought a cocoon of possessions with them, some in caravans so big that Bertram Mills Circus would have been proud to have owned them.

I told Peter how a group next to my tent arrived on evening: from the back of a bus-cum-caravan, a woman spread out a stair carpet and then shook out a large mat beyond. Having set up a table and chairs, she and the family then prepared the evening meal. During the whole of the first evening she had never set foot on the valley floor. Next morning, with her husband, she set off for the supermarket on a motorbike unhitched from the front of the caravan. There were rumors that some families even brought maids with them—black blouses, white lace aprons and all!

Peter led up next morning towards the belay below the roof. Although it was our fourth day, I regretted that the end was in sight. It was, after all, as the result of a good deal of hard work that we were up there enjoying the climb. I reached Peter's stance and looked with some misgiving at the belay pegs poking out of shallow pockets. I was glad to leave him to put more pegs between us. The roof reared out in three steps and, though the pegging was reasonable, it was difficult to rationalize the situation; I was glad to pass over the roof to the head wall, for I found the sheer drop of 2,500 feet to the trees below quite harrowing. It was certainly more exposed than any other roof I had climbed, including the direct on the Cima Ovest. We were both surprised to find the head wall overhanging for some 200 feet above, and now when the topo indicated slings for stances it meant just that. Some of the nailing was quite thin on the head wall, but with a light haul sack we could move together, and soon Peter was traversing right to the first ledge in four pitches. Those hanging belays were very exhilarating, in retrospect. Quite a wind buffeted the face, throwing us from side to side. Clouds gathered at both ends of the valley, and wisps blew off, diffusing the sun's rays which slanted down and across the quartzy granite, giving a sheen of rippled light.

Although the climbing was getting easier and was no longer actually overhanging, the threatening weather reminded us of our vulnerable position and made us hurry. Earlier in the month we had seen snow storms and six inches of snow. The clouds disintegrated towards evening as Peter led the last pitch, a 5.9 chimney. We scrambled up the last few feet of easy slabs and the climb was over—but not the whole experience, for our body chemistry kept on reacting hours after we had stopped climbing.

As the light faded, we went our separate ways on to the dome of El Cap. My walk slowed to a half pace as I stepped out, feeling my boots sink into the soft, friable earth that had only recently emerged from the melting snows. Heaps of pine cones crackled and crunched loudly in the still evening air as I walked over them. Stopping, I smelt the pine trees with an intensity I had never before experienced. I lifted my head to take in this sensation, like an animal sniffing out its quarry.

I saw for the first time, the full range of subtle, mellow colors in that evening light. The wind-scalloped surface of lingering snow patches twinkled like jewels in the facing light and all to the east the peaks of the High Sierra were pink above a purple haze of forested valleys. The brown of the soils, and the green of the forest ahead, exhibited innumerable facets. There were browns that were darker and browns that were lighter, and greens that stood out against other greens. Something enabled me to discern colors where before I had only seen one. I stood guzzling in these new sensations like a greedy child, hoping this beautiful experience would never end.

Our paths came together and we walked silently along a vague track, finally getting lost in the snow. As we settled down for the night in a forest clearing, I nibbled with relish at my shrunken salami. I can still recall the succulence of each mouthful. Next morning we made our way down towards the Lost Arrow and by a zig-zag path to the camp. Like the man who has come down and out of his LSD trip I found the experience at first to be beyond words, but like him I have searched hard to express what I felt—naively perhaps. As with him, a glimpse of my experience is recreated vividly months afterwards, sparked off by a cloud pattern, an expanse of blue sky, a smell of lichen and any other such catalyst.

The day trippers, in their eight-hour ecstasy, lose all sense of time, and this happened on Salathe Wall, especially after the first bivouac. Hours would go by in a rhythm of effort that at times seemed eternal. We had little regard for the past or the future, and thought only of the patch of rock a few feet ahead whilst climbing, or about things quite unrelated to our present position whilst sitting on the belays.

We felt that, given enough food and water, we could have gone on for a long time to come, for stopping the routine to which our bodies and minds had become accustomed was just as difficult as starting it in the first place. Why didn't we go down and back up the Nose or another El Cap special? I suppose because the spell was broken when we reached camp and anyway Peter had to go back to Austria.

Probably there was no reason to go again, at least not until this trip had been digested and lived with. Not even the North American Wall, with the promise of newspaper articles and lecture fees, could tempt me to go again!

On any multi-day, big wall route, the climber will discipline his body and its appetites, in the manner of the ascetics. Like them, he will probably experience hardship through extremes of heat and cold laying uncomfortable and sleepless on a hard bed, go without washing, remain immobile in certain bodily positions for long periods, wear "chains or other painful bonds," and go in for a certain amount of self-mutilation. Most ascetics, of course, also go in for chastity, a reduction in their food and water intake, extended periods of solitude, abstinence from alcohol, and, in some cases, breath control.

Any climber will be aware of this list of sufferings and will be able to cite instances in which he was afflicted by some or all of them whilst climbing. Indeed, I have not said much that any climber home from a week-end's cragging doesn't know about. He returns relaxed after escaping the anxieties and pressures of city life. What I am trying to say, however, is that with longer and more demanding climbs there are added ingredients of both suffering and reward.

Some of the young hippies in Yosemite are so profoundly affected by the pills and potions that they take that they tend to opt out of ordinary living, or at least claim to do so. This seemed to me to be not only futile, but hypocritical, because for their worldly needs they are so obviously and willingly dependent on the society they say they are rejecting.

I am not suggesting that "the doors of perception" were opened in the same way, or as wide, for me as for the acid heads, but after the trip I did seem to know positively where to go next—and that was back into society, relaxed, but with a new zest and enthusiasm, and without any worries about "the current undesirable side effects" on mind or body.

If big wall climbing is pursued in a more hostile environment and for longer periods, or if the big wall climber climbs alone, as Bonatti did on the Dru, then the doors of perception will be opened wide. The climbers involved may experience a more lasting state of heightened awareness, and may even reach a truly visionary, if not mystical, state of being which transcends normal human comprehension.

Most of us will never make such climbs, but that is not to say that less demanding climbs could not have a similar effect. The climber who is willing to extend himself to the limit of his technical skill and endurance on any long climb, is en route up the profundity trail.

Doug Scott

David Roberts (b. 1943) is recognized as one of America's best climbing writers. He is also an excellent mountaineer, having climbed extensively in Alaska including the first ascent of the West Face of Mount Huntington. He has also climbed the Wickersham Wall on Denali. His many books include *Deborah: A Wilderness Narrative*, *Moments of Doubt*, *The Mountain of My Fear*, and *The Lost Explorer: Finding Mallory on Mount Everest* with Conrad Anker, *Four Against the Arctic*, and *True Summit*.

DAVID ROBERTS: MOMENTS OF DOUBT

The most basic issue a mountaineer faces is the risk of death. In my case, the issue had an early immediacy, for by the time I was twenty-two I had witnessed three fatal climbing accidents. Not surprisingly, however, it took me fourteen years to face the issue in print.

"Moments of Doubt," which I sent in unsolicited, was my first piece published in Outside. I worked hard on it, and there is a certain gratification in the fact that, of all the articles I have written, this one has gained approval from the most readers.

The account here of Huntington overlaps with my earlier piece, "Five Days on Mount Huntington." For such repetition, I get indulgence: the "plot" of the article seems to need it, and I am bemused to discover that I told the story of Ed Bernd's death somewhat differently the second time round, after fourteen years of remembering it.

"When one is young, one trifles with death."
— Graham Green, at 74.

A day in early July, perfect for climbing. From the mesas above Boulder, Colorado, a heat-cutting breeze drove the smell of the pines up onto the great tilting slabs of the Flatirons.

It was 1961; I was eighteen, had been climbing about a year, Gabe even less. We were about six hundred feet up, three-quarters to the summit of the First Flatiron. There wasn't a guidebook in those days; so we didn't know how difficult our route was supposed to be or who had previously done it. But it had gone all right, despite the scarcity of places to bang in our Austrian soft-iron pitons: sometimes we'd just wedge our bodies in a crack and yell "On belay!"

It was a joy to be climbing. Climbing was one of the best things—maybe the best thing—in life, given that one would never play shortstop for the Dodgers. There was a risk, as my parents and friends kept pointing out; but I knew the risk was worth it.

In fact, just that summer I had become ambitious. With a friend my age whom I'll call Jock, I'd climbed the east face of Longs Peak, illegally early in the season—no great deed for experts, but pretty good for eighteen-year-old kids. It was Jock's idea to train all summer and go up to the Tetons and do the route: the north face of the Grand. I'd never even seen the Tetons, but the idea of the route, hung with names like Petzoldt and Pownall and Unsoeld, sent chills through me.

It was Gabe's lead now, maybe the last before the going got easier a few hundred feet below the top. He angled up and left, couldn't get any protection in, went out of sight around a corner. I waited. The rope didn't move. "What's going on?" I finally yelled. "Hang on," Gabe answered irritably. "I'm looking for a belay."

We'd been friends since grade school. When he was young he had been very shy; he'd been raised by his father only—why, I never thought to ask. Ever since I had met him, on the playground, running up the old wooden stairs to the fourth-grade classroom, he'd moved in a jerky, impulsive way. On our high school tennis team, he slashed at the ball with lurching stabs, and skidded across the asphalt like a kid trying to catch his own shadow. He climbed the same way, especially in recent months, impulsively going for a hard move well above his protection, worrying me, but getting away with it. In our first half-year of climbing, I'd usually been a little better than Gabe, just as he was always stuck a notch below me on the tennis team. But in the last couple of months—no denying it—he'd become better on rock that I was; he took the leads that I didn't like the looks of. He might have made a better partner for Jock on the Grand, except that Gabe's only mountain experience had been an altitude-sick crawl up the east side of Mount of the Holy Cross with me just a week before. He'd thrown up on the summit but said he loved the climb.

David Roberts

At eighteen it wasn't easy for me to see why Gabe had suddenly become good at climbing, or why it drove him as nothing else had. Just that April, three months earlier, his father had been killed in an auto accident during a blizzard in Texas. When Gabe returned to school, I mumbled my prepared condolence. He brushed it off and asked at once when we could go climbing. I was surprised. But I wanted to climb, too; the summer was approaching, Jock wasn't always available, and Gabe would go at the drop of a phone call.

Now, finally, came the "on belay" signal from out of sight to the left, and I started up. For the full 120 feet Gabe had been unable to get in any pitons; so as I climbed, the rope drooped in a long arc to my left. It began to tug me sideways, and when I yanked back at it, I noticed that it seemed snagged about fifty feet away, caught under one of the downward-pointing flakes so characteristic of the Flatirons. I flipped the rope angrily and tugged harder on it, then yelled to Gabe to pull from his end. Our efforts only jammed it in tighter. The first trickle of fear leaked into my well-being.

"What kind of belay do you have?" I asked the invisible Gabe.

"Not too good. I couldn't get anything in."

There were fifty feet of slab between me and the irksome flake, and those fifty feet were frighteningly smooth. I ought, I supposed, to climb over to the flake, even if it meant building up coils and coils of slack. But if I slipped, and Gabe with no anchor. . . .

I yelled to Gabe what I was going to do. He assented.

I untied from the rope, gathered as many coils as I could, and threw the end violently down and across the slab, hoping to snap the jammed segment loose, or at least reduce Gabe's job to hauling the thing in with all his might. Then, with my palms starting to sweat, I climbed carefully up to a little ledge and sat down.

Gabe was now below me, out of sight, but close. "It's still jammed," he said, and my fear surged a little notch.

"Maybe we can set up a rappel," I suggested.

"No, I think I can climb back and get it."

"Are you sure?" Relief lowered the fear a notch. Gabe would do the dirty work, just as he was willing to lead the hard pitches.

"It doesn't look too bad."

I waited, sitting on my ledge, staring out over Boulder and the dead-straw plains that seemed to stretch all the way to Kansas. I wasn't sure we were doing the right thing. A few months earlier I'd soloed a rock called the Fist, high on Green Mountain above Boulder, in the midst of a snow storm, and sixty feet off the ground, as I was turning a slight overhang, my foot had come off, and one hand. . . but not the other. And adrenaline had carried me the rest of the way up. There was a risk, but you rose to it.

For Gabe, it was taking a long time. It was all the worse not being able to see him. I looked to my right and saw a flurry of birds playing with a column of air over near the Second Flatiron. Then Gabe's voice, triumphant: "I got it!"

"Way to go!" I yelled back. The fear diminished. If he'd been able to climb down to the snag, he could climb back up. I was glad I hadn't had to do it. Remembering his impatience, I instructed, "Coil it up." A week before, on Holy Cross, I'd been the leader. "No, I'll just drape it around me. I can climb straight up to where you are."

The decision puzzled me. Be careful, I said in my head. But that was Gabe, impulsive, playing his hunches. Again the seconds crept. I had too little information, nothing to do but look for the birds and smell the pine sap. You could see Denver, smogless as yet, a squat aggregation of down-town buildings like some modern covered-wagon circle, defended against the emptiness of the Plains. There had been climbers over on the Third Flatiron earlier, but now I couldn't spot them. The red, gritty sandstone was warm to my palms.

"How's it going?" I yelled.

A pause. Then Gabe's voice, quick-syllabled as always, more tense than normal. "I just got past a hard place, but it's easier now."

He sounded so close, only fifteen feet below me, yet I hadn't seen him since his lead had taken him around the corner out of sight. I felt I could almost reach down and touch him.

Next, there was a soft but unmistakable sound, and my brain knew it without ever having heard it before. It was the sound of cloth rubbing against rock. Then Gabe's cry, a single blurt of knowledge: "Dave!"

I rose with a start to my feet, but hung on to a knob with one hand, gripping it desperately. "Gabe!" I yelled back; then for the first time in half an hour, I saw him. He was much farther from me now, sliding and rolling, the rope wrapped in tangles about him like a badly made nest. "Grab something." I yelled. I could hear Gabe shouting, even as he re-ceded from me, "No! Oh, no!"

I thought, there's always a chance. But Gabe began to bounce, just like rocks I had seen bouncing down mountain slopes, a longer bounce each time. The last was conclusive, for I saw him flung far from the rock's even surface to pirouette almost lazily in the air, then meet the unyielding slab once more, headfirst, before the sandstone threw him into the treetops.

What I did next is easy to remember, but it is hard to judge just how long it took. It seemed, in the miasma of adrenaline, to last either three minutes or more than an hour. I stood and I yelled for help. After several repetitions, voices from the Mesa Trail caught the breeze back to me. "We're coming!" someone shouted. "In the trees!" I yelled back. "Hurry!" I sat down and said to myself, now don't go screw it up yourself, you don't have a rope, sit here and wait for someone to come rescue you. They can come up the back and lower a rope from the top. As soon as I had given myself this good advice, I got up and started scrambling toward the summit. It wasn't too hard. Slow down, don't make a mistake, I lectured myself, but it felt as if I were running. From the summit I down-climbed the eighty feet on the backside; I'd been there before and had rappelled it. Forty feet up there was a hard move. Don't blow it. Then I was on the ground.

I ran down the scree-and-brush gully between the First and Second Flat Irons, and got to the bottom a few minutes before the hikers. "Where is he?" a wild-eyed volunteer asked me. "In the trees!" I yelled back. "Somewhere right near here!"

Searching for something is usually an orderly process; it has its methodical pleasures, its calm reconstruction of the possible steps that led to the object getting lost. We searched instead like scavenging predators, crashing through dead fall and talus; and we couldn't find Gabe. Members of the Rocky Mountain Rescue Group began to arrive; they were calmer than the hiker I had first encountered. We searched and searched, and finally a voice called out, "Here he is."

Someone led me there. There were only solemn looks to confirm the obvious. I saw Gabe sprawled face down on the talus, his limbs in the wrong positions, the rope, coated with blood, still in a cocoon about him. The seat of his jeans had been ripped away, and one bare buttock was scraped raw, the way kids' knees used to look after a bad slide on a sidewalk. I wanted to go up and touch his body, but I couldn't. I sat down and cried.

Much later—but it was still afternoon, the sun and breeze still collaborating on a perfect July day—a policeman led me up the walk to my house. My mother came to the screen door and, grasping the situation at once, burst into tears. Gabe was late for a birthday party. Someone had called my house, mildly annoyed, to try to account for the delay. My father took on the task of calling them back. (More than a decade later he told me that it was the hardest thing he had ever done.)

In the newspapers the next day a hiker was quoted as saying that he knew something bad was going to happen, because he'd overheard Gabe and me "bickering," and good climbers didn't do that. Another man had watched the fall through binoculars. At my father's behest, I wrote down a detailed account of the accident.

About a week later Jock came by. He spent the appropriate minutes in sympathetic silence, then said, "The thing you've got to do is get right back on the rock." I didn't want to, but I went out with him. We top-roped a moderate climb only thirty feet high. My feet and hands shook uncontrollably, my heart seemed to be screaming, and Jock had to haul me up the last ten feet. "It's OK, it'll come back," he reassured.

I had one friend I could talk to, a touch-football buddy who thought climbing was crazy in the first place. With his support, in the presence of my parents' anguish. I managed at last to call up Jock and ask him to come by. We sat on my front porch. "Jock," I said, "I just can't go to the Grand. I'm too shook up. I'd be no good if I did go." He stared at me long and hard. Finally he stood up and walked away.

That fall I went to Harvard. I tried out for the tennis team, but when I found that the Mountaineering Club included veterans who had just climbed Waddington in the Coast Range and Mount Logan in the Yukon, it didn't take me long to single out my college heroes.

But I wasn't at all sure about climbing. On splendid fall afternoons at the Shawangunks, when the veterans dragged us neophytes up easy climbs, I sat on the belay ledges mired in ambivalence. I'd never been at a cliff where there were so many climbers, and whenever one of them on an adjoining route happened to yell—even if the message were nothing more alarming than "I think it goes up to the left there"—I jerked with fright.

For reasons I am still not sure of, Gabe became a secret. Attached to the memory of our day on the First Flatiron was not only fear, but guilt and embarrassment. Guilt toward Gabe, of course, because I had not been the one who went to get the jammed rope. But the humiliation, born perhaps in that moment when the cop had led me up to my front door and my mother had burst into tears, lingered with me in the shape of a crime or moral error, like getting a girl pregnant.

David Roberts

Nevertheless, at Harvard I got deeply involved with the Mountaineering Club. By twenty I'd climbed McKinley with six Harvard friends via a new route, and that August I taught at Colorado Outward Bound School. With all of "Boone Patrol," including the senior instructor, a laconic-British hard man named Clough, I was camped one night above timberline. We'd crawled under the willow bushes and strung out ponchos for shelter. In the middle of the night I dreamed that Gabe was falling away from me through endless reaches of black space. He was in a metal cage, spinning headlong, and I repeatedly screamed his name. I woke with a jolt, sat shivering for ten minutes, then crawled, dragging my bag, far from the others, and lay awake the rest of the night. As we blew the morning campfire back to life from the evening's ashes, Clough remarked, "Did you hear the screams? One of the poor lads must have had a nightmare."

By my senior year, though, I'd become hard myself. McKinley had seemed a lark compared to my second expedition—a forty-day failure with only one companion, Don Jensen, on the east ridge of Alaska's Mount Deborah. All through the following winter, with Don holed up in the Sierra Nevada, me trudging through a math major at Harvard, we plotted mountaineering revenge. By January we had focused on a route: the unclimbed west face of Mount Huntington, even harder, we thought, than Deborah. By March we'd agreed that Matt Hale, a junior and my regular climbing partner, would be our third, even though Matt had been on no previous expeditions. Matt was daunted by the ambition of the project, but slowly got caught up in it. Needing a fourth, we discussed an even more inexperienced club member, Ed Bernd, a sophomore who'd been climbing little more than a year and who'd not even been in big mountains.

Never in my life, before or since, have I found myself so committed to any project. I daydreamed about recipes for Logan bread and the number of ounces a certain piton weighed; at night I fell asleep with the seductive promises of belay ledges and crack systems whispering in my ear. School was a Platonic facade. The true idea of my life lay in the Alaska Range.

At one point that spring I floated free from my obsession long enough to hear a voice in my head tell me, "You know, Dave, this is the kind of climb you could get killed on." I stopped and assessed my life, and consciously answered, "It's worth it. Worth the risk." I wasn't sure what I meant by that, but I knew its truth. I wanted Matt to feel the same way. I knew Don did.

On a March weekend Matt and I were leading an ice climbing trip in Huntington Ravine on Mount Washington. The Harvard Cabin was unusually full, which meant a scramble in the morning to get out first and claim the ice gully you wanted to lead.

On Saturday I skipped breakfast to beat everybody else to Pinnacle Gully, then the prize of the ravine. It was a bitter, windy day, and though the gully didn't tax my skills unduly, twice sudden gusts almost blew me out of my steps. The second man on the rope, though a good rock climber, found the whole day unnerving and was glad to get back to the cabin.

That night we chatted with the other climbers. The two most experienced were Craig Merrihue, a grad student in astrophysics, said to be brilliant, with first ascents in the Andes and Karakoram behind him, and Dan Doody, a quiet, thoughtful film maker who'd gone to college in Wyoming and had recently been on the big American Everest expedition. Both men were interested in our Huntington plans, and it flattered Matt and me that they thought we were up to something serious. The younger climbers looked on us experts in awe; it was delicious to bask in their hero worship as we nonchalanted it with Craig and Dan. Craig's lovely wife Sandy was part of our company. All three of them were planning to link up in a relaxing trip to the Hindu Kush the coming summer.

The next day the wind was still gusting fitfully. Matt and I were leading separate ropes of beginners up Odell's Gully, putting in our teaching time after having had Saturday to do something hard. I felt lazy, a trifle vexed to be "wasting" a good day. Around noon we heard somebody calling from the ravine floor. We ignored the cries at first, but as a gust of wind came our way, I was pricked with alarm. "Somebody's yelling for help." I shouted to Matt. "Think they mean it?" A tiny figure far below seemed to be running up and down on the snow. My laziness burned away.

I tied off my second to wait on a big bucket of an ice step, then zipped down a rappel off a single poorly placed ice screw. Still in crampons, I ran down into the basin that formed the runout for all five gullies. The man I met, a weekend climber in his thirties who had been strolling up the ravine for a walk, was moaning. He had seen something that looked like "a bunch of rags" slide by out of the corner of his eye. He knew all at once that it was human bodies he had seen, and he could trace the line of fall up to Pinnacle Gully. He knew that Doody and Merrihue were climbing in Pinnacle. And Craig was a close friend of his. During the five minutes or so since the accident he had been unable to approach them, unable to do anything but yell for help and run aimlessly. I was the first to reach the bodies.

Gabe's I had not had to touch. But I was a trip leader now, an experienced mountaineer, the closest approximation in the circumstances to a rescue squad. I'd had first-aid training. Without a second's hesitation I knelt beside the bodies. Dan's was the worse injured, with a big chunk of his head torn open. His blood was still warm, but I was sure he was dead. I thought I could find a faint pulse in Craig's wrist, however, so I tried to stop the bleeding and started mouth-to-mouth resuscitation. Matt arrived and worked on Dan, and then others, appeared and tried to help.

For an hour, I think, I put my lips against Craig's, held his nose shut, forced air into his lungs. His lips were going cold and blue, and there was a stagnant taste in the cavity his mouth had become, but I persisted, as did Matt and the others. Not since my father had last kissed me—was I ten?—had I put my lips to another man's. I remembered Dad's scratchy face, when he hadn't shaved, like Craig's now. We kept hoping, but I knew after five minutes that both men had been irretrievably damaged. There was too much blood. It had been a bad year for snow in the bottom of the ravine; big rocks stuck out everywhere. Three years earlier Don Jensen had been avalanched out of Damnation Gully; he fell 800 feet and only broke a shoulder blade. But that had been a good year for snow.

Yet we kept up our efforts. The need arose as much from an inability to imagine what else we might do—stand around in shock?—as from good first aid sense. At last we gave up, exhausted. I could read in Matt's clipped and efficient suggestions the dawning sense that a horrible thing had happened. But I also felt numb. The sense of tragedy flooded home only in one moment. I heard somebody say something like "She's coming," and somebody else say, "Keep her away." I looked up and saw Sandy, Craig's wife, arriving from the cabin, aware of something wrong, but in the instant before knowing that it was indeed Craig she was intercepted bodily by the climber who knew her best, and that was how she learned. I can picture her face in the instant of knowing, and I remember vividly my own revelation—that there was a depth of personal loss that I had never really known existed, of which I was now receiving my first glimpse.

My memory has blocked out Sandy's reaction. Did she immediately burst into tears, like my mother? Did she try to force her way to Craig? Did we let her? I know I saw it happen, whatever it was, buy my memory cannot retrieve it.

There followed long hours into the dark hauling the bodies with ropes back toward the cabin. There was the pacifying exhaustion and the stolid drive back to Cambridge. There was somebody telling me, "You did a fantastic job, all that anybody could have done," and that seeming maudlin-who wouldn't have done the same? There were, in subsequent weeks, the memorial service, long tape-recorded discussions of the puzzling circumstances of the accident (we had found Dan and Craig roped together, a bent ice screw loose on the rope between them), heated indictments of the cheap Swiss design of the screw. And even a couple of visits with Sandy and their five-year-old son.

My strongest concern was not to let the accident interfere with my commitment to climb Huntington, now only three months away. The deaths had deeply shaken Matt; but we never directly discussed the matter. I never wrote my parents about what had taken place. We went ahead and invited Ed, the sophomore, to join our expedition. Though he had not been in the ravine with us, he too had been shaken. But I got the three of us talking logistics and gear, and thinking about a mountain in Alaska. In some smug private recess I told myself that I was in better training than Craig and Dan had been, and that was why I wouldn't get killed. If the wind had blown one of them out of his steps, well, I'd led Pinnacle the day before in the same wind and it hadn't blown me off. Almost, but it hadn't. Somehow I controlled my deepest feelings and kept the disturbance buried. I had no bad dreams about Doody and Merrihue, no sleepless nights, no sudden qualms about whether Huntington was worth the risk or not. By June I was as ready as I could be for the hardest climb of my life.

It took a month, but we climbed our route on Huntington. Pushing through the night of July 29-30, we traversed the knife edged summit ridge and stood on top in the still hours of dawn. Only twelve hours before, Matt and I had come as close to being killed as it is possible to get away with in the mountains.

Matt, tugging on a loose crampon strap, had pulled himself off his steps: he landed on me, broke down the snow ledge I had kicked; under the strain our one bad anchor piton popped out. We fell, roped together and helpless some seventy feet down a steep slope of ice above a 4,500-foot drop. Then a miracle intervened; the rope snagged on a nubbin of rock, the size of one's knuckle, and held us both.

Such was our commitment to the climb that, even though we were bruised and Matt had lost a crampon, we pushed upward and managed to join Ed and Don for the summit dash.

At midnight, nineteen hours later, Ed and I stood on a ledge some fifteen hundred feet below. Our tents were too small for four people; so he and I had volunteered to push on to a lower camp, leaving Matt and Don to come down on the next good day. In the dim light we set up a rappel. There was a tangle of pitons, fixed ropes, and the knots tying them off, in the midst of which Ed was attaching a carabiner. I suggested an adjustment. Ed moved the carabiner, clipped our rope in, and started to get on rappel. "Just this pitch," I said, "and then it's practically walking to camp."

Ed leaned back on rappel. There was a scrape and sparks-his crampons scratching the rock, I later guessed. Suddenly he was flying backwards through the air, down the vertical pitch. He hit hard ice sixty feet below. Just as I had on the Flatiron, I yelled, "Grab something, Ed!" But it was evident that his fall was not going to end—not soon, anyway. He slid rapidly down the ice chute, then out of sight over a cliff. I heard him bouncing once or twice, then nothing. He had not uttered a word.

I shouted, first for Ed, then for Don and Matt above. Nothing but silence answered me. There was nothing I could do. I was as certain as I could be that Ed had fallen 4,000 feet, to the lower arm of the Tokositna Glacier, inaccessible even from our base camp. He was surely dead.

I managed to get myself, without a rope, down the seven pitches to our empty tent. The next two days I spent alone—desperate for Matt's and Don's return, imagining them dead also, drugging myself with sleeping pills, trying to fathom what had gone wrong, seized one night in my sleep with a vision of Ed, broken and bloody, clawing his way up the wall to me, crying out, "Why didn't you come look for me?" At last Don and Matt arrived, and I had to tell them. Our final descent, in the midst of a raging blizzard, was the nastiest and scariest piece of climbing I have done, before or since.

From Talketna, a week later, I called Ed's parents. His father's stunned first words, crackly with long-distance static, were "Is this some kind of a joke?" After the call I went behind the bush pilot's hangar and cried my heart out-the first time in years that I had given way to tears.

A week later, with my parents' backing, I flew to Philadelphia to spend three days with Ed's parents. But not until the last few hours of my stay did we talk about Ed or climbing. Philadelphia was wretchedly hot and sticky. In the Bernds' small house my presence—sleeping on the living room sofa, an extra guest at meals was a genuine intrusion. Unlike my parents, or Matt's, or Don's. Ed's had absolutely no comprehension of mountain climbing. It was some esoteric thing he had gotten into at Harvard; and of course Ed had completely downplayed, for their sake, the seriousness of our Alaska project.

At that age, given my feelings about climbing I could hardly have been better shielded from any sense of guilt. But mixed in with my irritation and discomfort in the muggy apartment was an awareness of a different sort from the glimpse of Sandy Merrihue that I was in the presence of a grief so deep its features were opaque to me. It was the hope-destroying grief of parents, the grief of those who knew things could not keep going right, a grief that would, I sensed, diminish little over the years. It awed and frightened me, and disclosed to me an awareness of my own guilt. I began remembering other moments. In our first rest after the summit, as we had giddily replayed every detail of our triumph, Ed had said that yes, it had been great, but that he wasn't sure it had been worth it. I hadn't pressed him; his qualifying judgment had seemed the only sour note in a perfect party. It was so obvious to me that all the risks throughout the climb, even Matt's and my near-disaster-had been worth it to make the summit.

Now Ed's remark haunted me. He was, in most climbers' judgment, far too inexperienced for Huntington. We'd caught his occasional technical mistakes on the climb, a piton hammered in with the eye the wrong way, an ice axe left below a rock overhang. But he learned so well, was so naturally strong, complemented our intensity with a hearty capacity for fun and friendship. Still, at Harvard, there had been, I began to see, no way for him to turn down our invitation. Matt and I and the other veterans were his heroes, just as the Waddington seniors had been mine three years before. Now the inner circle was asking him to join. It seemed to us at the time an open invitation, free of any moral implications. Now I wondered.

I still didn't know what had gone wrong with the rappel, even though Ed had been standing a foot away from me. Had it been some technical error of his in clipping in? Or had the carabiner itself failed? There was no way of settling the question, especially without having been able to look for, much less find, his body.

At last Ed's family faced me. I gave a long, detailed account of the climb. I told them it was "the hardest thing yet done in Alaska," a great mountaineering accomplishment. It would attract the attention of climbers the world over. They looked at me with blank faces; my way of viewing Ed's death was incomprehensible. They were bent on finding a Christian meaning to the event. It occurred to them that maybe God had meant to save Ed from a worse death fighting in Vietnam. They were deeply stricken by our inability to retrieve his body. "My poor baby," Mrs. Bernd wailed at one point, "he must be so cold."

Their grief brought me close to tears again, but when I left it was with a sigh of relief. I went back to Denver, where I was starting graduate school. For the second time in my life I thought seriously about quitting climbing. At twenty-two I had been the firsthand witness of three fatal accidents, costing four lives. Mr. Bernd's laborious letters, edged with the leaden despair I had seen in his face, continued to remind me that the question "Is it worth the risk?" was not one any person could answer by consulting only himself.

Torn by my own ambivalence, studying Restoration comedy in a city where I had few friends, no longer part of a gang heading off each weekend to the Shawangunks, I laid off climbing most of the winter of 1965-66. By February I had made a private resolve to quit the business, at least for a few years. One day a fellow showed up at my basement apartment, all the way down from Alaska. I'd never met him, but the name Art Davidson was familiar. He looked straight off skid row, with his tattered clothes and unmatched socks and tennis shoes with holes in them; and his wild red beard and white eyebrows lent a kind of rundown Irish aristocracy to his face. He lived, apparently, like a vagrant, subsisting on cottage cheese in the back of his old pickup truck (named Bucephalus after Alexander's horse), which he hid in parking lots each night on the outskirts of Anchorage. Art was crazy about Alaskan climbing. In the next year and a half he would go on five major expeditions-still the most intense spate of big-range mountaineering I know of. In my apartment he kept talking in his soft, enthusiastic voice about the Cathedral Spires, a place he knew Don and I had had our eyes on. I humored him. I let him talk on, and then we went out for a few beers, and Art started reminding me about the pink granite and the trackless glaciers, and by the evening's end the charismatic bastard had me signed up.

We went to the Cathedral Spires in 1966, with three others. Art was at the zenith of his climbing career. Self-taught, technically erratic, he made up in compulsive zeal what he lacked in finesse. His drive alone got himself and Rick Millikan up the highest peak in the range, which we named Kichatna Spire. As for me, I wasn't the climber I'd been the year before, which had much to do with why I wasn't along with Art on the summit push. That year I'd fallen in love with the woman who would become my wife, and suddenly the old question about risk seemed vastly more complicated. In the blizzard-swept dusk, with two of the other guys up on the climb, I found myself worrying about their safety instead of mere logistics. I was as glad nothing had gone wrong by the end of the trip as I was that we'd collaborated on a fine first ascent.

Summer after summer I went back to Alaska, climbing hard, but not with the all-out commitment of 1965. Over the years quite a few of my climbing acquaintances were killed in the mountains, including five close friends. Each death was deeply unsettling, tempting me to doubt all over again the worth of the enterprise. For nine years I taught climbing to college students, and worrying about their safety became an occupational hazard. Ironically, the closest I came during those years to getting killed was not on some Alaskan wall, but on a beginner's climb at the Shawangunks, when I nearly fell head-first, backwards out of a rappel the result of a carabiner jamming in a crack, my own impatience, and the blase glaze with which teaching a dangerous skill at a trivial level coats the risk. Had that botched rappel been my demise, no friends would have seen my end as meaningful: instead, a "stupid," "pointless," "who-would-have-thought?" kind of death.

Yet in the long run, trying to answer my own question "Is it worth it?," torn between thinking the question itself ridiculous and grasping for a formulaic answer, I come back to gut-level affirmation, however sentimental, however selfish. When I imagine my early twenties, it is not in terms of the hours spent in a quiet library studying Melville, or my first nervous pontifications before a freshman English class. I want to see Art Davidson again, shambling into my apartment in his threadbare trousers, spooning great dollops of cottage cheese past his flaming beard, filling the air with his baroque hypotheses, convincing me that the Cathedral Spires needed our visit. I want to remember what brand of beer

I was drinking when that crazy vagabond in one stroke turned the cautious resolves of a lonely winter into one more summer's plot against the Alaskan wilderness.

Some of the worst moments of my life have taken place in the mountains. Not only the days alone in the tent on Huntington after Ed had vanished—quieter moments as well, embedded in uneventful expeditions. Trying to sleep the last few hours before a predawn start on a big climb, my mind stiff with dread, as I hugged my all-too-obviously fragile self with my own arms-until the scared kid inside my sleeping bag began to pray for bad weather and another day's reprieve. But nowhere else on earth, not even in the harbors of reciprocal love, have I felt pure happiness take hold of me and shake me like a puppy, compelling me, and the conspirators I had arrived there with, to stand on some perch of rock or snow, the uncertain struggle below us, and bawl our pagan vaunts to the very sky. It was worth it then.

George Spenceley (b. 1921) was born in Yorkshire, England and took up mountain walking and rock climbing in his early teens and was very active on British mountains until the beginning of World War II. In 1939 his open air activities ceased when he joined the R.A.F., training as a pilot. He served in Bomber Command and was shot down over Germany in 1942 after which he suffered three years as a prisoner-of-war. After the war he returned to his mountain activities and had several seasons in the European Alps before joining the South Georgia Survey 1955-56. In 1987 he became deputy leader of an expedition in the Jugal Himal of Nepal where he suffered a tragedy in which he was the sole survivor. During the following years, George was active in the mountains of Norwegian and Swedish Lapland, Turkey, Ethiopia and East Europe. In 1968 he was on an expedition to the Watkins Mountains of East Greenland. In more recent years has become an enthusiastic long distance canoeist, first across the Barrens of Arctic Canada, and later with his wife, Sylvie, the full length of the Danube and Mississippi rivers. Now 83, he still continues to be active, although in a more modest and leisurely manner.

THE NEW GENERATION
BY G.B. SPENCELEY

"THERE WAS A TIME," said my companion, his voice raised above the raucous shouting that came from a party above, "when all whom you met on the hills were people pleasant to know." We were sitting separated from the crowds on a ledge some twenty feet about the foot of the crag and sheltered by an overhang from the descent of any unheralded missile. Below, a little way down the scree, in the "cave" among the orange peel and paper sat the young members of yet another new club.

We had finished our sandwiches and while waiting to see which of the four buttresses would be kept occupied, we had been discussing the behavior of some of the recent recruits to the climbing world. Later we found solitude above the climbs on the summit of the mountain and as we watched the sun sink behind the western hills, my friend, a mountaineer of distinction and twice my age, told me of his own novitiate. He described his feelings on seeing for the first time high mountains and how in came as a revelation to learn that their remote summits, could through toil and skill, be attained. The years that followed were a period of careful schooling for the ultimate purpose but his adventures were as yet lived vicariously in the pages of mountaineering literature on which he fed hungrily. In his later teens, hardihood and endurance were tested on long walks over northern moors, alone and in all weathers; and there were holidays too in the Lakes and Wales with here and there a little scrambling. But during all this time he knew no climbers, indeed had never even spoken to one, although he had seen them at work, remote figures clinging to Napes Ridge, and once in a hotel room he had stood back and listened in respectful silence to an account of a winter ascent of the Old West on Pillar.

However, in those days people never passed one by on the hills without a friendly though and it was just such a casual meeting that brought my friend his first offer of a climb. He was taken in hand and with infinite care taught the basic principles. For some time he was not allowed to lead and from the first there was instilled into him an awareness of the potential danger that lay in every step of a climb and a respect for even the smallest of mountains. Being a man of imagination, fear took a prominent part in those early expeditions, until with experience he began to distinguish between apparent and actual danger, and with increased mastery of his craft to reduce, if not quite eliminate, the latter. With new friends then and a new rope, working through all the moderates and then the difficults, and so upwards through all the standard courses my friend was launched on what was subsequently to become a great mountaineering career.

I have often thought of this man's approach and attitude to mountains, of his respect for them and love of them; love for their unearthly beauty as well as for the adventure they give, and inspired not only by the mountains themselves, but as much by the breed of men who were mountaineers in those days, forty years ago. Then, more than today, there was a very real and personal relationship between the experienced climber and the novice, and the older man's influence was a powerful factor in forming, in the budding mountaineer, the correct outlook and values.

George Spenceley

No sport has greater traditions than mountaineering; traditions not only of courage and high endeavor but also of unpretentious and gentlemanly behavior. I could not do better than quote the words of Geoffrey Young from an article in the *Alpine Journal*. He wrote:

Mountaineering was a discover. . . it was perhaps fortunate that the discovery was not made until Victorian days and then by a number of leaders of thought. By the authority of their of their writings and by their dignity of approach to the new activity, they set a seal of distinction upon climbing; and this preserved it as a practice respectable, if inexplicable, during the decades of popular derision and criticizm. They established a notable tradition of the spirit in which mountains must by climbed; and this in our country alone, and in this sport more than in all others, has served to protect its force for good from the progressively corrupting infection of competition and publicity hunting.

Mountaineering failed to become a popular sport and its recruits continued for many years to by largely drawn from the cultured and moneyed class. But if forty years ago climbing was for the few, now it is for the many and at the same time it is no longer the perquisite of the leisured and learned. That this is the case will be welcomed by all of open mind who have at heart the common good, but the most tolerant cannot help but feel regret at the resultant loss of values and standards of behavior.

Perhaps it is impertinent of me to criticize a group of climbers belonging to a generation so little removed from my own, but living as I do on the edge of the Lake District I may have a better opportunity than most of our members for observing the actions of those who tend to bring disrepute upon our sport. Perhaps a certain sense of superiority over the mere walker may be afforded and allowance made for the climber's boisterous spirits after a good day on the "Very Severs" within sight of the road, but the mature climber and the tourist will feel irritation and sometimes disgust at the noisy and affected behavior of many young climbers who haunt the popular valleys of the Lake District.

Climbers they may be, but mountaineers no; although they have been heard discussing in loud voices their plans to do that year the Eperon Walker. Bring them to the point and they will probably admit to a complete lack of interest in mountains as such; the most stirring of mountain aspects will leave them utterly cold; their interest may not even extend as far as the major crags of the Lake District except perhaps where conditions are suitable for the ascent of some notoriously difficult route of

The New Generation

when there is the prospect of knocking pitons into ten feet of unclimbed rock. Their playground is the low crag, close both to road and gazing crowds and to hotel bar and awestruck listener. They are essentially fair weather climbers; when the wind is too strong or the rocks too wet and cold for the ascent of climbs sufficiently hard, then all day will the hotel visitor hear their ringing voices.

There was a time when the rope was not seen until the foot of the climb was reached. It is now not only the practice of these young climbers to carry ropes in a prominent position on all possible occasions but literally to drape themselves with slings and karabiners and even pitons (used for display purposes only, in most cases) before they consider themselves suitably attired for public viewing. Thus garbed it is their custom to talk loudly, for all to hear, of super severes, new routes and sometimes, as was heard recently, of accidents, comparing and boasting of distances fallen.

Is there a remedy to combat this general lowering of standards and loss of values? Writing thirty years ago George Mallory expressed the belief that the time had come when is should be the principle of a climbing club to suppress the propagation of a gospel already too popular. It is certainly tempting to view the situation thus selfishly and to wish the hills only for those completely deserving. We can well imagine what the feeling of Mallory would be today, nevertheless the principle is the wrong one, now, as it was then. The invasion of the hills by young people from the cities should not, and indeed cannot, be halted. Whether we like it or not, we have to accept the fact that rock climbing, and to a lesser extent mountaineering, have in the last few years, become popular sports. Nothing but profit can come of it and if we feel at all for the common good that we should rejoice. The answer lies not in any attempt to arrest this movement by in education, not the education of the schoolroom, but rather the education in mountain manners and in the tradition and values of what is really not merely a sport but a religion, and this can only be given when there is re-established that close and personal relationship between the experienced mature mountaineer and the novice.

For prospective climbers of an earlier generation it was not easy to get started. The only clubs were what today we call the senior clubs and admission to them was closely guarded and limited only to the experienced; there was in existence no organization or machinery by which the inexperienced climber could be brought into contact with others of similar interests. The young recruit to the climbing world was dependent

George Spenceley

on his good fortune in meeting kindred spirits and on the good nature of others in devoting their few and precious hours in the hills to his instruction. I myself owe a debt of gratitude to those brilliant climbers Colin Kirkus and Alf Bridge, who in between forcing new routes up the most precipitous cliffs in Wales found time to take me, then aged seventeen, and many other equally youthful, on crags and routes of lesser difficulty. No doubt most climbers then and to some extent today, felt it a duty to encourage and train the beginner, and perhaps the flow of newcomers into the sport was so small that the unselfish efforts of these experienced and older cragsmen was sufficient to meet the demand.

Now it is different; the way of the would-be climber is made smooth and the situation is less satisfactory. The number of small local clubs whose membership is open to all and who will undertake the responsibility of training their new members in mountain craft or in rock gymnastics must now be close on a hundred and every month sees the birth of others. At the same time there are a number of other bodies who have interested themselves in mountaineering and the sport is now regarded as an educational benefit with the Ministry itself giving its official blessing. Local Education Authorities in some areas run courses both for children and adults in mountain craft and rock climbing; the Central Council of Physical Recreation have a permanent center in the Cairngorms where at holiday times the general public may receive skiing and mountaineering instruction; nearer home is the Outward Bound Mountain School with the accent more on discipline, team work and toughness, where the coalminer's son will rub shoulders with the boy from Eton; since the spate of postwar accidents the Youth Hostel Association who have made training in rock climbing their special province.

Necessary though a more widespread knowledge of mountain craft is, some criticism can be leveled, not only at the training offered by the Junior clubs—often extremely dubious training—but also at some of the bigger organizations, well-meaning though they may be. The climber of an earlier generation learned his craft behind men usually much his seniors, not only were they of adequate experience, but they were fully imbued with the highest traditions of the sport. Now, while men of character, ability and experience are lending themselves wholeheartedly to the training of beginners, the need is so great that others hardly out of their teens, some having little over a year's experience, are given the responsibility of running an instructional course; not only are they not qualified to giving the technical instruction but their attitude to the hills and their conduct is not always the best example for the young and impressionable novices under their care.

Sufficient is being done by these organizations both in fostering the spirit of adventure and in training the young in its path, but is enough interest and care for the new generation being taken by the individual? It is the personal relationship between mentor and pupil that really matters and will in the end do more good than a thousand lectures and all the collective training. Is it not the duty of all who feel deeply about the hills and who love adventure simply and purely for its own sake, free of all competitive elements and of exhibitionism and sensationalism, to pass on to the new generation, by their influence and example, the traditions and spiritual values that the true mountaineer holds so dear?

George Spenceley

MIKEL VAUSE:
KNIGHTS OF NOTHINGNESS

The Transcendental Nature of
Mountaineering and Mountain Literature

Humans, in their search for knowledge and dominion, have struck out on many memorable expeditions to achieve these desires, many times at great risk. The old adage "Nothing ventured; nothing gained" summarizes the attitudes that rationalized the risk factor. But another element attached to the idea of risk was that there must be some purpose connected to the venture, i.e.: land, gold, science and personal fame. The idea of risk-taking for anything other than material gain or for science was sheer lunacy.

This is also clearly represented in other forms of activity that are risky such as Arctic exploration. Roald Amundsen, after being the first man to reach the South Pole, had little to show for it; he was greatly in debt and physically worn out. His only reward was the fact that he had done it.

The very birth of alpine climbing came as a result of an offer made by the Geneves scholar Horace-Benedict de Saussure, who, after first reviewing Mont Blanc, in 1760, offered a reward to anyone who reached the summit. It is ironic that an activity that, in the late part of the present century, is practiced for intrinsic, almost solely spiritual reasons, was the child of materialism. Material motive no longer accounts for mountaineering, yet the encouragement of individuality and personal liberty, the sort of romantic freedom that led visionary humans to great achievements and rewards in science, industry and exploration is still questioned when applied to mountaineering. This is possibly due to mountaineering being so purely visionary as well as so lacking in any material recompense. Robert Frost examines the idea of climbing for its own sake in his poem "The Mountain":

> It doesn't seem so much to climb a mountain
> You've worked around on foot of all your life.
> What would I do Go in my overalls,
> With a big stick, the same as when the cows
> Haven't come down to the bar at milking time?
> Or with a shotgun for a strong black bear?
> Twouldn't seem real to climb for climbing it
> —(*Lathem* 40-44).

Even in a time of constant thrill-seeking and "adrenalin highs," the most adamant adventurer sees climbing as a sure-fire path to suicide. Those generally associated with mountain climbing are seen as somewhat deranged, having a death wish. In a television documentary dealing with the American Everest North Face Expedition, the American climber, Jim Wickwire, was asked why death seemed to override his wish to live, a question naturally directed to him as a mountaineer. His answer was that the death wish attributed to climbers is a fallacy, that, in fact, climbing is an affirmation of life and all of its goodness and joy.

The careful reading of essays dealing with ascent clearly illustrate that the climbers are more than just sportsmen, they are artists, poets and philosophers. Like Emerson, Wordsworth and other great thinkers and poets who believed in the divine nature of humans, they reach their god-like potential through such challenges as those found climbing, not only in the wild back country of the remote mountain ranges of the world, but many times in local crags as close to home as Walden Pond was to Thoreau's Concord.

Wilfrid Noyce, a prolific writer as well as active participant in mountaineering, states that the desire for risk and adventure is innate:

> If adventure has a final and all-embracing motive, it is surely this:
> we go out because it is our nature to go out, to climb mountains,
> and to paddle rivers, to fly to the planets and plunge into the depths
> of the oceans . . . When man ceases to do these things, he is no
> longer man (quoted in Schultheis 33).

Mikel Vause

But the climber must realize that with the commitment to climb comes responsibility and possibly death as a result of his choices.

An examination of the literature of mountaineering provides not only many exciting tales of high adventure, but also, if closely examined, one comes to understand the psychology and philosophy of those who wish, through the medium provided them by the ice-covered faces of nature's grand and timeless monuments, to ply their art in places of limited access. It is my intent to focus on the intellectual and social implications found in mountain writing as offshoots of the romantic essay rather than adventure stories only.

The literature of the mountains is transcendental by nature. Because language is limiting it contains the inevitably incomplete record of the climber/writer's sojourn in the ideal world, which though incomplete, still proves the reader with a vicarious account of enlightenment achieved by the climb, and a written vision of the climber's art achieved through his travels in the Earth's wild places and a record of the physical exhilaration felt by the climber fortunate enough to reach the summit. It matters not if it be a first ascent or the hundredth visit to the top, the experience is the end in itself.

The promise of reward to those willing to risk possible catastrophe is of little extrinsic value, but the intrinsic reward is beyond value or price. This gift from activity in wild nature is possibly best explained by John Muir, who constantly sought after the prize found at the tops of mountains:

Climb the mountains and get their good tidings. Nature's peace will flow into you as sunshine flows into trees. The winds will blow their own freshness into you, and the storms their energy, while cares will drop off like autumn leaves (Wolf, *Unpublished —Journals* 317).

The mountaineer is glad for every opportunity to return to the mountains in search of the divinity only available to the hardy. Muir put into words the inner feeling of all climbers upon their return to the mountain wilderness:

I am always glad
to touch the living rock again
and dip my head in the high mountain sky
(Wolf, *Unpublished Journals* 221).

This communion of humans with nature does not have to be unique to the climber, but to all who are willing to make the efforts needed—

who willingly reach deeper within themselves to overcome the most difficult problems for the sake of the spiritual reward. In this study of writings which are the works of climbers, the purpose is to show that mountaineers are not only superb athletes, but also deep thinkers rather than demented and suicidal, and who, through their writing provide those who lack the climber's gift a record of the experience and possibly the understanding of the motives that drive the climber to scale the few high places and break from the otherwise natural horizontal existence of the generic human both literally and figuratively. The climber, by providing the record of his climb, acts as a proxy for those who, for various reasons are unable to go into the wilds. The philosophy of the mountaineer is very clearly presented by the Italian climber, Walter Bonatti, who explains the psyche of the climber as being set for high achievement, unwilling to settle for the mediocrity so commonly found in industrialized humans; who willingly takes risks, not for anything material, but for the uplift of the inner spirit which directs the character of humans in all of their aspects. This is not to say that the climber is a superhuman or semi-divine, but that their philosophical perspective is an explanation of why the climber undertakes such risks.

Bonatti refers again and again to the effects of industry on society and how humans have come gladly to settle for a mere reaction of their whole potential. He contrasts this dull, over-civilized humanoid with the climber whose rebellion directed against the morbid effects one sees in "collective society" is manifest in their willingness to risk their lives in order to issue their protest against such an anesthetized existence as if found in most human settlements. This philosophy is not unique to Bonatti but is patently romantic and could as easily be the words of Wordsworth who in his poem "The Old Cumberland Beggar" states his concern of how industry affects man.

Along with recognition of the romantic ideal that is clear in climbing philosophy, it must be remembered that the rewards of the adventure do not come easy. Rob Schultheis explains the efforts of achieving spiritual growth by adventure this way, "Adventuring requires determination, curiosity, toughness, and—especially—the ability to solve problems with real creativity" (34), the same elements found anywhere there is success. It is with this in mind that the climber/writer writes.

All humans need to participate in adventure, to pioneer new frontiers, sometimes even at the risk of life, and to do it under their own power using few and possibly none of technology's products to add an even greater feeling of accomplishment and contribute to their ascent—physically and spiritually.

The philosophy of unencumbered progress as advocated most clearly by Henry David Thoreau, in *Walden,* is also the philosophy of Walter Bonatti, who states that though climbing starts out as a sport, the end result can be great spiritual rewards, and that the less material baggage one takes in the mountains, the greater possibility of reward.

Bonatti's belief is that mountaineering is an activity which provides inspiration and fulfills requirements set by his temperament, and which follows a tradition established "out of sacrifice, suffering and love," which does not allow for the easy win or to win at any cost. Bonatti's philosophy fits the theory of risk exercise (RE) of Dr. Sol Ray Rosenthal, who after many years of research and study has found "that there is something in risk that enhances the life of the individual—something so real, something with such impact that people who have experienced it need to experience it again and again" (Furlons 40).

The idea of risk must be clarified; it is more than just "the joy of survival or a sense of self-validation. It [is] a powerful psyche and visceral kick—an exhilaration, a euphoria, a sense of heightened awareness" (Furlons 93).

Heightened consciousness is reward of the transcendental experience common to Emerson, Thoreau and Muir. Dr. Rosenthal indicates that such "transcendent" experiences are common to the risk taker. Risk-taking results in a very personal revelation about one's limitations and abilities. What is "risky" to one may be commonplace to another, but regardless, "risk . . . heightens perceptions because it enforces an absolute concentration on the moment, as opposed to the ennui. This can pervade any endeavor in which there's nothing important at stake" (Furlons 94).

Dr. Rosenthal, in an interview with *Outside* magazine's William Berry Furlons, explains the differences between RE and risk taking this way: "Risk exercise differs from the common concept of risk taking in that it is measured. Rosenthal is not talking about a mindless pursuit, such as diving off the Golden Gate Bridge to see if, just this once, you can survive. "In the manic risk, terror or despair is the only predictable emotion," he says. One of the assumptions of RE is that the risk taker has the skills to match or overcome the risk. "Otherwise terror simply overwhelms the RE response."

In essence, this response is a sensation that envelops the risk taker, usually, though not inevitably, after the activity. The sensation varies in intensity and duration according to the individual and to the degree of risk. Rosenthal is careful to distinguish the RE response from the "adrenalin high" some risk takers say they have experienced. Adrenalin, notes Rosenthal, is simply a "fight or flight" secretion that speeds up the body or gives it more energy. The RED response goes further, taking on both a strong sensory and strong cerebral dimension.

Sensory: "In talking with people who've had an RE response," says Rosenthal, "you find that they describe a very pronounced sense of well-being. In most people it's a feeling of exhilaration, even euphoria. They talk of having achieved more of their potential as human beings, of feeling fulfilled and yet having a greater expectancy of their lives." They talk, he adds, not only of feeling keenly aware of the world around them, but also of themselves and their own awareness. They not only see, for example, but they know what they see. And they know that they know. This accounts for the risk taker's vivid feeling of potency—he can control his increased sensory power beyond anything he ever knew. Unlike someone who is drunk or otherwise mind-altered, he is not separated form reality. "Reality doesn't intimidate him, because he feels so good within himself," says Rosenthal. "He has the strong feeling that his whole life has been enhanced, that he has been enhanced."

Cerebral: With the pronounced RE response, the individual enjoys the power and pleasure of summoning up the "wholeness" of his thought. His mind, given more information from his senses, somehow seems to give it all greater meaning. At the same time, the mind discriminates among the various sensations and meanings so that there is less mental clutter and an increased capacity for setting priorities. "The result is that people find their concentration is increased immensely," says Rosenthal. "They find that they can go to the heart of a problem and find a solution." What if the problem is emotional, not cerebral? "They manage to take the hardest step in meeting such a problem—they recognize that it involves their emotions, not their reason, which is an enormous discipline in itself."

For generations, risk activities were thought to be for the inane or the insane. "We've all been taught from infancy that danger, the presence of risk, is the signal to stop, to turn back, to cease whatever we're doing," says Rosenthal. People who persisted in risk taking were said to be unbalanced in a dazzling variety of ways Some were said to have death wishes, the favorite cliche of journalism. Some were said to be exhibiting super-masculinity as a way of overcoming subconscious feelings of inadequacy. Some were said to be counter-phobic, seeking to conquer their own worst fears by exposing themselves to whatever caused those fears. Rosenthal, on the other hand, believes that measure risk becomes understandable and even desirable when seen simply as the act of a person seeking to enhance his life by exploring inner resources (Furlon 40-93). Mountaineering, clearly, is more closely related to RE (risk exercise) than to risk taking, because its effects or rewards are mostly intrinsic.

The influence of mountaineering and the results of the influences are the creation of a more spiritual and ultimately responsible individual who is given over to spiritual intrinsic betterment which comes from increased personal awareness and self-control in all situations rather than a self-indulgent, self-centered being who receives uplift only through ratification of worldly appetites achievable by no effort or at best the slight effort it takes to unloose his purse strings.

The comparison made by Galen Rowell in his essay "Storming a Myth," dealing with the physical and spiritual, explains in elegant terms the necessary philosophical approach to climbing:

I know that climbing is merely a vehicle, a tool, and the climber a tool user. As a tool, climbing can be used to over-come 5.12 cracks, the difficulties of a Grade 6 wall, or an 8000 meter peak. But held only to this narrow definition, it can eventually bring boredom and despair.

The climbing tool has a spiritual component as well. At the heart of the climbing experience is a constant state of optimistic expectation, and when that state is absent, there is no reason to continue climbing. "I have found it!" can apply not only to those who feel they have found God, but to those who, like me, continue to find Shangri-Las where we experience fresh, child-like joy in everything that surrounds us, including memories that are the most long-lasting and intense of our lives (quoted in Tobias, —*The Mountain Spirit* 85-91).

It is the purpose of climber/writers to provide the reader with at least some information that was uplifting to them during the climb and which not only provides extrinsic justification for climbing, but also is an intrinsic reward, that comes from sharing their experiences with others. No matter how eloquent or profound writer are they cannot live the total experience for their readers, but through their writing they can entice the reader to an active involvement, possibly on a firsthand level. This tactic was used, with great effect, by John Muir during his campaign for national parks in America. His glowing reports of America's wild places attracted a great deal of attention. He invited all "over-civilized" people into the wilderness and promised them "terrestrial manifestations of God." Because of Muir's writings many national parks were established like Yosemite.

Doug Scott is a leader in modern British climbing and an active climber/writer. His essay, "On the Profundity Trail," an account of his climb of El Capitan's Salathe Wall with Peter Habeler, carries the idea of participation and calculated risk to the more limited audience of the climbers, but is applicable to non-climbers as well and again illustrates Bonatti's mention of the harmful effects a collective society can have on man.

Not only does Scott support Bonatti's basic philosophy, but his ideas also tie in with the Emersonian theory of the transcendental experience from contact with wilderness. This results in personal growth as well as a "higher conduct of life" when one returns to the social world. But according to Scott the chances of achieving such spiritual and intellectual heights come from one's willingness to risk something of value—the longer the trip the more risk involved and the greater the possibility of growth.

These examples represent the psychological and philosophical ideas that help connect the realities of mountaineering, mountains, and travel. The next step is to see the effects mountains have had on literature. One can hardly read the works of the romantic writers, regardless of nationality, without coming across numerous references to mountains or wild terrain: man being naturally impelled to ascent in all it forms. This literature could hardly exist without reference to mountains and attempts to ascend them. As before mentioned, after man put aside the need for justification for climbing mountains, i.e. science and material wealth, mountains become a source of spiritual riches. The effort made to climb them was rewarded by spiritual uplift and a triumph of the inner man over himself. Samuel Taylor Coleridge, in 1802, made what has been recorded as the first descent of Scafell Crag in the Lake District of England. Just the small entry in his notebooks that recorded the event is filled with awe and wonder: "But O Scafell, thy enormous Precipices." The description of Coleridge's climb appears under the dates of August 1 and 9, 1802:

The poet Samuel T. Coleridge made what he described as a "circumcursion" from Keswick by Newlands to Buttermere and St. Bees, up Ennerdale, thence by Gosforth to Wasdalehead, from where he climbed Scafell, descended to Taws in Eskdale, and the continued by Ulphand, Coniston to Brathay and so back to Keswick. It is clear from his notebooks, now in the British Museum, that he descended from the summit of Scafell to Mickledore by the route we now call Broad Stand. He got down by "dropping" by the hands over a series of "smooth perpendicular rock" walls, got "cragfast" or nearly so, and finally slid down by a "chasm" or "rent" as between two walls. He recorded too that on reaching Mickledore his "limbs were all of a tremble," a phenomenon not unknown among modern cragsmen (*Mountain* 30:17-18).

It was sixty years before the next climb of Scafell was recorded. The myth of mountains being terrible and the hiding places of evil was dispelled by the men who climbed and returned with a report of the sublime rather than dread. As John Ruskin explained:

Thus the threatening ranges of dark mountains, which in nearly all ages of the world, men have looked upon with aversion or with terror, are in reality sources of life and happiness far fuller and more beautiful than the bright fruitfulness of the plain (Smith *The Armchair Mountaineer* 182).

Lord Byron, in his poem, "Solitary," written in 1820, takes the idea of Ruskin further: "To climb the trackless mountains all unseen, the wild flock that never needs a fold, alone o'er steeps and foaming falls to lean, This is not solitude; 'tis but to hold Converse the Nature's charms, and view her stores unrolled" (*Styles* 337).

Byron, in "Solitary," mentions the extrinsic beauties of the mountains but in "The True Shrine" he explains the intrinsic blessing derived from mountains by those who climb them:

Not vainly did the early
Persian make
His altar the high places and
The peak
Of earth-o'er gazing mountain,
And thus take
A fit and unwalled temple,
There to seek
The Spirit, in whose honour shrines
Are weak.

Upreared of human hands. The awesome power of nature is also recorded by Wordsworth in his poem, "England and Switzerland, 1802,"
in which he deals with the sea and the mountains and the freedom that
wild places provide for the man who is willing to venture out:

Two voices are there; one is of the sea,
One of the mountains, each a mighty voice;
In both from age to age thou didst rejoice,
They were the chosen music, Liberty!
There came a tyrant, and with holy glee
Thou fought'st against him—but hast vainly striven:
Though from thy Alpine hides at length and riven
Where not a torrent murmurs heard by these.
—Of one deep bliss thine ear hath been bereft;
Then cleve, O cleve to that which still is left—
For high-soul'd maid, what sorrow would it be
That Mountain foods should thunder as before,
And Ocean bellow from the rocky shore,
And neither awful Voice be heard by Thee!

As early as 1668 William Penn recognized the virtues and necessity
of wild nature even from a religious point of view:

Christ loved and chose to frequent Mountains, Gardens, Sea-sides.
They are requisite to the growth of piety; and I reverence the virtue
that feels and uses it, wishing there were more of it in the world
(*Styles* 157).

As mentioned before man seeks ascent; whether viewed from an evolutionary perspective or a religious perspective the need to more up is
there. The whole society of man is built on advancement. In 1740, Alexander Pope talked of the inborn need for man to ascent in the lines of his
poem, "Alps on Alps":

So pleas'd at first, the tow'ring Alps we try,
Mount o'er the vales and seem to touch the sky;
The eternal snows appear already past,
And the first clouds and mountains seem the last,
But those attain'd, we tremble to survey
The growing labours of the lengthening way;
The' increasing prospect tires our wond'ring eyes—
Hills peep o'er hills, and Alps on Alps arise!

Even in times of sorrow and tragedy directly resulting from climbing the mountains, there comes intrinsic beauty. In 1903, three climbers were killed while attempting to climb Coleridge's Scafell Crag. Here is the epitaph from the gravestone in Wasdale Head churchyard:

One moment stood they as the angels stand
High in the stainless immanence of air;
The next they were not, to their Fatherland
Translated unaware (*Styles* 165).

The number of references to the grandeur and beauty, the strength and power, and the spiritual necessity derived from mountain travel are many. And many of the poetic lines are direct results of firsthand experience of the poets in the mountains; but the writings of those who live to climb and participated in the ascents of the extremely high and wild mountains provide even better insight into the need to climb—for humans to continually scrape and pull themselves toward the clouds by way of the eternal rocks and snow and ice of which the mountains are made.

Basically, it is a romantic tendency: this emphasis on individuality, on close contact with nature as a spiritual matter, on the release and freedom that comes from this kind of experience. And all this tends to be put in an elevated language, a kind of inspirational "chant." The selections also produce elevated ideas which are the result of serious craftsmanship not as mountaineers only, but as artists, as writers.

As Hilair Belloc said: The greater mountains, wherein sublimity so much excels our daily things, that in their presence experience dissolves, and we seem to enter upon a kind of eternity. (Styles 153)

History illustrates the special place mountains have held in the past. Is it any surprise that humans naturally look to mountains as sources of inspiration? Mountains represent a place of renewal, of rebirth which draw humans toward them. This desire to visit and climb the mountains will always be alive in humanity regardless of the efforts of technology to make humans soft; their mind, their memory will pull them toward the pearls. Human potential is unlimited and climbing recognizes it:

However mechanized, or automatized, the conditions of human life may become, the same number of human beings will, I believe, continue to carry this inherited memory, reinforced for action by the new awareness of mountains and of mountaineering which has come with this last century. There will be men and women who find among hills forgetfulness of fear and of their anxieties, in the restoration of their sense of proportion, the recovery, of reasonable measure, which was the mountains' original gift to men; or who, like Smuts and like so many, will see again upon the mountains spirits of religion—true symbols, founded upon the same inspiring mountain principles of measure, proportion, order, and of an uprightness which points a way beyond clouds and, at least, towards the stars. (Young 115-116)

WORKS CITED

Furlons, William Berry. "Doctor Danger." Outside January 1981: 40-42, 92-95.

Lathem, Edward Connery, ed., The Poetry of Robert Frost. New York: Holt, Rinehart and Winston, 1969.

Rowell, Galen. "Storming a Myth." Mountain Spirit, eds. Michael Charles Tobias and Harold Drasado. New York: The Overlook Press, 1979.

Schultheis, Rob. "The Adventurers." Outside" January 1981: 33-34.

Scott, Doug. "On the Profundity Trail." Mountain 15 May 1971: 12-17.

Smith, George Alan and Carol D. The Armchair Mountaineer. New York: Pitman Publishing Corp., 1968.

Styles, Showell. The Mountaineers Week-End Book. London: Seeley Service and Co. LTD., 1960.

Wolf, Linnie Marsh, ed. John of the Mountains: The Unpublished Journals of John Muir. Madison: University of Wisconsin Press, 1979.

Young, G.W. "The Effects of Mountains Upon the Development of Human Intelligence." W.P. Ker Memorial Lecture, University of Glasgow, 2 May 1956.

SELECTED BIBLIOGRAPHY PERMITS AND CREDITS

Ament, Pat—*High Endeavors*: La Crescenta, CA: Mountain 'n Air Books

Bartlett, Phil—*The Undiscovered Country*: London: Ernest Press

Blum, Arlene—*Annapurna: A Woman's Place*: San Francisco, CA
Sierra Club Books

Bonington, Sir Chris—*I Chose to Climb*: London: Victor Gollancz, Ltd.

Brown, Hamish—*The Last Hundred*: London: Trafalgar Square

Brown, Joe—*The Hard Years: Seattle*: The Mountaineers

Child, Greg—*Thin Air*: Layton, UT: Gibbs Smith Books

Curran, Jim—*K2: The Story of the Savage Mountain*: London:
Hodder and Stoughton

Gervasutti, Giusto—*Gervasutti's Climbs*: Seattle, WA: The Mountaineers

Gifford, Terry—*The Joy of Climbing:Caithness*: Whittles Publishing Ltd.

Greig, Andrew—*Summit Fever*: London: Hutchinson and Company

Harrer, Heinrich—*The White Spider*: London: Harper Collins

Haston, Dougal—*In High Places(1997)*: Eiger Direct. Reprinted by permit of Curtis
Brown Group Ltd

Herzog, Maurice —*Annapurna* (translated by Nea Morin and Janet Adam Smith)©
19953 by Maurice Herzog. Used by permission of The Lyons Press, Guilford,
CT.

Hunt, Sir John—*The Ascent of Everest*: London: Hodder and Stoughton

Long, Jeff—*The Ascent*: NY, NY: William Morrow and Company

Lowe, Jeff —*The Ice World*: Seattle, WA: Mountaineer Books

MacInnes, Hamish—*Beyond the Ranges*: London: Hodder and Stoughton

McCarthy, Jeff—*The American Alpine Club Journal*

Mitchell, Ian—*The Mountain Weeps*: Leicester: Stobcross Press

Pritchard, Paul—*Deep Play*: London: Baton Wicks

Roberts, David —*Moments of Doubt*: Seattle, WA: The Mountaineers

Roper, Steve—*Camp 4*: Seattle, WA: The Mountaineers

Robinson, Doug —*A Night on the Ground, A Day in the Open*:
La Crescenta, CA: Mountain 'n Air Books,

Rowell, Galen—*The Mountains of the Middle Kingdom*: NY, NY
Random House—Reprinted by permission of Galen Rowell/Mountain Light.

Scott, Doug—*Himalayan Climber*: London: Baton Wicks

Shipton, Eric—*Upon That Mountain: London*: Hodder and Stoughton

Sayre, Woodrow Wilson—*Four Against Everest*: New York, NY:

Prentice Hall

Spenceley, George—*The Yorkshire Ramblers Club Journals*

Stephen, Sir Leslie—*The Playground of Europe*: Oxford: Basil Blackwell

Vause, Mikel—*On Mountains and Mountaineers*: La Crescenta, CA:
Mountain 'n Air Books

Whymper, Edward—*Scrambles Amongst the Alps* Layton, UT:
Gibbs M. Smith Books

Yates, Simon—*The Flame of Adventure*: Seattle, WA: The Mountaineers

Young, G. Winthrop—*On High Hills*: London: Methuen and Company